E		F		G	
Acerrae (Acerra)	D4	Cales (Calvi)			B1
Aenaria (Pithecussae/Ischia)	C4	Calor Fl. (Calore)			D4
Abella	D4	Cannae (Canne)			C4
Alba Fucens (Albe)	C2	Canusium (Canosa)			B3
Ameria	B2	Capreae (Capri)			C3
Amiternum (San Vittorino)	C2	Capua (S. Maria Capua Vetere)	D3	Puteoli	D4
Amsanctus L. (Mefite)	E4	Casinum (Cassino)	C3	Pyrgi	B3
Anagnia (Anagni)	C3	Circeii	C3	Roma (Rome)	B3
Antium	B3	Clusium (Chiusi)	A1	Rufrae (Presenzano)	D3
Ardea	B3	Cora (Cori)			D3
Arpi (Arpi)	E3	Corfinium (Corfinio)			D4
Arpinum (Arpino)	C3	Cortona (Cortona)			D4, E4
Atella (Atella di Napoli)	D4	Cumae (Cuma)			C3
Atina (Atina)	C3	Falerii (Civita Castellana)			D4
Aufidena	D3	Formiae (Formia)	C3	...ca)	C3
Aufidus Fl. (Ofanto)	E3, F3, E4	Gravisca	A2	Sulmo (Sulmona)	C2
Barium (Bari)	F3	Herculaneum (Ercolano)	D4	Surrentum (Sorrento)	D4
Beneventum (Benevento)	D3	Larinum (Larino)	D3	Tarentum (Taranto)	G4
Brundisium (Brindisi)	G4	Lavinium	B3	Tarquinii (Tarquinia)	A2
Caere (Cerveteri)	B3	Liris Fl. (Liri)	C2, C3	Tarracina (Terracina)	C3
Caieta Gaeta)	C3	Liternum	D4	Teanum Sidicinum (Teano)	D3
		Minturnae (Minturno)	C3	Tiberis Fl. (Tiber)	B1, B2, B3
		Misenum	D4	Tibur (Tivoli)	B3
		Neapolis (Naples)	D4	Trasimenus L. (Trasimene)	B1
		Nola (Nola)	D4	Trerus Fl. (Sacco)	C3
		Ostia	B3	Velitrae (Velletri)	B3
		Paestum	E4	Venusia (Venosa)	E4
				Mt. Vesuvius	D4
				Volsinii (Bolsena)	B2
				Volturnum	C3
				Volturnus Fl. (Volturno)	D3

LARINUM

ARPI

CANNAE
CANUSIUM

CALOR FL.

AUFIDUS FL.

BARIUM

N I A

BELLA   L. AMSANCTUS

VENUSIA

A P U L I A

SALERNUM

SILARUS FL.

BRUNDISIUM

TARENTUM

PAESTUM

Vergil's Italy

VERGIL'S
ITALY

by Alexander G. Gordon McKay, 1924-

NEW YORK GRAPHIC SOCIETY LTD.
Greenwich, Connecticut

FRONTISPIECE:

Aeneas at sacrifice.
Detail of the Ara Pacis Augustae, Rome,
13–9 B.C.

Aeneas sacrifices to Juno in thanks for his safe arrival in Italy and in hopes of peace. Augustus records the annual sacrifice at the Ara Pacis in his *Achievements:*

When I returned to Rome from Gaul and Spain after successfully settling the affairs in these provinces, during the consulship of Tiberius Nero and Publius Quintilius [13 B.C.], the Senate voted that an Altar of Augustan Peace should be consecrated for my return in the Campus Martius and ordered that magistrates, priests, and Vestal Virgins should bring an annual sacrifice to it.

(*Res Gestae Divi Augusti,* 12)

International Standard Book Number 0–8212–0367–3
Library of Congress Catalog Card Number 76–125595
© 1970 by Alexander G. McKay
MANUFACTURED IN THE U.S.A.
BY THE BOOK PRESS.
Design by Philip Grushkin.
Maps by Margaret Bostwick Vaill.

CONTENTS

HISTORICAL OUTLINE

7

ca. 350	Rome completes the "Servian" wall enclosing largest city in Italy.
343–341	First Samnite War.
340–338	The Latin War.
321	Battle of the Caudine Forks.
316–304	Second Samnite War.
298–290	Third Samnite War, including Etruscans and Gauls.
264–241	First Punic War, with Carthage.
239–169	Ennius, Father of Latin Poetry.
234–149	Cato the Elder, *Origines* and *De Re Rustica*.
218–201	Second Punic War; Hannibalic occupation (218–203).
216	Battle of Cannae (Apulia), Rome's worst disaster.
214–210	Recovery of Sicily; capture of Syracuse. Death of Archimedes.
202	Scipio Africanus defeats Hannibal at Zama (North Africa).
200–196	Second Macedonian War; Flaminius proclaims "freedom of Greece."
197–191	Recovery of Cisalpine Gaul.
171–167	Third Macedonian War; Roman victory at Pydna.
157–86	Gaius Marius, of Arpinum.
149–146	Third Punic War; destruction of Carthage.
138–78	L. Cornelius Sulla "Felix."
133	Attalus III wills Pergamum, art center of Asia Minor, to Rome. Tiberius Gracchus, tribune, institutes land reforms in Italy.
123–122	Tribunate of Gaius Gracchus.
106–48	Gnaeus Pompey.
106–43	M. Tullius Cicero, of Arpinum.
100–44	C. Julius Caesar.
97–54	Lucretius, *De Rerum Natura*.
91–88	Social or Marsic War: Rome v. Italic allies.
89–85	First Mithridatic War.
89	Lex Plautia Papiria gives franchise to Italians.
88	Sulla's march on Rome; flight of Marius.
87–54	Catullus, lyric poet, of Verona.
86	Marius' seventh consulship and death. Athens sacked by Sulla; Mithridates defeated.
82	Sulla captures Rome; Battle at Colline Gate and collapse of Samnite cause.

82–79 Dictatorship of Sulla; death at Cumae (Lake Lucrinus).

82–30 Mark Antony.

73–71 Spartacus leads a slave revolt in Italy; overcome by Crassus and Pompey.
Verres, governor of Sicily, plunders art.

70 Consulship of Pompey and Crassus. Trial of Verres.

70–19 VERGIL, of Pietole/Andes (b. October 15, 70).

67 Lex Gabinia confers on Pompey command against the pirates.

66 Lex Manilia confers on Pompey command against Mithridates.

65–8 Horace, of Venusia.

65 First Catilinarian Conspiracy.

63 Consulship of Cicero; Second Catilinarian Conspiracy; Pompey's settlement of the East; birth of C. Octavius, later Augustus (63–A.D. 14); birth of Agrippa (63–12 B.C.).

62 Death of Catiline.
Caesar elected praetor.
Pompey's return from the East; army disbanded.

60 First Triumvirate: Pompey, Crassus, and Caesar.

59 Caesar's consulship.

58–50 Caesar in Gaul and Britain (55, 54).

58 Clodius, tribune, procures Cicero's exile (58–57).
VERGIL in Cremona.

56 Conference at Luca.

55 Consulship of Pompey and Crassus. Theater of Pompey, Rome's first permanent theater.
VERGIL in Mediolanum (Milan); assumes *toga virilis*.

54 Crassus in Mesopotamia. Death of Julia, Caesar's daughter, Pompey's wife.
VERGIL in Rome; rhetorical school of Epidius.

53 Crassus defeated and killed by the Parthians at Carrhae; loss of the legionary standards.
Caesar crosses the Rhine.

53–50 VERGIL at Rome; studies rhetoric; some forensic activity; begins philosophical study with Siro the Epicurean.

52 Pompey, sole consul.

49 Caesar crosses the Rubicon (January 11); reaches Rome in April.
VERGIL leaves Rome for Naples and Garden of Siro; *Catalepton 5*.
Pompey and his senatorial followers leave Italy.

48   Battle of Pharsalus (Thessaly); Pompey killed in Egypt; Caesar in Alexandria.

46   Pompeians defeated in Africa; suicide of Cato at Utica.

46–44   Dictatorship of Caesar.

45   C. Asinius Pollio, praetor.

45–43   VERGIL leaves Rome for Mantua.

44   Assassination of Caesar (March 15).
Cicero's *Philippics,* against Antony.
VERGIL leaves Naples for Mantua.
Octavian in Rome; quarrels with Antony; raises an army against Antony.

43   Defeat of Antony at Mutina (April); Octavian marches on Rome; elected Consul in August.
Formation of the Second Triumvirate: Antony, Lepidus, and Octavian.
Proscriptions; death of Cicero (December 7).

43–41   VERGIL in Mantua; composes *Eclogues* 2, 3, 5, 7.
C. Asinius Pollio, governor of Cisalpine Gaul.

42   Battle of Philippi; defeat of Brutus and Cassius.
Death of Siro at Naples (?).

41   Octavian distributes land to veterans; Antony in the East. Outbreak of war with the consul L. Antonius; siege of Perusia (Perugia).
VERGIL and his father leave for Rome and Naples; *Catalepton* 8.

41–40   Confiscations of territory in Cisalpine Gaul; VERGIL'S estates lost.

40   Surrender of L. Antonius at Perugia; Octavian controls Italy. Consulship of C. Asinius Pollio. Peace of Brundisium: reconciliation of Octavian and Antony.
VERGIL composes *Eclogue* 4 ("Messianic").
VERGIL, prey to melancholy, composes *Eclogues* 9 and 1.

39–36   War with Sextus Pompey; construction of Portus Julius (37 B.C.).

39   VERGIL composes *Eclogue* 6, addressed to Alfenus Varus, suffect consul, and *Eclogue* 8. Pollio victorious in Illyricum.

38   Diplomatic mission, headed by Maecenas, includes VERGIL, Horace, Varius, Plotius Tucca, etc. VERGIL joins the delegation at Sinuessa.

37   Treaty of Tarentum. VERGIL composes *Eclogue* 10 and publishes the collection; begins *Georgics* (1).

36   Sextus Pompey defeated off Sicily; Lepidus deposed and re-
        sides, as Pontifex Maximus, outside Rome.

36–32 Antony in the East; marries Cleopatra.

31   Battle of Actium (September): defeat of Antony and Cleo-
        patra.

30   Octavian in Egypt; deaths of Antony and Cleopatra; annexa-
        tion of Egypt.

29   VERGIL publishes *Georgics* and plans *Aeneid*.
        Temple of Janus closed; Octavian celebrates triple triumph
        over Dalmatia (35–4), Actium (31), Egypt (30).

27   Octavian receives title "Augustus"; reorganizes the Roman
        state and rebuilds Rome.

26   Propertius extols Vergil's work on *Aeneid*.

23   Establishment of the Augustan Principate; Augustus rules with
        tribunician power and proconsular imperium.
        Death of Marcellus, nephew and son-in-law of Augustus, at
        Baiae.
        VERGIL reads *Aeneid* 2, 4, and 6 to Augustus and Octavia at
        Nola.

22–19 Augustus in Greece and Asia Minor.

20   Diplomatic settlement with Parthia and Armenia; recovery of
        the lost standards.

19   VERGIL leaves for Greece and Asia Minor to refine the
        Aeneid and resume philosophical studies; joins imperial party
        upon request of Augustus; contracts illness and dies after land-
        ing in Brundisium (mod. Brindisi), September 21st; burial in
        Naples.
        Aeneid published posthumously by Varius and Plotius Tucca.

LIST OF ILLUSTRATIONS
AND MAPS

MAPS

FOREWORD

ITALY was Vergil's ultimate and abiding love. Unjustly deprived of his boyhood home near Mantua in the aftermath of civil war, Vergil often reflected wistfully, sometimes bitterly, on his exile from the Arcadia of his youth. Throughout his writings he eulogized his land, from the Alps to the southern shores of Sicily. Its peoples, Greek, Etruscan, Celtic, and Italic, are his major concern and his main inspiration. For behind the imposing facade of late Republican and Augustan Rome shimmers the reality of a war-torn and anarchic Italy, crying out desperately for order and renewed productivity. The vision of the Golden Age, of Paradise lost and regained, permeates his writings.

Filled with melancholy and a sense of life's tragedy, Vergil's poetry nevertheless comes alive with glimpses of the wondrous aspects of the landscape and with tributes to heroism. There is a sure sense that Italian, not merely Roman, patriotism carried the country through its times of strain with Greek and Etruscan, Gaul and Carthaginian, and finally through internecine strife. Vergil finds hope for the future in the ancient abilities of the Italians, and he pleads for a new recognition of the antique virtues, for a renewal of the dignity that formerly was attached to the plow, and for an intelligent, almost reverential, pursuit of agriculture. For Vergil, the foundation of Rome and the rule of Augustus marked the culmination of Destiny, a progression that had begun with Aeneas, the faithful Trojan, seeking a new land for his dispossessed family and for the remnants of his people.

Vergil's Italy is designed to highlight Vergil's genius as landscape artist and as Italy's most sensitive interpreter. His achievement as a poet will first be discussed in detail. Arcadia Revisited, the Religion of Work, and the National Epic—these are his three major concerns. Matters of characterization and poetic method are studied, along with an inquiry into the poet's melancholy and the tragic design of his masterpiece, the *Aeneid*. Religion and imperialism, and the legacy of Vergil to subsequent European literature are explored. Subsequent chapters, arranged geographically, provide a detailed commentary on Vergil's use of various regions in his writings, from Cisalpine Gaul to Sicily. Throughout, the reader is introduced to social and political factors in the areas under review as Vergil would have experienced them, to historical and archaeological matters that are important to a more thorough grasp of the poet's genius and intention. A variety of translations by English poets and scholars mingle with the discourse. The illustrations testify to the fidelity of Vergil's writings to the topography and nature of the land.

Vergil's poems offer a vision unparalleled in ancient writings: the recovery of an Italy almost forgotten, of gods men had once trusted, of a beauty that would not die; and they give a prophetic glimpse of peace guaranteed by an enlightened, merciful ruler. The sensitivity of this Roman poet who lived through the death throes of the Republic, who knew and helped to shape the Augustan Principate and the new idealism, underlines the bitter realities of the human condition, frail in the face of evil, but part of a larger and hopefully benevolent pattern.

The comprehensive genius of Vergil still reverberates in our literature and art after two millennia. His landscape is an evocation of an ancient and a future world, with all the rampant vitality and heady confidence of the Augustan Principate, "but with some qualities which the Roman world lacked, some half-lights, some backward glances."[1]

---

[1] Kenneth Clark, *Landscape into Art* (Penguin ed., 1961), 68.

I

The Achievement of Vergil

T. S. ELIOT'S high regard for Vergil stemmed from two great achievements: his guidance of Dante towards a vision he could never himself enjoy, and his guidance of Europe towards the Christian culture which he could never know.[1] As a classical humanist, Eliot emphasized Vergil's unique position on the threshold of the Christian world. To some critics, Eliot's "pre-Christian" reading was out of focus, and to assess Aeneas' *pietas* as "an analogue and foreshadow of Christian humility" seemed anachronistic and even myopic. But his other observations seemed to give a fair estimate of Vergil's importance, for example his statement that "Vergil was among all authors of classical antiquity, one for whom the world made sense, for whom it had order and dignity, and for whom, as for no one before his time except the Hebrew prophets, history had meaning."[2] Eliot's criteria for the designation "classic" include a maturity, a comprehensiveness, and a universality which Vergil alone provides among the ancients.[3] His definition acknowledges Vergil's determining role in the creation and refinement of Augustan "classicism," which was a rebirth, but with enormous alterations, of the classical norms of Periclean Athens.

Brooks Otis supports Eliot's view of the *Aeneid* as the mature classic of Western society. "On a human, political, and even poetical level," says Otis, "we still face the problem of civilization in terms very like those of Virgil himself."[4] In fact, a great portion of Otis's recent book on Vergil[5] is an attempt to account for the poet's preposterous design to resurrect the heroic-age epic in the absence of a living tradition, in a cosmopolitan, urban civilization which had more in common with New York than Mycenae. Otis finds Vergil's "civilized" nature as poet in his "unromantic combination of humanity with moral realism—of justice with sympathy—that gives that 'ideology' of the Aeneid its balance, its fluidity, its richness and complexity of texture. There are tears for Dido, for Nisus and Euryalus, for Camilla, for Mezentius and Turnus: yet they all pay the penalty for their excesses. There are also tears for Marcellus, Pallas, and Lausus: these are examples of a much higher order of self-sacrifice. . . . But Aeneas is the *hero* in that he looks beyond such tragedy to a peace that will in some sense overcome it and, at the least, serve to mitigate it."[6] Otis's book, alongside the recent studies by George Duckworth, W. F. Jackson Knight, Jacques Perret, Viktor Pöschl, and Karl Büchner, has done much to shatter the Victorian sense of homage and breathless admiration, and has substituted an acutely critical approach, explaining and evaluating Vergil along modern lines.

But voices of disapproval have also been raised recently. Robert Graves, in an iconoclastic mood, launched a scathing attack on Vergil's anti-poetic nature. He summed up by saying, "Publius Vergilius Maro, *alias* Virgil, has for two thousand years exercised an influence over Western culture out of all proportion to his merits either as a human being or as a poet. Vergil's pliability; his subservience; his narrowness; his denial of that stubborn imaginative freedom that the true poets who preceded him had valued; his perfect lack of originality, courage, honour, or even animal spirits—these were the negative qualities which first commended him to government circles, and have kept him in favour ever since."[7] Throughout his withering lecture, Graves vilified the poet. He accused Vergil of being a "patronizing city-man" in his *Georgics:* "a more honest poet would have anticipated Goldsmith's *Deserted Village,* in distress that Augustus' victories had dealt another heavy blow to traditional Italian agriculture by further encouraging the growth of large estates run on slave labour." The *Aeneid,* Graves feels, was an entirely uncongenial task for the poet laureate. Such high-pitched derogatory protests (foreshadowed in Graves' earlier *Homage to Sextus Propertius*) have by their excessiveness done more to invalidate Gravesian criticism and poetic notions than they have to dislodge the Roman poet from any primacy that he may claim.

Although the polemic intent of Graves is unmatched, others have felt uneasy about Vergil's epic, about his hero and course of action. E. M. Forster has said that "the art of Virgil seems the wrong way up—if we assume that the art of Homer is up the only right way. He loves most the things that profess to matter least—a simile rather than the action that it illustrates, a city full of apple trees rather than the soldiers who march out of it, the absent friends of a dying man rather than the dying man."[8] Again, disturbed by overemphasis on heroism in the last six books, in which Turnus and Aeneas are the exemplars of two societies, E. A. Havelock remarks that "if Aeneas is a symbol flexible enough to accommodate not only Rome's past but Rome's present, surely it was the poignancy of recent memory (viz. the experiences of the first century B.C.) that inspired that half of the poem which is Vergil's *Iliad* (7–12), and adds moral ambiguity to his conception of Rome's role and her destiny."[9]

To judge by the scarcity of imitators, Vergil has not won much adulation recently. But works derived from Vergil have been created by some of the century's best poets: Sacheverell Sitwell, Robert Frost, Allen Tate, Robert Lowell, Edith Sitwell, Archibald MacLeish. More significant evidence of current standing are the fresh translations of Vergil's works, sometimes—happily—by writers who are both poets and scholars. Reasons for this sudden burst of enthusiasm are undoubtedly varied and often personal, but the parallels between the reconstruction of the western world after World War II and the energetic rebuilding after Actium in 31 B.C. are surely partly responsible for the renewed admiration of Vergil, particularly of the *Aeneid,* the testament of Augustan Rome. The universality of the situation, the heroic response, and on the poetic side, Vergil's allusiveness of language, brilliant use of metaphor and symbolism, and his mastery of structure and proportion have all had a strong effect on the renewed interest in Vergil.[10]

Scholars have always sensed, perhaps more perceptively today than earlier, the synthesis of Greek and Roman culture in Vergil's writings. There is a characteristic retrospective, imitative ingredient in Vergil's poems which to some readers, like Graves, has suggested poverty of imagination, but to others, a maturity and developed consciousness. Theocritus, Hesiod, and Homer—Greek poets of pastures, cultivated fields, and heroes—did in fact provide the pattern of composition, but Vergil moved beyond them and created more durable, more influential models for his own culture. Even his earliest works, the *Bucolics* (37 B.C.), Vergil's pastoral counterparts to the *Idylls* of Theocritus, reflect another state of mind and another age. They are brought sharply, sometimes painfully, into the context of Roman history, of Roman rule and the benign ruler. The pastoral setting tends to dissolve in an anti-Arcadian world where shepherds grieve for lost property, for displaced man and beast, and where their songs are addressed to a silent, non-resonant nature. "I can remember that as a boy, I used to fill the long day with singing. Now I've forgotten my songs. Even his voice has fled from Moeris" (E. 9, 51). Such is the originality of Vergil in only one small segment of his varied productivity, and herein lies his unique nature.

Before examining the works of Vergil, in particular the *Bucolics,* the reader should be aware that the misery and despair beneath the surface of Vergil's pastoral poems still persist in contemporary Sicily and southern Italy. Gavin Maxwell's clinical study of the depravity, ignorance, and oppression in modern Sicily, besides reflecting age-old problems in Italy, also highlights some of the persistent customs and behavior of the Sicilian. In *The Ten Pains of Death,* Maxwell reports an interview with a young cowherd (*vaccaru*) who describes his life in the Sicilian highlands. The passage reveals the timeless as well as the timely features of the Vergilian counterpart.

> While the animals graze, I pass the time playing my flute and singing, lying in the shade of a rock or a tree. All the herdboys like me have flutes—we make them ourselves out of thick bamboo stems and when we make a good one, we keep it forever. I can do bird songs on my flute, too, and you can have a wonderful time doing that, getting the birds to answer you one after another. I play herd songs a lot of the time, and when I meet another herdboy, we play part songs. I can sing hundreds of verses of songs—I love them—and I've learned dozens and dozens from other herdboys I've met in the mountains. The songs

go on forever, and there's as many verses as grains of sand on the seashore. . . . Then there's songs you sing in alternate verses with some-
one you can hear, but most times can't see. These are called *botta e
risposta.* We herds don't often meet each other in the mountains—
each of us takes his animals to different places because there's not
enough grass to go round, but we can play games together even if
we're far apart. You hear the voice of another herd singing far away
and you wait for the right moment and answer him. If he hears you,
start up alternate verses like this:

> Who are you that's singing up there?
> You sound like a yapping puppy.

and he answers:

> And who are you wailing away down there?
> You sound as if you had a toothache in every tooth.

> I: You know nothing about singing—
>   You'd better go and learn at school in Palermo.

> He: You say I don't know how to sing—
>   You'd better go to school at Monreale. (etc.)

Sometimes I've sung a *botta* for the whole night—one's voice sounds
better at night. We don't take offence at what we sing to each other—
if we did, we wouldn't sing them, or else we'd go and beat each other
up. If you're clever enough, you can invent new verses, but you have
to make them rhyme properly.[11]

THE PASTORAL POEMS: ARCADIA REVISITED

Although the *Bucolics,* sometimes called *Eclogues* ("selections"), are
certainly not Vergil's first work, they remain our earliest finished token
of his verse mastery and creativity.[12] Composed in an environment of
war, during the tumultuous years following Caesar's assassination, the
Eclogues provide moving testimony to the unhappy, distorted life of
the Italian peasant in a land devastated by civil war and by repeated
partition. They offer extraordinary insight also into the poet's sympathies.

The ten poems offer a mélange of pastoral vignettes, of painful recollections and heartbreaking concern for the displaced farmers, innocent victims of the civil wars, and a comparable feeling for his beasts. They also reveal hero worship for Octavian, as potential redeemer and restorer of peace.[13] The beguiling surface of the poems is Alexandrian, deriving from the Hellenistic poet Theocritus and his *Idylls* ("little pictures"),[14] which Vergil knew and loved. The *Bucolics* have absorbed some of their artifice, but not their artificiality, and show the same concern for symmetry and careful design. The Theocritean originals are often genre pieces, reminiscent of the Comedy of Manners that flourished then, and of certain types of Hellenistic sculpture.[15] Often they lack poetic force. But the two poets have much in common. Both are masters of a complex verse form, product of a sophisticated age, and both are ready to assume the mask of innocence in an age of tumult.

Pastoral verse has been traditionally a literature of escape, and it is always potentially dramatic, for it depends upon a perspective of sharp contrasts. The town or city is depicted in terms of the country, the rich in humble guise, the complex as something simple, almost abstract. Pastoral poetry makes its impact through the sense of conflict, of opposed viewpoints, through ironic differences between peoples and classes. Both Theocritus and Vergil use the debate, the conversation between shepherd-lovers, and the singing contest as formal devices. But Vergil's product is more impressive, for his shepherds are vocal in a different way. They share the unexpected eloquence, artful and refined, of Theocritus' peasants, but Vergil's are far more than idle shepherds engaged in the contest of verse and love. They are vehicles for political protest.[16] They enable Vergil to comment critically on his own time and perhaps on his own predicament,[17] for in 40 B.C. Vergil's father lost his estate in the confiscations for the Triumvirate's veterans.

Although the shepherd swains of Theocritus may be familiar figures, creatures of comedy as much as pathos, Vergil's shepherd-lovers, Corydon and Damon, Menalcas and Damoetas, are capable of genuine anguish and passion, composers of *chansons tristes* imbued with genuine melancholy. Vergil's love idylls are no longer pastoral comedies, but treat the emotionally charged predicaments of men with real involvement.

But bucolic poetry offered more than a vehicle for irony and protest.

It also provided a means whereby the poet and his literary friends could partly at least regain the Golden Age, the paradise of primeval benign nature.[18] Poetry and love are united in the pastoral retreat. Here are the ideal conditions for the writing of poetry, an Arcadian milieu where poets, like Gallus, may even enjoy the company of gods and shepherds in the expression of their love's lament. The pastoral poems are vital to Vergil's development, and are the earliest indication of his imaginative, creative genius. Vergil's Arcadia, vastly different from the native Greek haunts of Pan and the Muses in the central Peloponnese, is more a spiritual landscape than a physical reality, a landscape "set half-way between myth and reality . . . a no-man's land between two ages, an earthly beyond, a land of the soul, yearning for its distant home in the past."[19]

Herein lies Vergil's innovation, product of a mature understanding and of a deep-seated compassion for the human and the animal condition, far removed from the Alexandrian Idylls. Alongside the need for repair and redemption which appears as a tragic leitmotif throughout the lines, there is a wish-fulfillment world of plenty, where the rural calm of shade and quiet brook exists, and a love that is unimpassioned, gentle, and touched with sadness.

The Vergilian landscape in the *Eclogues* is more difficult to locate than any other landscape in his writings. It combines aspects of Vergil's homeland near Mantua, and the territories watered by the Mincius and the Po. But there are suggestions too of the Campanian green acres, and of the environs of Naples; and sometimes, perhaps by derivation, of Sicilian terrain. The harsher notes of rock and crag are a match for the discordant notes in the shepherds' world. Tragedy thrusts into the mellow light and sensitive world of the pastoral, emotional and political reality shatters the Arcadian vision, and one is left finally with the impression of despair countered by fervent hope, of love and affection undercut by separation and death.

The *Eclogues* provide the guide-lines for proper understanding of the structure of Vergil's subsequent works.[20] Throughout the collection, the poet evidently sought variety and contrast, in scenery, in presentation, and in subject matter. The following outline reveals, in part, the structure:

Eclogue 1. Country life: confiscation and recovery of homesteads (non-Theocritean, Roman emphasis; Italian scenery).

Eclogue 2. Corydon's love song (Theocritean; Arcadian setting).

Eclogue 3. Singing contest between Menalcas and Damoetas; no decision (Theocritean; Italian scenery).

Eclogue 4. "Messianic" Eclogue; the world to come; the Age of Saturn; religion and philosophy (non-Theocritean; Arcadian setting).

Eclogue 5. The Lament for Daphnis (=Caesar); the shepherd becomes a god (Theocritean, but with Roman associations).

Eclogue 6. The Song of Silenus: the world that was; the fall from the Golden Age; philosophy and mythology (non-Theocritean; Arcadian setting).

Eclogue 7. Singing contests of Corydon and Thyrsis; decision awarded to Corydon (Theocritean; Italian scenery).

Eclogue 8. Two songs of love; Damon and Alphesiboeus (Theocritean; Italian scenery).

Eclogue 9. Country life; confiscation of territory (non-Theocritean; Italian scenery).

Eclogue 10. The lovelorn Gallus; the friend who becomes a shepherd (=Daphnis) (Theocritean, with Roman emphasis; Arcadian setting).

Several features of the organization emerge very clearly. The odd-numbered poems use Italian or local scenery; the even-numbered poems use the Arcadian setting; the odd-numbered poems are dialogues, the others monologues, which also implies an alternation and distinction between dramatic and nondramatic poems. There is also a close correspondence between the poems of the first and the second half of the collection (excluding *Eclogue* 10, which appears to have been a later addition to the collection to balance *Eclogue* 5). Poems 1 and 9, 2 and 8, 3 and 7, 4 and 6, deal with related subject matter. Another organizational principle may be detected in a triadic arrangement of the poems: 1, 2, 3 deal with shepherds and personal themes; 4, 5, 6 deal with divine

beings and cosmic themes; 7, 8, 9 deal, as in the first triad, with shepherds and personal themes. Poem 10 not only honors Vergil's poet
friend Cornelius Gallus, but also provides a correspondence for Poem 5
and ends the collection with heightened interest. Brooks Otis has recently discovered another compositional design: "*Eclogues* 1–5 are
relatively forward-looking, peaceful, conciliatory, and patriotic in the
Julio-Augustan sense. *Eclogues* 6–10, on the contrary, are neoteric,
ambiguous or polemic, concerned with the past and emotively dominated
by *amor indignus,* love which is essentially destructive and irrational and
is implicitly inconsistent with (if not hostile to) a strong Roman-
patriotic orientation."[21] Otis's scheme reinforces one's general impression that the later poems show a weakening of the pastoral dream. The
overtones of brutality and intrigue, of elegiac despair and disenchantment, are markedly different from the pastoral *otium* and the surface
involvements of the earlier half.

The fourth *Eclogue* remains the most famous and the most enigmatic
of the bucolic poems.[22] Composed in 40 B.C. and dedicated to one of the
year's consuls, C. Asinius Pollio, it is unique among the other pastorals.
In a solemn style charged with epic anaphora and phraseology which
may derive from Sibylline prophecy, Vergil announces that Pollio's
magistracy will witness the arrival of a new dispensation, the rebirth of
the Golden Age, symbolized in the birth of a divine child. Vergil de-
clares that his poem must transcend the old limitations of tamarisks and
woods (*myricae, nemus*) and find a Muse more congenial to themes of
broader compass (*paulo maiora*) and greater moment. His larger tone,
more solemn, and quasi-religious, foreshadows the *Aeneid.* The birth of
the child (perhaps the offspring of Antony and Octavia, married in
40 B.C.) will bring to pass the cleansing of evil, the spontaneous productivity of the earth. But there will still be the few remnants of sin,
and Rome, in a reversal of the heroic age, must launch a second Argonautic Expedition (E. 4, 32–5) and another Trojan War (35–6). Thereafter, with the child grown into a philanthropic hero, a divinized man,
each land will be self-supporting, the world will be free of the need for
marine involvements, commerce, agriculture, and (the poet adds somewhat challengingly) artificially dyed materials. The age of innocence,
a soft primitivism, will succeed the age of Iron and wars. To herald the
child's coming:

Goats shall walk home, their udders taut with milk, and nobody
Herding them: the ox will have no fear of the lion:
Silk-soft blossom will grow from your very cradle to lap you.
But snakes will die, and so will fair-seeming, poisonous plants.
Everywhere the commons will breathe of spice and incense.
But when you are old enough to read about famous men
And your father's deeds, to comprehend what manhood means,
Then a slow flush of tender gold shall mantle the great plains,
Then shall grapes hang wild and reddening on thorn-trees,
And honey sweat like dew from the hard bark of oaks.

(E. 4, 21–30. Day Lewis)

Many readers have been struck by apparent ties between the Vergilian prophecy and Isaiah's Messianic prophecies. To be sure, Vergil may have been acquainted with the sizable Jewish communities in Rome and Naples, but there is no firm evidence that Jewish literature in the shape of the Septuagint was available to him.[23] One must simply suppose that Vergil and Isaiah provide us with parallel manifestations of the yearning for peace, for prosperity and natural productivity that was felt throughout the Mediterranean after centuries of conflict. E. V. Rieu states the problem of interpretation with due caution: "The Fourth Eclogue is a lyrical rhapsody. It is a Roman oracle, too. It is also a vision, conditioned by its date, but influenced nonetheless by those mysterious forces which, even as Vergil wrote, were gathering strength in Palestine to shape the future of mankind."[24]

THE GEORGICS: THE RELIGION OF WORK

Long before the *Georgics,* Vergil's "Treatise on Agriculture," the archaic Greek poet Hesiod had countered the concept of the heroic pursuit of glory as life's transfiguration with a more systematic gospel of work, which he supported by prudent maxims.[25] Hesiod's *Works and Days* is a sermon delivered with intensity by this dour Boeotian to his somewhat malign brother Perses, who had profited in an untidy lawsuit over property. The admonishments are threefold: that justice be the foundation of the city; that prosperity is the product of hard work; and that hard work must be directed by knowledge. The social and political system, peace and prosperity, and productive agriculture are for Hesiod all part of the same divine dispensation. The wise man who conditions his agriculture and seafaring to harmonize with the Seasons directs his social and political life by Justice:

> Perses, put this in your heart and listen to Justice and forget violence altogether. For Zeus appointed this custom (*nomos*) for men: that fish and beasts and winged birds should eat each other, because there is no Justice among them, but to men he gave Justice which is for the best.[26]

Though Hesiod's example was paramount, there were other influences on Vergil's *Georgics*. Both the *Phenomena* and the *Diosemeia* (Weather Signs) of Aratus had been translated by Cicero and were available to Vergil; other possible influences were Nicander of Colophon—who wrote poems on bee-raising, animals, and farming—and even the genius Eratosthenes, who had dabbled in the realm of didactic poetry.[27]

However much the works of these poets influenced Vergil, one of the main spurs to his imagination was surely the didactic poem of Lucretius, *On the Nature of Things*.[28] Vergil knew and respected the work, and in the *Georgics* there is a stirring tribute to the Roman poet:

> Lucky is he who can learn the roots of the universe,
> Has mastered all his fears and fate's intransigence
> And the hungry clamour of hell.
> But fortunate too the man who is friends with the country gods—
> Pan and old Silvanus and the sisterhood of nymphs:
> The fasces have no power to disturb him, nor the purple
> Of monarchs, nor civil war that sets brother at brother's throat,
> Nor yet the scheming Dacian as he marches down from the Danube,
> Nor the Roman Empire itself and kingdoms falling to ruin.
> He has no poor to pity, no envy for the rich.
> The fruit on the bough, the crops that the field is glad to bear
> Are his for the gathering: he spares not a glance for the iron
> Rigour of law, the municipal racket, the public records.
>
> (G. 2, 490–512. Day Lewis)

The model of the Georgics was certainly Hesiodic; the inspiration was undoubtedly Lucretian.

Lucretius had set about presenting the scientific basis of Epicureanism in verse, as support to the philosophical tenets of the gentle, unworldly system. But Epicurus stood for noncommitment to leader or party, and just as Horace (*Odes* I, 34, 2) questioned this position as an *insaniens sapientia* politically, so Vergil also found cause for objection.[29] Farrington has argued, with sense, that "it was hatred of the City, of the corruption of political life, that took Horace and Vergil into the Epicurean movement. It was the revival of political hope in the Augustan age which took them out of it."[30]

The areas of conflict between Vergil and Lucretius were numerous: on the definition of the godlike man as statesman rather than as philosopher of the retired life; on the primary importance of political life and involvement as opposed to defeatism; on the purposeful intervention of the gods in the world; on the use of force, as opposed to friendship, to combat one's enemies, at home and abroad; and on the necessity of an ethic of *virtus* rather than *voluptas*.

Vergil imagines a spiritual and political regeneration of his prostrate world, a world which he locates in the neglected fields of Italy. The vision is one of plenty and conditioned order, as systematic as the progress and demands of the seasons. His attitude towards the taming of nature to men's needs is completely different from that of Lucretius. The latter's tone is defeatist and as morose as Hesiod at his worst:

> What land remains Nature, if left to herself, would cover with briars, unless man prevented, accustomed as he is to maintain his life by groaning over the heavy two-pronged mattock and by cleaving the earth with the deep-pressed plowshare.[31]

Vergil's attitude is more courageous and has an almost militant air:

> Much does he help his fields, moreover, who breaks with a mattock
> Their lumpish clods and hauls the osier-harrow; on him
> The golden goddess of corn looks down from heaven approving.
> He helps them too, who raises ridges along the plain
> With a first ploughing, and then cross-ploughs it, constantly
> Exercising the soil and mastery over his acres.
>
> (G. 1, 94–9. Day Lewis)

Vergil's models were not restricted to Lucretius and the Greeks. Cato's treatise *On Agriculture* and Varro's contemporary *Three Books on Agriculture* were obviously part of Vergil's reading, and there are evidences of their influence.[32]

When Vergil wrote the bulk of the *Georgics,* he was resident in Naples, in the fertile Ager Campanus, a terrain fertilized by aeons of volcanic activity and endlessly productive. It was also a unique agricultural zone in his contemporary Italy because it consisted of small tracts leased by the state to small farmers, or *coloni.* Gentle, diffident, and conformist by nature, Vergil responded enthusiastically to the Imperial effort to revitalize the agricultural economy and to regain the moral stability of Republican Italy. The Augustan policy of "back to the land" has been challenged by many as insincere, anachronistic, and fruitless. But Vergil must have been quick to sympathize with the almost desperate recourse. A victim himself of State confiscation, his sympathies remained with the land and with the farmer class, the last great remnant of the Italic folk to which he belonged and which he celebrated later in the *Aeneid.*

No one believes anymore that Vergil wrote the *Georgics* to provide members of the rural proletariat with a useful compendium for farm activities. Admittedly, Augustus and Maecenas must have welcomed the finished work. But here was no solution to the aggravated problem of farming in Italy, where the countryside was largely deserted by the small farmer class. Vergil's audience was by design the imperial circle, above all the educated landowners, who had renounced the land in favor of the city but were still, as absentee landlords, tied to their rural holdings. The poet's intention was to restore a sense of pride in the farmer, to accord the proper dignity to the plough, and to provide exhortation and suggestion for the improvement of the desperate condition of the land. He aimed to rouse the landlords; to awaken them to the necessity of refertilizing the soil of Italy; to excite them to a patriotic determination to resurrect a world that was demoralized, anarchic, and moribund; to give them a sense of Divine intervention in the ordering of Nature, and in man's salvation by labor.

Vergil's didactic poem is in a sense anti-Arcadian. Idleness, reclining in pastoral quietude, plaintive love songs and sylvan notes are far removed from the world of the *Georgics.* They offer not a sentimental rapture but a call to work to realize the moral values that are associated with the farm life. The exhortation to work, the gospel of the *Georgics,* is resumed in the first poem:

> For the Father of agriculture
> Gave us a hard calling: he first decreed it an art
> To work the fields, sent worries to sharpen our mortal wits
> And would not allow his realm to grow listless from lethargy.
>
> (G. I, 121–4. Day Lewis)

There follows Vergil's picture of man as the creator, the developer of the arts, responding through experience and intelligence to the perversities of nature. Once again, as in the fourth and sixth *Eclogues,* Vergil harks back to the Golden Age, when there was no necessity for toil, but with the new suggestion that God imposed unremitting toil on mankind to induce him to strain for survival and to create a civilization by his arts. The idea was not original with Vergil. Hesiod, Aeschylus, and Sophocles had all been concerned with the painful progress of man from primitive ignorance to civilized power—in short, with the problem of human progress and the divine involvement. Vergil's theodicy, however, moves beyond his predecessors' in accenting the pleasures that attach to man's diverse activities, and the variety of produce that stems from man's labors.[33]

A brief digest of the four poems will provide some evidence of their complexity and their rich content:

Georgic 1. Dedication to Maecenas; followed by advice on the preparation of the soil, ploughing, crop rotation, manuring, burning stubble; the best conditions for grain and the work after sowing; the farmer's pests; the myth of the origin of labor; further practical suggestions are followed by almanac notices (204–310), weather lore and signs (311–462), and an epilogue on the prodigies which attached to Caesar's death and foretokened the civil wars (404–514); a final prayer requests that Octavian, with the gods' help, save the shattered world.

Georgic 2. The first section deals with tree cultivation, the vine and the olive, with attention to grafting; the soils and climate best suited to certain types of trees; and the *Laudes Italiae* (9–176); the next section deals with the planter's work (177–345), the nature of different soils, soil-testing, and the preparation for a vineyard, and it closes with a hymn to spring (323–45); the third section (346–540) concerns work in the country, manuring, hoeing, ploughing, vine-raising, etc., and includes a panegyric of country life; Vergil gives a lyric avowal of his desire to sing the secrets of nature (475–82), and pays tribute to Lucretius (490–2).

Georgic 3. The preface discards hackneyed mythological themes and invokes the herdsman's deities, with promise of a new subject and ultimately a work on Caesar's wars. The first section (49–285) deals with horse-breeding, the care and training of horses, and the need for sexual deterrents for bulls and stallions. The scene of battle between rival bulls for a heifer (219–41) is illustrative of the powers of love (cf. Lucretius *DRN* 1, 1–20, and *Georgic* 4). The second section deals with smaller beasts, sheep and goats, with digressions on African nomad shepherds (339–48) and Scythian cowboys on the frozen steppes (349–83); the final section deals with the uses of farm animals, a warning about snakes, diseases among sheep and other animals; the epilogue treats the horrors of the Noric cattle-plague and a racehorse's death agony, and also offers poignant reflections on the death of a steer.

Georgic 4. The first section introduces an account of bee culture (8–314), with particulars on the hive, the activities and governmental system of bees, and their favorite flowers; a digression (116–148) deals with the old Corycian beekeeper and prefaces a long account of the community of bees and their alleged participation in the Divine Mind (219–27). This section concludes with advice on gathering honey, pest control, the diagnosis and treatment of diseases, and a recipe for renewing a lost swarm from the carcass of a steer. The second section, the myth of Aristaeus (315–558), details Aristaeus' discovery of the method of regeneration through his nymph-mother, Cyrene, and Proteus, the sea-god.[34] Proteus tells Aristaeus he has unknowingly caused Eurydice's death, and then relates the story of Orpheus and Eurydice in a larger context. Aristaeus sacrifices cattle to propitiate the spirit of Orpheus; the cattle putrefy quickly and produce a miraculous rebirth of bees. The poem ends with Vergil's literary signature.

Agriculture, arboriculture, animal husbandry, and bee culture would appear to offer intractable subject matter for even the most inspired poet, and their organization into an intelligible, palatable unit would dishearten the most dauntless. Otis has seen through the didactic poem to a "most intricate structure of symbols whose major concerns are those most central in both human life and Augustan Rome: work, play, and man's relation to nature in both, and beyond these, life, death and rebirth. It is the transformation of Hesiodic and Lucretian didactic into a single homogeneous poem."[35]

When one gets beyond the abstruse, technical vocabulary and the occasionally monotonous details of the metrical treatise, there is apparent an order and progression in the *Georgics,* a symmetrical structure that lends additional meaning.[36] There is, to be sure, a startling progression in the emphases which sound at the close of each book: 1—War; 2—Peace; 3—Death; and 4—Resurrection. Books 1 and 2 deal with inanimate nature, fields, trees and vines, while 3 and 4 are concerned with living creatures, herds, flocks, and bees. Books 1 and 3 end with a mournful note: 1, with the menace of civil war; 3, with the description of the ravages of the plague and the representative deaths of horse and bull. Books 2 and 4 end more joyfully, with the praise of country life and with the regeneration of the bees. Vergil inserts a tribute to Rome in 2, 534 ff., and to Octavian in 4, 560 ff. The revival of the Golden Age at the close of *Georgic* 2 finds its counterpart in the miraculous birth of the bees to the representative farmer, Aristaeus. There are many links in the shape of similarities and contrasts between *Georgics* 1 and 3, and 2 and 4. Austin has noted, "Vergil's method was to construct a great series of word-paintings based on a single unified theme, and arranged with consummate skill in contrast; his domestic pictures are the more significant for their juxtaposition with some foreign scene, and technical descriptions are offset by the contemplation of pure loveliness."[37]

The second half of *Georgic* 4 is the story of Aristaeus (281–558). The question naturally arises why Vergil should have chosen to close his detailed account of the farmer's occupations with a myth. The practice of using a myth as the culmination of an extensive, often technical or philosophic argument was not unknown to Vergil's readers, but the enigmatic aspect clears only when the entire context of the *Georgics* is considered. Myth, as the ancients knew it, was a means of subsuming larger meanings, of representing universal truths symbolically and within an almost timeless setting, or of making general statements on the human condition. The figures of myth are, in short, universal types—a composite of the human and the poetic. Aristaeus, whose associations are with Greek pastoral, may be imagined as the universal farmer, whose labors may one day enjoy heaven's favor, but on another be assailed by disaster. So Aristaeus, the shepherd-god, finds one day that all of his bees are dead. Eventually Proteus tells him the reason for his loss: the gods punished Aristaeus for his unknowing role in the deaths of Eurydice and Orpheus, for in trying to elude the amorous grasp of Aristaeus, Eurydice stepped on the deadly serpent. The story of the double tragedy occupies a considerable portion of Proteus' tale to Aristaeus. The artful construction of the Orpheus and Eurydice episode, set within the framework of the Aristaeus story, has all the elegance and measured development of an Alexandrian epyllion, or "miniature epic" (cf. Catullus 64, "Peleus and Thetis").[38]

The meaning of the Orpheus myth remains problematical. Vergil, perhaps because of his Neo-Pythagorean attachments, made frequent allusion to Orpheus in the *Eclogues,* and he also figures in the *Aeneid*.[39] For the ancient world, Orpheus was a teacher, a philanthropic figure, a civilizer, a mystic, a lawgiver, and an artist.[40] Art imagined him as a figure capable of charming trees, rocks, streams, fishes, birds, and beasts by the power of music. And these are of course the associations which are relevant to the *Georgics* and just cause for his appearance. Vergil portrays him as an artist, capable of defeating the powers of death and of giving the challenge of love to death's finality. His descent into and ultimate ascent from Hades become an adventure of the human spirit and of the civilized world. Poet-artist and Everyman-farmer are united in this great myth of resurrection and rebirth. The tragic pattern of the *Georgics*—War-Peace-Death—ends with the triumph over death of the undying power of love and with the rebirth of the lost community of bees by divine intervention. The implications of the myth, recast so often in later times, in art, music, and literature, were potent and various, and immensely suggestive for Vergil's incomparable sixth *Aeneid*.[41]

THE AENEID: THE NATIONAL EPIC

Vergil's epic of "arms and the man" cannot be separated from his earlier works. The Arcadian world of the *Eclogues,* with its hymn to love and tranquillity, yielded to the harsher world of the *Georgics*. There love survives in a more heroic guise in Orpheus, but a harder primitivism and a more industrious regimen prevails. There are even traces of military associations in the lines: Vergil must have sensed that farming could serve as an outlet for man's aggressive instincts, for he frequently describes it as a physical battle against weeds and overgrowth, a battle waged with iron weapons, often divinely made, in which the farmer is ultimately victorious over the fields.[42] As with men, so with nature's creatures—the battles of bees are of equal moment with battles of Roman legionaries.[43] And there are other facets of the *Aeneid* which first emerge in the *Georgics*. Not only had Vergil discovered how he must write the *Aeneid*, he had also found the way to delineate Aeneas: behind the culmination of destiny represented by Aeneas' victory in Italy lay a sadness, a pain, a sense of exile, which his earlier writings had accented. "The problem of pain," writes R. G. Austin, "never absent in all the happiness of the *Georgics*, finally became an overmastering thought. But behind the inescapable grief, the *lacrimae rerum*, is the indestructible force of beauty; otherwise the struggle against pain that we do not understand would be unendurable."[44]

The *Georgics* are also linked to the *Aeneid* in another way, for in the prelude to the third *Georgic*, Vergil provides a programmatic forecast of his subsequent epic, specifically a forecast of the *Aeneid*, the poem of Aeneas and Augustus.[45]

The design of the *Aeneid*, product of a meticulous revision from the original prose version, is "classical" in the best sense. There is a monumentality and an architectural order implicit in the composition which never fail to impress the reader on closer view.[46] The principles of "classic" structure in Vergil's epic are, in the simplest terms, symmetry and proportion, order and contrast, measured control (imparted by the dactylic hexameter), and a generalizing character.[47]

Epic as a genre was centuries old. Homer's *Iliad* and *Odyssey* launched a great literary tradition which accepted heroic myth as the proper subject of poetry. Achilles, Hector, and Odysseus were imperishable figures, archetypal and symbolic. The successor epics, continuations of the Epic Cycle, and Apollonius Rhodius' *Argonautica* (centered on Jason's winning of the Golden Fleece and his love for the Colchian Medea) extended the repertoire and strained the form. The symbolic power of myth, though still active in the fifth-century tragedians and the lyricists of the Archaic period, waned markedly in later writers. Alexandrians like Callimachus and Apollonius Rhodius, who were trying to modernize antique material, avoided the mythological setting, and their poetic invention rested on more realistic, sentimental details which were not part of the original stories.[48]

The Roman approach to epic was as practical as the Roman way of life. Ennius simply juxtaposed Homeric thology and annalistic narrative; Cicero undertook to clothe a political pamphlet in epic trappings.[49] The "New Poets" of Italy, part of a cultural revolution and reaction to the decadent literary and personal practices of their poet-contemporaries, approached the older verse forms of lyric, epigram, and epic with a will to novelty and infused a new autobiographical element. The love poems of Catullus, addressed to Lesbia, provide an epic account of a lover's physical and spiritual progress to disenchantment and damnation, and though they were written separately, they are obviously interconnected.[50]

Hailed by Vergil's contemporary Propertius as "something mightier than the *Iliad*,"[51] the *Aeneid* has an Odyssean (1–6) and an Iliadic half (7–12). But there are vestiges and recollections everywhere of Ennius, of Apollonius Rhodius, of the Greek tragedians, of Catullus, and of the incomparable Lucretius. All the elements of Greek and Roman literary history combine in the *Aeneid*.

Readers have sensed worlds of difference between Homer and Vergil. Their epics are, of course, the products of different times and designed for different societies. The Homeric narrative, deriving from an oral tradition, is characterized by a strong, simple progression and by passages of great impact (cf. *Beowulf, La Chanson de Roland*). But the Vergilian epic, written for a literate audience likely to subject it to close scrutiny, reveals more interest in details than in overall design. Homeric (or authentic) epic is the product of an unformed, nomadic society which is impressed with the personal prowess of a strong man— one whose powers of initiative and independence and physical strength could lead such a society through a time of troubles. Vergilian (literary) epic is the product of a stable society; the hero is less a brilliant soloist than a pattern for organized civic behavior, one who makes and abides by the rules.[52] But both forms are concerned with the record of man's noblest achievement. So in Vergil, Aeneas is the embodiment of the literary epic hero; Turnus, Dido, Camilla, and Mezentius, however, are characters of the authentic epic, obsolete and foredoomed in the new environment and in the new literary form. Vergil's subject, unlike that of Homer or Apollonius Rhodius, was political. The whole emphasis is on the state, upon Rome, the embodiment of heaven's will and more important than any individual, even Aeneas. There is a constant sense of Rome as pacifier, as organizer, as civilizer, and Aeneas is the representative Roman.[53]

Vergil pioneered in composing poetry on a consciously symbolic level on the grand scale that epic requires. There is a new emphasis in the *Aeneid* which shifts from the external to the inner existence of the principals. Viktor Pöschl goes so far as to say that "everything—landscape, morning, evening, night, dress and arms, every gesture, movement, and image becomes a symbol of the soul."[54] The tempest that occurs at the outset of the poem sets the emotional key like an operatic overture. But alongside the tumult the theme of pacification appears in the mastery that Aeolus, father of the winds, exercises over the fractious blasts; and similarly, in the political simile wherein Neptune calms the sea with the dexterity of a statesman respected for his personal prestige (*auctoritas*) appeasing a rebellious mob. This statesman is praised for an essentially Roman quality—*pietate gravem ac meritis*— and for a virtue, *pietas,* that is the persistent epithet of Aeneas.[55] The allusive, enlarging style of Vergil is apparent from the beginning.

The struggle to establish a new home and to subdue the forces that contest its establishment is the primary theme of the epic. The theme has implications as much for the past, which is Trojan and Italian, as for the present, the aftermath of a century of civil war, and for the future, the Age of Peace at home and abroad, in a humanely directed world. Vergil recalls the agony and the moral deterioration associated with the life-and-death struggle between Rome and Carthage in the first six books; in the last six, he seems to show his personal reaction to the civil wars of the first century B.C. which finally yielded to Octavian a countryside ravaged and inert, and a nation, still divided, exhausted by war.[56] There is little happiness or exultation in Vergil's epic. Aeneas is finally triumphant, but he must surrender to the loneliness of the summit and of the divinely born and guided.

The design of the poem, composed first in prose then adapted as a verse epic, is intricate.[57] The obvious division is based on the acknowledgment of Vergil's indebtedness to Homer's *Odyssey* and *Iliad* and accepts the poem as composed of two halves. But there are other, perhaps more compelling reasons, to accept the poem as a triadic structure: 1–4, 5–8, 9–12. A précis will provide a basic insight into the poem's construction:

Aeneid 1. The Storm and the Arrival at Carthage.
> Juno, inimical to Troy and friendly to Carthage, rouses the storm to delay the hero's arrival in Italy; the landing in the strange country is peaceful, and the security of the Trojans is assisted by omens and prophecies; Venus, the goddess mother, prevails over Juno and ensures that Aeneas' party will be safe. Aeneas confronts Dido and begins his narrative.

Aeneid 2. The Destruction of Troy.
> Aeneas' narrative at Dido's banquet recalls the villainy of the destructive Greeks, the helplessness of Laocoön, of Priam, and the Trojans generally, deserted by the gods and overwhelmed by the energy and the inhumanity of the Greeks, especially Neoptolemus, Achilles' son; Aeneas maintains his "heroic" role against almost insuperable odds; Aeneas flees with his father, son, and wife; Creusa is lost in the escape and prophesies a great future for Aeneas in the West.

Aeneid 3. The Wanderings.
> Anchises assumes direction of the overseas passage, to Thrace, Delos, Crete, Epirus, and Sicily, where he dies at Egesta (Mt. Eryx); every stage is marred by adverse signs and incidents; the episode at Buthrotum, with Trojan Helenus and Andromache, Hector's widow, is joyful; the escape from Scylla and Charybdis, and from the attack of Polyphemus and the Cyclopes, is partly assisted by the counsel of a Greek castaway, Achaemenides. Aeneas' story ends.

Aeneid 4. The Tragedy of Love: Dido.
> Venus and Juno strike a compact to instill love for Aeneas in Dido; Aeneas succumbs and forsakes his duty to Ascanius-Julus and to the divine will out of his affection for the Carthaginian Queen; Dido, in turn, is guilty of impiety to the memory of her deceased husband, Sychaeus; Mercury recalls Aeneas to his duty, and Aeneas, a prey to emotional turmoil, leaves Carthage; Dido reacts in grief and outrage, and after fruitless appeals, commits suicide.

Here ends Part I of the triadic design, a portion devoted to the Tragedy of Dido, Aeneas' first encounter with the powers opposed to his Italian destiny and to his "Roman" person.

Aeneid 5. The Funeral Games of Anchises.

 Various athletic contests serve to ease the tension of the preceding narrative. Disputes among the contestants are allayed by Aeneas. Juno's scheme to prevail upon the women, weary of travel and anxious for a fixed abode, leads to the firing of the ships; Ascanius intervenes, and with the assistance of a miraculous rainfall most of the ships are saved. The passage from northwest Sicily to Italy requires the loss of one Trojan as sacrifice to Neptune; the death of the helmsman Palinurus follows.

Aeneid 6. The Visit to Hades and the Revelations.

 Aeneas, at Cumae, worships Apollo and requests the Sibyl to provide escort into Hades. The passage through Hades, beset with terrors and encounters, notably with Dido and Palinurus, is granted after the burial of Misenus, Aeneas' trumpeter, who challenged Triton and lost. The meeting with Anchises provides Aeneas with his commission and with a revelation of Rome's destiny. The march-past of heroes-to-come includes young Marcellus, Augustus' heir-apparent, who died prematurely in 23 B.C.

Aeneid 7. The Arrival in Italy.

 The initial landing is peaceful; Latinus offers friendship to the Trojans, and their security is assisted by omens and prophecies; Juno, unable to impress Heaven, incites Allecto, the Fury, to instill war in Amata, Turnus, and the Latins; Venus is thwarted by Juno's plans. Juno rouses hostility to the Trojans; the stag of Silvia is slain by Ascanius and general conflict follows.

Aeneid 8. The Beginnings of Rome.

 Aeneas leaves the Trojan camp to visit Pallanteum, the site of future Rome; Evander, the Greek king, welcomes Aeneas, guides him around the city, and promises assistance from Greek and Etruscan allies. Venus provides Aeneas with divine armor, particularly a shield which depicts future events in Roman history and, at center, bears an image of Augustus, victor at Actium, crowned with a fiery comet.

Here ends Part II, the core of the *Aeneid,* with its main emphasis on the establishment of the Trojans in Italy, the union of peoples, Trojans, Greeks, and Etruscans, in a military organization, and the beginnings of the hostilities with the Latins and the Rutulian and Etruscan allies.

Aeneid 9. Trials in the Trojan Camp.

During the absence of Aeneas at Pallanteum, Ascanius assumes the command; Nisus and Euryalus, two young volunteers, endeavor to carry a message to Aeneas requesting his return; their desire for glory and prizes results in their discovery by the enemy and their deaths; the Rutulian commander Turnus, confined within the Trojan walls, escapes after considerable slaughter by leaping into the Tiber.

Aeneid 10. The Tragedy of War: Pallas, Lausus, and Mezentius.

Venus and Juno are unable to find a compromise; Turnus, overcome by *violentia,* kills Pallas, youthful son of the aged Evander, and strips him of his belt, an action which ultimately leads to his death (A. 12). Aeneas, in an agony of remorse and prey to vengeance, kills the youthful Lausus, son of Mezentius; Mezentius, unable to live without his son, dies at the hands of Aeneas.

Aeneid 11. The Truce between Trojans and Latins.

A truce serves to ease the tension of the preceding narrative; the dead are buried. Latinus is unable to reconcile the factions in the Italian forces siding with Turnus and Drances; the tension finally erupts into fighting; Camilla, the warrior maiden in the service of Turnus, yields to a desire for glory and spoils, and dies at the hands of Trojan Arruns.

Aeneid 12. The Final Combat and Revelations.

Turnus issues a challenge to Aeneas to let single combat determine the issues of marriage with Lavinia, daughter of Latinus, and of peace. Juno persuades Juturna, goddess sister of Turnus, to prevent the duel. A Latin act of treachery renews the hostilities; Aeneas, wounded, temporarily withdraws from battle; Turnus kills many opponents; Laurentum, the Latin capital, undergoes a surprise attack by the Trojans; Amata, believing Turnus to be dead, commits suicide; Turnus agrees once more to single combat; Juturna and Venus both intervene to save their champions;

finally Jupiter intervenes. Juno and Jupiter are reconciled and sanction the creation of the "Roman" people. The death of Turnus follows after Aeneas sees him wearing the belt of Pallas, symbol of the Rutulian's frenzy and violence. Turnus' soul flies unreconciled to the shades below.

Here ends Part III of the triadic design, a portion devoted to the Tragedy of Turnus and to Aeneas' encounter with the last of the demonic powers opposed to his Italian destiny.

The foregoing scheme may be viewed in several ways. The halves of the two-part design are obvious, each moving towards a climax central to the epic theme, the ordained birth of the nation. There is also an interlocking between the various books, both by alternating mood and corresponding subject matter. The odd-numbered books have a lighter, almost Odyssean, character, and the even-numbered books have a contrasting darker, graver mood, often touched with tragedy, and a climactic finale (2 and 4, tragedy; 6 and 8, revelation; 10 and 12, triumph). The parallels between the halves are equally significant and contribute a powerful sense of unity and balance—1 and 7, 2 and 8, 3 and 9, 4 and 10, etc. The symmetry is obtained both by similarity and by seemingly deliberate contrast in the corresponding books.

Vergil keeps the outward trappings of Homeric, or authentic oral, epic: the stock phrases for commonplace situations, the epithets, the repeated lines and phrases. The occupational necessities of the bard have become mannerisms, even willful archaisms, in the Vergilian epic, a more intellectual form. But Vergil's method of creating poetry, pastoral or didactic or epic, is no easy matter of imitation and alteration. Vergil's mind, filled with all the learning of his age, as Servius remarked, was guided by associations of incident, historical circumstance, and, above all, of sound. As Jackson Knight has shown, Vergil seems as alert to recollections of earlier poetry (Ennius, Accius, Aeschylus and Euripides, Catullus and Lucretius) as to his own earlier writings. Syllables, words and phrases, and their sounds, rhythms, and thoughts, remained imbedded in his mind. This thought-process and the associational technique constitutes one of the unique aspects of the poet. It is also partly the explanation of the complex meanings in his lines, for occasionally Vergil worked with pairs of derivations, memories, or thoughts, and combined them to form something new.[58]

THE CHARACTERS OF THE AENEID

Aeneas is the embodiment of the Roman spirit and conduct: pious and faithful to the gods—for *pius* has a mainly sacerdotal sense—and faithful alike to parents, family, and state; he is priest, father, warrior, and ruler of men.[59] He is also the embodiment of civilization as opposed to disorder and barbarity, to blind heroic valor and impiety. The basis of western civilization was, as Vergil indicates throughout his writing, local and racial. The Italic "material," energetic, ambitious, and unadulterated, was for Vergil and for many of his contemporaries the source of Rome's greatness and reason for her success in agriculture and in war.[60] But the need for order and the "settled ways of peace" required a leader, a godlike Alexander. Organization man seems almost antiheroic to the present age, but to a society longing for national recovery the pattern of discipline, obedience, and devotion required by a militant, temperate authority was acceptable. Aeneas and his company are the exemplars for Vergil's contemporaries—for Augustus, *pius* and *felix,* for his counselors and the country's *Patres* (senators). Vergil repeatedly implies a likeness of his hero Aeneas to Hercules, the patient, enduring, philanthropic hero who faced even more horrendous labors than Aeneas, who explored the reaches of the world, founded cities, rid the world of terror, who visited Hades and attained ultimate divinity. Vergil's account in *Aeneid* 8 of the celebration of the Hercules rite at Pallanteum is often seen as a transparent allusion to the popular identification of Hercules with Octavian-Augustus.[61]

Notwithstanding these intimations of divinity and the parallels to Augustus (or Caesar), Vergil's hero has seemed to many a disappointment, a static or sleepwalking character, bowed down by the weight of destiny and immune to physical hurt or significant reversal.[62] His solitude, except for the company of Anchises, Achates, and Ascanius, all of whom lack vivid characterization or active roles in his progress, is inescapable. His isolation lends him a tragic character: deprived of wife and father, and of his beloved Dido, his piety and allegiance to the future Rome seem excessive. Aeneas is chosen by Heaven as the instrument to establish a new world. His is not the glory, but Rome's. His function is to originate, to bring something new into being by his actions. But the colorless aspect of the hero has probably been over-emphasized. There are pathetic qualities which claim respect and under-standing. Vergil has revealed depths of Aeneas' inner life that are unique in epic writing, suppressed desires and deep-seated doubts that humanize him.[63] The relationship with Dido has brought him criticism—as cold-hearted, deceitful and irresponsible. In fact he is compelled by Heaven and by a sense of responsibility to history to renounce Dido. Affection and duty are at war in him; though capable of passionate relations and selfish abandon, he realizes, too, that his own happiness is outweighed by the demands of his son, of the society around him, and by his mission. Bowra's view is reasonable: "Aeneas gains in appreciation, when we think of him not as a perfect character, but as a good man, who is hardly tested and sometimes fails."[64] His perils are not those of an Achilles or Hector in battle or of an Odysseus in his wanderings. They are "modern" confrontations—the stress of office, the agonies of spiritual dilemmas which give rise to melancholy and to resignation. But the heroic will, pride, and ambition are alive in him, and Aeneas often reflects the ideals popularly ascribed to Augustus—*virtus, clementia, justitia,* and *pietas.*[65] And for some, Aeneas is Everyman, suffering and dutiful, serving a nation yet unborn, accomplishing an unknown destiny.

The tragedy of Aeneas has much in common with that of Orpheus and with Vergil's own experience. Basically, it required the loss of the most cherished human ties: home, wife, family, friends. Aeneas' cause is just and certain of success; his sufferings are limited by divine will for he must be saved for the future. Yet he does suffer, and he does act independently. Dido and Turnus live out their lives in passionate sur-render to their human instincts; Aeneas is not permitted this and is required to make sacrifices that cause far more lasting spiritual anguish. He is often ready to deny the will of Heaven, but he is also concerned to save his *figura,* his reputation—to live up to the now-outmoded code of the Homeric heroes. He can find the resolution to renounce his destiny temporarily, but ultimately he must bring peace into a troubled society. He finds scope for heroic behavior in a foreign environment. His triumphant effort, his ability to surmount weariness of body and soul, to seek divine assistance and to act freely as an independent agent on a mission which will bring happiness and peace for mankind after his time, are altogether new and uniquely Roman. Maguinness has stated the ultimate intention concisely: "Vergil had travelled far from the illusory optimism of the Fourth *Eclogue* and so it is that we have an *Aeneid* which in the end was written, not for the benefit of Augustus and the Caesarian party, or even for the glorification of the Roman people, but for the enrichment, enlightenment and comfort of all mankind."[66]

Vergil has profound sympathy for defenders of the lost cause, of the obsolete and doomed society: for Dido, the Carthaginian queen, Camilla, the virgin warrior, and Juturna, the water-nymph sister of Turnus, and even for the Etruscan Mezentius, *contemptor deum,* monster of impiety and perverted cruelty who is at the same time an affectionate father and heroic figure . . . *Victrix causa deis placuit, sed victa Maroni*—"The victorious cause found favor with the gods, the lost cause with Maro (Vergilius)."[67]

The characterization of Dido brought tears to St. Augustine and has induced many to downgrade Aeneas for his callous actions towards her. The view of Otis is more charitable and accurate: "Dido is obviously an *alter Aeneas.* Like him she had a mission to found a new city overseas; like him she had a special pietas toward the dead (Sychaeus is, in effect, Aeneas' Anchises); like him she was lonely and vulnerable. She is, thus, the great example of *pietas* worsted by the *furor* of passion. She does what Aeneas finally was saved from; she sacrificed her duty to love (all for love)."[68] Kenneth Quinn has tried to redress the balance of sympathy by remarking that "those who think ill of Aeneas for deserting Dido are often the same people who think ill of Mark Antony for not deserting Cleopatra."[69]

Dido's tragedy is that she sought to lead a private life at an impossible juncture. She is the embodiment of the great and passionate Eastern queens, as much Medea as Cleopatra, as much Ariadne, bride of divine Dionysus, as deserted heroine of elegy, as much Helen as lost love. Dido is an instrument, a stage in the spiritual history of Aeneas. Like Latinus later, she suffers for her simple nature (the simile of the wounded deer in the Arcadian setting is pertinent) and for her generosity; her tenderness and love are hopeless in the face of destiny.[70]

Turnus, the representative Italian at war with the Trojan invaders for the sake of his country and of his love for the somewhat colorless

Lavinia, is outwardly more attractive than Aeneas. Youthful, with an air of audacity, he surrounds himself with remarkable women—his divine sister Juturna, the Latin queen Amata, and the warrior maiden Camilla. Turnus moves like a lion, recklessly and courageously against the Trojan intruders. Resigned (like Dido) to the possibility of death in the hope of fame, finally discouraged and deserted by the divine powers, he finds a heroic death at Aeneas' hand. Turnus stands for the antique land of Italy; his sister is a nymph of the river Numicus; he is part of the elemental forces of Italy, and the similes which Vergil associates with him, the lion, the bull, and even bloodstained Ares, are revealing of his primitive nature and energy.

Turnus' lineage is Greek, and this enables Vergil to mark the war in Italy as a continuation of the Trojan war. He has the firm resolve of the warrior—determined to live and die by his heroic, now-obsolescent ideals, in support of a lost cause. And like Homer's Hector, his tragedy is the more affecting because he cannot live up to the ideals. His last effort to counter the future and to save his world is wonderful. Alone and disarmed, but with his strength and courage remaining, he stares at his nemesis. He lifts a huge stone which twelve men could scarcely raise to their shoulders and hurls it at Aeneas. But the last desperate effort is in vain, like Priam's attempt to halt Neoptolemus in dying Troy; the stone misses its target, and Turnus' heroic world ends in the darkness of death. With the premature flight of his complaining spirit to the shades, the pastoral civilization and the Homeric ethos are superseded.[71]

The tragic career of Turnus, which occupies the last third of the epic, is interrupted and enlarged by the agonies of others, both Italian and Trojan. The tragic experiences of the lesser figures are like choral responses or parallel actions that provide mounting comment and generalizing statements on the greater theme. The intrusive stories of Camilla, of Nisus and Euryalus, Pallas and Evander, Lausus and Mezentius, play a role similar to that of the complementary panels on the Ara Pacis. For as on the Augustan monument, so here there is a larger program to be detected by viewing the self-contained "side-panels" within the work as a whole. Mezentius' career, for example, is the other side of Aeneas' piety. Mezentius is oblivious to the divine will; he gives vent to a self-confidence that verges on blasphemy; yet his ultimate piety towards his son's self-sacrifice is as memorable as any of Aeneas' actions.[72] Nisus and Euryalus provide another miniature tragic drama of friendship and rash ambition.[73] Their story is a counterpart to the Damon and Pythias story, or, in Vergil's own time, to the lamented deaths of the consuls Hirtius and Pansa in 43 B.C. Vergil's insights into man's frailty, his problems, aspirations, and weaknesses, is searching and personal.

The designation "tragic" applied to the stories of Dido, Turnus, and lesser figures is significant. The design of the tragedies of Dido and Turnus, which essentially frame the central theme,[74] is, with allowance for the epic context, tragic in the Euripidean sense. Furthermore, the recollections of Euripidean tragedy are numerous and suggestive throughout the epic. The parallel scenes involving Sinon and Priam in Book 2 and Anchises and Achaemenides in Book 3 are greatly indebted to Euripides' *Philoctetes,* whose hero's possession of the bow of Heracles ultimately ensured Troy's fall. The story of Nisus and Euryalus is indebted without doubt to Euripides' *Rhesus.* The Andromache-Helenus episode in Epirus, a mock Troy with pathetic recollections of past glories, owes much to Euripides' *Trojan Women, Andromache,* and *Hecuba. Aeneid* 2, the Fall of Troy (like *Aeneid* 8, the Birth of Rome), has theatrical elements that recall the physical setting of stage buildings, as well as the conventions of chorus, three actors, and *deus ex machina* (Creusa) at the close.[75] The conflicts which confront Dido and Turnus lead them to new awareness of themselves and their worlds; they suffer and die, as representatives of their respective societies, but without gaining the wisdom that their tragedy communicates to others. Turnus dies because he stands in the way of destiny and the fateful union of people, Trojans and Italians, in peace.

Camilla, fated victim, courageous and lovely, is a typical Italian and Vergilian invention: daughter of an Etruscan villain, brought up in an Arcadian exile, she goes to her doom gorgeously arrayed in scarlet and gold, like a barbaric queen, with all the associations of the Amazonian Penthesilea, tragically loved and killed by Achilles. Her irresistible *cupido* for glory and for finery brings her to ruin.[76] Turnus, as De Witt once pointed out, is a composite figure also who stands for the major enemies of Rome—Hannibal, Sertorius, Vercingetorix—examples of frustrated valor, possessors of courage without good fortune (*infelix* is the repeated epithet of many of Vergil's tragic characters), all imbued

with the pathos of the ill-starred.[77] Dido's links with Medea, in both
Euripides' play and the *Argonautica* of Apollonius Rhodius, have frequently been detected. Her characterization is another amalgam, this
time of the feelings and careers of Phaedra and Alcestis.[78]

TIME REMEMBERED

Past and present are inextricably interwoven in Vergil's epic. Although
Aeneas' adventures are part of a late Mycenaean context, eleven centuries past, there are Roman associations as well, allegorically or directly
stated. There are parallels between the agony of Troy's fall and both
the destruction of Carthage (146 B.C.) and the recent war-racked history
of Italy. There are similarities between the characters, ideal and actual,
of Aeneas and Augustus (Frontispiece, Fig. 1) of Turnus and Mark
Antony (Fig. 2), of Dido and Cleopatra, of Achates and Agrippa
(Fig. 3), etc. And elements of contrast and comparison are evident
between the Saturnian pastoral world of Evander and the alleged Golden
Age of Augustus.[79]

But there are shadows in the vision as well. The attainment of the
promised land is curiously joyless. Along the entire route, Aeneas is
reminded of a past that was peaceful, productive, and normal—one
might say, Arcadian. Arcadia, Vergil's first creation, remains a vital
element in his creative process. His personal tragedy of displacement
remained a disquieting factor and a source of regret and anxiety in his
later years. The bitterness of the *Eclogues,* in which the displacement
is first reflected, is succeeded by a sense of loss, of exile from the
pastoral world. The repeated instances of Aeneas' hopeless attempts to
recover, to embrace, the loved and lost, Venus in *Aeneid* 1, Creusa in
Aeneid 2, and Dido in *Aeneid* 6, seem to emphasize this enforced re-
nunciation. The most obvious statement of this sense of loss appears in
the Orpheus-Eurydice epyllion. Herein lies the pattern of Aeneas' repeated spiritual crises as he moves towards the fulfillment of destiny.[80]
Ironically, though Aeneas, like Vergil, seeks to regain the bliss of
Arcadia, he is himself a party to its dissolution. In his effort to regain
the past he is responsible for the outbreak of hostilities in Italy. His son
Ascanius-Julus kills the pet stag of Silvia, and the force of arms disrupts
the bucolic world. Evander's Pallanteum, described in the language of

the Golden Age, is subjected to war and bereavement, most poignantly in the loss of Pallas. Gossage has suggested the poet's dilemma: "Vergil strove to adjust himself to the world as he found it, with its cruel realities, and sometimes experienced a strange hesitation, a bewilderment, and even a stagnation of spirit in the face of those realities; but he was able to find consolation in the recollection of a land of peace, the Arcadia and the Golden Age that his spirit longed for; this manifests itself throughout his poetry and is the explanation of much that might seem strange or inconsistent."[81]

The sense of loss is repeatedly evidenced, but there is a sense of achievement as well. Like his Trojan hero, Vergil had known the travails of the birth of a nation, the ordeal of civil and world conflict, and finally the triumph of a new society. An awareness of the implications of Rome's role as successor to the classical world and the Hellenistic political powers undoubtedly did much to fire the poet's national pride and to strengthen his poetic impulse. The *Aeneid* has been called "patriotism raised to religion," and Aeneas appears as the symbol of the new national character and aspirations.

THE DIVINE MACHINERY

The gods of Vergil are difficult for our age to understand.[82] Venus and Juno, who contrive the major action of the *Aeneid* outside the will of Jupiter and Destiny, are a sinister, unattractive pair. Jealous of their own status, cruel, embittered, conniving, deceitful, they are nonetheless accepted by the heroes as embodiments of divine goodness and agents of succor. Their interventions on behalf of their favorites are officious. But even so, they have the power to inspire fear. Aeneas in Carthage is prey to the conflict between love and devotion to duty. His piety extends as much to his family and friends as to his goddess mother and the gods who intervene on his behalf. The prudential commands of the gods are fundamental to his role in history and his divine mission.

For Jupiter, whose will equates with destiny, and for Apollo, there is greater veneration. Apollo is especially revered. His prophecies are Aeneas' main guide during his wanderings, and culminate in the revelation at Cumae (*Aeneid* 6).[83] As god of moderation, of guiding counsel and of colonization, he is essential. And Apollo's role in recent Roman history made his part in the epic all the more pertinent because the god was associated with the crucial naval victories over Sextus Pompey, and over Antony and Cleopatra at Actium, and thus won special reverence from Augustus. Apollo became, almost overnight, the tutelary deity of Rome and of the Princeps. The splendid Temple of Apollo on the Palatine, dedicated in 28 B.C., was an object of awe.[84] The Palatine triad of Apollo, Diana, and Latona became a new focus for worship alongside, perhaps partly eclipsing, the ancient Capitoline triad of Jupiter, Juno, and Minerva.

Oracles, omens, and prophecies are also an essential part of the fabric of the *Aeneid,* and they repeatedly underscore the inevitability of Rome's establishment and ultimate primacy among the nations.[85] For Aeneas, and for Vergil, there is a divine purpose in the universe. Men's evils, their contests with sickness and death, are the result of their failure to seek out and comply with the divine purpose. *Fatum,* the "utterance" of the gods, determines the destiny of nations and of individuals. And mortals may become divine agents. Such is the career of Aeneas, who is the instrument of God's will; his survival is the result of his intellectual vigor, courage, versatility, strength, and endurance. His opponents, Dido and Turnus, and lesser figures as well, are also vouchsafed oracles and omens that directly reveal their proper courses of action, but their passions and their neglect of divine wisdom eventually bring them to ruin. Vergil, if Anchises' dictum on Rome's mission (A. 6, 847–53) may be taken as expressing the author's views, is convinced that man has the power to remedy his sufferings by his own efforts. More than this, each individual has the responsibility to dissipate every obstacle to perfection, to happiness, and to peace of mind. *Quisque suos patimur manes*—"We each endure our ghosthood as individuals," says Anchises; what man does not learn in his earthly existence, he learns in the afterlife.[86]

Vergil did not set out to be a religious or philosophic teacher. He was impressed with the resurgence, however temporary, of Italic cult and the simple agricultural worship of the post-war era. He was aware also of the brilliant advent of Apollo as redeemer divinity in the Roman pantheon, and the Emperor's association with the god. And he was no doubt impressed—as the Emperor had intended—by the basis of Octavian's claim to rule: his right as an adopted son of the deified

Julius, an assertion which capitalized on the deep-seated Latin sense of family. The Emperor's person remained mortal, but his office and the attributes that surrounded him were objects of veneration because of his divine sanction.

TRAGEDY AND HISTORY

A celebrated mosaic from Sousse, ancient Hadrumetum, in Tunisia, depicts Vergil seated pensively on a throne, looking outward, abstractedly awaiting the inspiration of the two Muses at his elbow: Clio, the Muse of History, and Melpomene, the Muse of Tragedy (Fig. 4). The Muses symbolize at least two components of his poetic invention.

The mosaic artist has shown considerable insight into his subject, for, as we have seen, both history and tragedy are deeply imbedded in the epic—to the concern, sometimes to the outright distaste, of many readers. The narrative of the *Aeneid,* within which multiple meanings and associations cluster, is a basically simple story of the migration of Trojan refugees to find a new home and a new sanctuary for their gods. (The Mayflower parallel is apposite, for Aeneas has much of the Pilgrim Father in his character.) But the divine purpose is superior to human design. Destiny shapes the future which is repeatedly, though often abstrusely, revealed by Apollo and his agents. The founding of Rome is divinely ordered, but the goal is evasive and hardly understood; it becomes manifest only by progressive revelations of the divine purpose. The road to Rome is beset with obstacles—storms, inhospitable lands and peoples, plague, and psychological terrors. Vergil comments tersely at the close of his preface: "Such was the cost in heavy toil of founding the Roman nation."[87]

Aeneas' departure from Troy involves the loss of his wife, Creusa; the wanderings are laden with disappointment and climaxed by the death of Anchises. Dido's tragedy is both private and political; there are intimations of Cleopatra and Julius Caesar in the lines of *Aeneid* 4, just as there is surely a direct summons by Dido of Hannibal as her avenger for the future. Every landfall of Aeneas in Hesperia is marked with death and the loss of a dear companion—Palinurus, Misenus, Caieta, the helmsman, the trumpeter, the nurse.[88] Youth is sacrificed repeatedly to war: Pallas, Lausus, Nisus, Euryalus, and Camilla. In Vergil's view, failure and loss seem implicit in every success. (Even in the *Georgics,* conceived in wartime with a prophetic vision of hope, there is unlikely slaughter in the destruction of the bees.) "Vergil realized," Maguinness has observed, "that conquest cannot be made, and the domination of a people or man established, without the sacrifice of beautiful and innocent creatures, suffering noble victims, and treachery and heartlessness on the part of those ambitious for power."[89] To build the massive reality and ordered unity of Rome, Priam and Polites, Mezentius and Lausus, Dido and Turnus, must die. But violence, passion, and chaos are succeeded by new ideals—ones which characterize the community of the bees in the *Georgics*—courage, industry, loyalty, order, and love for the leader.[90]

The source of Vergil's melancholy and compassion defies definition. But the poet's sensitivity to the appalling, sacrilegious sacrifice of life in the preceding century of war must have been a potent factor. His own lifetime also witnessed an accelerating incidence of war, proscription, and violent death.[91] The slave revolt under Spartacus, with its terrible aftermath of miles of crucified slaves, took place just before Vergil's birth. Further violence followed: the Catilinarian conspiracy, the First Triumvirate, the death of Crassus, caught with his legions in a Parthian sandstorm; Pompey's death in Egypt; Caesar's dictatorship and assassination; Cicero's beheading by Antony's minions at Formiae; Philippi, where Brutus and Cassius died gallantly on their swords; the Perusine War with its mass execution of senators who opposed the Julian tide; and finally Actium and the defeat of Cleopatra and her Roman paramour. The Ptolemaic kingdom and the post-Alexandrian Hellenistic Age yielded to Rome, to a sober, determined world of Italian patriotism and to a new kind of god-man ruler.

THE ROMAN IMPERIAL MISSION

Vergil's Roman epic was designed for a specific juncture in history when, outwardly at least, a new order had arrived, a new morality, and a wider sympathy with and understanding of the condition of man. The *Aeneid,* in effect, relates the achievement of Italy's destiny under the favor of heaven and is an account of how "faithful" Aeneas, against seemingly hopeless odds, fulfilled his mission as founder of the Roman world. Anchises' charge to Aeneas during their interview in Hades is apt both for Aeneas, whose subsequent career in the Italian conquest fulfills the commission, and for Augustan Rome and its imperial mission:

> Others will, I believe, fashion bronze more gracefully into breathing forms, or draw living features from marble. They will be better pleaders and will mark out the course of the heavens with their pointer and name the rising stars. But thou, O Roman, remember to rule the peoples under your sway—these will be your arts—to add to peace a settled way of life, to spare the conquered and to beat down the proud.
>
> (A. 6, 847–53)

Anchises' seven-line summation of Rome's mission is a concession, realization, and definition of purpose. Both Horace and Vergil were ready to concede to Greece the formative influences on Italian civilization. Horace is even more forceful than Vergil, remarking, "Captive Greece led captive her fierce conqueror, and brought the arts into agrarian Latium."[92] Anchises concedes to the Greeks literature and the fine arts, specifically sculpture in bronze and marble, and the theoretical sciences, represented by astronomy. But the Roman arts will be magisterial in a stricter sense: in the realms of government and empire, conquest and rule, and of settled organization and peace. Anchises does not sound the war cry of past imperialistic society, to conquer and aggrandize; he emphasizes government which, by implication at least, will be enlightened and merciful. Conquest is but the first stage to peace.

Vergil's imperialistic fervor sounds several times in the *Aeneid*. Rome's imperial mission is defined with pride in Book I in Jupiter's prophetic promise to Venus:

> To these I set no bounds, either in space or time;
> Unlimited power I give them. Even the spiteful Juno,
> Who in her fear now troubles the earth, the sea and the sky,
> Shall think better of this and join me in fostering
> The cause of the Romans, the lords of creation, the togaed people.
>
> .   .   .   .
>
> From the fair seed of Troy there shall be born a Caesar—
> Julius, his name derived from great Iulus—whose empire
> Shall reach to the ocean's limits, whose fame shall end in the stars.
> He shall hold the East in fee . . . .
>
> (A. 1, 278–82, 286–9. Day Lewis)

Aspirations for conquest, for booty, for the prestige and office which attend the successful general, were part of the Roman Republican development. But the process was impeded by traditional senatorial resistance to overseas commitments. Isolationist in sentiment and practice, the Republican Senate feared the rise—a frequent occurrence—of individualistic generals who would undermine the constitutional strengths of Roman government. Even popular enthusiasm was diminishing during the second and first centuries B.C. The masses, from whom soldiers had occasionally to be conscripted, did not like prolonged campaigns, although Caesar's projected revenge against Parthia, which had been responsible for Crassus' defeat in 53 B.C., did arouse popular enthusiasm. But one statesman at least, Cicero, expressed concern and criticism of Caesar's designs of becoming the new Alexander.[93]

What was Vergil's attitude to contemporary imperialistic plans? Like many Roman writers, Vergil had thoughts of remote conquests and supposed that Augustus would be the agent to accomplish Rome's mission to exercise dominion unlimited in space or time—such was Jupiter's promise to Venus regarding Aeneas and his descendants. Of the current imperialistic ventures, two areas commanded most popular attention, Britain and Parthia, both responsibilities carried over from the Republican era. Vergil (and Horace as well) suggested boldly that Augustus' divinity could only become manifest by a career of conquest in these territories.[94] But Britain was judged too remote for conquest and of questionable value. Parthia was a more terrific prospect; by clever diplomatic maneuvers the Parthians were finally induced to make concessions to Rome in 20 B.C. and to accept Roman dictates. Augustus was honored with a triumphal arch in the Forum, and the event is also commemorated in the great Prima Porta statue (Fig. 5). The Emperor was not shy of conquest, for his *Achievements* place special emphasis on his military gains.[95] But the romantic dream which Vergil, Horace, and their contemporaries promulgated was set aside for more urgent, less drastic objectives. The policy of co-existence with the Parthian kingdom, which Augustus inaugurated, lasted for two centuries, except for the reign of Trajan from 98 to 117 A.D. The problems of the Hellenistic monarchies, of the Seleucids and the Ptolemies, with their huge, heterogeneous states, were sensibly deferred by Augustus.

THE AFTERMATH

The *Eclogues, Georgics,* and *Aeneid* found an instant, if not unanimously favorable, reception among Roman society. Graffiti on the walls of Pompeii testify at least to the availability, and most likely to the popularity, of the poems in Flavian times. More important perhaps are the poems of the so-called *Appendix Vergiliana,* once defined as "second-rate pieces, pleasantly perched somewhere between an Alexandrian Vergil and a Vergilian Ovid"; they are at least a clue to what Julio-Claudian and later readers enjoyed in Vergil and thought worthy of imitation.[96] Lucan, in his *Pharsalia,* the epic on the Civil War between Pompey and Caesar, and Seneca, in his extravagant dramas and moral essays, offer additional evidence of Vergil's influence in Neronian days. Even more derivative and deferential to the master are Statius, Valerius Flaccus, and Silius Italicus. Tacitus and Juvenal, the greater masters of the Silver Age, echo and parody the Augustan poet with sophisticated artistry. Petronius' *Satyricon* is saturated with Vergilian reminiscences and hilarious reversals of incident and tone.[97]

To the Middle Ages, Vergil was a marvelous magician rather than a literary model. The fourth *Eclogue* was regarded as a prophecy of Christ's Nativity; the Golden Bough (*virga*) of *Aeneid* 6 had occult connotations and at the same time Christian reference to the Virgin. Vergil was remembered as the architect who built the tunnel under Posillipo, the Castel dell'Ovo on the Bay of Naples, and a bronze tower that reflected every conspiracy against the person of the Princeps. His words, like the Bible, were consulted at random, with confidence, for guidance and consolation. Dante turned to Vergil as master and equated the Roman poet with earthly wisdom that lacked only the vision of Love which Dante saw as the ordering principle of the Universe.[98] In the Renaissance, Vergil was part of the core of the school curriculum, "Prince and purest of all Latine Poets." In the seventeenth century appeared Milton's *Paradise Lost,* the best commentary on the *Aeneid* of any age, an epic that could never have existed without the *Aeneid.* It is hard to imagine a more thoroughly classical epic poem in English, and its architecture is as strict as Vergil's. To Dryden, and to most seventeenth-century critics, the true heroic poem was "undoubtedly the greatest work which the soul of man is capable to perform." Dryden's *Aeneid,* in heroic couplets, is infused with a sprightliness and vigor which often undermine the grandeur of the hexameter, and yet it remains a durable monument of poetic translation. His version of the *Georgics,* "the best poem of the best poet," is superb.[99]

Imitators, translators, and heirs to Vergilian characters and pathos are legion. The landscape, the mood of Arcadian tranquillity, the poetry of earth and the religion of labor, personal sacrifice and heroism, the wisdom that comes from suffering, the adult nature of inner conflict and resolution of doubts in action, the rationale of rule, and the compassion which attaches to the lost cause—all of these, and the mastery of the verse, the complexity of imagery, the patterned structure—combine to influence the poet-translator in his adaptive, but at the same time critical and innovating, art. C. Day Lewis, whose verse translations of the works of Vergil are the most expert and sensitive of our time, writes that the most rewarding passages to translate were those in which, writing of country scenes and pursuits, Vergil raised his language to lyric utterance, and those where he charged the classical epic with romantic feeling.[100] Vergil has been called the greatest of all those landscape painters who have used words rather than paint. His landscapes are not, however, studies of nature in the raw, of great open spaces, majestic mountains, primeval forests. The scene that attracts Vergil is one in which man and his works form an integral part.[101] Our task now is to take a comprehensive view of Vergil's landscape, his seascapes, lakes, and rivers, and of the peoples who were constituents in the colorful mosaic of ancient Italy and of the Augustan society of his day.

I I

Cisalpine Gaul
and Lombardy

PUBLIUS VERGILIUS MARO (Fig. 45) was born on October 15th, 70 B.C., at Andes, a small community usually identified with modern Pietole, near Mantua in Cisalpine Gaul. In its simplest definition, Cisalpine Gaul, i.e. Gaul "on the Roman side" of the Alps, was the valley of the Po, delimited by the Alps and the Apennines, by the Tyrrhenian and Adriatic seas, and by a number of rivers. Four of the later Augustan regions were within the Cisalpine territory: XI (Transpadana) and X (Venetia), both north of the Po; IX (Liguria) and VIII (Aemilia), south of the Po.

The poet's family has interested many scholars and critics, and its origins have been sought among Oscan, Ligurian, Celtic, and Etruscan forefathers. Mary Gordon's conjectural reconstruction of the history of Vergil's family[1] has won considerable acceptance, and it now seems almost certain that the Vergilii were an important family at Mantua, descended from Etruscan forebears who had founded the city. The family acres at Pietole were probably extensive, and the traditional ascription of the potter's trade to Vergil's father no doubt stemmed from the production of pottery on the estate for use in merchandising its produce. Vergil's father seems to have married, perhaps late in life, the daughter of another landowning mercantile family belonging to the local aristocracy of Cremona. Vergil, the eldest son, inherited the family cognomen, Maro, which commemorated the tenure of an Etruscan priesthood (*zilath maruchva*) at Mantua. The second son, Silo ("snub-nosed"), and the third, Flaccus ("flap-eared"), may have drawn their names from the mother's relatives. Both brothers died young, and because Vergil remained unmarried, his father adopted Valerius Proculus, member of an aristocratic family of Cisalpine Gaul.

Most scholars favor Pietole-Andes, approximately two miles southeast of Mantua, as the birthplace of the poet, though there is still lively debate on the question. Besides the biographical testimony, supplied most authoritatively by a fourth-century grammarian, Aelius Donatus, who drew primarily on a life by Suetonius (69–140 A.D.), there are clues to the identification of his birthplace in the poet's writings, particularly in *Eclogues* 1 and 9, where Vergil alludes to evictions in the territory of Cremona and Mantua. Though the *Eclogues* were composed in Rome or Naples, one may assume that these poems provide a fair, though wistful, reflection of the poet's homeland. The details in *Eclogue* 9 suggest an estate perched on high ground, with adjacent low ground stretching down to the banks of the Mincius river:

> all the land, from the place where
> That spur with its gentle slope juts out from the recessive
> Hill-line, as far as the water and the old beech-trees with
> Their shattered tops . . .
>
> (E. 9, 7–10. Day Lewis)

A swampy stretch, the plot of Tityrus which was exempted from the confiscations because it was unproductive (E. 1, 46–48), apparently lay between the Vergilian farm and Mantua. There are several allusions to hills descending gently into the arable plains. While the express location of Vergil's birth at Andes by the author of the "Life" should not be disregarded, attempts to sharpen the poetic vagueness of the *Eclogues'* description of such a locale are misguided. One cannot expect precise details of landscape or mileage in a poetic masque, but the realistic features, which are the poet's way of awakening responses in his audience, seem to provide a summary sketch of the countryside of Vergil's youth:

> Fortunate old man!—so your acres will be yours still.
> They're broad enough for you. Never mind if its stony soil
> Or the marsh films over your pastureland with mud and rushes.

At least no queer vegetation will tempt your breeding ewes,
And there's no risk of their catching disease from a neighbour's flock.
Ah, fortunate old man, here among hallowed springs
And familiar streams you'll enjoy the longed-for shade, with cool shade.
Here, as of old, where your neighbor's land marches with yours,
The sally hedge, with bees of Hybla sipping its blossom,
Shall often hum gently to sleep. On the other side
Vine-dressers will sing to the breezes at the crag's foot;
And all the time your favourites, the husky-voiced wood pigeons
Shall coo away, and turtle doves make moan in the elm tops.

(E. 1, 46–58. Day Lewis)

Vergil evidently took considerable pride in the origins of Mantua. Certainly his allusions to the Etruscan role in the foundation of the city are historically sound. The Etruscans subjugated the Po valley during the sixth century, and according to Livy, had ventured deep into the Alpine valleys, affecting the area so strongly that traces of the Etruscan language still persisted in the tribal speech of Lombardy in early Imperial times. Alert to the necessity for protection and organization in this remote terrain, the Etruscans formed an alliance of twelve cities, a dodecapolis, which no doubt included Mantua and Felsina (mod. Bologna). A colony was also established at Marzobotto on the Reno river; recent excavations there have revealed impressive indications of the Etruscans' abilities as town-planners, hydraulic engineers, and domestic architects. Mantua must have shared in this cultural awakening in the sixth and fifth centuries B.C. The coastal cities on the Adriatic, Adria (Hadria) and Spina, at the ancient mouth of the Po, were cities of enormous wealth and influence. Strabo records that Spina was built on piles with a grand canal leading into an inner harbor, and a network of smaller canals forming a gridiron pattern of houseblocks. Like an ancient Venice, Spina prospered from her Adriatic trade, and the recent finds of Attic vases and other luxury articles offer eloquent testimony to Etruscan enterprise in the Po valley. However, during the fourth century the Etruscan domination of the Po valley began to disintegrate, and the twelve cities were overrun by barbaric Gallic tribes from central Europe. They soon occupied most of the productive open country of the valley, and a Gallic way of life superseded the Etruscan by the middle of the fourth century. Only Mantua remained outside the Gallic conquest, and Vergil refers to its freedom as proudly as an Athenian would assert his freedom from the Dorians.

By Vergil's time Mantua sought distinction in a pedigree that asserted that Ocnus, son of the Theban prophetess Manto and an Etruscan river god, gave the city its walls and—with characteristic Etruscan respect for the maternal side—bestowed on it his mother's name.

> There too was Ocnus, who'd whipped up a force from his native land:
> He, the son of the Tuscan river and the seeress Manto,
> Founded the city of Mantua and gave it his mother's name—
> Mantua, rich in its forefathers, who were not all of the same stock:
> Three clans it had, each clan ruling over four townships,
> With Mantua, by reason of its Etruscan blood, as the capital.
> They sailed in warships following a figurehead of the river
> Mincius wreathed with the grey-green rushes of Lake Benacus.
>
> (A. 10, 198–206. Day Lewis)

Although Vergil preferred the legendary tradition, the place-name actually derives from Mantus, the Etruscan Pluto. Mary Gordon has surmised that his Etruscan background may have stimulated Vergil's capacity to see visions and dream dreams, because "Mantua was the city of Pluto, and the Etruscan mind, like the mediaeval, seems to have been preoccupied with the next world."[2] Maybe the apocalyptic strain in Vergil's writings and his interest in ritual also derive from his Etruscan background.

Rome founded her first Latin colonial outposts at Placentia and Cremona in 219 B.C. Both colonies proved of value to Rome during the Hannibalic war, but thereafter Rome had to face a coalition of the Cenomani, Roman allies since 225 B.C., and the Insubrian Gauls. The coalition's attempt to dislodge the Romans from the north failed, and the final defeat came on the banks of Vergil's Mincius river. Cremona and Placentia were further strengthened with military contingents in 190 B.C.; Latin colonies were lodged at Bononia (Etruscan Felsina, mod. Bologna) in 189 and at Aquileia in 181, and Roman colonies at Mutina and Parma in 183 B.C. Transpadane Gaul was thoroughly policed and became heavily occupied by Romans who streamed into the organized territories as settlers, merchants, and tax collectors. The Social War

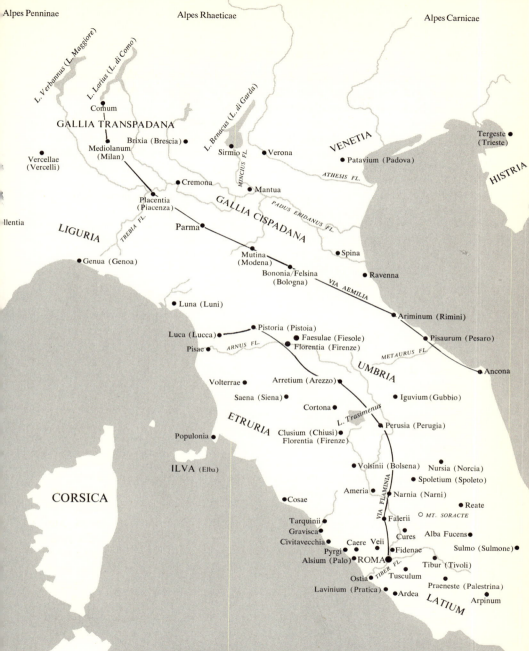

Alpes Penninae   Alpes Rhaeticae   Alpes Carnicae

L. Verbanus (L. Maggiore)
L. Larius (L. di Como)
Comum
GALLIA TRANSPADANA
Brixia (Brescia)
L. Benacus (L. di Garda)
Sirmio FL.
Verona
VENETIA
Patavium (Padova)
Tergeste (Trieste)
Mediolanum (Milan)
Vercellae (Vercelli)
MINCIUS FL.
ATHESIS FL.
HISTRIA
Cremona
Mantua
Placentia (Piacenza)
GALLIA CISPADANA
PADUS ERIDANUS FL.
LIGURIA
TREBIA FL.
Parma
Spina
Genua (Genoa)
Mutina (Modena)
Ravenna
Bononia/Felsina (Bologna)
VIA AEMILIA
llentia
Luna (Luni)
Ariminum (Rimini)
Pistoria (Pistoia)
Pisaurum (Pesaro)
Luca (Lucca)
ARNUS FL.
Faesulae (Fiesole)
Florentia (Firenze)
Pisae
METAURUS FL.
Ancona
UMBRIA
Volterrae
Arretium (Arezzo)
Iguvium (Gubbio)
Saena (Siena)
Cortona
ETRURIA
L. Trasimenus
Populonia
Clusium (Chiusi)
Florentia (Firenze)
Perusia (Perugia)
ILVA (Elba)
Volsinii (Bolsena)
Nursia (Norcia)
Spoletium (Spoleto)
CORSICA
Ameria
Narnia (Narni)
Cosae
VIA FLAMINIA
Reate
Tarquinii
Falerii
○ MT. SORACTE
Gra_visca
Cures
Alba Fucens
Civitavecchia
Caere Veii
Cures
Sulmo (Sulmone)
Pyrgi
Fidenae
Alsium (Palo)
ROMA
TIBER FL.
Tibur (Tivoli)
Ostia
Tusculum
Praeneste (Palestrina)
Lavinium (Pratica)
Ardea
Arpinum
LATIUM

NORTHERN ITALY AND ETRURIA

SARDINIA

(91–89), that ambiguously named war of Rome's allies (*socii*) against Rome, their treaty partner, involved northern cities along with many other restive areas in the peninsula. Although the franchise was granted to almost all of the contestants throughout Italy, in the northern regions there was a piecemeal settlement in 89 under the direction of Gnaeus Pompeius Strabo. In all likelihood *civitas* (Roman citizenship rights) was conferred on the old Latin colonies, and Latin rights were awarded the native *oppida* (towns). The Via Aemilia serviced both Roman and Latin colonies. North of the Po only Cremona and Aquileia acquired citizenship rights.

In the years subsequent to Pompeius Strabo's regime, Cisalpine Gaul emerged as a full-fledged Roman province. But the partial extension of Roman citizenship suggests that a deep-seated prejudice against the Gauls as an inferior civilization still persisted. From the standpoint of productivity, Cisalpine Gaul had much to offer. Well-watered by the Po and the Mincius, its fertility was proverbial, almost as staggering as Campania's. Wheat, vine, and olive production were maintained at a high level during Republican and Imperial times, although in Vergil's day one must imagine that large tracts were still consigned to pasturage and cattle ranches. The geographer Strabo, a contemporary of Vergil, wrote: "As for the excellence of the regions, it is evidenced by their goodly store of men, the size of the cities and their wealth, and in all these respects the Romans in that part of the world have surpassed the rest of Italy, for not only does the tilled land bring forth fruits in large quantities and of all sorts, but the forests have acorns in such quantities that Rome is fed mainly on the herds of swine that come from there." Even today Emilia, Lombardy, and Venezia have the largest wheat production in Italy.

Small landholders in Vergil's time existed alongside the wealthier landowners who maintained extensive pasture lands close to the central and southern margins of the Apennines in order to have both winter and summer grazing. Vergil's frequent allusions to sheepherding are certainly more than a Golden Age vision. Pliny confirms that the white wool of the Po valley was without rival. Patavine wool, used in carpets and rough cloaks, and in the clothing industry generally, was widely exported. Sheep were therefore an important factor in the economy of Cisalpine Gaul. The most profitable crops were grain and grapes, and wines were always an important export. The best wine, the so-called Rhaetic, was produced at Verona from smoke-dried grapes. Strabo made exaggerated claims for it, and Augustus, according to Nepos, favored the wine, but Vergil was not overwhelmed even though it was a product of his native district:

> What poem can do justice
> To Rhaetian? Yet even this cannot compete with Falernian.
> (G. 2, 95–6. Day Lewis)

Vergil alludes to bean crops (G. 1, 215–6), which were important in Cisalpine Gaul; they were used in breads and cakes to soften the taste of rougher cereals. His references to alfalfa (Median Clover) are associated by Servius (in the fourth century A.D.) with its extensive cultivation in Venetia, and this produce may well have served as an alternative crop to wheat or barley. Columella, writing about 60 A.D., informs us that trees and vines were usually planted at the edge of furrows of corn; that vines and trees were the farmer's primary concern, and then grain, which was planted to make use of the surface soil above the roots, which were deliberately set deep. Presumably Vergil's farm followed much the same system, for all these crops receive informed notice in the *Georgics*.

Cisalpine Gaul also made an important contribution to literature. Before Vergil's birth and during his lifetime there emerged in this region a group of poets distinguished for their avant-gardism, their fresh sophistication and novel subject matter. They revolutionized Roman poetry during their generation and greatly affected Vergil throughout his career. This remarkable Transpadane School included Valerius Cato, called "Latin Siren," one of a number of celebrated teachers of literature in the region; he taught several of Catullus' literary compatriots of North Italy, and Vergil may even have known this inspirational figure during the master's advanced years. Northern poets who took part in the revolution were Helvius Cinna from Brescia; Furius Bibaculus and Alfenus Varus, from Cremona; Catullus himself, from Verona; Ticidas and Varius Rufus; and Caecilius of Comum. Besides the Transpadane School, there were a number of influential literary figures, Vergil's contemporaries, from the same area: Cornelius Nepos, historian and biographer; Quintilius Varus, the distinguished literary critic and close friend of Horace and Vergil, from Cremona; Asinius

Pollio, consul of 40 B.C. and a man of marked literary interests, perhaps an early patron of Vergil; and Cornelius Gallus, the love poet and elegist, from Forum Julii (mod. Fréjus) in nearby Gallia Narbonensis.

Vergil grew up in an area which was still largely unassimilated, still a mixture of origins and loyalties, and there assumed the *toga virilis,* the clothes of manhood, in 55 B.C. This right was accorded exclusively to Roman citizens, and since Mantua enjoyed only Latin rights at that time (full citizenship was conferred on the province in 49 B.C.), one must suppose that Vergil's father had qualified for Roman citizenship by holding public office in Mantua or was an immigrant with Roman citizenship; the latter seems unlikely. After exhausting the educational offerings of Mantua, whose facilities as a minor municipal town were undoubtedly limited, Vergil proceeded to Cremona in 58 B.C. for more advanced schooling. He no doubt travelled over the kind of roads described in *Catalepton* VIII (a parody of Catullus IV):

> O cold Cremona and muddy Gaul, Sabinus says that this was and is well known to you; he claims that from his earliest birthtime he stood in your mire, in your marsh unloaded his packs, and thence over so many miles of rutty roads drove his team.

Cremona's distinction as a Latin colony, established in 190 B.C., no doubt resulted from her strategic situation, her great opportunities for agriculture and commerce, as well as her military record. Livy records that Cremona offered asylum to Scipio after his defeat by Hannibal at the Trebia river (218 B.C.), and remained faithful to her Roman alliance during Hannibal's occupation of Italy in spite of heavy attacks from the insurgent Gauls. Colonial status enabled her to heal her wounds and to repair the war damage to the point where she had become a populous, flourishing city during the early Empire, enjoying the rich produce of her territories and the income from her industries and commercial involvements. The splendid forum and the other evidences of wealth must have greatly impressed Vergil in his youth, and the opportunity to continue his education there, perhaps under the care of his mother's family, was no doubt readily offered. After two years' study in Cremona (58–56), Vergil proceeded to Mediolanum (Milan) to spend another year (55) in the study of literature, philosophy, and history. Milan was the major city of the Insubrian Gauls in Cisalpine

Gaul and was for a long time capital of the area. Strabo calls it a considerable city in Augustan times, and although Pliny's evidence stems from a century later, one might suppose that the educational resources there would have complemented or surpassed those at Cremona. With the attainment of adult status, Vergil proceeded to Rome to receive the equivalent of a university education; the year was 54 B.C., the year Catullus died and Lucretius' posthumous *De Rerum Natura* was made public. Vergil's father had provided him with the best education possible, and after a training in rhetoric under Epidius (54–53), the best instructor of the time for young men with ambitions for a career in law or politics, Vergil began to plead in the Roman lawcourts (53–52). But the career of advocate and politician did not appeal to Vergil, and in his early years he turned to the study of philosophy, at first in Rome (51–50), then for a longer period at Naples (49–44), where he entered the academy of the Epicurean teacher Siro, under whom he had studied originally in Rome.

Even before his departure for Rome, Vergil had known troublesome and explosive times in northern Italy. The Transpadane Gauls were clamoring for the right of citizenship; Celts and Etruscans and Italians all demanded their rights from Rome. And they found an advocate in Julius Caesar. Cisalpine Gaul became Caesar's administrative headquarters during his Gallic campaigns and the Italians were recipients of his favors. Cremona was enlarged by the foundation of a colony of five thousand householders and granted citizenship. Rumors circulating in 52 B.C., when Vergil resided in Rome, when Pompey was sole consul, suggested that Caesar had used his own initiative, without Senatorial consent, to award suffrage and the right to hold office to other Transpadane cities. The breaking point in the relations between Caesar and the Senatorial Republic came in 49 B.C., when Caesar crossed the Rubicon and marched on Rome. The government, with most of the senators, evacuated the city. Vergil's dismay at the general disorder, the breakdown of the juridical system, the limitations on free speech, and the impending confrontation of Caesar's and Pompey's armies, motivated his departure from Rome in 49. Impressed with the poetics and the Epicurean message of Lucretius, he retreated to Naples, to the Garden of Siro, center of Epicurean teaching in this Athens of the West. Finally, alarmed by the ominous sequels to Caesar's assassination, by the rising tide of proscriptions of property and judicial murders, Vergil left Naples in 44 for his father's estates near Mantua, perhaps out of concern for his family's security and his own as well in an age of increasing turmoil.

The Triumvirs, Mark Antony, Lepidus, and Octavian, had guaranteed to their troops before Philippi that Italian farmland would be their prize. The victory of 42 therefore meant that thousands of ex-servicemen had to be located on small landholdings in various parts of Italy, including Lombardy. Cremona had been loyal to the cause of Brutus and along with seventeen other Italian cities was compelled to provide allotments for some of the one hundred thousand veterans of the Philippi campaign. Cremona's territory proved inadequate, and the partitioning was extended to include Mantua. The rich properties of Vergil's father yielded sixty allotments. Although the account of the confiscations and evictions is confused, certain salient facts emerge. Alfenus Varus was almost certainly Octavian's agent in charge of the assignment of land to the veterans; he was evidently appointed to the post after Lucius Antonius (Mark Antony's brother), who had supported the victims of the confiscations, was defeated at Perugia in February, 40 B.C. *Eclogue* 9 is usually credited with being the poet's way of recording Varus' unsuccessful appeal on behalf of the Mantuans to have their territory excluded from the confiscations:

LYCIDAS
Where are you footing it, Moeris? to town? this trackway leads there.

MOERIS
Oh, Lycidas, that I should have lived to see an outsider
Take over my little farm—a thing that I had never feared—
And tell me, 'You're dispossessed, you old tenants, you've got to go.'
We're down and out. And look how Chance turns the tables on us—
These are *his* goats (rot them!) you see me taking to market.

LYCIDAS
Can this be true? I had heard that all the land, from the place where
That spur with its gentle slope juts out from the recessive
Hill-line, as far as the water and the old beech-trees with
Their shattered tops—all this had been saved by Menalcas' poetry.

MOERIS
So you heard. That rumour did get about. But poems
Stand no more chance, where the claims of soldiers are involved,
Than do the prophetic doves if an eagle swoops upon them.
Indeed, but for a raven which croaked from a hollow ilex
On my left hand, and warned me to stop this last dispute
Whatever it cost, neither I nor Menalcas would be alive now.

LYCIDAS
Good God, what a scandalous thing this is! So we might have lost
Menalcas himself and the heartening pleasure his poetry gives us!
Who then would have written about the nymphs, the flowering grasses
That feather the earth, and the springs thatched over with leaves to
    shade them?
Who then would have written those lines I overheard you singing
Not long ago, on your way to your sweetheart, Amaryllis?—
Tityrus, till I return (I'm not going far), look after
My goat flock, When they have browsed, take them to water: only
Keep away from my he-goat—a terror he is with his horns.

MOERIS
Why not these lines, from a poem to Varus he's not yet finished—
Varus, if but Mantua remains untouched—but Mantua
Stands far too close for comfort to poor Cremona—choirs of
Swans shall exalt your fame right up to the starry heavens.

                              (E. 9, 1–29. Day Lewis)

Menalcas is almost certainly to be identified as Vergil; Varus is surely
Alfenus Varus, the officer in charge of the redistribution.

So Vergil was expelled from his ancestral domain, and like Horace
at Venusia in Apulia, became one more victim of the Triumvirate's program of confiscations. The ancient biographies and commentaries state
that the Vergilian farm was later restored through the efforts of some
influential friends; most prominently mentioned are C. Asinius Pollio,
the poet Cornelius Gallus, and Alfenus Varus, the land commissioner.
Asinius Pollio was governor of Cisalpine Gaul from 43 to 41, and
judging by Vergil's allusions, he was a close friend and supporter; he
may even have been a patron of the poet. But Pollio's military and
political activity was closely tied to Mark Antony, and Tenney Frank is

undoubtedly correct in asserting, "We may safely conclude that Pollio was neither governor nor colonial commissioner in Cisalpine Gaul when Cremona and Mantua were disturbed, nor could he have been on such terms with Octavian as to use his influence in behalf of Vergil." As for the other supporters mentioned, *Eclogue* 6 is respectful to Alfenus Varus, though in fact far more cordial to Cornelius Gallus. The lines addressed to Varus, however, may be an indication of his efforts to retrieve Vergil's fortunes:

> Since there'll be bards in plenty desiring to rehearse
> Varus' fame, and celebrate the sorrowful theme of warfare,
> I shall take up a slim reed-pipe and a rural subject;
> And not unasked. If anyone—if a single reader falls
> In love with this little poem of mine, it is you, Varus,
> Our tamarisks, all our woods, will be singing about. No page
> Could charm Apollo more than a page inscribed to Varus.
>
> (E. 6, 6–12. Day Lewis)

Cornelius Gallus may have intervened on Vergil's behalf with Octavian at the time. Gallus did take issue with Varus in the matter of unjust confiscations of lands adjacent to Mantua for when ordered to leave unoccupied a district of three miles outside the city Varus included within the district eight hundred paces of water lying about the walls.

What was the outcome of the appeals and the interventions? There is no certain answer, but Vergil's own words would suggest that the original estate was lost permanently (G. 2, 198–9; E. 9, 26–30). One may reasonably suppose that Vergil received some sort of compensation, but henceforth his residences were fixed at Rome, Naples, and Nola, all of them perhaps acquired through the settlement offered by Octavian after the appeal. The *Georgics* and the *Aeneid* provide eloquent proof of the trauma caused by the eviction. The *Eclogues* were published in 37 B.C., and some, possibly 2, 3, 5, and 7, antedated the time of troubles (43–41), but the majority touch on the contrasting worlds of cruel reality and the lost "Arcady," the serenity which Vergil had experienced in his North Italian home. The consequences were considerable, for, as Gossage has argued, "If it is assumed that Vergil was compelled by political and military circumstances to leave his native place and that he never returned to live there, it was in exile, in a special but important sense, that most of his work was composed."

Northern Italy had the advantage of major waterways to expedite communications and trade. Like arterial highways, watery counterparts of the Via Aemilia, the Po and the Mincius played important roles in the consolidation and enrichment of Cisalpine Gaul. The Po delta had been dredged and drained in 109 B.C. The streams had been carefully controlled, and much of the marshy terrain between the Po and Parma was reclaimed for effective agricultural uses. Drainage operations in the lower stretches of the Po had safeguarded the cities against flood and also quickened the tempo of river traffic, and this operation was still in effect under Augustus. The Po became navigable, as it is today, as far as Turin. Ravenna, at the river mouth, was converted into a naval base of importance, accommodating two hundred and fifty ships, supplementing the military bases at Misenum, near Naples, and at Forum Julii (Fréjus). Ravenna became the leading naval arsenal and marine station on the Adriatic, and Spina, the onetime Etruscan Venice, sank further into obscurity.

The Po, which rises in the Cottian Alps, follows a course of almost four hundred miles eastward towards Ravenna. Called Padus by the Romans, and Eridanus, the "amber river," by the Greeks, Vergil shared the general Italian awe for the mighty stream, following its proud course to the point where the alluvial efflux discolored the sea:

> Eridanus, depicted with gilded horns on his bull-head—
> Eridanus, than which through fertile lands no river
> Rushes with more momentum to the pansy-purple sea.
>> (G. 4, 371–3. Day Lewis)

> Po, the king of rivers, in maniac spate whirled round
> Forests, washed them away, swept all over the plains
> Herds and their byres together.
>> (G. 1, 481–3. Day Lewis)

In another marvelous simile Vergil recaptures the raucous sounds of seabirds at the mouth of the Po where the fishing fleets ply their trade:

> A monstrous din
> Went up now all over the town as men argued and wrangled together:
> So it is when a flock of birds have alighted upon
> The tree-tops in some wood, or the fish-haunted river Padusa
> Resounds with the harsh screaming of swans till its pools are a bedlam.
>> (A. 11, 454–8. Day Lewis)

The clamoring sea birds find analogy in the uproar which distracted the Italian assembly in *Aeneid* 11 and finally excited Turnus to rash action. The memorable picture almost certainly stems from Vergil's experience at the river mouth and among the marshy pools which fringed the river. The gilded horns of the river are Vergil's elaborated reference to a common mythical representation of great streams, especially rivers in torrential flood, as rampaging bulls.

The evidence suggests that the flatlands and borders of the Po were well wooded in antiquity and admired and used by the natives. Ovid called the Po *populifer* ("poplar-bearing") and located the fall of Phaeton there. Vergil compares the warriors Pandarus and Bitias to mighty oaks along its banks:

> Pandarus and Bitias, sprung from Alcanor of Ida,
> Reared by the dryad Iaera in Jupiter's sacred wood—
> Young men as tall as their native pine trees and mountains—these two,
> Confident in their weapons, threw open the gate which their general
> Had given them to guard, positively inviting the foe to enter
> The ramparts; while they, swords drawn, flaunting the plumes on their
>   tall heads,
> Stood just inside, to left and right, in front of a turret.
> So by some flowing river—by the banks of the Po, it might be,
> Or Athesis' genial waters—twin oaks stand, head in air,
> Soaring up side by side, raising their leafy crowns
> Into the sky, their tops dizzily nodding.
>
>   (A. 9, 672–82. Day Lewis)

Vergil also refers to the Po being used as an artery for the movement of timber:

> The alder too, when you launch it upon the Po, rides lightly
> That boiling stream.
>
>   (G. 2, 451–2. Day Lewis)

The Athesis, which he links with the Po, is the modern Adige river, second only to the Po in length. It rises in the Rhaetian Alps and after a long meandering course emerges in the plains near Verona, which, rather like Mantua, stands on a promontory, a peninsula almost surrounded by water. (Fig. 6)

Vergil has a profound affection for his native river, the Mincius (Mincio), tributary of the Po, with its grey-green reeds and meandering flow. It rises from the southern tip of Lake Garda and joins the Po about eleven miles southeast of Mantua. Even today the riverbanks are in many places lined with willows, poplars, and alders, sometimes with hazel and birch trees. The upper reaches offer rapidly moving water, with power enough to sustain mills along its modern course. Originally the Mincio spread out around Mantua forming swampy areas, but dams and irrigation measures have confined them to form three lakes. The ancient city, superbly protected by the moatlike marshy areas, was situated on a narrow-necked peninsula. Today, below the Castello, small fishing craft dot the surfaces of the lakes as they must have the marshes in antiquity. Vergil etches the scene with sympathy and fidelity:

But if your business be rather the keeping of calves and cattle,
The breeding of sheep, or goats that burn up all growing things,
You should try the woodland pastures and the prairies of rich Tarentum
And plains such as unlucky Mantua has lost
Where snow-white swans among the river weeds are feeding:
Here neither springs of water nor grass will fail your flocks,
And all that the cattle consume
In a long day is restored by the cool dew during the short night.
                    (G. 2, 195–202. Day Lewis)

In the prelude to the third *Georgic*, in which the *Aeneid* is foreshadowed, the poet vows to build a shrine to Octavian at Mantua by the Mincius:

If life enough is left me,
I'll be the first to bring the Muse of song to my birthplace
From Greece, and wear the poet's palm for Mantua;

And there in the green meadows I'll build a shrine of marble
Close to the waterside, where the river Mincius wanders
With lazy loops and fringes the banks with delicate reeds.
                    (G. 3, 10–15. Day Lewis)

Although the Mincius and the Po are his most celebrated northern rivers, Vergil honors the Mella river, which flows past modern Brescia, and the *aster amellus,* a purple flower favored by bees:

There's a flower of the meadow, too, that our farmers call "amellus":
It's easy enough to find,
For it raises up from a single stool a forest of stems;
Golden the disk, raying out into petals whose dark violet
Is shot with a purple shine:
Often the gods' altars are adorned with garlands of it:
Its taste is rough to the tongue: shepherds gather it on the close-cropped
Valley slopes and beside the meandering stream of Mella.
Boil the roots of this flower in fragrant wine, and serve it
In basketfuls at their door, a tonic food for the bees.

(G. 4, 271–80. Day Lewis)

Vergil's account of the two Lombard lakes, Como and Garda, is rhapsodic. Como, ancient Larius, he inaccurately salutes as the largest of the lakes: "Lake Larius the greatest of them all." (G. 2, 159) Though greatest in depth and of extraordinary length, some sixty miles, Como in fact is not so large as Garda. But Vergil's compliment suggests that Como, the popular vacation area for the modern Milanese, must have been equally attractive to the poet during his student days in ancient Mediolanum. The region of dramatic slopes, lovely shoreside villas and gardens, and blue waters of great depth and icy coolness was extolled by the Younger Pliny a century later. Writing to his friend Caninius Rufus, he recounts some of the advantages of a retreat on the Lake: "How is my friend employed? Is it in study, or angling, or the chase? Or does he unite all three, as he well may on the banks of our favourite Larius? For the Lake will supply you with fish; as the woods that surround it will afford you game; while the solemnity of that sequestered scene will at the same time dispose your mind to contemplation." (Epist. 2–8, 1–3) Comum became a popular port of embarkation for travellers bound for the North who were unwilling to endure the agonies of travel by land through the rugged countryside.

Lake Garda, in antiquity Benacus, is Italy's largest body of fresh water. It is exposed to the north winds which sweep down from the Alps, rousing violent storms. Garda at the mercy of the Alpine gusts is one of the most dramatic sights in Italy. Vergil alludes to it, undoubtedly from personal observation: "Lake Benacus, that tosses and growls like a little ocean." (G. 2, 160) Sirmio, at the south end of the lake, a short distance from Desenzano by foot or water, was the site of Catullus' villa on the *limpidum lacum* (Fig. 7).

And fallow deer with hounds:
Often their barking will start a wild boar and drive him
From where he wallows in the wood; or in full cry they'll hunt a
Noble stag over the uplands and manoeuvre him towards the nets.
(G. 3, 404–13. Day Lewis)

The boar of the simile which enlarges the imaginative scope of Mezentius' catalogue of opponents slain in combat is specifically associated
with the Cottian Alps (Mount Vesulus) and Laurentum in Latium:

The coast of Laurentum holds Mimas, a stranger to it,
Like a boar driven out by the biting of dogs from high mountains,
Whom pine-bearing Vesulus defended for many years
And the Laurentine swamps fed on reedy growth,
When he has come among snares stands and growls fiercely,
His shoulders a-bristle, so none has the courage to vent his
Anger on him and approach, but safe at a distance
They press upon him with javelins and shouts, but unfrightened
He stands, facing in each direction and grinds his teeth,
Shaking the spears from his back.
(A. 10, 735–44. L. R. Lind)

Beekeeping and the details of agriculture almost certainly derive from
Vergil's experiences in the Mantuan countryside, and in addition to
Georgic 4 where the details are supplied fully, Vergil refers to the bees
elsewhere as patterns of industry and as models for moral behavior.
Disasters on the farm are often recalled in more cataclysmic circumstances involving cities. The holocaust at Troy is brought into the
context of nature's destroyers, fire and flood:

As when a flame
By South wind madly driven falls on the wheat,
Or some swift torrent down a mountain channel
Smashes the fields and good crops, work of oxen,
And drags the trees headlong, which from his crag
A shepherd hears in bewildered awe.
(A. 2, 316–21. L. R. Lind)

Similarly, a passage in the *Aeneid* suggests the experience of equi-
noctial gales and deluges in northern Italy. Hail besets farmers and
travellers:

It was like when the storm-clouds burst, scattering down their shrapnel
Of hailstones; all the ploughmen and labourers have dispersed
Hurriedly from the fields, and the traveller is sheltering somewhere
In safety—beneath a river-bank maybe, or a corner of rock—
While the downpour drenches the earth; and they wait for the sun to
    come back
And let them get on with their work. Aeneas, snowed under with
    missiles
From every angle, endured the blizzard of war and waited
For it to be spent . . .

                      (A. 10, 803–10. Day Lewis)

Occasionally the destruction is made by the country folk for useful ends.
So Vergil describes a farmer's burning over his fields with scattered fires
igniting the stubble:

Just as, in summer-time, when the winds he has prayed for have risen,
A shepherd may light fires at intervals over the heathland;
All of a sudden the interspaces catch fire, an unbroken
Line of crackling flame is spread across the broad acres;
He sits and reviews the exultant flames like a conqueror.

                      (A. 10, 405–9. Day Lewis)

Though born in the shadow of the Alps and near the Apennines,
Vergil is curiously reticent about his mountainous environment. Though
mountains are featured occasionally in similes, they are like the mountains in Pompeian wall paintings, hilly or rocky backdrops to the principal subject, less dramatic than illusionistic in style. Vergil certainly
knew the Alpine and sub-Alpine country from Mount Vesulus (Monte
Viso) in the west right across to the Venetian lowlands. Vesulus is
somewhat menacing in the passage quoted above (p. 73), the haunt of
wild boars, pine-crowned. Curiously, it is the only Alpine peak which
Vergil chooses to name, perhaps because it was loftiest of all to the west
of the Po basin.

One of the most poignant passages in the Georgics, the account of
the Noric pestilence which ravaged the cattle ranches of North Italy, is
placed in an Alpine setting:

Thicker and faster than squalls of wind that tear at the sea's face
Come many diseases of cattle,
Killing not one here and there, but a whole summer pasture—

The lambs, the dams, the whole lot of them root and branch.
You'd bear me out, if you went to look at the lofty Alps,
The hill forts of Bavaria, the fields beside Timavo;
It happened long ago here, but you'd see the derelict ranches
Of sheep, old grazings empty up to the far horizon.

(G. 3, 470–7. Day Lewis)

The poet provides two vivid sketches of the northeastern coast of Italy. In one he describes the waves of the boisterous Adriatic racing to the shore before the east wind:

Or count the waves that break along Adriatic coasts
When an easterly gale comes down in gusts upon the shipping;

(G. 2, 107–8. Day Lewis)

In the second he evokes the turbulent gales that roar down from the mountains of Friuli:

Like a north wind when from the frontiers of ice in gathering force
It swoops, drives helter-skelter the cold dry northern clouds:
The cornfields deep and the deepsea
Shudder with the gusts that flick them, and treetops in the forest
Cry aloud, and long rollers ride to the beach:
So flies that wind, sweeping field and flood as it goes.

(G. 3, 192–201. Day Lewis)

Vergil has special notice for one of the most ancient and prosperous road centers of Venetia, Patavium, modern Padua, subject to Rome by 174 B.C. When Venus complains to Jupiter that the endless wanderings of her favorite Aeneas seem an injustice in contrast to the happier fate of Antenor, Vergil records the following tradition of a Trojan founding:

Antenor, slipping away through the Greek army, could safely
Sail right up the Illyrian gulf, pass by the remote
Liburnians, and pass the source of river Timavus
Where tidal water, roaring aloud below rock, spouts up
Through nine mouths, and the fields are hemmed with a sound of the sea.
He was allowed to found Padua, make a home for
Trojans there—could give his people a name, and nail up
His arms, could settle down in peace and quiet.

(A. 1, 242–9. Day Lewis)

The historian Livy, who was born in Patavium, gives a detailed account of his city's origins and states, correctly, that it was founded by the Veneti:

> Antenor joined forces with the Eneti, who had been driven out of Paphlagonia, and, having lost their king, Pylaemenes, at Troy, wanted someone to lead them as well as somewhere to settle. He penetrated to the head of the Adriatic and expelled the Euganei, a tribe living between the Alps and the sea, and occupied that territory with a mixed population of Trojans and Eneti. The spot where they landed is called Troy and the neighboring country the Trojan district. The combined peoples came to be known as Venetians.
>
> (Livy I, I, 3. de Selincourt)

This Trojan tradition, parallel to the Aeneas tradition for Rome, may have been as old as Sophocles, to whom a tragedy entitled *Antenorides* has been ascribed. Vergil does not expand further on the city's origins, but there are allusions by other writers to anniversary games for Antenor being celebrated every thirty years in the city. Patavium acquired a reputation for conservatism and puritanical behavior, owing, at least in part, to its being the home of the somewhat reactionary Livy, called a "Pompeian," and of the staunch Republican Paetus Thrasea, voice of the Stoic opposition under Nero. It was also distinguished for its Republican sentiments during the Civil Wars, along with Mediolanum. The citizenry's spirited opposition to Mark Antony cost them dearly, for Asinius Pollio exacted reparations. However, by hard work Patavium managed to re-emerge as a wealthy mercantile city, heavily involved with the wool trade and the clothing industry.

"Patavinity," of which Asinius Pollio accused Livy, has never been satisfactorily explained on ethical or grammatical grounds, though many have favored the view that Asinius Pollio implied rusticity of expression. A rusticity of appearance was certainly attributed to Vergil, and Servius (*ad. Georg.* I, 104) alleged that Vergil also kept certain stylistic features of his Cisalpine background even in his later writings.

The descriptive passages and similes which reflect aspects of North Italy in Vergil's time are often incredible to the modern traveller. The area of Cisalpine Gaul has altered markedly in two millennia. The naturally productive Arcadian aspect has yielded to intensive cultivation in most areas, and the factories and industrial enterprises of Milan and Brescia, along with the other major communities, have changed the region enormously. There can be no hope of recovering the Vergilian landscape in any extensive area; the wilderness and the great tracts of pasturage which were commonplace in Vergil's time are now almost nonexistent. But the soil remains fertile and still capable of quick renewal in the moist environment around Mantua, just as it was after heavy grazing in the poet's time. Actually, the radical changes in the region have been comparatively recent. Sixteenth-century wall maps in the Vatican Gallery show zones still heavily wooded, and the marshy terrain east of Ostiglia and around Mantua still undrained. Canals and drainage ditches criss-cross the modern Lombard plain like legacies from the Etruscan engineers; but the wooded areas, except along the river banks, are virtually destroyed. Poplars and plane trees are deliberately planted today to serve as borders, as windbreaks, and as shade trees. However, in Vergil's woodlands—the area of the modern Prealpi Bresciane and Prealpi Benacensi Occidentali, but particularly of modern Brescia—there are still marvelous stands of ash, birch, and hazel, and on the higher slopes, oak and chestnut, and comparable vegetation appears in the western Apennines on the southern fringes of the Po valley.

Vergil's affection for the North Italian landscape manifests itself repeatedly throughout his poetic life. The susceptible years spent in these glorious surroundings, where Vergil appears to have ranged widely and alertly, yielded rich returns as a source of illustration and of the nostalgic recollections which appear in another, totally different environment, that of Naples and the south.

III

Etruria

ETRURIA and the Etruscans play an important role in Vergil's epic. He assigns to these mysterious early settlers of Italy, founders of his native Mantua, an important role in the defense and ultimate unification of central Italy.

Our own curiosity regarding the origins and lifespan of Etruscan culture in Italy was no doubt felt by Romans in Vergil's time. The Etruscan heritage of Maecenas, "descended from ancestral kings" (Horace, *Odes* I, I, I), may have quickened men's interest. Maecenas' evident pride in his Etruscan Arretine background and his desire to emulate the elegant style of living suggested by the banqueting scenes in Etruscan tomb paintings must have excited the admiration as well as the outraged criticism of his contemporaries. Certainly the story of the Etruscan people remained in men's minds; their past glories and defeats were recounted by Vergil, Livy, the geographer Strabo, Dionysius of Halicarnassus, and—with most tragic intensity—by Propertius, the elegiac poet from the environs of Perugia. The Etruscan language was probably a mystery to most Romans (as it remains to us). Aulus Gellius remarks that Etruscan, in the second century A.D., was a strange relic from the past, an unintelligible country tongue. One must assume that its use, except for religious services and for augury, was very restricted in Vergil's lifetime. However, in the *Aeneid*—although the epic should not be pressed for definite historical information—there is no problem of verbal communication between Latin and Etruscan, or indeed, between Trojan and any other language stock.

Shortly before Vergil's birth the Etruscans had been virtually erased as a free people by the thorough measures of Sulla, who exacted vengeance because they had tended to favor the cause of Gaius Marius. Their cities were razed and their language and practices suppressed. Etruscan was not the only language to succumb to Roman demands: Oscan, Umbrian, and Messapic were also outlawed early in the first century B.C., after the Social War, and Latin became the official tongue of all the Italian tribes and communities.

Rome had gained much from the Etruscans in both the material and spiritual spheres; they influenced Roman art and architecture, religion, and governmental forms and regalia. But the Romans felt strongly the marked differences between the two cultures—and for certain aspects of Etruscan *mores* they could have entertained only disgust. Sometimes, too, the cultural legacy had been attained violently. Pliny tells that when the Romans plundered Volsinii (mod. Bolsena), ca. 300–250 B.C., they stripped the town of more than two thousand statues. Propertius testifies even more poignantly to the ruthless devastation wrought by the Romans in suppressing Etruscan resistance near Perugia and Assisi in Umbria. He laments his dead countrymen, whose bones lay strewn over the mountainside of Etruria, near their cold hearths and plundered homes.[1]

Scholars are still divided over the origins of the Etruscans. The Herodotean tradition, that they came from Lydia in Asia Minor, has probably won more supporters than the view of Dionysius of Halicarnassus that the Etruscans were aboriginal, or the less tenable thesis that they were a trans-Alpine folk. Vergil beyond a doubt subscribed to the Herodotean version.

Vergil also disagreed with Dionysius, even more strikingly, about the origins of the Trojan royal house. He relates the legend that Dardanus, forefather of the Trojans, was born in Italy, along with his brother Iasius, in Etruscan Corythus (mod. Cortona?). The details of the connection between Etruria and Troy are reported circumstantially by Latinus to the Trojan embassy headed by Ilioneus, Aeneas' official ambassador on several occasions:

> I indeed remember, though time has dimmed
> The legend, Auruncan elders telling how Dardanus
> Was born here, and hence migrated to the towns of Phrygian Ida
> And into Thracian Samos, which men call Samothrace now.
> His beginnings were here, in the Tuscan home of Corythus: now
> He has his throne in the golden palace of the star-glistering
> Heavens, and adds one more to the altars of the gods.
>
> (A. 7, 205–11. Day Lewis)

Again, in a vision of the Penates which came to Aeneas in Crete, the Italic tradition of Troy's origins was rehearsed:

> There is a place—the Greeks call it Hesperia—
> An antique land, well warded, possessed of rich soil.
> Oenotrians colonized it; whose heirs, so rumour says now,
> Have named it, after their first founder, Italy.
> There is our real home: there was Dardanus born,
> And old Iasius; there did our line begin.
> Rise up then, with a cheerful mind repeat to your father
> These sure and certain sayings: let Corythus be his bourne
> And Italy, for Jove forbids you to colonize Crete.
>
> (A. 3, 163–71. Day Lewis)

Dionysius, on the other hand, adhered to the theory expounded by Varro that Dardanus, Troy's founder, was a native of Arcadia and that his descendants were therefore Greek (cf. the allusion to this tradition in A. 8, 134–7). Vergil may even have invented the opposing "tradition" that Dardanus came originally from Italy, since he was anxious to discover links between the Trojans and the Italians. There may, however, be a kernel of fact behind the generally untenable thesis, for he does reconcile the principal hypotheses for the origin of the Etruscans, the Lydian and the autochthonous.

The Asiatic theory is most likely correct: the Etruscans probably came in several waves, settling in the coastal and nearby interior cities of Tuscany. Herodotus no doubt preserves the accurate tradition. He lived in Asiatic Halicarnassus in the fifth century B.C., a time closer to the rise of the Etruscans than the era of Dionysius (who was born in the same community five centuries later). Dionysius testifies to the rapid assimilation of the native peoples, the Villanovans, into the Etruscan pattern of life. One can therefore imagine several waves of smallish colonial parties—with Antenor's settlement at Patavium (Padua) as model—making preliminary conquests and then merging successfully with the natives to form a new society with a twofold cultural aspect. Vergil's version is no bolder than that of Dionysius. Taken together and reviewed in the light of the ever-increasing archaeological evidence, these traditions of Etruscan origins in Italy may be construed as complementary rather than exclusive.

Vergil is consistent in his Trojan associations for Dardanus' birthplace, Corythus. Aeneas absents himself from the *castrum* near Ostia in order to find aid among his alleged kinsmen:

> Aeneas, leaving town, comrades and fleet, seeks the Palatine realm, and Evander's dwelling. Nor does that suffice; he has won his way to Corythus' utmost cities, and is mustering in armed bands the Lydian countryfolk.
>
> (A. 9, 8–11)

But considerable problems attach to the identification of ancient Corythus with modern Cortona: Cortona undoubtedly developed late as an Etruscan center, a fact which belies Vergil's ascription of antiquity to it; and it is located inland. Ancient sources are conflicting. According to Dionysius of Halicarnassus (1, 26), Cortona was an Umbrian city before the coming of the Etruscans; he supplies Corthonia as its Hellenic name. Solinus (third century A.D.) and Martianus Capella (fifth century A.D.) allege that Dardanus founded Cora (mod. Cori). Silius Italicus, writing in Naples in the first century A.D., in the shadow of Vergil, associates Cortona with Gravisca in his Etruscan catalogue. Since Gravisca was the port of Tarquinii, Hardie has associated this last interesting juxtaposition with Boccaccio's remark (*Geneal. Deor.* VI, 1) that Corythus is Corneto (i.e. Tarquinii).[2] Certainly the demonstrable antiquity of Tarquinii and its seaside location would make it a more acceptable site for Vergil's Corythus than inland Cortona.

Vergil's reconstruction puts Caere (mod. Cerveteri, i.e. *Caere vetus*) in the forefront of the Etruscan cities. And the poet seems personally acquainted with its site. He resurrects the ancient center, once called Agylla, as a wealthy, powerful city which falls prey to the despotic Mezentius. Actually in Vergil's time, according to Strabo, the city had sunk into such insignificance that the adjoining spa, Aquae Caeretanae, surpassed the ancient city in population. Caere owed its wealth to sea trade and to the export of bronze articles, both domestic and military. The monumental grave mounds, or tumuli, dating from the mid-seventh century, are impressive testimony to the wealth of the Caeretan warlords, or *lucumones*. The tumuli, the most striking landmarks of modern Cerveteri, recall, perhaps, the hills and customs of the settlers' homeland in Asia Minor (where great mound burials have been recently excavated at Gordium [Phrygia] and Sardis [Lydia]). The base of the mound is usually a drum constructed of masonry or carved out of the soft tufa and ornamented with moldings. Brightly painted sculptured lions once guarded the tomb entry, and steps led to the summit of the mound where an altar and other monuments originally stood.

Because Caere and Veii had helped the Latins and Sabines against Tarquinius Priscus, their territories were devastated and tokens of submission were required: "the insignia of their own kinds; a crown of gold, an ivory throne, a sceptre surmounted by an eagle, a scarlet tunic embroidered with gold, and a golden-embroidered purple cloak like that worn by the kings of Lydia and Persia, except that it was not rectangular but semicircular—something the Romans called a toga." (Dion. Hal., 3, 51) Other authorities note that the Etruscans also surrendered to Tarquin the twelve axes, one from each city, for it seems to have been their custom for the king of each city to be preceded by an attendant carrying an axe in a bundle of rods (*fasces*). Paraphernalia of rule of Etruscan origin persisted into Roman Republican and Imperial times and included the *sella curulis,* the ivory folding chair for men of rank; twelve lictors with *fasces* attending the consuls; and the golden crown, sceptre, tunic, and toga, prerogatives of triumphant generals.

Caere, along with Veii, was a distinguished center for the production of terra-cotta sculpture, for pottery and elaborately carved sarcophagi. The tombs, occasionally with stuccoed and painted walls, seem to have been patterned after the houses of the living. Architectural details, columns, capitals, chairs, beds, roof paneling, and porch, are often translated directly into the tufa underground tombs (Figs. 8, 9). The wealthiest tomb at Caere was the so-called Regolini Galassi. Gold jewelry, masterpieces of granulation and repoussé work, exotic, sizable —to modern taste sometimes overwhelming and hideous—was part of the tomb's treasure. An outer burial, perhaps the warrior son of the couple entombed in the principal burial, yielded, *inter alia,* a four-wheeled catafalque, eight parade shields nailed to the wall, an iron sword, ten bronze javelins, and a table service for festivities in the afterlife.

Vergil brings Aeneas to the vale of Caere to receive the divine armor —perhaps because of the city's reputation for metalwork. Caere produced bronzework of high quality as early as 550 B.C., and the superb war chariot found at Monteleone, near Perugia, now in the Metropolitan Museum in New York, was almost certainly a Caeretan product (Fig. 10). But the export market and even the materials dwindled rapidly during the wars with Rome, and by the second century B.C. Caere seems to have entered its decline; this onetime center of handicrafts, of gold and bronze works, became a rural community, self-supporting but without distinction. When the Via Aurelia, the military highway along the west coast north from Rome was constructed, it bypassed Caere and its citadel, leaving the city some two and a half miles to the east.

In his catalogue of the Latin Allies at the close of *Aeneid* 7, Vergil assigns the former king of Caere, Mezentius, to the primary position, Turnus' chief ally:

> The first to arm his men and enter the war was Mezentius,
> A Tuscan exile, a man embittered and irreligious.
> Beside him marched his son, Lausus, who far excelled
> All others in personal beauty, except for Laurentine Turnus.
> Lausus, the tamer of steeds, the mighty hunter, was leading
> A thousand men from the town of Agylla—an enterprise
> Doomed to disaster. Well he deserved to live under a better
> Regime and to have a better father than Mezentius.
>
> (A. 7, 647–54. Day Lewis)

Mezentius is the first historical personality in Agyllan-Caeretan annals.[3] He figures in Cato's history of Rome: on Aeneas' arrival in Latium he is pitted against a Latin-Rutulian alliance, as in the *Aeneid,* but in Cato's version Latinus was killed in the first engagement, and Turnus and his troops had to seek asylum with Mezentius at Caere. Together they renewed the war against the upstart Trojans, and during the fighting both Turnus and Aeneas were killed. The outcome was finally decided by a single combat between Mezentius and Aeneas' son, Ascanius-Julus, in which Mezentius was either slain or was induced to make a peace treaty and alliance with the Trojans. Livy gives a slightly different version of the same story.

Vergil, however, has created a new image of Mezentius, a sinister villain whose recent history (described by Evander) as an arch-tyrant and sadist ultimately dethroned by his subjects equates him with Tarquinius Superbus. And yet his heroism, his effective assistance in the lost cause, his piety towards his son's memory, and finally his valiant death are redeeming features. Evander's account of Mezentius' tyrannical rule at Caere is intriguing both for its narrative value and for the motivation it provides in Vergil's epic for the large-scale Etruscan subscription to the Trojan cause:

> Not far away lies Caere, a populous city, founded
> On ancient rock: a tribe from Lydia, renowned in war,
> Settled it long ago upon a hill in Etruria.
> For many years they flourished; but there rose a king, Mezentius,
> Who with insolent tyranny and cruel force opposed them.
> I will not enlarge on that despot's brutish acts or his damnable
> Massacres—may the gods keeps such things for himself and his breed.
> Why, he would even have live men bound to dead bodies,
> Clamping them hand to hand and face to face—a horrible
> Method of torture—so that they died a lingering death
> Infected with putrefaction in that most vile embrace.
> At last the townsfolk could stand it no more: they rose in arms
> Against the criminal maniac, besieged him in his palace,
> Put his friends to the sword and set the place alight.
>
> (A. 8, 477–90. Day Lewis)

Near Caere, Aeneas eventually confronts his ally Tarchon and the latter's Etruscan troops bivouacked in a grove sacred to Silvanus.

> There's an extensive woodland near the cool stream of Caere,
> Reverenced by all around in the faith of their fathers: encircled
> By hills, that wood of dark green fir-trees lay in a hollow.
> The legend is that the ancient Pelasgians, the first settlers
> Of Latium in the old days, had dedicated the wood
> And a festival day to Silvanus, the god of field and cattle.
> Not far from here were Tarchon and his Etruscans, camped in
> A good defensive position; and now from the hills above
> They could see the whole of his army, their tents all over the plain.
>
> (A. 8, 597–605. Day Lewis)

Here in this haunt of Silvanus, Vergil also brings Aeneas into Venus' presence to receive the miraculous armor. Vergil clearly regarded Silvanus as an ancient Italian deity, one equated with the Greek Pan, and, if the etymology is proper, with the Italian god of woods and gardens as well; perhaps, too, he is patron of the hunt, although Vergil assigns him to fields and cattle, rather like Aristaeus. There may also have been a definite association of the Etruscan nature god, Selvans, with this same grove, for Vergil connects him with Caere. Vergil appears to locate the grove of Silvanus or Selvans on the banks of the Vaccina River, perhaps in the woodlands which once covered Mount Abbatone on the east side.

The Etruscan landscape, once heavily forested, had provided abundant ship timber and building material in earlier times, but with reckless overcutting and the consequent exposure and soil erosion, the forests that once clothed the hills of Tuscany became merely a hallowed memory. This had already occurred by Vergil's time, and the poet looks back regretfully to the days when the heroes of yore enjoyed forests with cool, shady clearings, sparkling springs and limpid brooks.

The erosion along the Minio river (mod. Mignone) (A. 10, 182–4) is a perfect example of the gradual soil depletion common in Italy today. The stream is bordered with lush vegetation which receives quantities of dust from hill slopes and field topsoil exposed by grazing and tillage. The rich foliage along the riverside catches the dust, and the river, yellowish-white with river wash, carries off the irreplaceable topsoil in endless quantities to the sea. The Tiber and Po rivers, which are frequently mentioned in antiquity as silt-laden and sandy, remain today as they were then, voracious consumers of valuable soil.

The ports of Caere, Pyrgi (Santa Severa), Alsium (Palo), and Gravisca were immensely important to Caere's industrial and mercantile enterprises.[4] (Today all three have yielded to Civitavecchia as the major shipbuilding port in the vicinity of Rome.) Though the Etruscans of earlier times had been pirates—for piracy was frequently equated with trading in the ancient Mediterranean—Strabo affirms most emphatically that the Caeretans were not. Dionysius, the tyrant of Syracuse, stated—truthfully or not—that it was with the intention of suppressing Etruscan piracy that he landed to sack the temple at Pyrgi in the territory of Caere in 383 B.C. (Diod. Sic. 15, 14). This sanctuary, sacred to

Leucothea or Eileithyia, local marine goddess or patroness of childbirth, has recently been located. The pedimental figures, a rare feature in Etruscan temples, are the earliest Etruscan examples extant, and are almost certainly indebted to the west pediment at Olympia (Fig. 11).[5]

Gravisca, which Vergil aligns with the Minio river and ancient Pyrgi, he designates as "unseasonable," "unhealthy." Day Lewis's choice, "malarial" (A. 10, 184), is probably the most accurate description of the condition of the ancient strongpoint. Cato in fact derives the name of the colonial settlement in 181 B.C. from *gravis* and *aer,* suggesting that the heavy atmosphere at the site made it an unpleasant spot. The depopulated state of many of the southern areas of Etruria, and of Campania and Lucania during the second century B.C., stemmed partly from malarial conditions, but partly also from the threat of pirate raids along the coasts. The reduced numbers prompted the Romans to establish a loose chain of colonies to protect the shores from invasion. Pisarum, Potentia, and Gravisca all had to house colonies when the investigators on a tour of inspection into Bacchanalian rites in 186 reported that the coast was underpopulated at a number of points. Vergil may have recalled the necessity for these second foundations at Pyrgi (ca. 194) and at Gravisca, for he stipulates that their entire complement of assistance to Aeneas, including Caere and the territory around the river Minio, was limited to three hundred. By Vergil's time these colonial settlements must have been sadly depressed, further depopulated by the duress of the Civil Wars and the failure of the land to support its inhabitants properly.

When Aeneas displays the captured arms of Mezentius, the cuirass is described as pierced in twelve places, a reference to the fact that the contest had also brought Mezentius into conflict with the twelve cities of the Etruscans (A. 11, 9 f.). Vergil's catalogue of Etruscan heroes includes a description of the colorful regatta of thirty ships with contingents from Etruria's finest cities:

Massicus led a squadron, sailing in his bronze-beaked vessel
The *Tiger;* his contingent, a thousand strong, had come from
Clusium and the town of Cosae; their arms were a deadly
Bow and a light-weight quiver of arrows slung over the shoulder.

Grim Abas came too, his whole detachment in glittering armour,
A gilded image of Apollo gleaming on his poop:
Populonia had given him six hundred of her sons,
Expert fighters all;
Ilva had furnished three hundred—
That isle so rich in mines of inexhaustible iron.

Third came Asilas, a medium between mankind and the gods,
A master at divining from the entrails of sacrificed beasts,
The stars in the sky, the songs of birds, the presage of lightning:
He hurried to war a thousand spearmen in close formation;
Etruscan Pisa, whose founders had come from the river Alphaeus,
Had raised them for him to command. Then followed the handsome Astyr,
Confident in his charger and many-coloured accoutrements.

Three hundred more, who were all of one mind in their wish for battle,
Came from their homes in Caere, from the country around the Minio,
The ancient town of Pyrgi and malarial Graviscae.

(A. 10, 166–84. Day Lewis)

Vergil set Massicus of Clusium in the lead ship. Clusium (mod. Chiusi) is inseparable from Macaulay's Lars Porsena, who laid siege to Rome. His burial place (although Pliny doubted the reliability of Varro's account) was probably the most conspicuous in Tuscany: the tomb, on a rectangular stone base, measured three hundred feet on each side, fifty feet in height, and was hung with bells. It has never been found, but many other tombs have been unearthed at Chiusi. An ancient Villanovan settlement in the hills at the southern end of the Val di Chiana, Clusium found renewed life under the Etruscans. A productive bronze industry developed, modelling its monumental works on South Italian and Campanian products, and continued to flourish until ca. 450 B.C. At this time another school of decorative bronzework appeared, specializing in braziers and candelabra. A great center of limestone sculpture also developed, particularly for use as grave monuments, which were often in the form of evocative figures of mourning women, or were ash urns or sarcophagi. The finest sarcophagi and urns were created in the second century, in terra cotta, travertine, and alabaster. The walls of the tombs in which they were placed were often painted with banqueting scenes and games.

In several respects, however, modern Chiusi is not completely acceptable as the ancient site of Clusium. Vergil associates Clusium with
Cosae in the naval catalogue, which perhaps implies some easy access to
the sea. Polybius' account of the Gallic defeat at Telamon in 225 B.C.
specifically locates Clusium by the sea. Accordingly, Porsenna's Clusium
might better be sought on the shoreline, north of Tarquinii, possibly at
Orbetello, or even more likely at Marsiliana d'Albegna, obviously a
wealthy and populous site of the early Etruscan period. Clusium's associations with Rome, after the Porsenna incident, were amiable and help-
ful. This fact probably explains why Vergil assigns Clusium, possibly
Pliny's Clusium Vetus, the leadership among the naval allies. When the
Gauls crossed the Apennines and attacked Clusium in 390 B.C., the
citizens appealed to Rome for help. Clusium, in turn, supplied grain and
ship-building timber to Scipio in 205. But by the time of the Social War,
Clusium was a sadly depleted city. The citizens sided with Marius along
with Arretium and most other Etruscan cities, and in 82 B.C. shared the
final stand at Volaterrae, which held out for two years against Sulla's
inept siege-craft. After the fall of the city the Etruscan allies suffered
confiscation of territory and a revision of their citizenship rights. Colonies were planted at Faesulae, Florence, Arretium, and Volaterrae, and
probably also at Clusium.

Vergil cites the contingents of Clusium and Cosae as a single force.
Until recently, Cosae was something of a mystery, as Etruscan city or
Latin colony. But the recent excavations by the American Academy in
Rome at the promontory of Ansedonia have exposed splendid remains
of the colony of 273 B.C., contemporary with the similar establishment
at Paestum, south of Naples. The colony was evidently established as
a marine station to guard the coastal area near Etruscan Vulci. It went
through one period of significant urban renewal and enlargement of
facilities in 197, but thereafter subsided gradually, and by Vergil's
time it had fallen into comparative anonymity. The town in its original
design was formidable. The thirty-three-acre site was provided with
splendid fortifications, polygonal walls with eighteen towers and three
main gates (possibly an Etruscan town-planning legacy), and capacious
cisterns ensured an adequate water supply in case of siege. The commanding peninsular site, with a carefully designed harbor which was
kept clear of silt by means of tidal sluices and finally by breakwaters,

offered a superb station for the systematic surveillance of the offshore
waters that might be invaded by the fleets of Magna Graecia or
Carthage. The city plan adopted the gridiron pattern, comparable to that
from an earlier date discovered at Marzobotto, south of Bologna.
Vergil's recollection of Cosae's naval importance during the third and
second centuries explains her inclusion in the epic fleet that followed
Aeneas.

Populonia and Ilva (mod. Elba) are linked in Vergil's catalogue
militarily, as they were in fact industrially, for the iron ore of Ilva was
shipped to the smelting furnaces of Populonia. Campiglia Marittima,
northeast of Populonia, also had important iron and lead mines, as had
nearby Monte Valerio, which in addition produced the only tin found
in Italy. Populonia's location, on a rocky promontory overlooking the
bay of Porto Baratti, was unique among Etruscan cities; although the
Etruscan founding fathers usually sought locations near the coast, it is
the only city actually on the Tyrrhenian Sea. Situated between Cecina
and Follonia, it served as the port for Volaterrae, some distance to the
north. Servius suggests that Populonia was Volaterrae's colony. In any
case, at the time of the Hannibalic Wars, Populonia helped to provide
the hard-pressed Scipio with sufficient iron to undertake the amphibious
operations which lay ahead in North Africa. Today Populonia is a
popular seaside resort on a peaceful bay, with a weird medley of archaic
tumuli and slag-heaps. The latter are being reworked to extract the
metallic content that ancient methods could not redeem.

Vergil alludes to the tradition of a Greek foundation at Pisa (A. 10,
179–80). In fact there are traces in the earliest Villanovan cemeteries
of Greek penetration, but an actual Greek foundation at Pisa is doubt-
ful. Situated on the borderland between Etruscan and Ligurian territory,
Pisa owed her influence and prosperity basically to her coastal position
at the mouth of the river Arno, though today the city lies six and one-
half miles from the coast. Strabo says that Pisa had declined as a seaport
by late Republican times, no doubt for a variety of reasons, but primarily because the silting problem could no longer be controlled. Strabo
does indicate, however, that Pisa's stone quarries, in the hills of the
Catena Metallifera, the ore-bearing chain between Pisa and Luca, were
noteworthy, and that timber resources and agricultural productivity kept
the economy alive. Rome founded a colony at Luca in 180 B.C. on

land provided by the city of Pisa, and another at Luni (mod. Carrara) in 177 to keep watch on the Ligurians, who were a troublesome element during the second century. Probably both cities undermined Pisa's primacy in the northwest.

Two other sites in Etruscan territory enter the Vergilian narrative, Ameria (G. 1, 265) and the river Clitumnus. Although technically in Umbria, Ameria was located fifteen miles south of Tuder and seven miles west of Narnia, on an eminence between the Tiber and Nar valleys. Cato assigns its foundation to 1135 B.C., a specific but incredible antiquity. Polygonal walls survive from the ancient stronghold, but its importance in historical accounts starts with the time of Cicero. In his defense of Sextus Roscius, a native of Ameria, Cicero indicates that Ameria was a flourishing municipality at that date (80 B.C.). Its territory extended to the Tiber and was rich in willows and orchards, and Amerine willow-ties were widely used as supports for grapevines.

The Clitumnus (mod. Clitunno) river, halfway between Spoleto and Foligno, was noted particularly for the snow-white sacrificial cattle which were raised on its banks.

> Here the charger gallops onto the plain in his pride,
> Here the white-fleeced flocks and the bull, a princely victim
> Washed over and over in Clitumnus' holy water,
> Head our Roman triumphs to the temples of the gods.
> (G. 2, 145–8. Day Lewis)

Though a small river, it ultimately fed into the Tinia and Tiber. It was renowned for the clarity of its waters, implying that soil erosion in the area was under control or nonexistent. The cypress groves at the source were an evocative setting for the sanctuaries which lined its banks and attracted numerous visitors, but the area was especially desirable for pasturage of exceptional richness. Pliny remarks that Augustus gave the Temple and Grove of Clitumnus to the inhabitants of Hispellum, who sought to make the religious site more remunerative by erecting public baths and buildings.

Aeneas' land support served under the eponymous hero of Messapia, or Iapygia, the territory forming the heel of Italy. The poet remarks that the cities involved were pacific by disposition, long retired from the battlefields, and certainly the communities were of the second rank compared with those offering naval support to Aeneas.

> Messapus, tamer of horses, the seed of Neptune—he
> Whom no man might lay low with fire or steel—now calling
> All of a sudden to arms his tribes that had long been torpid
> And lost the habit of fighting, took up the sword again.
> They lived on Fescennae's jagged skyline, at Falerii
> The just, in the field of Flavinium, or the hill-country of Soracte,
> By the lake and mountain of Ciminus, in the woodland of Capena.
>
> (A. 7, 691–7. Day Lewis)

Fescennia and Falerii (Aequi Falisci) are barely noticed in Roman history, though Fescennine farces, an ingredient of Roman comedy and satire, may owe something to Etruscan inspiration. Soracte (mod. Sant' Oreste), immortalized in Horace's *Ode* 1, 9, engages Vergil's interest primarily for the fire-worship traditionally celebrated on its heights in honor of Apollo. Priests of Apollo at the site were able, with the confidence of Indian fakirs, to pass unharmed through fire and to tread on the hot cinders with bare feet. At the moment before striking down the warrior maiden Camilla, Arruns prayed to his protector Apollo:

> Most worshipful god, Apollo, guardian of blest Soracte,
> Where we, your chief devotees, heap up in your honour the blazing
> Pine logs and walk through the midst of the flames, sure in our faith,
> Treading the high-piled embers as we perform your rites—
> Apollo, puissant in battle, grant that I may rub out
> This stain on our escutcheon!
>
> (A. 11, 785–90. Day Lewis)

As a feature of the Etruscan landscape, Soracte, 2420 feet high, is distinctive as the only major outcrop of the Apennines west of the Tiber in the southern Etruscan environs (Fig. 12). Twenty-six miles north of Rome, visible from the city in wintertime with snow glistening on its five craggy peaks, Soracte seems to have been regarded as Etruscan, although almost certainly the residents spoke an Italian dialect from earliest times. The open-air sanctuary atop the height was dedicated to Apollo Soranus. The picturesque limestone height rising abruptly from the tableland between Falerii and the Tiber has long been a favorite of artists working in the Roman Campagna.

The Flavinian ploughlands, mentioned in the passage about Messapus, Vergil has coupled with the heavily wooded Ciminian mountains, north of Lake Vico. The Ciminian Forest survives today as token of what Etruria must have looked like in antiquity when the Etruscan fleet could depend on the local timber resources. Livy's account of the surprise attack of the Roman consul Quintus Fabius on the Etruscan forces besieging Sutrium (mod. Sutri) is enlightening on this score. According to Livy, the consul's brother Caeso Fabius, accompanied by a single slave who was like his master disguised as a shepherd, forced his way through dense forests, closed even to merchants before that date, to the territory of the Umbrian Camertes (mod. Chiusi). The Via Claudia, built ca. 300 B.C., skirted Lake Bracciano and the Montes Sabatini on the west and reached the Ciminian mountains above Lake Vico. It was designed to serve as a military highway to help Rome safeguard her alliances and interests against the possibility of a third Samnite War.

Vergil's allusion to the Groves of Capena involves the larger area of Capena and the Ager Capenas. The latter covered a stretch of land north of Rome which may be adequately defined by the line of the Via Flaminia, Mount Soracte, and the lower Tiber valley. Capena's location on the Etruscan side of the Tiber bend meant that it played an important role as distribution center for Etruscan, Sabine, and Umbrian articles of trade. After the fall of Veii in 396 B.C., Capena's position, however defensible on the heights, was doomed by systematic Roman ravages in the outlying countryside. The city finally surrendered and entered the Roman orbit. Dennis's description of the site, still heavily wooded, supports the implications of Vergil's allusion:

> The view from the height of Capena is widely beautiful. The deep hollow on the south with its green carpet; the steep hills overhanging it, dark with woods . . . the bare swelling ground to the north, with Soracte towering above; the snow-capt Apennines in the eastern horizon; the deep silence, the seclusion; the absence of human habitations (not even a shepherd's hut) within the sphere of vision, save the distant town of S. Oreste (mount Soracte), scarcely distinguishable from the grey rock on which it stands;—it is a scene of more singular desolation than belongs to any other Etruscan city in this district of the land.[6]

The groves Vergil alludes to may also include the celebrated religious center of Lucus Feroniae at nearby Scorano on the Via Tiberina, near the modern Fosso di Grammiccia (anc. Capenas river). Feronia, who had another celebrated cult at Tarracina (Anxur), was a rural Italic goddess, honored with the first fruits of the season but revered especially for her involvement with the liberation of slaves and as protectress of freedmen. Her shrine in the Campus Martius, established by 217 B.C., was inspired by the Capenate center. G. D. B. Jones has speculated that the joint evidence of newly excavated buildings in the Forum area, a recently discovered amphitheater, and a land-settlement scheme reflected in Cicero's correspondence during 46 may indicate that both Capena and Lucus Feroniae became *coloniae* in the same year, as part of Julius Caesar's program of settling his disbanded soldiers in organized areas.[7] More veterans were added to the colony at Lucus Feroniae during the Augustan period.

Vergil's reconstruction of the "historical" scene for his war in Italy is distinctly interesting in the light of archaeological finds and recent hypotheses. The theory of Lydian or Asiatic origin for the Etruscans, the Herodotean argument which Vergil appears to accept, is very well supported by the oriental nature of Etruscan art, architecture, dress, and social and religious customs. Even though the recent excavations at Sardis, the ancient capital of Lydia, have not yielded any striking indication of similarities to the language and culture of the Etruscans during the sixth and fifth centuries, there are some remote parallels. With continued ferreting in other sites in Greek Asia Minor, stronger links may yet be found.

There are, to be sure, remarkable similarities between the odyssey of Aeneas and the suggested route of the Etruscans. Both progressed first through the northern Aegean, thence through the central Aegean to the straits, and then, by different routes, to the western shores of Italy, the Hesperia of poetry and oracles. Certainly the Tyrrhenian migration to Italy had no connection with Aeneas and late Mycenaean times, nor with the history of the Achaeans. But it remains at least a remote possibility that two completely unrelated movements into the western Mediterranean, centuries apart, may have fused and been suggestively identified in the poetic imagination. Epic, however actual the settings and circumstantial matters like behavior and speech, is nonetheless projected against the flat screen of an almost timeless past. And there is an unquestionable historical parallel to Aeneas' alliance with the Etruscans upon his arrival in Italy, uniting his own Trojan forces with the Etruscan in the occupation of Latium.

There are also other details in the Vergilian account of the Etruscans which reflect his awareness of historical realities. Tarchon, obviously the eponymous founder of Tarquinii, bears the name of the divine Thunderer, whose associations are certainly Asiatic. The emphasis on military organization, splendid equipment, chariots, and ships, and on religious practices are all consonant with the findings of archaeology and are, in their way, further support to the argument that the Etruscans came as sea invaders from Asia Minor. The Etruscan incursion ca. 850 B.C. into the peaceful agrarian communities of Tuscany and Umbria, into the sequestered, almost Arcadian communities of the Villanovans, was as shattering as Aeneas' arrival in Latium. Mezentius' efforts to conscript the native farmers for his military ends may also reflect historical Etruscan practice. The priestly Asilas from Pisa (A. 10, 175–8), expert in divining the future from the livers of animals (hepatoscopy), from the stars, the songs (and flight) of birds, and from ominous lightning flashes, is obviously very much in the tradition of historical Etruscan religion, which was, almost surely, composed of remembered or borrowed elements of oriental practices.

Alongside Vergil's sympathetic view of the Etruscans as constant supporters of Rome's establishment, there are darker recollections. Vergil was certainly sensitive to the long, spirited opposition to Rome of the Etruscan warlords, both in their confederation of twelve city-states and in their separate encounters. The war with Veii, concluded in 396 B.C., was Rome's counterpart to the Greek siege of Troy. There must have been repeated hostilities between the struggling Roman community and the superbly organized military states of the Etruscans. When Rome was merely a hamlet, and later a collection of villages, the Etruscan coastal cities lived elegantly behind superb fortifications, with all the amenities and elegant appointments of the Asiatic Greeks, in an advanced, sophisticated society. Violence and superstition, appalling savagery and inhuman cruelty, were part of their heritage and their society. Wall paintings, like those in the Tomb of the Baron at Tarquinii, offer vivid illustrations of the Etruscan fondness for bloody spectacle, for gladiatorial combats, and for the lustier themes of drama at funeral games. The subject matter of Etruscan bronzes and imported Greek pottery are also indicative of their somewhat bloodthirsty nature. Mezentius seems close to the historical Etruscan character.

Into the description of Aeneas' shield Vergil inserts an account of the time of strain after the expulsion of the Tarquins:

> Again, you could see Porsenna telling the Romans to take back
> The banished Tarquin, and laying strenuous siege to Rome,
> While the sons of Aeneas took up the sword for freedom's sake:
> He was pictured there to life, pouring out threats and wild with
> Chagrin, seeing that Cocles dared to break down the bridge
> And Cloelia had slipped her fetters and was swimming across the river.
>
> (A. 8, 646–51. Day Lewis)

If the character of Mezentius may be regarded as containing elements of Tarquinius Superbus, a belligerent renegade in exile, that of Turnus may equally well involve general, maybe even specific, traits of Rome's oldest enemy. Dionysius of Halicarnassus calls Turnus "Tyrrhenus" ("the Etruscan"), which may be a fortunate explication on his part, for the incidents which involve Aeneas with the allied Mezentius and Turnus seem almost certainly to be folk recollections of early wars between the settlement in Latium (Lavinium or Roman Pallanteum) and two Etruscan *lucumones*. The hostility between the settlement of Romulus and the neighboring Sabine communities has much the same aspect as these border hostilities in the epic narrative, which often seem more like raids than large-scale military operations. Deeply versed as he was in Etruscan religious and sacerdotal lore, Vergil may also have been aware that Aeneas played some "heroic" role in the Etruscan scene. A series of small terra-cotta statuettes, probably votive offerings to a hero's cult, recently excavated at Veii, provide startling parallels to the description of Aeneas' escape from Troy with his aged father borne on his shoulders.[8]

George Hanfmann has stated with admirable compression and definition the scope of the Etruscan contribution to Rome, a legacy which Vergil unquestionably perceived and greatly respected: "The Etruscans have contributed in three ways to the greatness of Rome. Politically, they have helped Rome to become a state; racially, they have enriched the Romans with qualities which this sturdy peasant stock would otherwise have lacked—imagination, enthusiasm for life, religious fervor; artistically, they transmitted knowledge of Greek art and culture to early Rome and bequeathed to the Romans many monumental forms to which the Romans conservatively clung. Artistic influence of more subtle character may have been transmitted through racial heritage—the feeling for decorative color, for impressive mass, for Baroque excited scenes, for pompous representation of ceremonies. As educators of the Romans, the Etruscans have contributed their share to European culture."[9] (Fig. 13)

1. C. Julius Caesar Octavianus
(?) (63 B.C.–14 A.D.). Marble
bust, ca. 30 B.C. Height 15¾
inches. New York, The
Metropolitan Museum of Art,
Rogers Fund, 1919.

*This bust, said to have been
found at Nola, probably
represents the young political
upstart Octavian, who came to
be venerated as Augustus,
victor, peacemaker, and
traditionalist.*

2. M. Antonius (ca. 82–30 B.C.).
Marble. Narbonne, Musée d'Archéologie.

*A realistic portrait of the triumvir. Mark
Antony was arrogant and a faulty
politician but he was a popular champion
and the soldier's favorite next to Caesar.*

3. M. Vipsanius Agrippa (ca. 63–12 B.C.). Bronze bust, first century B.C. Height 12 inches. New York, The Metropolitan Museum of Art, Rogers Fund, 1914.

Agrippa was the military genius of Augustus and husband of the Emperor's daughter Julia. His portraits are, like this one, characterized by a furrowed brow and sombre expression.

4. The Vergil Mosaic, found at Sousse (ancient Hadrumetum), Tunisia. Third century A.D. Tunis, Musée du Bardo.

An allegorical portrait of Vergil, with Clio, Muse of History, reading to the pensive Melpomene, Muse of Tragedy.

OPPOSITE PAGE:

5. Augustus of Prima Porta, detail of the cuirass. Ca. 14 A.D. Height of statue 6 feet 9 inches. Rome, Musei Vaticani.

The elaborate breastplate of the posthumous statue depicts the cosmic setting of Augustus' reign, the subjection of Spain and Gaul, and the recovery of the Parthian standards in 20 B.C. At center, an Oriental returns a standard to a Roman soldier; below, the Earth goddess nourishes the Roman twins; Apollo and Diana, astride a griffin and stag, move towards the center.

6. Verona: Roman theater and Athesis (mod. Adige) river, with remains of the Roman bridge.

Verona commanded the routes to the Brenner Pass. The theater is of Imperial date; the five-arched Ponte Pietra, heavily damaged in World War II, is of the Republican period.

7. Sirmio: remains of the double cryptoporticus
of the Imperial villa overlooking Lake Garda.

*The Imperial villa is an enlargement of a Republican U-shaped
villa which may have been the home of the Valerii, Catullus'
family.*

8. Cerveteri: Tomb of the Capitals, Banditaccia necropolis. Archaic period.

Interior of the subterranean "porch." The Aeolic capitals and columns recall the wooden construction of Etruscan architecture.

9. Cerveteri: Tomb of the Painted Reliefs, Banditaccia necropolis. Hellenistic period.

The interior recalls the luxury of patrician homes. The couch for the deceased couple provides a bench for sandals; bowl, cylix, satchel, helmet, sword, shields, greaves, a lady's fan, walking-stick, and a demonic, fish-tailed dog complete the repertoire of impedimenta.

10. Etruscan chariot (reconstructed) from Monteleone, near Perugia. Mid-sixth century B.C. New York, The Metropolitan Museum of Art, Rogers Fund, 1903.

The bronze repoussé reliefs are generalized heroic scenes: the central scene is the presentation of armor before battle (cf. Venus and Aeneas); the left panel shows the warrior defeating his enemies.

11. Terra-cotta group from the pediment of the Etruscan temple at Pyrgi. Ca. 460 B.C. Rome, Museo di Villa Giulia.

The goddess Minerva dominates the group; a striding Jupiter is alongside, and a god and giant are wrestling in the foreground.

12. View to Mount Soracte from the Via Flaminia.

13. Ash urn from Chiusi, terra cotta. Mid-second century B.C. Worcester (Mass.), Art Museum.

A baroque scene of combat between Greeks and barbarians, no doubt influenced by the Altar of Zeus in Pergamum.

14. Cn. Pompeius Magnus (106–48 B.C.). Bust of Imperial date. Height 11½ inches. Collection of Frank E. Brown.

Pompey's portrait reveals the dichotomy of his character: the complacent face, with small, suspicious eyes and pursed lips, suggests the arrogant and vacillating nature which hastened his decline.

15. M. Tullius Cicero (106–43 B.C.). Bust of Imperial date. Rome, Museo Capitolino.

This somewhat idealized portrait is more just to the character of this skillful reconciler of men than any veristic treatment.

16. C. Julius Caesar (100?–44 B.C.), wearing a laurel wreath. Sard intaglio of Imperial date. Length 15 mm. Boston, Museum of Fine Arts.

Suetonius (Divus Julius 45) remarks that Caesar was tall and fair, had a large mouth, keen black eyes, and an embarrassing baldness.

17. Theater of Pompey and the porticus garden, in foreground of reconstruction of the area. Model: Rome, Museo della Civiltà Romana.

Pompey's theater accommodated some 10,000 spectators. The porticus garden included the Curia Pompeii (for meetings of the Senate), where Caesar died.

18. Reconstruction of an apartment block (*insula*), Ostia, of Imperial date. Model: Rome, Museo della Civiltà Romana.

The shop with added upper story or stories (taberna, *with* cenaculum) *was very common in Rome and Ostia. The tenement, incorporating commercial and domestic requirements, was no doubt a Roman creation.*

19. Reconstruction of the west end of the Forum Romanum.
Model: Rome, Museo della Civiltà Romana.

1. *Rostra*
2. *Arch of Septimius Severus*
3. *Temple of Concord*
4. *Temple of the Deified Vespasian*
5. *Tabularium*
6. *House of the Vestals*
7. *Temple of Vesta*
8. *Parthian Arch of Augustus*
9. *Temple of the Deified Julius*
10. *Temple of Castor*
11. *Basilica Julia*
12. *Temple of Saturn*
13. *Basilica Nova*
14. *Temple of Antoninus and Faustina*
15. *Basilica Aemilia*
16. *Senate House (Curia)*
17. *Temple of Venus Genetrix, in the Forum Julium*
18. *Forum of Augustus*

(The Fora were under construction in Vergil's lifetime.)

20. Temple of Vesta,
relief of Imperial date.
Florence, Galleria degli
Uffizi.

*The temple was reputedly
built by Numa Pompilius
and always rebuilt on the
original plan of circular
hut-and-hearth type.
However, the earliest
foundations discovered
contradict this tradition,
indicating a rectangular
construction.*

21. Hut of Romulus,
mid-eighth century B.C.;
reconstruction. Rome,
Palatine Antiquarium.

*Post holes discovered on
the Palatine Hill, where
the hut of Romulus was
maintained as a state
monument in Roman
times, permitted this
reconstruction in timber
and wattle-and-daub, with
thatched roof.*

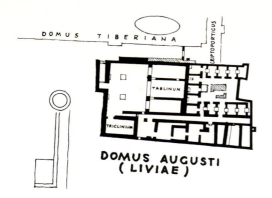

22. Plan of the House of Augustus on the Palatine Hill.

The modest house where the Emperor lived for more than forty years was acquired from the estate of Hortensius, Cicero's opponent. Like the hut of Romulus, the house was later safeguarded as a national monument.

23. House of Augustus: so-called tablinum.

The house has several wall paintings with mythological and Egyptian subjects; that on the southwest wall of the so-called tablinum depicts the story of Io and Argus.

24. Ancient Rome: reconstruction of the area around the
Capitoline Hill. Model: Rome, Museo della Civiltà Romana.

1. *Temple of the Capitoline Triad*
2. *Temple of Juno Moneta, on the Arx*
3. *Tarpeian Rock*
4. *Basilica Aemilia*
5. *Theater of Marcellus*
6. *Temple of Apollo "in Circo"*

7. *Pons Fabricius*
8. *Temple of Aesculapius*
9. *Pons Cestius*
10. *Forum Holitorium*
11. *Forum Boarium*
12. *Circus Flaminius*

IV

Rome

VERGIL was born into an age of revolution. In 70 B.C., the year of his birth, Pompey (Fig. 14) and Crassus were the consuls, militarist and millionaire in combination. Their regime heralded the end of the constitution of Sulla and of the entrenched position of the senatorial oligarchy in the government. A new era dawned, with new privileges for the business class, the equestrians, and there was a semblance of peace. The armies which had served in Spain and against the risings of slaves and gladiators at home were disbanded, and for three or four years Italy knew peace, however uneasily founded on the revised governmental structure. Also in 70, Cicero (Fig. 15) championed the Sicilians against Verres and emerged as Rome's foremost advocate. Outside Italy, Mithridates VI, King of Pontus, a Hellenistic kingdom on the Black Sea, was in retreat from Roman arms. But when Lucullus, the Roman general following in the steps of Alexander the Great, marched against Tigranocerta in Mesopotamia to press his advantage against the enemy, his troops refused to advance; the dream of a Roman Empire in the East was shattered. Piracy was rampant in the Mediterranean, product of the uneasy balance of power between Rome and the Near East and her inability to guard the sea lanes properly. The Senate was impressed by Cicero's championing of legislation which would give Pompey an extraordinary command against the pirates and later against Mithridates (67 and 66 B.C.), and overwhelmed by the popular and equestrian support for the appointments, it conferred both commands, though with reasonable hesitation and foreboding. For Pompey returned victorious against the pirates (as he would ultimately against Mithridates); he was now a titanic figure—a brilliant strategist and impressive personality, a skilled organizer of his conquests, and an ambitious statesman.

During Pompey's absence overseas, Rome witnessed increasing political unrest, bribery in elections and in the courts, revolutionary talk and outright violence. The city was on the verge of civil war in 63 when Lucius Sergius Catilina, a renegade aristocrat, embarked on an outrageous campaign which promised redistribution of property and cancellation, or at least scaling-down, of debts. Bankers and capitalists were allied with the conservative senatorial segment of Roman society, and in response to Cicero's indisputable evidence of a forthcoming revolution and of Gallic involvement with the conspirators, the Senate voted the death penalty for Catiline. Some of his followers were executed that same day in the dank, torchlit confines of the Tullianum prison, beneath the Church of S. Giuseppe dei Falegnami. Catiline died with the remnant of his forces at Pistoia, fighting gallantly under the legionary standards of Marius. Cicero took advantage of his success to cement a new Concord of the Orders, and a brief period of compromise and cooperation between the dissident strata of Rome's governing classes followed.

Pompey returned to Italy from the East in 62, and to everyone's surprise, disbanded his legions without incident, thereby winning Cicero's admiration but losing his political advantage for the future. Caesar (Fig. 16), born in 100, had managed to survive the proscriptions and violence of the period, and by dint of meritorious service in the East and in Spain, by the prestige attaching to his office as Pontifex Maximus, and not least by his personal magnetism, had won a place alongside Pompey and Crassus in the First Triumvirate of 60 B.C. The formation of this illegal, extraconstitutional league of gain-seeking statesmen meant the collapse of Cicero's harmony of orders and the gradual disintegration of the Republican constitution. In 59, as consul with the inconsequential Bibulus, Caesar ratified Pompey's conquests in the East, an action which had been postponed unwisely by the Senate, and also sought to settle the veterans on confiscated farmlands. Cicero was attacked by Publius Clodius Pulcher, a supporter of Caesar, on the ground that he had illegally executed the Catilinarians, and Ciecro had to leave the city he had so recently saved, a city which had honored him with the exemplary title *Pater Patriae,* "Father of his Fatherland."

Caesar waited outside Rome for Cicero to be exiled and then hastened northwards to assume the command of the legions in Provence, to begin ten years of campaigning, territorial aggrandizement and organization in France, Switzerland, and the Low Countries. Pompey and Crassus were soon at loggerheads. The former, anxious to regain his popular image and to win the support of the nobility, engineered the recall of Cicero. But Caesar's supporter Clodius unleashed riots and demonstrations against Pompey and confined him to his home. Crassus assisted Clodius with funds and relished the embarrassment of his rival. However, Pompey's efforts were ultimately successful, and the Assembly passed a bill for Cicero's return with uproarious enthusiasm. Caesar was concerned for his own prestige and for the security of his undertakings in the North and their ratification; he was aware, too, of Cicero's role in Pompey's growing popularity with the nobility. These factors induced Caesar to summon a conference at Luca. The deliberations had important results for the forthcoming years: Pompey and Crassus were to stand for the consulship of 55, with guarantees that Pompey should later become governor of the Two Spains and Cyrenaica for five years, with six legions under his command; Crassus, for an equal period, was to be governor of Syria with the right to campaign against the Parthians; Caesar's proconsulship and military command was to be renewed for another five years. Cicero's oratory was to be curbed, and mob demonstrations inspired by Clodius and his Pompeian counterpart, Annius Milo, were to be restrained.

Caesar left immediately to join his legions in Transalpine Gaul, and the seemingly reconciled parties returned to Rome. In the following year (55 B.C.) Caesar invaded Britain for the first time, and although the "commando" raid accomplished little, the communiqués were sufficient to excite the Senate to declare a public thanksgiving for a period of twenty days.

Three years later, in 52, Caesar had to face his stiffest opposition during the Gallic campaigns. Vercingetorix mustered the Gauls to a war of independence which adopted desperate but effective measures. Guerrilla warfare, a scorched-earth policy, the disruption of communications, the capture of military convoys, and the terror of ambush and sudden raids took their toll of Caesar's legions. But the Gauls, heartened by their victory over the besieging Roman armies at Gergovia, decided to meet Caesar in open warfare, and finally, at Alesia in 52, the future of Gaul was decided in favor of the Romans. The courageous Vercingetorix died later in the Tullianum, with a jest about the cold baths which Romans accorded their prisoners in the damp depths of the Carcer.

Meantime, at Rome, Pompey chose to remain in the city rather than transfer to Spain after the consulship. Crassus, hungry for spoils and for new prestige, invaded Mesopotamia in 54, crossed the Euphrates and returned to Syria with some minor victories to his credit. But in 53, Crassus made an ill-advised march across the northern desert of Syria, and during a dust storm the legions were ambushed by squadrons of heavily armed Parthian cavalry. The Parthian archers were triumphant finally, and to Rome's shame the standards of seven Roman legions were exhibited in Parthian temples. The young Publius Crassus, onetime lieutenant of Caesar in Gaul, died with his father. The triumvir's head was later used as a prop in a performance of the Bacchae of Euripides at the Parthian court.

The death in 54 of Julia, Pompey's wife and Caesar's daughter, further widened the breach between the two men. The marriage had been devised at the Luca conference, and for a time Julia's affability and charm helped to maintain a semblance of equilibrium between Pompey and Caesar. With the death of Crassus at Carrhae the relationship between the surviving pair grew more strained than ever. When Vergil arrived in Rome, probably in 54, disorder and violence were in the offing. For two years there was virtual anarchy in the city, with no consuls elected for either year. Clodius died in a roadside struggle, and his death excited his followers to arson and sacrilege in the Forum. The body was carried into the Curia, laid on a pyre of chairs and benches, and cremated amid the flaming ruin of the Senate Chamber.

Pompey's opposition to Caesar became more open and destructive. Caesar's concern for the eventual settlement of his veterans on farmlands and their reintegration in Italy after the long service across the Alps meant that he must act decisively on their behalf before long. Among those who opposed Caesar were the poets Catullus and Calvus.

Though acknowledged among the New Poets as a passionate and original genius, Calvus was also a skillful orator who had on at least one occasion heaped abuse on one of Caesar's partisans, Vatinius, the tribune of 59. Caesar also had smarted under the popular lampoons of Catullus, poems which were charged with slander and forthright abuse of Caesar and his henchmen, particularly the infamous Murena, Caesar's engineer and intimate associate. Catullus and the Neoterics—the Young Turks of the poetic scene—Lucretius, Cicero, and many others have left comments on the downfall of their society, a disintegration of political and social morality which they both assisted and deplored.

Meanwhile Vergil continued his rhetorical studies under Rome's best masters, in particular the rhetor Epidius who had established a school which had as pupils, beside Vergil, such later luminaries as Mark Antony and Octavian. After a brief and unhappy experience in the Roman courts, Vergil renounced an advocate's career, along with any political designs, for further philosophical study with Siro, the Epicurean who, according to Cicero, was teaching in Rome about 50 B.C.

Finally, in 49, the confrontation between Pompey and Caesar was at hand. With the rejection of his ultimatum to the Senate, Caesar led his troops across the Rubicon, with the resolution of a gambler playing for the highest stakes. Confused and dismayed by the blitzkrieg advance and success of Caesar, the Senate and Pompey evacuated Rome and prepared to transport themselves to Greece. Caesar's legions entered Rome, and after ensuring that administration both at home and abroad would be effectively maintained without his presence, the commander proceeded to Spain with six legions and seven thousand cavalry. His victories in Spain against the Pompeian forces led to jubilation in the Capital, only partly diminished by his failures in North Africa. Caesar's election as consul for 48 further enlarged his image as patron of the citizenry and as a clement, magnanimous statesman. Finally, at the battle of Pharsalus in 48, Caesar's superior strategy won the day. Pompey fled to Egypt at a time when that country was in an uproar of civil war. Ptolemy XIV and his elder sister, wife, and co-regent, Cleopatra VII, were contesting each other for the throne their father, Ptolemy the Fluteplayer, had willed to them. Pompey's arrival coincided with the moment when the opposing forces were about to engage. Ptolemy's advisers urged Pompey to land. But as he stepped ashore a Roman renegade stabbed him in the back, in full sight of his wife and young son Sextus. His head was cut off and preserved in brine for presentation to Caesar, the body left on the shore. Three days later Caesar arrived to view with mixed emotions the head of his former partner and son-in-law.[1]

Events moved quickly, and within three years Caesar's legions had suppressed all senatorial and Pompeian resistance in the Mediterranean region in Africa and in Spain. Affairs in Asia Minor were settled decisively and promptly. His campaign against Pharnaces, the son of Mithridates, lasted five days, and after the battle at Zela, Caesar immortalized his speedy victory with the laconic communiqué to his friend Matius—*Veni, vidi, vici,* "I came, I saw, I conquered."

Proclaimed Dictator for life, Caesar undertook a massive program of administrative and governmental reform, and of social and economic changes which would bring Rome to the forefront of the nations and establish her as worthy mistress of the expanded empire. But his actions and designs roused considerable enmity among the reactionary onetime governing class of Rome. And on the Ides of March 44 irate senators acted, and Caesar fell at the foot of Pompey's statue in the porticus gardens of Pompey's theater. (Fig. 17)

Whether or not Vergil was in Rome at this troubled time, we shall never know. The poet has certainly given evidence of favor for Caesar and regret for his passing. On the eve of his final encounter with Turnus, Aeneas embraces his son Ascanius and utters a famous apostrophe:

> From me you may learn courage and what real effort is;
> From others, the meaning of fortune. To-day this hand will see
> You're protected in war, and take you to where war's prizes are found.
> Be sure that when you have grown to your full manhood, you do not
> Forget; but rather, dwelling upon your kinsmen's example,
> Be inspired by your father Aeneas, your uncle Hector.
>
> (A. 12, 435–40. Day Lewis)

Aeneas would appear to prefigure Julius Caesar in this context, with the suggestion too of gentle counseling by Vergil of his imperial patron Augustus, appealing to him to follow the path of virtue and positive effort for his people, to ensure as well that the destiny of the past, of agonizing wars and a ravished nation, should not be repeated.

One must suppose that the years of civil war, 49–46, were not favorable times for the cultivation of the Muses in Rome. Vergil's nature was better attuned to the tranquillity of the Mantuan countryside and the family circle. Whether or not he witnessed any of the turmoil, we may be certain of the mounting horror and revulsion felt by the poet whose second book of the *Aeneid* translates into universal terms his tormented world. R. G. Austin[2] has captured the almost biographic nature of the second book with amazing sensitivity: "It is the poet's own experience: Virgil has lived through the last hours of Troy, knowing how the minds of men (civilians and military alike) work in war-time, familiar with the personal tragedies that war brings, sharing in the desolation of a city whose stones he has known and loved; he has seen men shot down in ignorance by their own side, old men murdered in their homes, women and children lined up for prison camps; he has endured the incomprehensible injustice of what must be interpreted as the will of heaven." For Rome and for Mantua Vergil has deep feelings of respect and love: for their depredation he has both sorrow and indignation.

The topography and monuments of Italy affected Vergil's imagination most dramatically in Rome. Here he spurned neither the greatness of the past nor the grandeur of the present. To be sure, the poet was always more interested in people than in the brick, stone, concrete, and wood which clothe the community, but he was also genuinely impressed with the "message" of the contemporary architecture of Rome, largely the product of Augustus and his lieutenant, Marcus Vipsanius Agrippa.

Between the deaths of Caesar in 44 and of Vergil in 19, Rome underwent architectural changes of a grandiose order, approximating the staggering changes in the cityscape of the twentieth century. Augustus, with the self-praise expected of eminent Romans, reported to the world in his epigraphical testament, the *Res Gestae,* that he had found Rome a city of unbaked brick and had transformed it into a city of marble. The assertion was partly true, for although the marble was often nothing more than a thin veneer laid over brick and concrete, he did alter the appearance of the city in its secular and religious monuments to a remarkable degree. As in the mediaeval city of later times, the fresh appearance and beauty of the new architecture must have compensated greatly for the mud and filth, the danger and poverty, the ignorance and servitude of the citizenry. Ferrero has called this quarter-century of Rome's existence "un véritable recommencement d'histoire." After Actium and the collapse of Ptolemaic Egypt, Rome became the new center of privilege, and the new scale of living demanded an architecture which would satisfy the needs and desires of the citizens and the Princeps. A picture of a veritable frenzy of building emerges from the pages of the historians, from the inscriptions, from the recovered remains, and not least, from the poet's enthusiastic allusions.

Vergil's biographer (*Vita Donati,* 11) states flatly that the poet did not enjoy Rome as a residence and that he lived there as little as possible. He preferred the serene heights of Posillipo overlooking the bay of Naples and the cultural environment of the city Cicero regarded as the Athens of the West, but he was also a recognized figure at Rome. The favor of Augustus and Maecenas, Princeps and Patron, and his association with the other literary lights made him a celebrity there— so much so that, by Suetonius' account, he would take refuge in the nearest house to avoid those who followed him and pointed him out. He kept a residence, the gift of Maecenas, on the fashionable Esquiline Hill, perhaps somewhere near the Carinae (keels) section, and was certainly welcome behind Imperial doors on the Palatine. Augustus was vitally interested in the progress of the poem which would one day substantially strengthen and defend the claims of the Julian family to the Principate.

Vergil's early reaction to the metropolis appears in his pastoral poetry, recalling the confiscations which had made him initially hostile to the Roman government:

> The city men call Rome—in my ignorance I used to
> Imagine it like the market town to which we shepherds
> Have so often herded the weanlings of our flocks.
> Thus I came to know how dogs resemble puppies,
> Goats their kids, and by that scale to compare large things with small.
> But Rome carries her head as high above other cities
> As cypresses tower over the tough wayfaring tree.
>
> (E. 1, 19–25. Day Lewis)

His first reaction, one of awe at the scale and soaring magnificence of Rome, strengthened still further after he had become more completely acquainted with the city. The gleaming white facades of the Roman government buildings, the well-sculptured spaces of the ancient Forum Romanum, of Julius Caesar's elegant new square, and of the Campus Martius, must have awakened new admiration in the poet. Here was thrilling confirmation of the return to the Golden Age, not so much Saturnian as Periclean, among the seven hills. The rebirth of classical building forms and orders accentuated the appearance of a great new society and a new age of enlightenment. Rome was to become, like Periclean Athens, the "education of the West," and the architectural marvels of Augustan Rome would inspire the ages.

On two occasions Vergil speaks of poetic composition in terms which seem to reflect the building craze of the first century. In *Georgic* 3, 12–39, after discarding the threadbare subjects of Greek mythology, he pronounces his poetic manifesto: to erect a temple, a circus, and a theater at his native Mantua, adorned with marble sculptures, ivory and gold, with historical reliefs and allegorical wall paintings, all to the honor and glory of Octavian. The physical monuments are, of course, symbolic and figurative: Vergil is proposing to "build" a temple of song, perhaps an historical epic, or to make a monumental offering of his poetry to his hero Octavian. His biographer also relates that "after writing a first draft of the *Aeneid* in prose, he divided it into twelve books, and proceeded to turn into verse one part after another, following his whim, in no particular order. And so as not to impede the flow of his thought, he left some elements unfinished, and, so to speak, bolstered others up with very slight words, which, as he jokingly used to say, were put in like props (*tibicines*) to support the structure until the solid columns should arrive." So, like Horace with his "monument more durable than bronze," Vergil too seems to have imagined his work as a memorial, consciously constructed and lasting, partner to the marble architectural monuments of Octavian and Agrippa and the contemporary *triumphatores*.

Vergil's perspective of Rome, past and present, does not include, for obvious reasons, the less desirable sectors of the city—areas like the Subura, the ghetto-like sector which Caesar preferred as residence, subject to frequent fires, lawlessness, and depravity. Behind the areas of renewal there were many malodorous and monotonous side streets, mean apartment blocks (*insulae*) (Fig. 18), and dilapidated *pensioni,* slum dwellings of the sort which Juvenal later fulminated against in his acerbic satires. Urban renewal could not blot out entirely the larger older city with its drawbacks and perils. But the administration was not blind to these evils. To compensate for the misery, the confinement, and the soul-destroying nature of the depressed areas of the city, the Augustan planners repaired the aqueducts and sewers, improved the parks and piazzas, and gave the citizens open-air galleries in the shape of colonnaded porticoes filled with sculptures and paintings, and new centers for the amusement of the gregarious, the circus and bath buildings.

The variety of new buildings and monuments make Vergil's imaginative recovery of the ancient site all the more remarkable, for behind the Imperial facade of the rehabilitated city, the costly enterprise of the Imperial philanthropy, Vergil saw the outline of a grassier, more expansive, less tumultuous Arcadian past. Just as natural settings were a frame for man and his works, so too the civic monuments of Augustan Rome were an elaborate frame for the simpler dignity of the past, and for men whose actions had brought Rome to the realization of her great destiny. Only once does Vergil express outright disdain for the city setting, for the strain and clamor of the Forum:

> The fruit on the bough, the crops that the field is glad to bear
> Are his for the gathering: he spares not a glance for the iron
> Rigour of law, the municipal rackets, the public records [office].
> (G. 2, 500–2. Day Lewis)

This moody rejection of the city which forms part of a larger diatribe (493–512) must have stemmed from a momentary disenchantment during his days as student and lawyer in Rome, or from his consternation at the gradual breakdown of constitutional government and his new awareness of the hollow "message" of the governmental buildings which rose new or refurbished in the administrative sectors of Rome.

In order to grasp the significance and the wonder of Aeneas' visit to Evander's Pallanteum, ancestor to Rome, one must have some awareness of the nature of the Forum Romanum in Vergil's day. Today, beneath Michelangelo's Senatorial Palace, the visitor's eye is attracted to the Tabularium, and beneath that to the Temple of Saturn and the Imperial Rostra. The Tabularium was built by Quintus Lutatius Catulus in 78 B.C. to house the state archives. The sturdy substructures of squared tufa masonry, even without their stucco, and the first story with its rhythmic arcade and Doric half-columns, offer a splendid clue to the original nature of the building, which even in this rear facade provides a monumental backdrop to the Forum below (Fig. 19). The Temple of Saturn, a deity whom Vergil associated with the Golden Age of an earlier Latium, was no doubt a fifth-century successor to an earlier shrine on the same spot. The present remains survive from a rebuilding by Lucius Munatius Plancus which was financed by the spoils of his Gallic triumph. The best date for the rebuilding is after Plancus' reconciliation with Octavian, between 31 and 22 B.C. This splendid Ionic temple with a high podium housed the Roman treasury (*aerarium*) in its basement; the door which once admitted the treasury officers (who at one stage included Horace, who worked here after Philippi) still survives near the temple steps, with the lock-holes intact.

To the right of the Saturn Temple stood formerly the Temple of Concord; according to tradition it was founded by Camillus in 367 to commemorate the harmony between the patrician and plebeian orders. Lucius Opimius rebuilt it after the demise of Gaius Gracchus in 121 B.C., and the present remains, which are scanty, date from the reigns of Augustus and Tiberius (7 B.C.–A.D. 10). This temple may have inspired Agrippa's Pantheon in the Campus Martius. To the right of the Temple of Concord was the open-air Comitium, the meeting place of the Populus Romanus, in front of the Curia, the Senate House. The Rostra, so-called from the ships' beaks which decorated its facade after the Roman victory over the Antiates (338 B.C.), stood between the Comitium and the Forum until Caesar and Augustus reordered the area, together with the patterns of government, and transferred the speakers' platform westwards towards the present, reconstructed remains.

The small rectangular temple of Janus Geminus, the god of beginnings who faced both front and back, stood near the Curia where the Argiletum entered the Forum. Along the northern side of the Forum, east of the Curia and Janus Temple, lay the elegant Basilica Aemilia, a magnificent lawcourt building erected in 179 by the censors Marcus Aemilius

Lepidus and Marcus Fulvius Nobilior. The building was repaired between 80 and 78, at the time of the building of the Tabularium, and was
rebuilt in 55–54 from funds advanced by Julius Caesar through the
offices of Lucius Aemilius Paullus and his son, who dedicated the building in 34. The courts were refurbished in Augustan times after a
catastrophic fire in 14 B.C. The lower Ionic order incorporated an historical frieze which related stories from Rome's early days—as evocative
as Evander's narrative or the pictorial review on Aeneas' shield. The
shops and colonnade along the southern flank of the Basilica Aemilia
were choice locations in the busy civic center.

On the opposite side of the square, across the Via Sacra and past the
sanctuary of Venus Cloacina, there stood, until 46, another lawcourt
building, the Basilica Sempronia, built by Tiberius Sempronius Gracchus, censor in 169, and father of the ill-starred Gracchan reformers.
Julius Caesar acquired the building and the site and began his own
Basilica Julia, another two-storied edifice, resplendent with a forest of
columns inside and out.

The Temple of Castor, which shared the same north-south orientation
as the Saturn Temple, stood on its high podium at the eastern end of the
Basilica Julia, near several smaller cult sites reserved to Juturna and
Asclepius. Castor and Pollux, the twin sons of Zeus, the Dios-kouroi,
were deeply involved in the Trojan-Roman and Latin religious traditions and were among Rome's most hallowed divinities. They had
allegedly intervened at the Battle of Lake Regillus in 496 and supported
the Romans against the Latins; after the engagement, according to re-
liable sources, they had watered their divine mounts at the Spring of
Juturna (Lacus Juturnae) in the Forum. The Temple of Castor served
as a state repository and housed the official weights and measures of
the Republic in its podium. It was restored by Lucius Caecilius Metellus
in 117 and remained intact until Tiberius' rebuilding in 6 A.D. The
Augustan victory arch, the so-called Parthian Arch, was erected after
20 B.C. at the northwest corner of the Temple of Castor, successor to
the earlier arch which rose between the Temples of Castor and of the
Deified Julius, in honor of the victory at Actium. Among other elements
it displayed the calendar lists (*Fasti*) of consuls and generals who had
celebrated triumphs from earliest times, a roll call of eminent Romans
and commanders.

The House of the Vestals (Atrium Vestae) and the Vesta Temple rose on the eastern flank of the Castor Temple. The Vestal virgins, housed magnificently in the Forum, were given the special privilege of being permitted to travel by wheeled vehicle through the civic square. Their chief function was to tend the sacred fire traditionally supposed to have been brought by Aeneas from Troy, along with the Penates. The Vestals served under the direction of the high priest (Pontifex Maximus) and assumed their role with nun-like dignity and reverent responsibility. Ovid (*Fasti* 6, 261–4) affirms that the Temple of Vesta (Fig. 20) assumed a tholos, or bee-hive, form because it was descended from a primitive circular hut, following the pattern of the Hut of Romulus (Fig. 21) and Palatine and Forum settlements. Certainly the rotunda of the Imperial period seems to hark back to a primitive hut form, with the same central hearth and smoke vent. However, earlier remains discovered in the immediate environs of the circular temple suggest a rectangular building, possibly contemporary with the temple which preceded the building of the Regia at the turn of the sixth century.

The temple of the state cult of the Penates stood on the Velia, not far from the Forum, on a short street leading into the wealthy residential sector of the Carinae. The cult statue there depicted the Great Gods as seated youths, in military dress, reminiscent of their original form at Lavinium and probably Tusculum. Augustus refurbished the Velian shrine with emphasis on the Trojan associations of the Julian family in order to impress the populace with the identification of the "household gods" of the Roman state with his own.

The Regia, repository of the regalia of the kings and administrative office and cult place of the Rex Sacrorum, stood near the Vestal cult site on the Sacred Way. Rebuilt in marble on the original sixth-century plan by Gnaeus Domitius Calvinus in 36, the building resembled a complete archaic house (*aedes*), with vestibule, two side chambers, and a courtyard. The original building, a pious construction of Republican founding fathers about 500 B.C., had an oblong, tripartite design, with a trapeziform courtyard furnished with a well and an impressive altar. Although it recalled the design of existing domestic buildings of Etruscan design, it was created for cult rather than residential needs. It is not known when the Pontifex Maximus assumed or superseded the functions of the Rex Sacrorum or indeed whether that "cross between theologician and civil engineer (i.e., 'bridge-builder')," as Sir James Frazer called the Pontifex Maximus, ever did assume the "regulating" and specific functions of the Rex Sacrorum. Certainly the official residence of the Pontifex Maximus in Republican times, the Domus Publica, lay eastwards on the Via Sacra. In fact, Julius Caesar and Augustus chose to live elsewhere, and the unfortunate Lepidus, that outmoded survivor of stormier days, lived out his pontificate defiantly at Circeii.

The Via Sacra, avenue of the triumphal processions which came with accelerated frequency after the Punic wars, moved somewhat irregularly from the east end of the Forum to the Capitoline slopes and ultimately to the temple of the Capitoline Triad. Several ancient cult sites were open to view from the road. One of these, the Lacus Curtius, onetime marshy depression in the Forum area, was imagined to be an avenue to the underworld, and coins were cast into it by Romans to ward off the evil day and, latterly, to safeguard the emperor. Although it owed its name to the consul of 445, Gaius Curtius, who consecrated the spot after lightning struck, it was popularly associated with Mettius Curtius who, in 362, in obedience to an oracle, leapt mounted and fully armed into the chasm which opened up in the Forum. Such a chasm is evidence of the original marshy nature of the square, a problem remedied by the Etruscan drainage measures; the great drain (Cloaca Maxima) was paved over by Sulla and monumentalized by a balustrade decorated with a relief depicting the "devotion" of the heroic Curtius. The location was close to the existing Column of Phocas (608 A.D.).

The Senate House (Curia) of Rome was located at the northwest end of the Forum. Called originally the Curia Hostilia, which suggests the involvement of the Hostilian family during the sixth or fifth century, it was restored and enlarged by Sulla about 80 B.C., burnt in 52 during the riots over Curio's cremation and burial, and rebuilt by Faustus Sulla. In 44 it was razed to provide a location for an expanded Senate house on a new site, the Curia Julia, which was eventually finished by Octavian in 29. The surviving Senate House, built by Diocletian, preserves the main design of Caesar's Curia, with its oblong hall, the marble steps for folding chairs along the sides, and the magistrate's dais opposite the central door.

The little temple of the Deified Julius rose in the middle of the

Forum, facing west towards the Rostra and the Tabularium, located, apparently, with a view to imposing some symmetry on the nondescript order of the square. The temple was begun in 42 and dedicated by Octavian in 29 on the spot where the mourning citizens cremated the body of Caesar. The entrance platform, decorated with ships' beaks captured at Actium, contained in a semicircular niche the altar which commemorated Casear's cremation and ultimate apotheosis.

Aeneas' walk through Pallanteum with his ruler-host, the aged Evander, takes him from the Great Altar of Hercules and the cult celebrations past the Porta Carmentalis in the so-called Servian wall, and so within sight of the place where the Corinthian Temple of Apollo will be consecrated, perhaps on Octavian's birthday, September 23, 32 B.C. The two then proceed to the foot of the Capitoline Hill, where they view the Asylum and the Lupercal, and also the Argiletum alongside the site of the future Basilica Aemilia and the Curia, both of which will be restored by Augustus; then they climb the Capitoline slopes by the later Clivus Capitolinus, and from the summit they survey the Tarpeian Rock and the sites where the Capitoline Temple of Jupiter, Juno, and Minerva, and the Temples of Jupiter Tonans and Juno Moneta will rise (Fig. 24). Thereafter they descend into the Forum Romanum area at its west end, then a pasturage for cattle, and continue past the route to the Carinae, the luxury quarter of Augustan Rome, arriving at Evander's modest palace, the Regia, alongside the ancient burial grounds of the Romulan or Villanovan community, and near the spot where Aeneas' descendant, Julius Caesar, will be cremated and the Temple of the Deified Julius will rise.

The Carmental Gate, which bears the name of Evander's mother, the Arcadian Muse, was located at the southwest corner of the Capitoline Hill where the Vicus Jugarius leaves the Forum and passes through the fourth-century "Servian" wall towards the Campus Martius and the partially visible Temple of Apollo and Theater of Marcellus. The cave of the Lupercal, restored by Augustus, was located on the steepest side of the Capitoline Hill, and commemorated the nurture of Romulus and Remus by the wolf, for it was here, according to Dionysius, that the wolf retreated when the shepherds discovered her with her nursling children. The large cave with a spring inside it was built over by

Augustus and monumentalized. The rite of the Lupercalia, involving naked patrician youths armed with strips of goatskin which they used to strike women in order to promote fertility, was a survival from a primitive festival of purification, associated with wolves and celebrated annually on February 15th. The Luperci, "wolf-controllers," were a natural outgrowth of a shepherd community which was prepared to take any measures to guarantee its herds against marauders. The Asylum, or refuge, lay between the twin peaks of the Capitoline Hill. Although the area was covered over during the rehabilitation of the Capitoline after 31 B.C., it was enshrined in men's memories as the site where Romulus tried to gather together non-Romans who would increase the population. (The Rape of the Sabines, recalled elsewhere by Vergil [A. 8, 635–6], was part of the same policy.) The Argiletum was a major city artery of Augustan Rome, terminating in the Forum between the Curia Julia and the Basilica Aemilia, both completed by Augustus. Legend told that the death of Argus (*Argi-letum*), the many-eyed guardian of Jupiter's beloved Io, was remembered here, but a more likely inspiration, though infinitely less romantic and bizarre, lay in the white clay (*argilla*) which forms part of the tufaceous floor of the Forum. The Tarpeian Rock was associated with Tarpeia's infamous surrender of the city to the Sabines in the time of Titus Tatius. The cliff behind the Capitoline Temple was the place of public execution for traitors, including the lamentable Tiberius Gracchus.

For the Capitoline Hill, Vergil's Evander shows special concern and appropriate awe:

The Capitol, golden today, but then a tangle of thicket.
Even at that time the timorous countrymen went in awe of

The god-haunted feel of the place, trembled at wood and rock,
Evander remarked:—This wood, this hill with its leafy crest
Some god inhabits; though which, we cannot be sure. The Arcadians
Believe that they have witnessed great Jove himself, seen him repeatedly
Shaking his dark aegis and summoning up the storm clouds.
Now look at those ruined walls: there used to be two towns there,
And what you see are the relics, the monuments of a past age.
Janus built a citadel here, there Saturn built one;
This was called the Janiculum, that other the Saturnian.

(A. 8, 347–58. Day Lewis)

Pride of the Capitoline Hill was the great Temple of Jupiter Optimus Maximus, the magnificent triadic temple housing Juno and Minerva as well as Jupiter which Rome had inherited from the Etruscans. The temple had a symbolic importance for Romans comparable to that of the Parthenon to Athenians or Westminster Abbey to Londoners. The massive substructures are evidence of the immensity of the building. The original temple, the largest ever undertaken by the Etruscans, was of the Doric order, hexastyle across the facade, and lavishly decorated with painted terra-cotta revetments and sculptures which were perhaps overseen by Vulca of Veii, the Etruscan Phidias. Fire destroyed the basically wooden structure in 83 B.C., ruining the now faded terra cottas and destroying the treasured books of Sibylline prophecy housed there since the time of its construction and purchased from the Apolline Sibyl at Cumae by Tarquinius Superbus for the Etruscan priesthood. The restoration after 83 incorporated some of the columns of the great Temple of Olympian Zeus in Athens, thwarted project of the Pisistratid tyranny. Quintus Lutatius Catulus dedicated the rebuilt version in 69, and Augustus undertook to repair the building at considerable cost in 26, a year after Agrippa had completed his controversial Pantheon in the Campus Martius. The gilded roof tiles of Evander's account are typical of the lavishness of Augustan redecoration.

Four years later, in 22, Augustus dedicated a new temple nearby on the Capitoline Hill to Jupiter the Thunderer (Tonans) as a thank-offering for deliverance from death by lightning in northwestern Spain (26 B.C.). Suetonius adds a rather entertaining footnote to the construction, asserting that Jupiter appeared to Augustus in one of his habitual dreams and complained bitterly that his worshippers were being taken away from him by the newly erected building. Augustus, who was as alert to dream admonitions as his Trojan ancestor Aeneas, replied that the new temple had been set alongside the greater edifice as door-keeper, and that the worshippers, like earthly clients waiting on their patrons, were thronging to see him.

Evander's archaeological review and reconstruction from the remnants of "ruined walls" is somewhat troublesome in the light of more scientific, though still incomplete, exploration. The difficulties are resolved, however, if the Janiculum ("the fort that Janus built") is identified with one of the summits of the Capitol, the well-known arx, or citadel, rather than with the hill across the Tiber. The Saturnian settlement is then the area covered by the Capitoline Temple with its outlying sanctuaries.

Vergil's detailed description of the palace of Latinus at the ill-defined Laurentum has much in common with the impressive Temple of the Capitoline Triad. Camps' observation on the marked similarity of palace and temple is suggestive and probably accurate: "Here at the very middle of the *Aeneid* Vergil has placed a symbolic counterpart of the great Capitoline Temple of Rome, which he has called to mind also at 8, 347 ff. and 9, 448."[3]

> The palace of Laurentine Picus was large and majestic. It stood at the top of the city on one hundred high columns; the people were awed by its ancient nearby forest. Here kings had received their sceptres, and taken up fasces, an omen for good; this temple was also their law court. Here was the place for their sacred banquets, and here, when a ram had been sacrificed, the fathers by custom sat down at long tables that stretched in unbroken line. Then too, here stood in the vestibule statues of ancient cedar-wood showing the ancestors set up in succession; Italus, Father Sabinus, the planter of vines, who kept his curved sickle as part of his portrait, Saturnus, the image of two-faced Janus, and other kings, from earliest times. They bore the wounds they had suffered defending their country. Upon sacred doorposts hung many weapons besides, captured chariots, and curved axes, crests from helmets, huge bars from gates, both spearheads and shields, and prows torn from ships.
>
> (A. 7, 170–86)

Ilioneus, Aeneas' dutiful ambassador at Laurentum as at Carthage earlier, offered Latinus the tokens of earthly and temporal power in the manner of a suppliant nation seeking alliance or surrendering its autonomy (A. 7, 243–8). The reference to the king's first appearance at the "palace" after his accession parallels the formal presentation of the Roman consuls after they took up office. And the banquet even finds its counterpart in the Feast of Jupiter (Epulum Jovis) which was celebrated annually on the Ides of September and November in honor of the Capitoline Triad. All of these circumstantial parallels, combined with the location, the impressive colonnade, the temple doors adorned with trophies, the statues of rulers and military heroes at the entrance, suggest that Vergil has placed the ancestral ruler of the Latins within a Roman context which would both excite and gratify his Italian audience.

The Temple of Juno Moneta and the story of Manlius and the warning geese on the Capitoline summit (*arx*) are given pride of place on Aeneas' divinely fashioned shield:

> At the top of the shield, Manlius, warden of the Tarpeian
> Fortress, stood before the temple, guarding the Capitol—
> The palace, just built by Romulus, being shown with a rough
> thatched roof.
> Here too a silvery goose went fluttering through a golden
> Colonnade, honking out an alarum, that the Gauls are on us.
> (A. 8, 652–6. Day Lewis)

The temple was actually dedicated in 344 when Rome was contending with the Aurunci, although both Vergil (*supra*) and Plutarch (*Camillus*, 27) imply that there was a less formal shrine on the height in 390. The cult title, which was commonly attached to the "warning" (*moneo*) provided by Juno's geese, was more likely a Latin version of the Greek Mnemosyne, the Remembrancer, appropriate to the formulae of prayer addressed to the goddess to "remember" her former benefactions. The temple housed the Libri Lintei, and after 269 was the site of the mint (cf. monetary). The Church of Santa Maria in Aracoeli covers the site today, as the temple had formerly replaced the house of Marcus Manlius Capitolinus, destroyed in 384. The Capitoline geese are strange company for Juno's "paycocks," and their presence is probably explained by their use for divination by the haruspices at the time of the Gallic incursion. Cicero describes the annual rite on the Capitol to reawaken memories of the saving grace of Juno's raucous sentries, and Vergil responds accordingly in his shield vignette.

The Temple of Janus Geminus, towards the west end of the Forum and close to the Curia, was a small rectangular building, with folding doors at either end appropriate to a double-faced divinity. It came into the limelight of the New Age with the ceremonial closing of the doors in 29 B.C. as token of the cessation of civil war after the victories at Actium, Dalmatia, and Alexandria. For this temple, Vergil's references are particularly contemporary:

There are twin gates of war, for that is the name which they give
them, sacred in worshipful fear of Mars, the fierce wargod. One
hundred bronze bars, the eternal resistance of iron, close the door,
nor does Janus, its guard, step away from the threshold. When the
elder's decision for war is entirely certain, the consul himself in his
Quirinal robe and the cincture of Gabii opens the screeching doors,
calls for battle. Then the rest of the young men take up the cue, and
the bronze horns breathe out their hoarse-voiced approval of what he
has done.

(A. 7, 607–15)

Peace over land and sea was signalized once again during Vergil's
lifetime when Augustus' campaigns in Spain (27–25) were brought to a
successful conclusion.

Evander's modest but accommodating house at the end of Aeneas'
walk through Rome recalls the Regia, although Vergil's description of
the modest dwelling also seems appropriate to the simple domesticity of
Augustus' house on the Palatine:

> Arrived at the palace, the king said:—Hercules stooped to enter
> This door: this humble palace received the conquering hero.
> Have the courage, my guest, to despise possessions: train yourself,
> As he, to be worthy of godhead: don't be intolerant of poverty.
> Evander, with these words, led tall Aeneas beneath
> The roof of his simple dwelling, and gave him a couch of leaves
> With a coverlet made from the skin of a Libyan bear, to sleep in.
>
> (A. 8, 362–68. Day Lewis)

> Evander was roused from his humble dwelling
> By the genial light and the dawn song of birds beneath his eaves.
> The old man got out of bed, clothed himself in a tunic,
> And laced the Tyrrhene clogs on his feet; then shouldered a baldric
> So that his sword of Tegea could hang at his side, and threw
> A panther-skin over his left shoulder to dangle behind him.
> Two dogs, his bodyguard, preceded him as he stepped
> Through the doorway, and went with their master on his errand.
> He made for the private room where his guest, Aeneas, was lodged.
>
> (A. 8, 455–63. Day Lewis)

Evander's son Pallas and the Greek place-name Pallanteum offered
Vergil an acceptable but inaccurate etymology for the Palatine Hill,

which overlooks the Forum on the south side. Behind the literary invention which sought to intrude Greek or Arcadian elements into the aboriginal setting, there lies a firmer etymology in a pre-Indo-European root, *Pal*—or *Fal*—implying a rock or hill (cf. Etruscan *falad,* "sky"). But etymologists have always been free with suggestions—some have even associated Palatium with Ba'alation, with intimations of the Phoenician Earth Mother at prehistoric Rome. Vergil chose from a number of possibilities for the origin of the hill's name.

There is, however, less controversy over the precedence of the hill in the chronology of settlement at the site of Rome. Vergil harks back to the primitive huts of the early settlement with an exactitude which one might expect from his acquaintance with the oft-renovated timber, thatch, and wattle-and-daub huts on the Palatine and Capitoline (cf. page 125). Excavations beneath the Flavian Palace on the Palatine disclosed traces of huts, with postholes extant, indicating that the Palatine community centered around the northwest corner of the hill. The earliest level, which dates from the first phase of the Iron Age in Rome, has been placed about 800–700, a date amazingly close to the traditional Romulan foundation of 753. The hut foundation discovered in 1948 between the Temple of Magna Mater and the Scalae Caci has been identified with the Hut of Romulus (Fig. 21), an antiquity which was always carefully tended during the lifespan of Rome (as was a comparable hut on the Capitoline). Chance finds in the Alban Hills had also brought to light a series of rough clay urns (*dolia*), each containing an ash urn in the shape of a miniature oval hut, reduced versions of the Hut of Romulus type. Not until the seventh century, apparently, did the hilltop communities of Romans and Sabines move down the slopes into the valley where the necropolis (*Sepulcretum*) had once been located on the north side of the Forum. During Etruscan times the marshy, potentially malarial forum area was drained, and a pebble pavement (ancestor of the Via Sacra) was laid down. The predecessors of two celebrated buildings probably came into being about this time: the temple which preceded the building of the first Regia, and the earliest Vesta shrine. Both buildings surmounted an area where a modest settlement of small huts had clustered during the seventh century.

Two notable temples stood on the Palatine in Vergil's time. One was the Temple of the Magna Mater, goddess of the Aeneadae in Vergil's account and savior of the ships from Turnus' firebrands (A. 9, 77 ff.). Advised by the Sibylline books in 205 to seek divine help outside the city, the Romans appealed to Attalus of Pergamum for the black meteoric stone of Cybele, Phrygian goddess of Ida and great mother of the gods. The stone rested originally in the Temple of Victory on the Palatine. Eventually—although the strait-laced Roman religious sensibilities must have been repeatedly shocked by the celebration of orgiastic rites by eunuch priests and the near-psychedelic ceremonies with the clanging cymbals—a temple was formally consecrated to the Great Mother in 191. The building was rebuilt in 109 and was restored under Augustus after a fire in 3 A.D.

The other Palatine temple of particular importance to the Augustan age was the Temple of Apollo, begun in 36 and completed three years after Actium. Octavian vowed its dedication during the hostilities with Sextus Pompey, and the victory over Cleopatra ensured its completion and its lavish decoration. Vergil pays due regard to the Apolline sympathies of Augustus in Aeneas' address to the Sibyl at Cumae:

> And you, most holy priestess, knowing the future, allow me (I ask for a kingdom not unallotted by Fates) to settle the Teucrians in Latium, my wandering divinities, the harassed powers of Troy. I shall build a temple of solid marble to Phoebus and Hecate, declare the days of a festival named after Phoebus. Great shrines shall await you in my realm. I shall place there your lots and hidden fates spoken to my people, and consecrate men who are chosen to serve you, O fostering one.
>
> (A. 6, 65–74)

The newest Temple of Apollo, a triadic shrine shared with Diana and Latona, vied with the Augustan Forum, the Temple of Mars the Avenger, and the Temple of Jupiter the Thunderer for elegance and novelty in design and furnishing. Augustus' piety to Apollo took an extreme form. He gave instructions that approximately eighty statues of himself, on foot, mounted, or borne in quadriga, should be melted down to provide funds for the donations which he deposited in the temple in his own name and in the names of the original donors of the statues. In 18 B.C. (the year after Vergil's death), Aeneas' promise became a reality: a new collection of Sibylline books of prophecy was lodged in the base of the Apollo cult statue; and in 17 B.C. Horace composed and conducted the Secular Hymn for performance before the temple.

Every authority who mentions the temple and its dedication on October 8th, 28 B.C., is rhapsodic over its facilities and splendid appointments: the libraries, Greek and Latin; the gilded portico with the intercolumnar statues of the Danaids and the sons of Aegyptus, and statues of Rome's heroes on its roof; behind the portico were Apollo Citharoedus (the Lyre-player) and Myron's oxen, masterpieces of Greek fifth-century bronzecraft. The temple was of Carrara (Luna) marble. The doors were extolled for their gold and ivory reliefs (ancient counterparts of Florence's Gates of Paradise), in the tradition of Daedalus' doors to the Apollo Temple at Cumae but representing the legend of Niobe and the Defeat of the Gauls at Delphi. The interior cult statues included one by the fourth-century Greek sculptor Scopas, another version of Apollo as lyre-player, patron of the Muses and of poets, symbol and guarantor alike of the Pax Augusta. At the close of *Aeneid* 8, Vergil finds occasion to provide what may be a "photographic" account of the triple triumph of Augustus in 29 B.C., culminating in the Emperor's appearance at the as yet unfinished Temple of Apollo Palatinus:

> Caesar, borne through Rome's walls in a triple triumph, was making a deathless vow to Italian gods: he would build three hundred great temples throughout the whole city. The streets were an uproar of laughter and clapping and games. In all of the temples a chorus of mothers, in all sacrifice lay on each altar. Slain bullocks lay sprawled on the earth before each. Caesar sat on the snowy white threshold of Phoebus to acknowledge gifts from the peoples, to hang them on the proud doorposts. The conquered races went by in a long procession, as varied in tongue as in dress and weapons.
>
> (A. 8, 714–23)

In Rowell's words, "The Temple of Apollo on the Palatine could not and was not intended to supersede the greatest temple of Rome's greatest god. It was meant to be a new center for religious interest which symbolized present and future blessings. It recalled that an age of force had given way to an age of order and reason. In the Sibylline Books the 'fate of Rome' had been placed under peaceful auspices. The Apollo of the Palatine was the Apollo of the secular games which introduced a new era."[4]

On the same southwest part of the Palatine Hill where the Temples of Magna Mater and the Palatine Triad rose, Augustus had lodged himself in simple style but deliberately (Figs. 22, 23). Because he had refused to live in the Domus Publica, he made part of his Palatine property public domain so as to conform to the rule that the High Priest should inhabit state property. Suetonius' remarks on the Emperor's way of life cannot be improved upon: "He could not bear gorgeous palaces. He ordered the demolition of an extravagant country house built by his grand-daughter Julia. . . . Later he lived on the Palatine, but even there only in the modest house of Hortensius, which was neither particularly big nor strikingly decorated. It had only short colonnades of Albanian peperino, a volcanic rock, and its rooms contained neither marble nor mosaic floors. He slept in the same bedroom, summer and winter, for over forty years. The furniture was hardly elegant enough for the average private citizens; and the clothes that he wore are supposed to have been woven in this house." Mackail first detected the relevance to the Domus Augusti of the passage in which Vergil forecast undying fame for the lost Nisus and Euryalus:

> The passage of time will never erase your memory, so long as Aeneas' dwelling shall have as neighbor the immovable rock of the Capitol, and the Father of Rome shall hold the supreme temporal power.
>
> (A. 9, 447–9)

Mackail writes: "Augustus, the descendant and representative of Aeneas, *pater patriae,* invested with consular and proconsular *imperium,* [had] his house on the Palatine facing the Capitoline rock across the valley, with the Capitoline Jupiter literally his *accola,* the dweller side by side with him."[5]

When Aeneas stepped ashore at Pallanteum he moved into an evoca-tive ambiance of tradition and perspective. The setting is the Forum Boarium—the Cattle Market—of Rome, Tiber-side, at the Great Altar of Hercules, and the occasion is the festival of Hercules' victory over the underworld demon Cacus. Evander relates the story: The fire-demon Cacus rustled eight of Geryon's cattle; Hercules, halting temporarily at Pallanteum en route to Greece, discovered the theft and strangled the bestial creature. Evander then says:

> Since then these rites have been practised, this day kept holy by grateful
> Posterity, headed by its founder, Potitius, and by
> The Pinarian family, wardens of the worship of Hercules.
> This altar, which he himself set up in the grove here, always
> Shall be for us, in name and truth, the Ara Maxima.
>   (A. 8, 268–72. Day Lewis)

Hercules, Evander, and Aeneas—benefactors in name and deed—are exemplary heroes for Roman Augustus, whose labors and philanthropy brought him divinization.[6] The Forum Boarium cult of Hercules, largely Greek, but with Italian elements, was addressed to Hercules as God of Commerce in a market environment; it was the private undertaking of two families until 312 when the State assumed its direction. Although a dozen temples in addition to the Ara Maxima once stood in the Forum Boarium, only two have survived: a rectangular Ionic temple near the Tiber, assigned without much reason to Fortuna Virilis; and a circular Corinthian temple, assigned with no real validity to Vesta, or Mater Matuta. Both are Republican buildings. The Ara Maxima, in spite of its vast scale, has never been certainly located, although a large tufa platform under the present Church of Santa Maria in Cosmedin (where the Bocca della Verità, an ancient well-head, still lures countless visitors) may have formed part of the sanctuary. The grove Vergil mentions (*supra*) may reflect the landscaping on the Velabrum in his time, but groves in Vergil are often merely atmospheric settings, locales for initiation or trial which may lead to death or renewed life. And indeed here at the Ara Maxima, as formerly at Cumae and Avernus, Aeneas is introduced to another great example and to a new role in Herculean guise—guardian of the destiny of Pallanteum-Rome.

Aeneas entered upon his destiny at the point where Ostian craft rested at their quays, where lighters and barges from time immemorial had landed their goods. The warehouse of the Aemilian family, constructed in 193 and rebuilt in 174, remained one of the most impressive commercial monuments in the late Republican city, a gigantic building with fifty stepped barrel vaults accessible through splendid arcades.

The most spectacular architectural additions to Vergil's Rome lay in the Campus Martius, so called from the ancient cult of Mars at the site, which was also the meeting place of the assembly "under arms," outside the religious confines of the city. This ancient zone, onetime drill and parade ground for the Roman army, and exercise area for the Roman cavalry (*equites*), now served for the revived Lusus Troiae, the ceremonial parade which Vergil assigns to Ascanius-Julus in honor of sainted Anchises. This great "wasteland," bounded by the Tiber on the west, the Flaminian Way on the east, the vegetable market (Forum Holitorium) on the south, and the later Porta Flaminia on the north, was the last area to be zoned for replanning and new buildings. Before Augustus and Agrippa had moved in with their planners and architects, earlier buildings had included: the Villa Publica (435 B.C.); the Temple of Apollo Medicus ("The Healer"), between the Forum Holitorium and the Circus Flaminius, established in 433 outside the pomerium because the cult was foreign (perhaps Cumaean) and rebuilt by Augustus either in 32 or after 20 B.C.; and the Circus Flaminius (220), between the Theater of Marcellus and the modern Piazza Cenci. Two theaters of great capacity and historic association must also have attracted Vergil's notice: One was the Theater of Pompey (55), Rome's first permanent theater, designed to accommodate 10,000 spectators in a grandiose setting; it had an extensive porticus-garden (where Julius Caesar fell in 44) and a temple of Venus Victrix housed in the topmost tiers and balcony. The second was the Theater of Marcellus, begun by Caesar to counteract the "democratic" victory of Pompey's theater, but completed by Augustus and dedicated to the memory of his recently deceased heir (Fig. 24).

The Augustan innovations in the Campus Martius were staggering in their scale and rapidity of construction: repairs were made to the Porticus Octaviae and the Theater of Pompey (33–32); among the new constructions were the Mausoleum of Augustus (28); the wooden stadium erected in the Campus for the Actian games (28); Agrippa's Pantheon (27); and the Saepta Julia (26), a great enclosure designed originally by Julius Caesar for the use of assemblies in the Campus Martius and to accommodate the tribesmen as they waited their turn to vote. Caesar's plan, which called for the use of costly imported marble and a mile of porticoes around the edifice, was scrupulously followed by Augustus' architects. By 25 B.C., Agrippa, acting as Augustus' representative, had completed the Pantheon, the Stoa, or Porch, of the Argonauts, with its murals relating the Argonautic adventures, and also the impressive Baths (*Thermae*), with a Sudatorium (or *Pyriaterion,* steam swimming pool), Rome's first public bath complex. Agrippa's Basilica of Neptune adjoined the Pantheon and the Agrippan Baths.

Although undoubtedly a witness to the building boom in the Campus, Vergil singles out only the Mausoleum of Augustus, which was also the only building which Augustus erected in his own name. The tomb (Fig. 25) was begun in 28 B.C. at the extreme northern end of the Campus, in an area which ultimately faced upon the colonnaded facade of Agrippa's Pantheon and its forecourt. Vergil alludes to the monument in the course of his heartbreaking eulogy of Marcellus, dead at Baiae in 23:

O son, do not search into the great sorrows of our descendants. The Fates will merely show him earth but forbid him to live there further. O gods above, Rome's stock would appear too powerful if your gifts should remain among men. What groans shall the Field of Mars carry to that great city, what funeral rites shall you see, river Tiber, when you flow past his fresh-made tomb.

(A. 6, 868–74)

One other Roman building, however, the Circus Maximus, seems to be reflected in Vergil's account of the anniversary games for Anchises at Segesta in Sicily.[7] The narrative is set within an environment which is both natural and man-made. There are suggestions of a mound at the center of the arena or games area which serves as a podium for the fanfare introducing the contests; the seating area, or "stands" (5, 288–9; 664) and the official, or "royal," box are remarkably similar to the arrangements in either the Circus Maximus (Fig. 26) or the Circus Flaminius. The first seems the more likely inspiration for the poet. Rome's earliest and most spacious arena lies between the Aventine and Palatine Hills, in an area first selected by the Tarquins. After 174 its central ridge (*spina*) had been equipped with two turning posts (*metae*) for the chariot races. Augustus lodged an obelisk which he had imported from Egyptian Heliopolis in the center of the spina and also installed an imperial box on the Palatine side. The metaphorical relationship between Vergil's ship race and a chariot race, and the constructional suggestions in the boxing, racing, archery, and cavalry events, all support the association with an actual Circus. But there may also be an even more direct reminiscence of Augustus' temporary wooden stadium erected in the Campus Martius, where he celebrated his Actian victory with athletic contests (cf. Aeneas' games at Actium: A. 3, 280–2).

Two other remnants of the past still active in men's minds in the Augustan age affected the poet's imagination. The Cacus episode was recalled by the existing Stairs of Cacus (*Scalae Caci*) located immediately to the east of the Hut of Romulus.[8] The steep, narrow passage was enclosed by walls and led from the Palatine to the valley of the Circus Maximus. Hercules' struggle with Cacus was customarily assigned to the Aventine Hill. Cacus sheltered himself and his stolen cattle in a cavern behind a divinely engineered portcullis. Hercules reacted in frenzy:

> Three times in a transport of fury
> He paced the whole Aventine hill, tried the stony threshold
> Three times in vain; three times he sat down in the valley,
> Tired. There was a sharp rock with the stone cut sheer round it
> That rose on the ridge of the cave, a vision most lofty
> And a home that was fit for the nests of fierce birds of prey.
> This hung on the left of the ridge slanting down to the river.
> Hercules pushed at the rock from the right side and wrenched it
> Off from its roots. He suddenly shook it. Great ether
> Resounded, the banks sprang apart, and the river ran backward
> In terror. The vast cave of Cacus appeared from its cover,
> His palace was seen, and the shadowy cavern lay open.
>
> (A. 8, 251–62. L. R. Lind)

The Aventine Hill actually lay outside the city walls and pomerium, and remained a derelict, lightly populated area until the mid-fifth century B.C. Servius Tullius founded the cult of Diana on the hill to serve the needs of settlers from Latium and further afield, and above all to cater to the religious demands of the plebs. The location of the Diana cult on the Aventine underscores her non-Roman origins; her temple, still undiscovered, probably lies near the famous old Church of Santa Sabina. Elsewhere Vergil introduces a hero Aventinus (A. 8, 659), son of Hercules and Rhea, product of Hercules' sojourn at Pallanteum. (A. 7, 655–63).

The Pons Sublicius (Bridge of the Wooden Piles) appears in the description of Aeneas' shield pictures (A. 8, 649–51). Horatius Cocles, the traditional defender of Rome at the Sublician bridge, gave the Romans time to demolish their bridge and, though wounded, swam across the Tiber to safety. The wooden bridge stood near the location of the later Pons Aemilius. Because Veii controlled the lower Tiber crossing at Fidenae, Rome found it necessary to provide her own bridge to safeguard her expanding economy founded on the Ostian salt-works at the river mouth. The often-restored bridge washed away during the flood in 23 B.C. and was replaced.

The visual arts of Rome, its sculpture and painting, profoundly affected Vergil's composition and illustration. The poet proclaims his intention to build a marble temple by the Mincius river, with Caesar's image central, and on the doors gold and ivory historical reliefs (G. 3, 26–33), lifelike statues of Rome's venerated ancestors, and a mélange of the Furies, Cocytus, Ixion tied to his wheel of torment, and Sisyphus straining with his "unconquerable" rock (G. 3, 34–9). Since Pales (god of flocks, and etymologically attached to the Palatine) and Apollo are both invoked at the outset of the poem, one may construe that the poet's temple reflects the splendid shrine of Apollo rising on the Palatine (36–28), where Myron's oxen, appropriate to Apollo's role as protector of herds, were prominently displayed. The gallery adjoining the temple, the so-called Porticus ad Nationes, contained a series of frescoes or reliefs depicting all of the nations owing allegiance to Rome (cf. A. 8, 720–8).

Sculpture frequently appears in Vergil, not always in examples as eye-catching or as monumental as the temple by the Mincius, but impressive nonetheless: Diana, with red hunting boots (E. 7, 31–2); Priapus, the gardener's scarecrow god, in marble ready for gilding (*ibid.,* 35–6); Silvanus, crowned with green reeds and large lilies (E. 10, 24–5), or carrying a young uprooted cypress (G. 1, 20). When Venus endows Aeneas with an appearance handsome enough to ignite

Dido's infatuation, the goddess is compared to a sculptor or celator:

> Venus herself had breathed
> Beauty upon his head and the roseate sheen of youth on
> His manhood and a gallant light into his eyes;
> As an artist's hand adds grace to the ivory he works on,
> As silver or marble when they're plated with yellow gold.
>   (A. 1, 589–93. Day Lewis)

The application of gilt to marble (and to bronze) was contemporary practice both in sculpture and architecture, for capitals were also often adorned with gilt. Chryselephantine figures, sculptures in gold and ivory, were equally part of the Roman sculptor's repertoire, and the addition of eyes, nostrils, lips, etc., in a material other than the basic marble or bronze was a long established craft. Aeneas and Dido are imagined in the guise of Apollo and Diana, and the description of their persons reflects the practice of embellishing marble with color, a device as old as Egyptian and as recent as Classical and Hellenistic Greek art. Vergil describes Dido, on the day of the Carthaginian hunt, in terms of a classical Diana, perhaps best paralleled by a Roman copy of the Praxitelean Artemis of Gabii, now in the Louvre (Fig. 27):

> She wears a Phoenician habit, piped with bright-coloured braid:
> Her quiver is gold, her hair is bound up with a golden clasp,
> A brooch of gold fastens the waist of her brilliant dress.
>   (A. 4, 137–9. Day Lewis; cf. A. 1, 318–29)

Aeneas appears in a guise strikingly comparable to the celebrated Apollo Belvedere in the Vatican Museum, again a Roman copy of a fourth-century Greek original:

> The god himself steps out on the Cynthian range, a circlet
> Of gold and a wreath of pliant bay on his flowing hair,
> The jangling weapons slung from his shoulder. Nimble as he,
> Aeneas moved, with the same fine glow on his handsome face.
>   (A. 4, 147–50. Day Lewis)

The best attested, though not uncontested, instance of sculptural association is the Laocoön scene (A. 2, 213–22). The struggle of Laocoön and his two sons with Juno's serpents is strikingly illustrated by the group found near the Baths of Titus in Rome in 1506. This group (Fig. 28), recently reconstructed, is usually dated after 50 B.C., although the new sculptural finds at Sperlonga (cf. Fig. 55) suggest a date anywhere from 150 to 80 B.C. Vergil was probably acquainted with the original Rhodian masterpiece, although there is also the possibility that he had seen a painting, perhaps a fourth-century work, which inspired the six versions of the same theme known to us. But the sculptural inspiration seems a more reasonable model than the hypothetical painting, and Vergil's variation on the sculptural theme, where one youth is represented moribund and the other trying to flee, is most appropriate to his poetic purposes.

Other sculptural "entries" may be detected throughout the epic. It has been suggested that Vergil's graphic description of Neptune's retinue (A. 5, 822–6) owed its inspiration to a sculptural group by Scopas exhibited in Vergil's time in the Circus Flaminius (cf. Pliny, *N.H.* 36, 26). Especially noteworthy are the statues of the ancestral rulers and heroes in the palace of Latinus; the palace is so closely modeled on the Temple of Jupiter Capitolinus in other respects that it seems likely that the sculptures described by Vergil (A. 7, 175–82) also owe something to portrait sculptures at the site. So also may the likenesses which are singled out for special description in the march-past of heroes in the Underworld: the Alban kings (A. 6, 760–2), Romulus (779–80), Numa (808–12), Brutus the tyrant-expeller (817–20), and the Marcelli (855–62). Father Tiber (A. 8, 31–4) has sculptural affinities with reclining figures of river gods, notably that of the Tiber, with oar, cornucopia, and the wolf with the twins, a sculptural group found in the sixteenth century near the Church of San Stefano del Cacco. This allegorical figure of Rome's pride is now in the Louvre (Fig. 29). The Shield of Aeneas constitutes a marvelous testimony to the pictorial artistry of Vergil's time, a mastery demonstrated with equal skill and allegorical flair on the breastplate of the Augustus statue from Prima Porta (Fig. 5). Moreover, it illustrates one of the most hallowed sculptural groups in Rome:

> He [Vulcan] had depicted the mother wolf as she lay full length in
> The green-swarded cave of Mars, with the twin baby boys fondling
> And suckling at her udders, fearlessly nuzzling their dam;
> She, her graceful neck bent sideways and back, is caressing
> Each child in turn with her tongue, licking them into shape.
>
> (A. 8, 630–4. Day Lewis)

The figure of the wolf with the twins found its inspiration in the group (no longer extant) which was set beside the Ficus Ruminalis during the third century B.C., by the fig tree where the twins were exposed to the floodwaters of the Tiber. The more ancient Capitoline Wolf, which guards the twins, a Renaissance addition, does not correspond to the description and was assuredly not Vergil's model (Fig. 30).

Mackail's interprets the multitudinous bogies in the Underworld (A. 6, 269 ff.) as sculptured figures of monsters—"a couchant hound, Cerberus; a female figure grasping serpents, Tisiphone; creatures hundred-armed, three-headed, serpent-haired, beaked, and clawed"; he is probably correct, although wall paintings and mosaics might also be imagined.[9] Charon, the ferryman of the dead, recalls the figures in Etruscan tomb paintings as well as the more theatrical sculptures of the Hellenistic age (A. 6, 299–304).

Painting seems to have been even more congenial to Vergil than sculpture or relief. The series of events from the Trojan War which Aeneas discovers to his surprise and sorrow depicted on Juno's temple walls at Carthage (A. 1, 453–63) has much in common with the celebrated Vatican Odyssey frieze, a series of partly isolated but related panel pictures which feature episodes from the adventures of Odysseus (ca. 50 B.C.). Such scenes as these and the subject matter and stylistic features of the shield panels support Vitruvius' assertion (7, 5, 2) that contemporary artists favored land- and seascapes, and also "detailed mythological episodes, or the battles at Troy, or the wanderings of Ulysses, with landscape backgrounds, and other subjects reproduced on similar principles from real life." (Fig. 31)

The sculptural simile which likens Dido to Diana (A. 1, 496–502), again recalling the Artemis of Gabii type, follows shortly after the description of the Trojan War cycle and underlines the unity of both spheres of reference in the poet's art of illustration. There may actually have been a contemporary inspiration for Vergil's Trojan pictures in the gallery of the Porticus Philippi in the Campus Martius. Lucius Marcius Philippus, Octavian's uncle by marriage, used the spoils of his successes in Spain to restore the Temple of Hercules Musarum and also to add a portico northwest of the existing Porticus of Octavia with the same orientation. Among the murals of the Porticus Philippi were pictures of Helen by Zeuxis, several paintings by Antiphilus of Dionysus

(Liber), the young Alexander, and Hippolytus, and scenes from the Trojan War by Theorus (Pliny, *N.H.* 35, 144). The last may have inspired Vergil's account in *Aeneid* 1, for these particular paintings were intimately associated with the Aeneadae and with the family of Octavian-Augustus.

The shield of Aeneas, with its story of repeated violence leading to ultimate peace, with the repeated confrontation of good and evil, is a vision of Roman history from Romulus and Remus, twin sons of Mars, to Augustus and Agrippa, triumphant at Actium and architects of the Pax Romana throughout the world. The rationale behind the choice of scenes and their arrangement on the shield remains a topic for debate, but the simplest solution may be best: that is, to accept a pattern of two concentric circles, each containing four panels, with a central boss. The centerpiece depicts Octavian's triumphal procession after Actium, whereas the panels relate to the historical adventures of the Romans, four from the regal period, four from the Republican era (A. 8, 626–728).

Allegorical subjects played a significant role in the art of Augustan Rome. The end panels of the Altar of Augustan Peace (13–9 B.C.) are most revealing. Italia (perhaps in the guise of Venus Genetrix) appears seated amid children, animals, and plantlife, flanked by the spirits of ocean and inland waters (Fig. 32); in the relief opposite (of which only fragments survive) the warrior goddess Roma appears seated, at peace, her arms laid aside.[10] These examples of personification in Roman art are counterparts to Vergil's delineation of Fides and Vesta, of Remus and his deified brother as lawgivers (A. 1, 292–3), and of the monstrous allegorical figure of civil war (A. 1, 294–6); all have a rhetorical quality and are designed to point a moral as well as tell a story. The allegorical creature of "fratricidal fury seated on a heap of savage weapons, with its hands tied behind its back in a hundred brazen knots, raging there with foaming, bloody mouth" draws on a work by the fourth-century artist Apelles, a panel painting lodged by Augustus in his own Forum.[11] Cupid, in the likeness of Ascanius, settled in the lap of Dido (A. 1, 715–19), recalls fourth-century Italian vase paintings which represent Eros on Helen's lap.

Wall paintings found in 1875 in the dovecot (*columbarium*) tomb of the Statilii on the Esquiline, now in the Terme Museum in Rome, are superb samples of late Republican continuous figure scenes, with landscape and architectural elements introduced but kept secondary to the human figures (Fig. 33). The subject matter parallels in a striking fashion Vergil's account of Rome's Trojan and Latin ancestry from the settlement at Lavinium to the foundation of Rome. Narrative paintings of this sort must have been the inspiration for many of Vergil's most memorable scenes, as, to be sure, Vergil's "pictorial" scenes would provide a rich repertoire for Claude, Poussin, and Turner.

The storm in *Aeneid* 1 (103–24) and the vision of Neptune calming the tumult of the waves (*ibid.*, 124–9); the landing in Africa (A. 1, 159–97); the scenes which relate Troy's capture and destruction throughout *Aeneid* 2; the Daedalus panels on the temple doors at Cumae (A. 6, 20–33), with the unfinished masterpiece of Daedalus' flight from Crete; the pastoral scene in Latium with Ascanius shooting the stag of Silvia (A. 7, 475–508)—these are only a sample of the artistry which identifies Vergil as an expert among landscape painters who have used words instead of pigments. Always there is the distinctly Roman feeling for the manifold aspects of peace and tranquillity, and for the mystery and barbaric strengths of the ancient land and people of Italy.

V

Latium

VERGIL is especially well informed on the topography and the contemporary condition of places in Latium. Legends, history, and religious survivals combine in his account to produce a veritable Baedeker on the antique centers of Latium.

Strabo's description, which is partly eyewitness, offers a mixed prospect along the Tyrrhenian shore, "entirely fortunate and productive of all plants, except for a few marshy and unhealthy places along the coast and such parts as are mountainous and rocky." (5, 3, 1) The most dismal and unsalubrious areas lay in the territory of the Pomptine Marshes, a constant source of concern to travellers and dwellers in the environs because of its noxious dampness and belligerent mosquitoes. The main communities clustered in the upland areas overlooking the Roman Campagna. Some areas were very productive, particularly in the southeastern sector, in the Liris river valley at the northwestern fringe of the mountain ranges, and in the Tiber and Anio river valleys. Eons of volcanic deposit had made the soil endlessly fertile, and Etruscan and Roman irrigation had ensured that it remained attractive and arable. The wines of Latium, particularly of Tusculum (mod. Frascati), won many enthusiasts.

The Queen of Highways, the Via Appia, Rome's earliest military road, was used often by Vergil during his residence in Rome. It followed the shortest possible line from Rome to Capua and thence to

Brundisium (mod. Brindisi). Procopius later estimated the distance from Rome to Capua as a five-days' march.

The wars of Aeneas in Italy have been thought to prefigure several periods of conflict in Italy's history, especially the wars of Rome against the Latin League in the early days, and against the Samnites, Volscians, Aequi, and Hernici. But they may equally foreshadow the damaging civil wars of the first century. No one of these conflicts can be the source of Vergil's vivid account of wars between Trojans and Italians, and yet the final conflict between Aeneas and Turnus does markedly underscore the implications of the Rutulian's defeat: his fall meant the demise of the Italian farms and their rustic religion, both areas which Augustus had specifically set himself to reawaken. During the final engagement Aeneas' spear sticks fast in the root of an olive tree consecrated to Faunus, and in answer to Turnus' desperate entreaty, Faunus and Earth hold the weapon fast until Venus has to wrench it clear for her son (A. 12, 766–87). Finally Turnus cries:

> You have won. The Italians have seen me
> Beaten, these hands outstretched. Lavinia is yours to wed.
> Don't carry hatred further.
>
> (A. 12, 936–8. Day Lewis)

Vergil was clearly troubled, along with Horace (cf. *Odes* 1, 14), by the thought of a recurrence of the civil wars from which Italy had only recently emerged. His own experiences had sharpened his awareness of the terrible cost of war, the senseless waste and the destruction of a placid, productive countryside.

The Latin War of 340–38 is also reflected in Vergil's choice of cities inimical to the Trojan designs. Angered by Rome's indifferent showing in the First Samnite War (343–41), resentful of Rome's abandoning her allies for a separate peace treaty, and irritated by other seeming or real injustices, the Latins offered Rome an ultimatum: one of the two consuls at Rome should always be a Latin. To strengthen their hand they formed a coalition with the Sidicini, the Campani, and the Aurunci, and with the Volscian remnants. But their demands were rejected, and the Latin War followed.

There is no evidence that Norba or Ardea, both close to Rome, took up arms against her. But other combatants can certainly be identified:

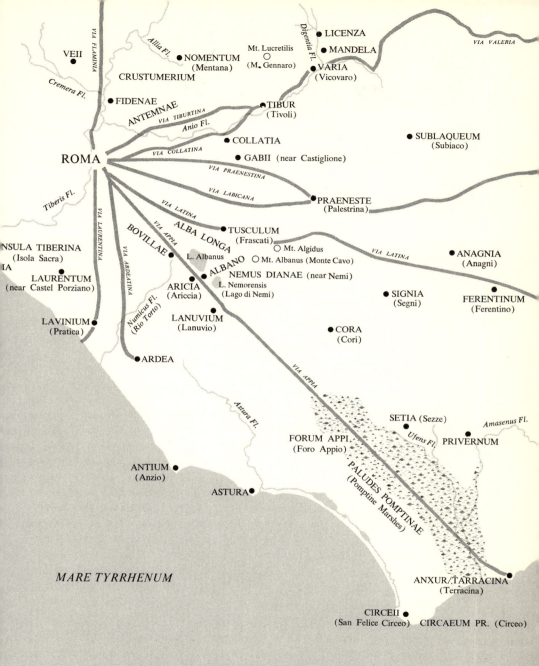

LATIUM

Lanuvium, Aricia, Nomentum, Pedum, Tibur, Praeneste, Antium, Setia, Cora, Circeii, Signia, Velitrae, Satricum and possibly Laurentum (Livy 8, 11, 3–4). The Roman victory in the war meant the dissolution of the Latin League. Ardea and Circeii, for various reasons, remained Latin allies of Rome; Tibur, Praeneste, and Laurentum became allied states (*civitates foederatae*) with reduced privileges; Tibur and Praeneste lost territory; Cora became an allied state; Lanuvium, Aricia, Nomentum, and Pedum all obtained citizenship, but probably without the franchise. Most of the Latin peoples, says Livy, including those of Satricum, Labici, Vitellia, Gabii, and portions of Velitrae and Antium, were deprived of the rights of mutual trade and of intermarriage. They became *municipia,* performing the duties but lacking the privileges of Roman citizens. As Salmon has shown, "the Latins were for the most part reduced to a state of complete inferiority, politically speaking. Their status must have seemed miserable to themselves and to other Italians: that is shown by the desperate resistance which the Hernici and the insignificant Aequicoli put up a few years later (in 304) rather than accept it (Livy, 8. 42–3)."[1] Nearly all of these communities figure in Vergil's account of Latin resistance to Aeneas and his Trojans.

Not all of the Latin sites in Vergil's account, however, are hostile. Some played useful roles in the peaceful consolidation of Roman suzerainty over Latium. Others were probably included because they were enshrined in the Roman mind as locations of important events in the past. Many of those chosen for hostile roles were communities which had only recently felt the heavy hand of Rome in the Social War (91–88) and had emerged from the trial weakened and diminished.

There is, therefore, no easy solution to the problem of why Vergil chose some sites for special mention; why, for example, he omitted Veii and Tusculum but included Bola and Collatia. Perhaps Vergil set out to extol his adoptive country and its antique customs and settings as part of a larger scheme of providing support for Augustus' peninsular policy; to beg for a lasting peace together with a renewal of the one-time affluence and prestige of the ancient communities, and to stress the heritage of culture and hardy virtues which their countrymen could offer Rome. But one cannot forget that the wars of Rome with the Latin League and with the Samnites, along with the Social War, had left a powerful imprint on Vergil.

Vergil brings his Trojans to shore near Ostia, at the mouth of the Tiber, and so introduces a new locale for their arrival and first settlement. There was, to be sure, some precedent for Vergil's relocation of the first settlement from Lavinium to the Tiber estuary. Troia was a place-name on the Latin shore near modern Zingarini, although the "Trojan" name, a source of much dispute, probably derives from a pre-Indo-European word signifying "a fortified place." But Vergil's Tiber-side settlement must also be indebted to the historical foundation at Ostia. The Sabine king, Ancus Marcius (642–617) was hailed as founder of a colony at Ostia, although archaeology has proved that the earliest remains discovered so far date from the fourth-century level, about 325 B.C., when the Roman maritime colony was founded, in fact. And yet the Sabine and regal tradition should not be discarded for want of evidence in an incompletely excavated area. Certainly Rome owed its early prominence and its first road, the Via Salaria, to the salt-beds at the river mouth on the right bank. So, although Ancus Marcius' foundation may be apocryphal, there must have been some sort of settlement at the mouth which promoted the salt trade before the fourth century.

Aeneas' landing on the Tiber banks introduces him to scenery in marked contrast to the horrific atmosphere of Circeii, the hero's most recent contact with the Italian mainland. The poet reconstructs an Arcadian setting, peaceful, verdant, and well forested, even when glimpsed from the sea, guaranteeing a surcease of travails and a fixed abode.

Vergil attaches two names to the river, Thybris and Albula. Thybris is certainly Etruscan (*Thebris*) and is apt for oracular pronouncements, with an ambiguous ring reminding his readers at the same time that the river formed the eastern frontier of Etruria and the northern frontier of Latium. The Etrusco-Lydian connection is a learned allusion, part of Vergil's archaeological lore, an expression of the romance of geographical history. The alternative name, Albula, is almost certainly the older, deriving not from the whiteness, or sulphurous character, of the water, but from a pre-Indo-European word meaning mountain (cf. *Alba Longa,* Alps). The replacement of the antique name with Thybris, and later Tiber, denotes the historical victory of the Etruscan language over the native speech. Vergil may possibly have attached the notion

of whiteness to the name, as reflected in the white sow and her brood
on the greensward, and in the subsequent foundation of Alba Longa.

The mouth of the river, subject to strong onshore winds, never offered
an easy road for shipping bound for Rome some fifteen miles upstream.
The foundation of a maritime colony at Ostia to safeguard the coastline against sea-borne attack followed upon the elimination of Caeretan
and Antiate naval power in the Tyrrhenian. The colony was modest
in size, judging by the tufa walls of the *castrum,* or encampment, which
enclose an area of less than six acres. The settlement adopted the
standard plan of a Roman military camp, a rectangular design with
the two main streets crossing at right angles at the site of the later
Forum. The colony's function was both military and commercial. As a
coastguard station it collected customs dues, landed and safeguarded
grain shipments from Sicily and North Africa, and witnessed the departure of the fleet for overseas operations. The earliest settlement,
neatly and symmetrically organized, is a more formal version of Aeneas'
careful foundation near the same site:

> Aeneas himself traced out the walls with a shallow trench,
> And breaking the ground, threw up a rampart and battlements as for
> A military encampment, round his first home there on the coast.
>
> (A. 7, 157–9. Day Lewis)

Sulla expanded the colony to 170 acres (of which 70 have been excavated) and brought the port town into new importance. Augustus
and Agrippa subsequently improved the city and its harbor facilities,
crucial to the provisioning of Rome. The theater and "corporation
square" (Fig. 34) were completed before 12 B.C., and Augustus lodged
another colony at the site. Whether he also undertook to dredge the
harbor to improve the port facilities is not known. Caesar had conceived the plan, but his assassination prevented its implementation.

The woods described in the *Aeneid* were almost certainly the poet's
contribution, to provide a setting suitable for both the initiation of
Aeneas into Italy and the revelations of Father Tiber. Silting and deforestation had already taken their toll of the river banks by Vergil's
time, and the river, rising in the Apennines near Arretium (mod.
Arezzo), became tawnier by the mile as it made its serpentine way to
the river mouth. But Vergil is duly respectful of the Tiber's virtues as

well, and knows all of its major tributaries, the Tinia-Clitumnus, Clanis, Nar, Anio, and Allia.

Aeneas' passage upstream is miraculous, almost an invasion of a wonderland. Both the river and the river god are Aeneas' guides to his destined Rome. Vergil seems determined to have Aeneas reach Pallanteum by water, and to make the feat possible Father Tiber arrests the adverse current of the river so as to offer a safe and easy passage, which nonetheless still requires a night and a day. The miracle vouchsafed to Aeneas reflects the difficulty of Tiber navigation, for the ordinary seaman with a ship of any significant draught could never navigate its length. Sea-going ships would normally transfer their cargoes at the river mouth to lighters or barges which were entrusted to rowers or tow lines. In Vergil's time the river banks were lined with villas, pleasure domes of the wealthy, all of them with beautifully landscaped grounds sloping down to the river.

Aeneas' preliminary settlement by the sandy Tiber (one recalls that Trojan Xanthus ["sandy"] and Simois were promised earlier: A. 3, 497–505) cannot be specifically located. Augustan Ostia was three miles inland from the Fiumara, the ancient Tiber mouth, and Vergil's description of the settlement may therefore be associated with the historical foundations of either the fourth or the first century. The Fiumicino, the present Tiber mouth, is in reality a canal dug by Claudius and Trajan to provide access to their new port facilities, designed to answer some of the inadequacies of the Republican port.

The site of the oracle of Faunus at Albunea has been much debated, some preferring a location at Tibur (mod. Tivoli), others a site closer to Lavinium and near the Tiber. Vergil offers a tantalizingly detailed sketch of the scene and of the oracular procedures:

> The king, greatly disturbed by this portent, goes to visit
> The oracle of Faunus, his prophet father, and questions
> The grove where Albunea towers above the forest, resounding
> With hallowed cascade and darkly exhaling a deadly vapour.
> Here the Italian tribes, all the Oenotrians, go for
> Advice in times of perplexity: hither the priestess brings
> The offerings, and couched at dead of night on the fleeces
> Of the sheep sacrificed there, she woos slumber; and then
> Visions appear to her, shapes are floating strangely about her,

And in her ear are many voices—she is conversing
With deity, addressing the powers of the nether regions.
This was where Latinus now went to consult the oracle.

                              (A. 7, 81–92. Day Lewis)

Some features of the account are above cavil. Vergil adopts elements
from several oracular procedures in his description: incubation, which
implies spending the night in a sacred place to receive the divine revelation; a dark grove where the river-nymph Albunea (counterpart to
Tiberinus in Aeneas' experience) makes her revelations; and a volcanic
exhalation which recalls comparable sites at Lake Avernus and at the
Valles Amsancti (A. 6, 273 ff.; 7, 563 ff.). The three main requirements
for locating the oracle are a wooded slope, resonant water, and volcanic
fissures or pools. Albunea, therefore, cannot be located in the landscape
of Tivoli by the farthest stretch of imagination, given these conditions.
Bertha Tilly in 1933 suggested the most likely site in the small sulphurous lake of the Zolforata (sulphur mine): "There is a large cave . . .
[with] a copious sulphur spring, which bubbles loudly and hisses like
a great cauldron. Reflected by the roof of the cave which acts as a natural
sounding board, the noise can be heard plainly at a distance of nearly
one hundred yards. The overflow trickles from the entrance, making
all the ground in front of it barren. This natural cave, with its weird
sounds, and mysteriously troubled waters, is by far the most remarkable feature of the region."[2] Albunea must therefore be sought about
two miles northeast of Lavinium, in the desolate area along the Via
Ardeatina.

     According to legend, the acropolis site of Lavinium (mod. Pratica
di Mare) derived its name from Aeneas' Italian bride. Located in
Laurentine territory, about sixteen miles from Rome and three miles
inland from the sea, Lavinium, with its grass-covered surface, is unquestionably less impressive than the rocky eminence of Ardea, although it remains richly evocative to its excavator, Ferdinando Castagnoli: "The landscape itself has been preserved relatively untouched
in its rustic simplicity and in its wide open spaces, and it is still possible
to gaze from the gentle heights on which the city was placed at the sea
and at those shores where sailors landed, bringing with them the first
objects of a much more advanced civilization, the Greek, and marvelous

tales of gods and heroes. Something still remains here of the fascination which has been destroyed in the Roman Campagna, and this is an extraordinary circumstance if one thinks of the sudden industrial transformation of so many other ancient cities, such as its neighbor Ardea (where unplanned urban development has most recently led to the construction of tall apartment houses, one next to the other, right in the center of the ancient city)."[3]

Vergil located the prodigy of the white sow and the thirty piglets on the Tiber bank (A. 8, 43–8), whereas Dionysius (8, 21, 1) favored Lavinium as the location. Dionysius also told of a thatched hut, after the pattern of the Hut of Romulus in Rome, where allegedly Aeneas sacrificed the white sow and her progeny to Juno, and lodged for the first time the Penates of Troy and the Hearth-goddess, Vesta (Fig. 35). Varro adds another intriguing notice (*LL.* 5, 144), mentioning that bronze versions of the sow and her offspring were exhibited at Lavinium in the civic center, and also that priests, on special request, would exhibit the sow's body, pickled in brine, to the credulous. The number of the piglets was probably associated with the thirty members of the Latin League, who paid special reverence to this ancient site (Fig. 36).

The tradition that located the first Trojan settlement at Lavinium was supported by an annual ceremony required of the leading officials of Rome—consuls, dictators, praetors, and generals: at the outset of their terms of duty they would proceed to Lavinium to offer sacrifices to the Trojan Penates and Vesta. The Romans were therefore ready to assign the original worship of both cults to the coastal settlement. The Penates, originally gods of the storehouse, were identified, between 520 and 480 B.C., with the Dioscuri, Castor and Pollux. The Dioscuri were usually rendered as seated youths, each holding a spear, and it is in this guise that the sculptor of the Altar of Augustan Peace represented them. There is also testimony that besides the cult images at Lavinium, heralds' wands and Trojan amphorae (storage vessels; in Latin, *dolia*) were lodged in their temple there. The Romans established the cult of the Penates and of Vesta in the Forum Romanum in the circular Vesta temple, consecrated in 484 B.C.

Even in her declining years Lavinium remained a sanctuary city, with cults of the Penates, Vesta, Juturna, Liber (Bacchus), Castor and Pollux, Ceres, Frutis-Venus, and Aeneas. The last was certainly

Greek-inspired, for there were cult sites at Aeneia in Macedonia, in Ambracia, at Zacynthus, and at Sicilian Segesta. Aeneas was especially venerated at Lavinium; he was worshipped under the name of Aeneas Indiges ("the Divine Ancestor"), and as Lar Aineias, he became identified with a local divinity who was regarded as the father of the Latin people. His earliest shrine was on the banks of the Numicus river, near Lavinium, but there was also a later cult site at Tor Tignosa, five miles inland from Lavinium. Sol Indiges also had a grove and sanctuary at nearby Tor Tignosa, which may have been the site of the two altars where Aeneas sacrificed upon landing (Pliny, *N.H.* 3, 56; Dion. Hal., 1, 55, 2). The cult of the Sun as ancestor recalls Circe's role in the origins of the Latins; the daughter of Helios, she became the mother of Agrios (=Silvius) and Latinus by the hero Odysseus.

Recent finds at Pratica di Mare have substantiated and clarified the traditional picture of Lavinium.[4] Traces of a fifth-century wall-system have appeared, along with two sanctuary sites outside the settlement's fortifications. A southern sanctuary, near the little Church of Santa Maria delle Vigne (which bears a variation of the place-name of a site once sacred to Venus in her guise as marine and fertility goddess), has yielded startling evidence of cult activity. Thirteen stone altars, oriented eastwards and mounted on a narrow platform, have been found (Fig. 37). The earliest of the altars dates from the sixth century, and Castagnoli, their discoverer, has wavered between accepting each as consecrated to a separate divinity, or (a more likely supposition) as designed to service numerous sacrifices required simultaneously, perhaps initially in connection with the federal cult, thereafter for the Roman magisterial rites. Though evidence is wanting, Alföldi has argued for the identification of this elaborate cult site with the temple of the Penates and of Vesta. An eastern sanctuary, still awaiting large-scale excavation, may yet disclose the sanctuary of the Sun and the two altars, still visible in Dionysius' time, which were accepted as memorials to Aeneas' gratitude for the life-saving water found at the site.

Latinus' Laurentum cannot be located as a community distinct from Lavinium in the ancient accounts, and we have seen that the palace of Latinus seems constructed along the lines of the Temple of Jupiter Capitolinus in Rome. If there was such a community, one must suppose that it was short-lived and was absorbed into the district of Lavinium.

Vergil couples the Tiber and Numicus as the frontiers of the Trojan settlement in Latium. The Numicus, which rises in the Alban Hills and flows across the Campagna, has been firmly identified with the modern Rio Torto, roughly midway between Ardea and Lavinium, and approximately two and a half miles from Pratica. A legendary battle between Mezentius and Aeneas, a tradition which Vergil could not support, occurred at the Numicus river on the eve of Aeneas' apotheosis. Several cults were associated with the river: one, the Ardeatine cult of Juturna, sister of Turnus, centered about a stream with therapeutic qualities; another, the cult of Pater Indiges, stood in a grove by the river, awaiting the annual visit of Roman consuls to the spot where Aeneas died. Holy water for the Vesta cult at Lavinium was drawn from the Numicus. The river's name, which is connected with *numen* ("divine power," "the power resident in a divinity"), almost certainly inspired the poet to describe it as *sacrum Numici litus,* "the hallowed shore of Numicus." (cf. Fig. 38)

Ardea was the legendary home of Turnus and tribal capital of the Rutuli, a people of Latin stock with strong Etruscan cultural ties. It lies approximately twenty-five miles south of Rome and about seven miles from the sea. Vergil's background information is romantic and wistful:

> The louring Allecto mounted at once on her sombre wings
> And made for the walls of hot-headed Turnus—the city which men say
> Danae founded and colonized with Acrisians, when she
> Was driven that way by the South wind. Our ancestors called the place
> Ardea; though it retains the great name of Ardea still,
> Its best days are far behind it.
>
> (A. 7, 408–13. Day Lewis)

Vergil's reflective comment on the venerable but moribund center fails to mention the sanctuaries and summer places which gave it a prolonged lease of life. Strabo comments that the Ardeates supervised the ancient sanctuary of Aphrodite (Frutis-Venus) at Lavinium and at the same time included Ardea among those places "devastated by the Samnites; and although traces of the cities are left, those traces have become more famous because of the sojourn which Aeneas made there, and because of those sacred rites which, it is said, have been handed down from those times." (5, 3, 5)

The poet's antiquarian curiosity is more active than the geographer's. Legend assigned Ardea's founding either to a son of Odysseus and Circe in Mycenaean times, or, as in Vergil's account, to Danae, bride of Zeus' golden shower, daughter of Argive Acrisius and mother of Perseus. Ardea won early distinction and affluence as a maritime city. Boethius's excavations there have proved that the original settlement was contemporary with Rome and Alba Longa. In 500 B.C., though now within Rome's orbit, Ardea remained an important harbor, with a superb system of fortifications around the citadel. The Temple of Juno on the acropolis may be imagined as home of Vergil's aged priestess Calybe, a guise assumed by the hellish demon Allecto, Juno's emissary to the apathetic Latins (A. 7, 419). The lower city, modern Civitavecchia, was probably the site of a Castor and Pollux temple and perhaps of a law court. The Castor and Pollux temple reputedly contained second-century murals relating to the Trojan war and may therefore have partly inspired Vergil's description of similar murals in Juno's temple at Carthage (A. 1, 453 ff.).

Active campaigning against the Volsci induced the Romans to make an alliance with Ardea in 444 and ultimately to establish a Latin colony at the strategic site in 442. Ardea remained loyal to Rome during the Gallic occupation and sheltered Camillus on several occasions. Samnite ravages of the third century were repeated during the first-century Sullan-Marian differences. In late Republican times Ardea's claim to fame rested in its venerated shrines, its pasturage for the imperial elephants, and its storied past.

The temples, judging by the finds, were decorated before the Roman colonial foundation with terra cottas in the Etruscan style. Curiously, as well as anachronistically, Vergil emphasizes an Etruscan link for Turnus, a name which almost certainly derives from Etruscan *turan,* meaning "tyrant's son," or "leader."[5] The Etruscan name has no relevance to the eighth-century foundation. Ardea's port town, Castrum Inui (A. 6, 775), at the mouth of the modern Fosso dell'Incastro, was in Strabo's time a declining center, ravaged by the anopheles. A temple of Aphrodite, reminiscent of the shrine at Lavinium, was no doubt located near the shore (Pliny, *N.H.* 3, 56), and Livy's mention of a state sacrifice at Ardea in 217 may relate to the arrival of the imported cult of Sicilian Venus Erycina. Inuus has been equated with Pan and with

Faunus (Servius, *ad Aen.* 6, 775), but the identification is debatable and the name is probably pre-Italic.

In his salute to the Volscian contingents which fought alongside Turnus, Vergil includes two rivers which empty into the sea from the Pomptine Marshes, the Satura, more commonly called the Astura, and the Ufens (mod. Ufente).

> Men from the parts around Anxur,
> Where Jove is patron, men from the greenwoods of Feronia,
> The fenlands dark of Satura, and the deep combes where Ufens
> Cold-running winds its way down and plunges into the sea.
> (A. 7, 799–802. Day Lewis)

Both rivers empty northwest of the promontory of Circeii, and both form, topographically and artistically, a matching pair to the Tiber and Numicus rivers. Taken together, they act as a frame to Vergil's coastal cities which are here under review.

Bertha Tilly[6] has surmised that when Vergil, Varius, and Plotius joined Horace and his diplomatic company at Sinuessa in 37, they had made the journey from Rome by sea, passing the very sites which he details in his epic review. Certainly the passage by sea was more reasonable than the discomforts of the Via Appia which Horace and the others had travelled, or even of the Via Latina, which runs inland by way of Teanum Sidicinum. However, one may wonder whether Vergil, whose stomach was weak, would have chosen a sea journey over the trials of the highway. The Via Appia did, in fact, traverse the marshlands, but for greater comfort and relaxation, travellers usually made the trip by barge-canal over a distance of nineteen miles. Horace's account of the passage between Forum Appi and Tarracina which he made in the spring of 37 is highly entertaining, a masterpiece of economical but memorable description:

> Never take a night boat, reader. You spend the first hour
> Paying fares and hitching up the mule. Then fearless mosquitoes
> And resonant swamp frogs keep sleep safely at bay.
> A sailor and a passenger, soused with cheap wine, compete
> In songs to their absent girl friends. The mule driver finally
> Drops off to sleep: the lazy driver lets the mule browse,
> Fastens the rope to a rock, stretches out, and snores.

Dawn was already at hand before we observed
That the boat hadn't budged an inch. Then a hot-tempered tourist
Leaped ashore, cut a switch from a willow, lit into the mule
And the driver, drumming on their domes and their bones.
Even so, it was ten when we finally got through the canal
And washed our faces and hands in your sacred spring,
Feronia, goddess of groves.

(Horace, *Sat.* 1, 5, 13–24. Palmer Bovie)

The unhealthy malarial nature of the zone should probably be associated with the breakdown of the drainage system during the long period of the Hannibalic occupation. Although Julius Caesar had plans for the proper drainage of the Pomptine Marshes and lagoons, the project was shelved after his assassination. Mosquitoes and frogs notwithstanding, Astura was a popular Roman summer resort, and even Augustus was numbered among its visitors. Cicero had a villa there which he used as a retreat in 45 after his daughter Tullia's death, and also as an escape from his political foes. The orator favored the location especially for its seaside attractions and the splendid views to Antium (mod. Anzio) and Circeii.

Rome's bitterest foes in the hinterland of Latium were the Volscians. Shakespeare's *Coriolanus* is a faithful reflection of their persistent enmity towards Rome and her imperialistic designs in Latium. The heyday of the Volscians was during the fifth century after they had made their descent from the highlands of central Italy into the Liris river valley and the regions southeast of the Alban Hills. For almost two centuries Rome was repeatedly involved in hostilities and counter-measures. They suffered most in their campaigns against Coriolanus, who led the Volscians successfully against Signia, Norba, and Ardea, between 495 and 442, and right up to the gates of Rome. Rome's predicament was made worse by famine and disease, both prevalent in fifth-century Mediterranean societies. A series of Latin colonies at Circeii (393), Satricum (385) and Setia (382) checked the Volscian advances, and by 304 they had submitted to Rome and were rapidly assimilated.

Aeneas' last landfall before he enters the Tiber mouth is Caieta (mod. Gaeta), a commanding cape with a suggestive topography. Capo Gaeta, from the sea, has the shape of a massive tumulus, and here, according to Vergil, Aeneas buried his aged nurse Caieta. The incident follows immediately after the experience at Cumae and in the underworld:

> Aeneas made his way back to the ships and his friends with all speed,
> Then coasted along direct to the harbour of Caieta.
> The ships, anchored by the bows, line the shore with their sterns.
>
> Caieta too, who was nurse to Aeneas, when she died
> Gave Italy's coast undying fame; for even now
> The place where she rests is preserved by her legend, she has an epitaph
> In a place-name of Great Hesperia—no small glory.
> When the ever-faithful Aeneas had paid her the last rites
> And heaped a burial mound over her, the deepsea now
> Being calm, he weighed from harbour and set course under sail.
>
> (A. 6, 899–901; 7, 1–7. Day Lewis)

Popular etymology derived the place-name from the Greek verb "to burn," so Vergil may have adapted Caieta's cremation to the place-name's implications. The five-hundred-foot cape was in fact an important burial place even in Vergil's time. It was crowned then, as now, with a stone tumulus which closely resembled the Mausoleum of Augustus in Rome. The tomb marked the last resting place of an occasionally errant, but always ambitious, statesman named Lucius Munatius Plancus, who was best remembered for his colonial foundations at Lugdunum (Lyon) and Augusta Raurica (Augst), and above all for his proposal of the name Augustus for Octavian in 27 B.C. A second mausoleum held the remains of Lucius Sempronius Atratinus, onetime prefect of Mark Antony's fleet (38–34) and a consul in 34. Vergil's rider on the future fame of Caieta—*si qua est ea gloria*—may imply some reserve towards these two contemporary politicians who had served several masters with equal zeal: Julius Caesar, Mark Antony, and finally Octavian. But the phrase also seems attuned to Vergil's recurrent melancholy and pessimism, perhaps even a Stoic resignation in the face of mortality. Vergil's readers would also remember that Marcus Tullius Cicero was executed at Capo Gaeta on December 7th, 43, and that his tomb was located outside Formiae.

Vergil's extensive familiarity with Latium by sea is obvious throughout the last six books of the epic. Certainly the sites of Latium visible from the sea are all given a careful look: the Volturnus river, Minturnae and the Grove of Marica, Anxur-Tarracina and the Pomptine Marshes, Circeii, Astura, Lavinium and the Numicus river, Ostia and the Tiber.

The Volturnus river, depicted as silt-laden and bordered with sedge, swift and many-shoaled (Lucan, *Phars.* 2, 423; A. 7, 728–9), was a match for the Tiber further north. The name, like Tiber, would appear to be Etruscan, deriving from the Etruscan god-name Vel. The river flowed past Casilinum and Capua, the onetime Etruscan capital in Campania.

Vergil makes only a passing reference to Marica, wife of Faunus and mother of Latinus, though her cult was a celebrated one during the Marian-Sullan civil war. The marshlands around Minturnae, especially at Marica's grove, served as haven of refuge for Marius in 88 and from there Marius took ship for Ischia and North Africa (Plut., *Marius* 37; Appian, *B.C.* 1, 57). The Grove of Marica (A. 7, 47) was located on the Liris River (mod. Garigliano) near Minturnae. Marica was regarded as mother of the Latins and, according to Servius, was the deified Circe. The ancient tufa shrine of the Italic goddess, a local sea-nymph or swamp-goddess, has been discovered and probably dates from the sixth century.

Minturnae, the capital of the Aurunci, had been linked with Formiae and Sinuessa by the Via Appia in 312. By 295 the Romans had established a maritime colony at Minturnae and nearby Sinuessa in order to safeguard the shoreline against Samnite attacks which might intercept Roman trade along the Via Appia as well as by sea. Minturnae's role, which was to combine the duties of a coast-guard station and fortress, ensured her prosperity, and the surviving monuments and civic buildings testify to her continued importance into Augustan times.

The Via Appia, Rome's main artery to the south, was built by the censor Appius Claudius Caecus in 312 and ran initially from Rome to Capua. Vergil must have travelled along the highway often and visited the venerable settlements which attached to the Trojan origins of Rome along the route. One of these, Alba Longa, twelve miles southeast of Rome, won his attention on several grounds: for its undoubted antiquity, as the reputed founder of Rome; for its religious associations; and for its primacy among the Latins.

Tradition held that in 1152 Ascanius-Julus, Aeneas' son, built the settlement at Alba Longa on the slopes of the Alban Mount, close to the present-day Papal summer residence at Castel Gandolfo. It remained, in Vergil's account, the capital of the Aeneadae until Romulus and Remus brought to pass the foundation of Rome:

> Ascanius for his reign shall have full thirty years
> With all their wheeling months; shall move the kingdom from
> Lavinium and make Alba Longa his sure stronghold.
> Here for three hundred years shall rule the dynasty
> Of Hector, until a priestess and queen of Trojan blood,
> With child by Mars, shall presently give birth to twin sons.
>   (A. 1, 269–74. Day Lewis)

The prodigy of the sow with the thirty piglets was interpreted by Vergil to mean that with the passage of thirty years Ascanius should found a white town, Alba, city of shining name (A. 8, 44–8). Although the etymology is incorrect—the stem "alb" almost certainly denotes height, or mountain—Vergil finds the whiteness suitable to his epic canvas. Following the same tradition, Vergil also establishes the Lusus Troiae for the first time in Italy at Alba Longa (A. 5, 596–603). Unquestionably the Julii, who came originally from nearby Bovillae but derived their gentile name from Alba Longa's Ascanius-Julus, were protectors, advocates, and propagators of the Trojan tradition.

Archaeological evidence offers surprising support to certain aspects of the tradition which Vergil favors, for persistent and gradually improving archaeological excavations in the tufa foundations of the topsoil at Alba Longa have revealed a series of large clay storage vessels (*dolia*), each containing a clay cinerary urn in the shape of a miniature oval hut. The necropolis finds are in the first place important clues to the nature of the simple agrarian life at Iron-Age Alba, but they are equally important as evidence of links between Alba Longa and Rome. Comparable hut-urns have also been found in the Forum necropolis, east of the Temple of Antoninus and Faustina. Equally relevant are post-hole finds on the Palatine which provide for huts identical with the cinerary urn designs. There is no doubt, judging by archaeological finds, that the settlement at Alba Longa did in fact precede the Romulan settlement at Rome.

The destruction of Alba Longa by Tullus Hostilius about 650 has not been supported by archaeological evidence, for there is no fundamental break in the stratification at Alba until later. Likewise Vergil's depiction on Aeneas' shield of Tullus' grisly execution of the deceitful Alban king, Mettus Fufetius (A. 8, 642–5), can find no parallel in Rome's record of criminal executions, although there are Etruscan parallels for its brutality.

The Alban Mount (mod. Monte Cavo, 3115 feet) nearby was the federal religious sanctuary for members of the Latin League, who from very early times gathered annually around the Temple of Jupiter Latiaris on the summit to celebrate the Feriae Latinae (Latin Festival). In Vergil's day Roman consuls continued to hold the festival on the mount in the presence of their fellow magistrates, and no ex-magistrate left for his provincial term of duty without attending the rites on the Alban Mount. The hill also witnessed the triumphal processions of returning generals.

At Aricia, beneath the Alban hills, the cult of Diana Nemorensis was celebrated. The cult, which inspired Sir James Frazer's monumental study of anthropology and religion, *The Golden Bough,* has always awakened curiosity and awe among students of religion. Vergil was certainly greatly moved by the antiquity and the mysterious nature of its rites. There are clearly links between the mistletoe (?) branch, emblem of kingship at the grove at Nemi, and the Golden Bough which Aeneas plucks and presents to the Queen of the Underworld in *Aeneid* 6, the bough which is his token of goodwill towards the nether powers, his passport to the upper world, and perhaps also symbol of his legitimate right to rule in Italy.

According to Cato the Elder, who provides the earliest testimony, a number of Latin communities formed a league about 500 B.C. to maintain the ancient cult site at Aricia. Rome was excluded because of her Etruscan associations. The earliest members of the League were Aricia, Tusculum, Lanuvium, Laurentum, Cora, Tibur, Pometia, and Ardea. The League (*Concilium Latinorum*) met annually at one of two sites: either at the archaic shrine of Lucus Ferentinae, south of modern Ariccia, or at Aricia itself, the location of the grove and shrine of Diana overlooking Lake Nemi (Fig. 39). The cult was notorious for its barbarous practices. Strabo is explicit about the Augustan point of view: "A barbaric and Scythian [Crimean] element predominates in the sacred usages, for the people set up as priest a runaway slave who has slain with his own hand the man previously consecrated to that office; accordingly the priest is always armed with a sword, looking around for the attacks, and ready to defend himself. The temple is in a sacred grove, and in front of it, is a lake which resembles an open sea, and round about it lies an unbroken and very high mountain brow which encloses both the temple and the water in a place that is hollow and deep. You can see the springs, it is true, from which the lake is fed—one of them is Egeria, as it is called after a certain deity." Strabo's account of the ancient crater lake, the so-called Speculum Dianae ("Mirror of Diana") is comprehensive.

The weird, barbaric character of the cult persisted until at least 150 A.D. The priest-king, Rex Nemorensis, was usually an escaped slave or convicted gladiator, who always gained his office by killing the incumbent after he had first violated the grove by plucking a sacred branch, probably mistletoe, from an oak tree. The Greek rationalization of the cult referred its origins either to Orestes, Iphigenia and the Crimean Artemis, or, as Vergil argues, to Theseus' bastard son Hippolytus. After his death as a consequence of his father's curse for alleged adultery with his step-mother Phaedra, Hippolytus was revived by Aesculapius and translated to the shores of Lake Nemi where he lived another life in concealment under the name of Virbius. His son appears in Vergil's Latin catalogue:

> The son of Hippolytus too, most beautiful, went to the wars—
> Virbius, a fine young man, sent by his mother Aricia,
> Who's brought him up near the shore of the lake in Egeria's wood
> Where stands an altar to Diana, rich and reverenced.
>
> But Diana was kind and hid Hippolytus in a secret
> Place, removing him to the grove of the nymph Egeria,
> Where he would live out his days a solitary unknown
> In Italian woods, having changed his name and become Virbius,
> Wherefore to this day horses are not allowed near Diana's
> Temple of sacred wood, because horses, scared by a sea beast
> Had spilt Hippolytus once and his chariot on the shore.
>
> (A. 7, 761–4; 774–80. Day Lewis)

The association with Hippolytus, a far-fetched link for an Italic cult figure, was no doubt partly confirmed by the proviso that no horses, the instruments of his death, might enter the precinct. The other cult figure attached to the site, Egeria, has her memorial in the stream which flows past the temple site. Although the extant remains of the Diana Temple are Sullan in date, there are indications that earlier cult buildings, begun in the fourth century, were fashioned along Etruscan lines in what must have been an archaizing style. The temple cult statue, according to Strabo, was modelled after the many-breasted Artemis of Ephesus type, but the outdoor sanctuary in the cypress grove sheltered an Etruscan-style cult image of Diana as huntress, set between two women, signifying thereby the threefold nature of the goddess as underworld deity (Hecate), huntress (Artemis), and moon goddess (Selene).

Aricia itself stands some sixteen miles southeast of Rome on a spur of the Alban Hills, about a mile and a half from Lake Nemi. The Appian Way crossed the fertile valley at Aricia, on a viaduct which became a beggars' haunt in Imperial times; they would harass the travellers there as they began their rather arduous ascent (Martial 2, 19; Juvenal 4, 116–8). Aricia was perhaps originally a colony of Alba Longa; its historical role was to offer resistance to Hernican, Volscian, and Etruscan thrusts into Latium. It assisted the allied Latins, along with the ambitious Aristodemus of Cumae, against an Etruscan force in 505 B.C., and by that victory ensured, among other gains, that Aristodemus should gain the tyranny at home. Aricia also provided effective leadership in a federal and religious league which was quite distinct from the religious community which met on Monte Cavo to celebrate Jupiter's cult. After playing the role of satellite for a century and a half, Aricia finally gained Roman citizenship in 338, and though sacked later by Marius, recovered and remained the respected custodian of the wealthy temple of Diana. The cult site was still affluent enough in late Republican times to induce Lucius Cornificius, Octavian's admiral, to "borrow" from the temple treasures to finance the campaigns against Sextus Pompey. Cicero also relates that Aricia provided Rome with many of its most distinguished governmental and equestrian families (Cic. *Phil.* 3, 15–6).

Octavian's mother Atia, daughter of Marcus Atius Balbus and Caesar's sister Julia, came from Aricia, and so the Emperor's associations were in fact Latin, though he was born at Velitrae (mod. Velletri).

This fact may have assisted the promotion of the Palatine cult of Apollo, Diana, and Latona in Rome during the Emperor's lifetime and may have inspired Vergil's detailed account of the comparable cult at Cumae and Lake Avernus.

Circeii, the enchanting promontory of Circe (mod. Monte Circello) is irresistibly appraised by Bertha Tilly: "No one who visits Monte Circeo can fail to experience something of its enchantment. The great mass of limestone gleaming and rising into sharp peaks silhouetted against clear skies; the shore-line where the sapphire waves of the Mediterranean break into white foam around its foot; the shore itself, strewn in one place with brilliant white pebbles which dazzle the eyes; the thick tangle of fragrant wild plants and shrubs—all weave spells to charm the senses. The profusion of growth was well known even to the Greeks, for the botanist Theophrastus writes of the lofty headland thickly grown with bushes, oak, laurel, and myrtle; this still characterizes all the slopes, especially on the landward side, where thick woods of cork oaks, ilexes, stone-pines, and many another small bush flourish in profusion."[7]

Vergil's account of the passage by Circe's promontory is one of the loveliest episodes in the epic:

> The wind blew steadily on into the night, a bright moon
> Favoured their voyage, its radiance dancing upon the water.
> Soon they were skirting close by the shore of Circe's land
> Where that luxurious daughter of the Sun, her song forever
> Thrilling through the spell-protected groves, in her proud palace
> Burns fragrant cedarwood during the night to see by,
> While the rattling shuttle runs through the gossamer warp.
> From this place could be heard through the small hours the groaning
> Roars of angry lions resentful at their captivity;
> Bristly boars and bears were heard from their enclosures
> Furiously raging, and wolf-like creatures howling—
> Men they had been once, but the terrible goddess had turned them
> Into beast faces, things on all fours, with her magic herbs.
>
> (A. 7, 8–20. Day Lewis)

Circe's perpetual song, with the zoological garden supplying its exotic accompaniment, is unforgettable.

Although the early history of Circeii is obscure, there is both literary and archaeological evidence for the foundation of a Latin colony there in 393, evidently an effort on the part of the Romans to safeguard southern Latium against Volscian advances from the interior. Remains of the colony appear on the eastern side of the cape at the modern village of San Felice Circeo. The polygonal walls of the citadel, 300 feet above sea level, still survive in small sectors. A paved precinct at the western edge of the ridge probably embraced the open-air sanctuary or temple of Circe. Strabo's account does confirm the existence of a temple at the site, together with an altar of Athena. But the ancient cults were probably incidental to most visitors, who came to enjoy the alluring coastline, dotted with porticus villas during Republican and early Imperial times. For Circeii was a rival to Formiae and Caieta, and with them, a precursor of present-day Capri and the Amalfi Drive, with cliffside villas along their slopes.

Anxur, on the coast beyond Circeii, had already enjoyed a long lifespan and colorful history of Volscian and Etruscan settlement before Rome occupied the site in 406 and changed the place-name to Tarracina. In 329 Rome lodged a colony on the height of San Francesco to guard against the threat of enemy advances from Volscian Privernum in the interior. Tarracina dominated the Tyrrhenian coastline between Ostia and Naples, and was also custodian of the Via Appia, which had to pass through the defile of nearby Lautulae. Tarracina's position at this strategic pass, a veritable Thermopylae between central and southern Latium, ensured her prestige and prosperity. The city became an important stage on the highway to Capua and the south, and served as a convenient stop-over for travellers both before and after their passage through the adjacent Pomptine Marshes (cf. Horace, *Sat.* 1, 5, 25–29).

The landscape and the highway have altered considerably since Vergil's time. The Pomptine Marshes were finally drained successfully in the time of Mussolini. The masses of rock which once stood below the height were removed in Trajan's time to permit an easier passage along the shore. In Vergil's day the road turned inland and crept up the slopes which dominated the harbor; then, by an inland circuit, the highway continued to Fondi and Formiae in the South. (Fig. 40)

On the citadel height of Monte Sant' Angelo, the ancient Volscian cult center of Jupiter Anxur was rebuilt by Sulla's architects along monumental lines comparable to the great constructions at Rome (Tabularium), at Tibur (Temple of Hercules), at Praeneste (Temple of Fortune) and at Baiae. The imprint of Hellenistic Aegean architecture is always strong in Sulla's architectural undertakings. The Jupiter temple at Tarracina stood on a sizable concrete platform which was supported in turn by arched galleries, so that the play of light on the seaward side, where eleven vaulted chambers lay open to view, was most impressive. The temple itself, built of white Circeian marble, was a gleaming marker on the headland. Cicero owned a villa at Tarracina and used it often for overnight stops between Rome and Naples.

The groves and clear water of Feronia (mod. Punte di Leano), about three miles from Tarracina, must frequently have won the gratitude of weary travellers emerging from the Pomptine Marshes (cf. Horace, *Sat.* I. 5.) Servius even ascribes to the grove and spring some of the characteristics of Lake Nemi, suggesting that the cult site offered sanctuary to runaway slaves and implying also that Feronia was perhaps a cult title of Diana. Elsewhere in the *Aeneid* Vergil introduces Feronia as mother of King Erulus, a despot slain by Evander before the walls of Praeneste, a triple-threat as enemy because he was endowed with three lives and three sets of equipment. Erulus has the earmarks of a demonic creature and probably reflects the untamed chthonic character of his mother's cult. There was an even more famous grove of Feronia in the Ager Capenas.

The Via Latina ran southeast from Rome, crossing the Alban Hills at Algidus, then continuing through the Trera valley and Hernican country to a point near Anagnia, where the Via Labicana joined it. It then proceeded through southern Latium and Campania by way of Cales to Casilinum (near Capua), where it linked up with the Appian Way. Vergil's account of the contingent of Caeculus from Praeneste includes several references to sites on the Via Latina:

> Warriors who dwelt in high Praeneste, or the Gabine district
> Where Juno is worshipped, or by the cold Anio, or in the stony
> Hernican brooklands; men whom fertile Anagnia reared,
> Or the river Amasenus.
>
> (A. 7, 682–5. Day Lewis)

The acropolis of Gabii, near modern Torre di Castiglione, twelve miles east of Rome, was a flourishing and important Alban foundation along the road from Veii. Local pride in its origins—for its foundation preceded Rome's—was fixed on the tradition that both Romulus and Remus were educated there. Even in Augustan times there was still extant a treaty between Tarquin and Gabii inscribed on a leather shield which was displayed in the temple of Semo Sancius. But the settlement's active, independent history had come to an end with the close of the regal period. Although Gabii was a satellite of Rome during the early Republic, there was a momentary resurgence of local patriotism during the fourth century. Thereafter it entered upon a rapid decline which even an ephemeral colony of Sulla could not resuscitate. Horace and Lucan both testify to the depopulated, moribund nature of the village site. Gabine institutions, however, abided in Rome as a reminder of the city's ancient distinction. The Gabine cincture, *Gabinus cinctus,* was a particular form of sacrificial dress in which the toga was gathered about the body in such a way as to leave the arms free, and then carried over the head (cf. Frontispiece). Strabo refers to the popular red stone quarried locally and always in great demand at Rome (5, 3, 10).

Labici was another of the moribund communities of Latium which Vergil honored by a reference in his epic. The ancient settlement (mod. Monte Compatri), on the commanding, defensible hill along the Via Labicana, had allied with Bovillae and Gabii at one stage (Cicero, *Pro Planco,* 23). It remained outside the Alban League, and the community had no importance except during the fifth century. Thereafter the decline was only briefly arrested by Julius Caesar's decision to construct a villa at the site.

Bola (probably mod. Zagorolo), near Labici and Tolerium, also enters Vergil's account of Alban colonies (A. 6, 775). Historically it was a member of the Alban League, but after its destruction by Camillus during the wars against the Aequi (389), it vanished from history.

Collatia (mod. Lunghezza), another of the Alban foundations, was important as a guard station at the Anio river crossing and as a post on the road between Veii and Gabii. It survived in a modest way into Imperial times, remembered always as the site where Sextus Tarquinius, "with ravishing strides," surprised the virtuous Lucretia.

Praeneste (mod. Palestrina) was, according to legend, founded by Caeculus, to whom Vergil assigns command of a Latin contingent:

Caeculus too was there, the founder of Praeneste,
The king whom men throughout the ages have believed
Was son of Vulcan, born among flocks and herds, and found
On the hearth.

(A. 7, 678–81. Day Lewis)

During the seventh and sixth centuries Praeneste, twenty-three miles east-southeast of Rome, surpassed the later capital in both political and cultural importance. After the Latin War, Praeneste lost territory and became a federated city state (*civitas foederata*), enjoying the right to house political outcasts without fear of Roman reprisals or extradition. Her strategic location, on a defensible outcropping of the Apennines, made her a pawn in the struggles between Marius and Sulla. Sulla's troops under Ofella finally sacked the city and massacred its twelve thousand inhabitants because the Praeneste had befriended Marius. The city was also moved to lower ground and was occupied by Sullan veterans. During late Republican and Imperial times it was immensely popular as a summer resort, enjoying cool breezes in summer, and was frequented by Augustus, Horace, and Tiberius.

Its most impressive monument was the sanctuary of Fortuna Primigenia ("the Firstborn") (Figs. 41, 42). Fortuna, "Lady Luck," was, according to Sulla, his goddess patroness. In his lost memoirs he no doubt chronicled the instances where Fortuna had befriended him and also his own activities in her honor at Tibur. For the Dictator rebuilt the Temple of Fortune on a colossal scale, embellishing the ancient site and the building by a splendid new series of arcades and ramps designed to glorify the oracular cult. The newly organized sanctuary exhibited aspects which are found in other Sullan undertakings: a merger of the Italic principle of axiality and symmetry with the masterly Hellenistic conception of landscape planning and terrace architecture. Clever use of concrete enabled Sulla's architects to impart a new monumentality to the sanctuary by vaulting, arches, and curved colonnades. At the same time Sulla located a garrison on the acropolis and established a Roman colony in the plain at the foot of the citadel. In such fashion did Sulla make amends for the ghastly siege of 82 B.C., when the Younger Marius committed suicide, when most of the inhabitants had been butchered, and the lovely city had been sacked and destroyed.

Vergil's allusion to the stony brooklands of the Hernici (A. 7, 684–5;

cf. p. 169) reflects the rugged nature of the terrain north of the Trerus (mod. Sacco) valley and the Via Latina. The Hernici, doughty Sabine mountaineers, were early allies of Rome and fought alongside them against their own neighbors, the marauding Volscians and Aequi. They also stood by Rome during the Latin War, but finally, renouncing their old ties, they joined Anagnia against Rome in 306. Both were quickly subdued.

Anagnia (mod. Anagni) was the chief town of the Hernici, occupying a fertile stretch of the corridor which separated the bellicose Aequi from the Volsci. Always uneasy in such a perilous environment, Anagnia favored good relations with Rome. Both Pyrrhus and Hannibal ravaged her fertile territory during their period of occupation. After the Social War, Anagnia enjoyed full citizenship and also retained some importance as a religious center. Cicero had a villa there, and some have speculated that *dives Anagnia* ("rich, wealthy Anagnia") may have been Mark Antony's principal Italian mint. When Marcus Aurelius, much later, visited Anagnia, he told his tutor Fronto that, though diminutive in size, it still housed many antiquities and numerous religious shrines and memorials.

Powerful Atina, one of Vergil's five arsenal towns, was an important community during the regal period and engaged in frequent combat with Rome during the fourth and third centuries. Cicero's comments on the community are most rewarding since he was acquainted with the citizenry, who were neighbors to his own staunchly moral, somewhat strait-laced, industrious Arpinates:

> It is a neighbourhood to be praised, and even to be loved, retaining the old-fashioned habits of kindness for one another; and not tainted with ill-nature, nor accustomed to falsehood, nor insincere, nor treacherous, nor learned in the suburban, or shall I say, the city artifices of dissimulation.
>
> (Cicero, *Pro Planco,* 22)

Cicero's comments parallel Vergil's own estimate of the Latin and Sabine stock whose virtues Augustus tried desperately to revive with his program or moral reform.

Besides the settlements on the east side of the Via Latina, Vergil cites several on the west. Privernum (mod. Piperno) enters the epic as the original home of the Volscian dictator Metabus. He fled from the revolution which unseated him to seek safety in the mountainous, wooded area in the hinterland of his home, carrying with him his baby daughter Camilla. Resolute and inventive in his efforts to save her, he strapped her to his spear and hurled her across the torrential Amasenus river (A. 11, 540–66). The river flows into the Pomptine Marshes after passing near modern Fossanova, where St. Thomas Aquinas died in 1274 at the Cistercian Abbey. The French tried to improve the marshy condition of the countryside by the Fossa Nova canal, which would regulate the Ufens and the Amasenus rivers. Rome's establishment of a colony at Anxur-Tarracina in 329 was largely designed to protect the coast from attacks by the Volscians based at Privernum.

Cora (mod. Cori) on the northwestern extremity of the Volscian ranges, was supposedly founded by Dardanus the Trojan, or by Coras, brother of the founder of Tibur. Its beginnings were certainly ancient, perhaps as old as Rome's. Isolated and secure with deep ravines on all sides save one, Cora was largely undisturbed except for a major assault by the Volscians in 330 and its capture and pillage by Marius. Sulla provided for the rebuilding and rewalling of the city, and during the first century it attained the apogee of its prosperity. The most impressive monument at Cori, dating from Sullan times, is a Doric temple in Italic style, a delicate but barbarous version of an architectural order unpopular in Italy.

Pometia (or Suessa Pometia, mod. Caracupo) lies on the Latin and Volscian frontier, south of the Alban Hills and north of the Pomptine Marshes, which may owe their name to Pometia. The Aurunci who inhabited the settlement maintained a loose suzerainty over the area south of the Volscians, between the Liris and Volturnus rivers. Pometia's life-span ended during the first century A.D.

The route of the ancient Via Salaria, "Salt Highway," ran along the left bank of the Tiber from the salt pans at Ostia to the Apennine range. It was lined with communities whose fortunes were involved with Rome's. Antemnae (A. 7, 621), cited by Vergil as one of the five arsenal towns of the Latins, was a natural fortress at the confluence of the Tiber and Anio rivers. Although remains include only local and Etruscan pottery of the seventh century and occasional outcroppings of squared masonry, the origins of the community can safely be assigned to the eighth century. Alban settlers would have found an easy and natural crossing at the site, which finally rivaled Fidenae further down-stream. It is even conceivable that Antemnae, with its long-distance view past Fidenae to the Capitoline Hill, served as a signal station for Rome during any hostilities between Rome and the Etruscans at Veii. Vergil's epithet *turrigerae* ("turreted, tower-bearing") may imply both wall turrets and signal towers. The site came into prominence in 82 B.C. after the Samnite defeat at the Porta Collina. The Samnites evacuated to Antemnae but were later surrendered by their embarrassed hosts to the Roman commander and were all executed on Sulla's order. Antemnae survived into Augustan times (Strabo 5, 3, 2), although considerably diminished in size.

The Via Salaria also ran close by the isolated height of Fidenae (mod. Castel Giubileo), only two miles distant from its rival Antemnae. One of Fidenae's wars with Rome was generated by an attack on grain barges which floated past the site, implying that Sabine traders guiding their rafts and vessels downstream must have suffered more than once from Fidenae's exactions and outright piracy. Her Etruscophile attitude finally prodded Rome into launching an allied military attack on the city, and to safeguard the victory the Romans lodged a colony there before 500 B.C. Hostility flared up again, however, and in 475 Rome took the city by storm and sold the inhabitants into slavery. Cornelius Cossus slew the enemy commander Tolumnius in personal combat, and for his valor was awarded the *spolia opima* (the Roman army's most highly valued war decoration) which Augustus was still able to view in Rome some four centuries later.

Saxa Rubra (mod. Prima Porta), five miles distant from Rome on the Via Flaminia, was the landing opposite Fidenae. In order to consolidate their operations with Fidenae, the military commanders of Veii established a camp there facing the Cremera valley, Veii's sole artery for access to the Tiber. The Empress Livia's estate at Prima Porta, which was probably part of her dowry to Augustus, yielded the celebrated portrait statue of Augustus now in the Vatican Museum, and also a marvelous garden fresco now in Rome's Terme Museum.

Crustumerium (mod. Marcigliana), about one mile north of Fidenae at another Tiber crossing-point, also dominated the Via Salaria and proved an embarrassment to Sabine and Roman river traffic. Its origins were assigned to Sicilian, Trojan, or Athenian initiative. The archaic necropolis was found in 1962. Crustumerium enters Vergil's catalogue as another Latin arsenal. It shared Fidenae's career and was absorbed into the Roman orbit by the late fifth century.

Cures (A. 6, 808–12; 10, 345) stood aloft on a hill beside the Via Salaria and the Fosso Corese. Vergil salutes its ancient lawgiver, Numa Pompilius. His reference to "humble Cures/A town in a poor area," matches the present-day scene. The Romans sometimes argued that their formal designation as Quirites derived from Cures, although the acknowledged ethnic name was Curenses.

Nomentum (mod. Mentana) lies thirteen miles north of Rome and is the terminus of the Via Nomentana (A. 6, 773; 7, 702). Vergil favors both Latin and Sabine affiliations for the center. Her productive fields and privileged municipal status assisted Nomentum to survive into Imperial times. It was a favorite villa resort for Titus Pomponius Atticus, Cicero's beleaguered correspondent, for Seneca, Martial, and others.

Vergil's passing remark on the Allia river (mod. Fosso della Bettina) as "ill-omened" (A. 7, 717) is a reminder of Rome's defeat by the Gauls on July 18th, 391. A local precinct and shrine dedicated to Aius Locutius ("sayer and speaker") recalled the warnings of an unknown divinity or hero who had tried to alert the Romans to the approach of the Gauls. The Roman commander, Quintus Sulpicius, stationed his forces on the left bank of the Tiber where the Allia fed into the river. His defeat, magnified by drownings after the battle, led to the occupation of Rome.

Vergil's failure to mention Etruscan Veii, on the left bank of the Allia, is particularly curious because Rome's war with Veii, eighteen miles distant, was often compared with the Greek siege of Troy.[8] Although Vergil does not introduce the site, some scholars have thought that the war between Aeneas and Mezentius may reflect the historical conflict at Veii. Both Mezentius and the ruler of fourth-century Veii were despised, hated for their impiety, and able to raise only meager support (Veii's came from the Falisci and the Capenates), and both leaders were abandoned ultimately by Juno. Veii survived the capture of the city in 396, but by Augustan times it had become a melancholy farmland, a sad decline from the days when Roman statesmen advocated the removal of Rome's government to Veii. Her natural assets far out-weighed Rome's:

> The city of Veii was not inferior to Rome as a place of residence. It had much fruitful land both in the mountains and on the plains. The air in the neighborhood was very pure and salubrious. There were no marshes near to throw off chill breezes in the early morning. Its water supply was sufficient, and vegetation flowered with rich luxuriance.
>
> (Dion. Hal. 12, frag. 21)

"Haughty Tibur," another of the five arsenal towns, is located on the Anio, eighteen miles east-northeast of Rome, and it was regarded as a Greek (Argive) or Siculan settlement. Tibur (mod. Tivoli) sided with the Gauls and Praenestines against Rome in early times but was finally subdued by Camillus and deprived of some territory in 338. Although technically subject to Rome thereafter, Tibur remained nomi-nally free and autonomous and enjoyed the right of exile (*ius exilii*) with a limited number of other sites. Roman citizenship was granted in 90, and thereafter Tibur developed rapidly as a flourishing summer resort for Romans, and a rival to its neighbor Tusculum. Catullus, Propertius' sweetheart Cynthia, Julius Caesar, Mark Antony, and Augustus all favored the city, and among its most notable exiles were Syphax, king of Numidia (201), and Cinna, after 44 B.C.

Today the fountains of the Villa d'Este and the spectacular remains of Hadrian's villa nearby are the major attractions. But the remains from Republican times are equally impressive for their excellent preser-vation and their location: the round Corinthian temple (of Vesta ?), dating about 50 B.C., and the rectangular Temple of Hercules Victor, misnamed the "Sibyl's Temple," dating about 70–60 B.C. The latter, which lies mainly beneath a paper factory, originally rested on a series of vaulted substructures like the Tabularium in Rome or the Temple of Fortune at Praeneste. It stood at the rear of a rectangular precinct surrounded on three sides by a two-story double colonnade. Entry into the sanctuary was gained by an impressive, theater-like semicircular staircase which was aligned with the temple axis.

Vergil subscribes to a rather recherché tradition which assigns the city's foundation to the three grandchildren of Argive Amphiaraus, Tiburtus, Coras, and Catillus:

25. Mausoleum of Augustus, air view. Begun 28 B.C.

Patterned after heroic tumuli and Etruscan burial mounds, the tomb contained a concentric series of concrete vaulted corridors surrounding a cylinder holding the ashes of the Princeps. The ash urns of the family and later rulers lined the corridor around the central cylinder.

26. Reconstruction of the Circus Maximus and surrounding area.
Model: Rome, Museo della Civiltà Romana.

*A view of the Circus (1) from the Aventine Hill, looking towards
the Imperial Palace (2). The Imperial box, pulvinar (3), overlooks
the starting and finishing line.*

27. Artemis of Gabii. Roman copy of a Greek original of ca. 350–320 B.C. attributed to Praxiteles. Paris, Musée du Louvre.

Vergil's description of Venus in the guise of a Spartan girl recalls this statue type:

In huntress wise she had handily strung her bow from
 her shoulder,
And her hair was free to blow in the wind, and she
 went bare-kneed
With the flowing folds of her dress kilted up and
 securely knotted.

(A. I, 314–20. Day Lewis)

28. Laocoön, by Hegesandros, Polydoros, and Athanadoros. Ca. 150–80 B.C. About life-size. Rome, Musei Vaticani.

The group, newly restored, recalls the excitement and baroque splendor of the Altar of Zeus at Pergamum.

29. Father Tiber. Roman copy of a Hellenistic original of ca. 240–200 B.C. Paris, Musée du Louvre.

30. The Capitoline she-wolf. Bronze, ca. 500 B.C. Height 2 feet 9½ inches. Rome, Museo Capitolino.

The vigorous, aggressive wolf, a compromise between naturalistic and abstract rendering, was made by an Etruscan bronze-worker. The twins are a Renaissance addition.

31. Odyssey landscape. Mid-first century B.C. Height about 5 feet. Rome, Musei Vaticani.

The panoramic landscape was discovered on the Esquiline in 1848; this section depicts Odysseus summoning the ghosts at the entry to Hades.

32. Italia. Detail of the east end of the Ara Pacis Augustae, Rome, 13–9 B.C. Height 5 feet 2 inches.

Italia, in the guise of Venus Genetrix, personifies maternity. This allegory of the Saturnian land parallels Vergil's glorification of Italy (G. 2, 136–76).

33. Wall painting from a tomb near the Sepulcrum Statiliorum, Rome. Augustan date. Rome, Museo Nazionale Romano (Terme).

The frieze illustrates the Aeneid *and the early annals of Rome. This section, from the south wall, depicts the building of Lavinium.*

34. Ostia: theater and square. Augustan date, and later.

The theater had three tiers of seats and an upper gallery, semi-circular orchestra, and raised stage. Behind lies the Corporation Square, with seventy trading offices; each had a floor mosaic indicating the business conducted there.

35. Aeneas sacrificing to the Penates. (Cf. Frontispiece.)
Relief on west end of the Ara Pacis Augustae, Rome,
13–9 B.C. Height (without border) 5 feet 2 inches.

*The small shrine at upper left contains the Penates. The
sow locates the scene at Lavinium, where thirteen altars
have been found (cf. Fig. 37). Aeneas' young companion is
probably Ascanius.*

36. The white sow with the piglets. Life-size marble. Second century A.D.
Rome, Musei Vaticani.

*The bronze original, ca. 300 B.C., decorated the forum of Lavinium, marking
it as the Latin metropolis. Vergil (A. 3, 389–93) describes the prodigious
beast as a wild boar rather than a domesticated sow.*

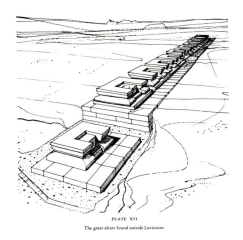

37. The thirteen altars outside
Lavinium, reconstruction by F.
Castagnoli.

*The stone altars, some of them
approximately thirteen feet long,
date from the mid-sixth century
B.C. Their number testifies to
periodic collective sacrifice in
the open air (cf. A. 12, 213–5).*

38. The cista Pasinati, a bronze toilet box cover, from Praeneste.
Ca. 200–175 B.C. London, British Museum.

Latinus, at center, wears the garb of Jupiter; to the left, victorious Aeneas grasps his hand (cf. A. 12, 161 ff.), and the slain Turnus is carried away; to the right, Lavinia, gesturing towards Aeneas, with Amata and Allecto (?); in the foreground, Tiber and two water deities, Numicus and mourning Juturna.

39. Lake Nemi.

The "mirror of Italy" was once surrounded by woods sacred to Diana Nemorensis and the cult of the Golden Bough. The Diana temple faced south onto the lake, on the site of modern Giardini.

40. Tarracina: the Trajanic passage and the substructures of
the Temple of Jupiter Anxur.

The temple substructures crown the heights far above the Via Appia
and the area that was once the Pomptine Marshes.

41. Reconstruction of the Temple of Fortuna Primigenia at Praeneste.
Model: Palestrina, Museo Nazionale.

Reminiscent of the multi-terraced Temple of Aesculapius on Cos, the
Temple of Fortune was the most splendid Republican edifice in Italy.

42. Battleship relief, related to Actium (31 B.C.) Frieze from the Temple of Fortune, Praeneste. Height 2½ feet. Rome, Musei Vaticani, Sala di Meleagro.

The relief shows a four-deck man-of-war with an artillery tower on the prow; the ship carries an officer and marines. The crocodile identifies it as part of the Libyan contingent attached to Mark Antony. (Cf. A. 8, 691–3.)

43. Maecenas (?) (died 8 B.C.). Detail from the Ara Pacis Augustae, Rome.

The Imperial adviser Maecenas, "descended from ancient Etruscan kings," was friend and patron of Vergil and Horace.

OPPOSITE PAGE:

44. Vergil's tomb and the Neapolitan tunnel.

The late Republican dovecot tomb to the left of the tunnel entrance has been identified for centuries as the tomb of Vergil.

45. Vergil (?) (70–19 B.C.).
Height 20¼ inches. Boston,
Museum of Fine Arts (Perkins
Collection).

*This late Hellenistic bust, known
in forty versions, conforms with
contemporary descriptions of
Vergil's rustic appearance and
deportment. This and the
Seminario Patriarcale bust in
the Museo Nazionale, Venice,
are the most convincing of the
extant portraits identified as
Vergil. (The Museum of Fine
Arts lists the portrait as "Herm
Bust of a Man of Letters,
identified by some as Menander,
by others as Vergil.")*

46. Etruscan helmet, found at
Olympia. Ca. 474 B.C. London,
British Museum, King Edward
VII Gallery.

*This bronze helmet, dedicated at
Olympia by Hieron of Syracuse
after his victory in 474, is
inscribed in Greek: "Hiaron, son
of Deinomenes, and the
Syracusans [dedicated]
Tyrrhenian spoils won at
Cumae to Zeus."*

47. Cumae: lower Temple of Apollo.

48. Cumae: plan of lower Temple of Apollo. Two stages of design: Greek (late sixth century B.C.) and Roman (Augustan). Drawing by R. F. Paget.

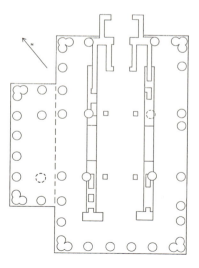

The Greek temple halfway up the Acropolis slope was reoriented and reconstructed by Augustus. The original Doric temple was oriented NE by SW. Under Augustus a porch was added on the northwest overlooking the forum (56 by 20 feet; 6 columns across and 4 inner columns). The interior of the temple was altered to a triple cella arrangement, with the main entry at the northeast. The Roman architect combined the original tufa columns and capitals with brick and concrete versions, providing unusual strengthening at the corners.

49. Cumae: the grotto of the Sibyl.

The evocative passageway was the oracular chamber for the Apollo-Trivia cult. Deiphobe ("terror to the enemy"?), daughter of Glaucus (a sea divinity of infallible prophecy), would supposedly have prophesied to Aeneas from the inmost recesses.

50. Cumae: the prophetic chamber at the rear of the Sibyl's grotto.

Here the Sibyl probably prophesied from her golden tripod while the lateral windows were opened and shut to enhance the eerie effect.

> Next, twin brothers marched from the walled city of Tibur
> Where lived a people named after their brother, Tiburtus—
> Catillus and mettlesome Coras they were, warriors born in
> Argos, and moving now in the van where the fire was hottest.
>
> (A. 7, 670–73. Day Lewis)

Cato's tradition, perhaps more plausible but incompatible with the Vergilian account, made Catillus the admiral of Evander. Archaeology has confirmed the antiquity of Tibur, however, for there was a settlement there during the Iron Age and a more formal community during the fifth and fourth centuries. The Sullan rebuilding of Tibur, as at Praeneste, greatly enriched the appearance of the city. Octavian seized the treasures in the Temple of Hercules Victor during his campaign against Lucius Antonius, the renegade brother of Mark Antony. Tibur's importance as a strategic site guarding the entrance to the Anio Valley and the road leading to the Abruzzi and the Adriatic coast was universally recognized, and there were other less minatory assets, natural assets which included the celebrated gorge and waterfall, productive orchards and vineyards, and elegant homes.

Sometime around 35 B.C. Maecenas (Fig. 43) gave Horace a large country house at nearby Digentia (mod. Licenza), between the villages of Vicovaro and Mandela. The villa commanded a sweeping panorama of the Sabine hills and was a cool Arcadian retreat for the poet from Rome's turmoil and long hot summers. Horace tends to understate the scale and appointments of his villa, for the residence in fact contained twelve rooms grouped about two courtyards, with a large walled garden and central pool (*piscina*), with a sparkling spring (*fons Bandusiae*), elms, oaks, cultivated fields, an orchard, vineyard, olive grove, and more than adequate pasturage. Five peasant families and eight slaves ministered to the needs of the bachelor poet and his friends, and one may be certain that Maecenas and later Horace must have entertained Vergil there frequently.

VI

Campania, Lucania, and Central Italy

THE TERRITORY of Campania lies between the Apennines and the Tyrrhenian sea and between Latium and Lucania, stretching from Sinuessa (mod. Mondragone) in the north to Surrentum (mod. Sorrento) and Salernum (mod. Salerno) in the south. The region attracted some of Italy's earliest settlers. Although the aboriginal Opici, Ausones, and Cimmerians were probably visited by Mycenaean Greeks, the first fixed Greek settlements were at Pithecusae (mod. Lacco Ameno) on Ischia about 770, and at the mainland site of Cumae almost immediately opposite, about 750. Campania flourished under the Greeks, though they were repeatedly challenged by the Etruscans who also settled in the area, at Capua, Nola, Nuceria, Atella, and possibly Pompeii and Herculaneum; but this prosperous phase came to a sudden end about 425 when the Osco-Sabellian Samnite invaders overran all the wealthy cities of Campania. After the Samnites had yielded to Roman legions, determined measures were taken by Rome to guarantee the security and prosperity of the region. The Via Appia served as a military and commercial highway linking Campania with Rome and with the southern regions of the peninsula. And not only did Campania give Rome promise of wealth and manpower, it also provided a good sea-front and year-round harbor facilities at Puteoli (mod. Pozzuoli) and Neapolis (mod. Naples). With the consolidation of their rule in Campania the Romans could move purposefully towards becoming a world power.

The fertility of Campania never faltered. The volcanic soil, rich in minerals and retaining moisture even during the dog-days of August, supplied the local farmers and the Romans with a rich array of grains, vegetables, olives and grapes, fruits and roses. Vergil was enthusiastic about the terrain:

> The soil that breathes forth wisps of floating fog,
> That drinks in dampness, drains it off at will,
> And wears a grassy robe of evergreen
> Yet never scores your tools with flakes of rust,
> This soil will weave your elms with joyous vines
> And yield an olive crop, and it will prove
> When cultivated, gracious to the herd,
> Submissive to the ploughshare's curving blade.
> Such arable rich Capua enjoys
> And the coast that borders on Vesuvius' ridge
> Where the Garigliano drifts past lone Acerrae.
> (G. 2, 217–35. Palmer Bovie)

By the time of Augustus, some of the country's most favored wines, including the strong, dry Falernian, came from the grapes nurtured on the slopes of Mount Massicus at the northwestern edge of the plain. But Gauran, Sorrentine, and Vesuvian wines were also highly regarded, and the olive oil of Venafrum was renowned at home and abroad. During his *annus mirabilis* as consul in 63, Cicero strenuously opposed any division of Campania into private holdings, arguing that the countryside was indispensable to Roman security and livelihood:

> Will you allow the one most beautiful estate of the Roman people, the source of your wealth, an adornment in peacetime, a support in war, the basis of your revenues, the granary of your legions, the relief of your grain supply—will you allow all this to perish?
> (*De Lege Agraria*, 2, 80)

Vergil, who resided at Naples while he composed his *Georgics* and *Aeneid,* was intensely fond of Campania; for him and many others, the Italian maxim *Vedi Napoli e poi muori* was a fair reflection of their sentiments about the captivating shoreline both south and north of Naples and on the islands. All year round the shoreline harbored a population of invalids and retired persons, and it was a favorite resort for wealthy

Romans who sought to escape the heat of the Roman summer. The volcanic regions offered abundant resources for the steam baths at Naples, Baiae, Puteoli, and on the island of Ischia (anc. Aenaria).

Vergil's epitaph, allegedly from his own hand, pays tribute to Naples as his last resting place—*tenet nunc Parthenope*.[1] For most of his productive career Naples was his favorite residence. Aside from the natural beauty of the setting, its restorative springs and surroundings, and its remoteness from Roman political upheavals, Vergil favored the city for its cultural assets. Throughout antiquity Naples retained its original Greek manner of life and institutions, its language and cultural inclinations, and it remained a perennial favorite for tourists, bohemians, philosophers, writers, and dilettantes of all nationalities and backgrounds. Cicero respected Naples for its avid pursuit of the Greek arts and sciences and regarded it as a center of Italian Hellenism, as the Athens of the West (*Pro Archia* 3, 5; 5, 10).

Vergil came to Naples probably for the first time around 50 B.C. and there became attached to the Epicurean philosopher Siro and the circle of Epicurean poets gathered at Naples. Philodemus (ca. 110–40 B.C.), the Greek-speaking Epicurean teacher from Gadara, made a decisive foray into Neapolitan cultural circles through the patronage of L. Calpurnius Piso (consul in 58). Fragments of his writings were found in 1752 in the excavations of Herculaneum in the so-called Villa of the Pisos.[2] They covered a wide range of subject matter, from naughty love epigrams to "*haute vulgarisation*" of Greek philosophy, and involved theology, ethics, aesthetics, and rhetorical theory. He was associated with Siro in Naples' Epicurean circle, which included at various times the poets Vergil, Varius Rufus, Plotius Tucca, and Quintilius Varus. The school, located on the hill of Pausilypon (mod. Posillipo) was modeled after the Garden of Epicurus in Athens and consisted of a small company of friends residing and studying together. Piso may have conferred benefits on Philodemus, but the members were mostly men of modest means. Epicureanism, which flourished in Naples, was not regarded as a respectable philosophy for men with political ambitions; although some may have yielded to the friendly, somewhat apathetic creed, they were ready to set it aside for Stoicism or some other eclectic code of ethics which would support their political aims. Caesar and Cassius were exceptions to the rule, for both men retained their

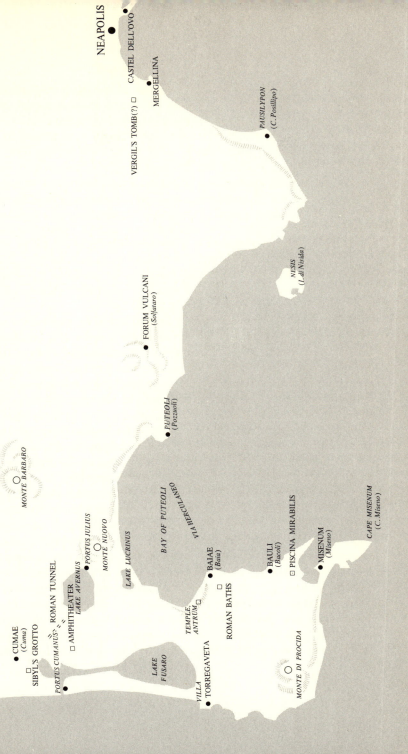

CAMPI PHLEGRAEI

NEAPOLIS

CASTEL DELL'OVO

VERGIL'S TOMB(?)

MERGELLINA

PAUSILYPON
(C. Posillipo)

NESIS
(I. di Nisida)

FORUM VULCANI
(Solfataro)

PUTEOLI
(Pozzuoli)

MONTE BARBARO

CUMAE
(Cuma)

SIBYL'S GROTTO

PORTUS CUMANUS
ROMAN TUNNEL
AMPHITHEATER
LAKE AVERNUS
PORTUS JULIUS
MONTE NUOVO

LAKE LUCRINUS

BAY OF PUTEOLI

VIA HERCULANEO

TEMPLE,
ANTRUM

BAIAE
(Baia)

ROMAN BATHS

BAULI
(Bacoli)

PISCINA MIRABILIS

MISENUM
(Miseno)

CAPE MISENUM
(C. Miseno)

LAKE FUSARO

VILLA
TORREGAVETA

MONTE DI PROCIDA

Epicurean tenets during their political careers. Among the poems of the Appendix Vergiliana, *Catalepton* 5 (8–10) may record Vergil's enthusiasm on first joining the Epicurean company at Naples:

> Now we set sail for the havens of bliss where by attending the learned lectures of Siro we will free our lives from all anxiety.

Another poem in the same collection, *Catalepton* 8, may reflect his sentiments at the time he transferred permanently to Pausilypon, lodging his dispossessed father and brothers there also:

> Little country house, once the property of Siro, a poor man's modest acre, yet a treasure to that esteemed master, I entrust myself to your care now and along with me those whom I have always cherished, my father foremost. Now you will become for him what Mantua once was and Cremona in earlier days.

Epicureanism and Lucretius' Epicurean didactic poem *On the Nature of Things* left as firm and lasting an imprint on Vergil as on Catullus and Horace. Some have detected in the account of Aeneas' love for Dido what may have been a fundamental struggle in Vergil's own ethical and philosophical development, the tension between the Epicurean tenets of his youth and the stricter discipline of Stoicism which he espoused in his maturer years.

The Donatus-Suetonius *Life* (11,14) mentions that Vergil's modesty in speech and thought earned him the nickname of Parthenias ("The Maid") at Naples. The somewhat ambiguous name probably derives from the poet's long association with the city, which was traditionally the site where the Siren Parthenope washed ashore after Ulysses had made his successful passage past the entrancing shores of the Sirens' song.

Founded originally by nearby Cumae during the sixth century, Neapolis ("New City") soon spread from the original site along the modern Via Partenope shoreline, to include Megaris (mod. Castel dell'Ovo) and the harbor area. The influx of Campanian immigrants and of refugees from Cumae after the Samnite capture of the city in 421 led to a large expansion of Neapolis along modern lines, for it adopted the regular gridiron pattern of streets introduced by Hippodamus into Thurii in South Italy in 444. After the city fell to Roman armies in 326 it remained loyal to its treaty with Rome, offering resistance and help against Pyrrhus and Hannibal during the third century. Neapolis enjoyed a favored status somewhere between absolute independence and absorption by Rome, able to hold to a somewhat isolationist stand during the Civil Wars (save for the loss of her fleet and a massacre of her citizenry in 82) and to give a measure of support to Pompey in 50.

During the troubles with Sextus Pompey, Octavian and Agrippa turned to the engineering genius of Lucius Cocceius Auctus. He constructed a tunnel through Mons Pausilypus to allow the entry of the Via Puteolana, which connected Puteoli and Naples, into the city (Fig. 44). Though alterations have been considerable since that time, the tunnel's original dimensions have been calculated as twenty-one feet wide and seventy feet high along the half-mile passage through the volcanic rock. Light and air were admitted through vents inserted at regular points along the passage connected with the summit. Seneca's letter offers an entertaining and revealing glimpse of travel through the tunnel:

> When I had to leave Baiae to return to Naples it was easy for me to convince myself that a storm was raging so that I would not have to resort to a ship again; but the road was so muddy that I might appear to have made a sea-voyage nonetheless. For on that day I had to undergo the total regimen of the athletes; after the anointing I was sprinkled with sand in the Neapolitan tunnel. No place could be longer than that prison-cell; nothing could be dimmer than those torches which helped us simply to see the darkness rather than peer through the gloom. Even though the place might admit some light, the dust, which is oppressive and disagreeable even in the open, would dispel the light. What an experience it is there to have the dust roll back on itself and, because it is confined without any ventilation, blow back in the faces of the very individuals who stirred it up in the first place. We underwent two inconveniences at one and the same time, both of them diametrically opposed: we struggled with mud and with dust on the same road and on the same day.
>
> (*Epistles* 57, 1–3.)

Augustus was very fond of Naples, as he was of the entire Campanian littoral. Quinquennial gymnastic contests, in the Greek mode, were established at Naples in his honor, and he attended one such event in 14 A.D., on the eve of his death. He also showed his affection for the city when he provided funds to assist reconstruction after an earthquake (Dio Cass. 55, 10).

When in Naples, Augustus probably stayed at the mansion on the height of Pausilypon, overlooking the Bay of Naples,[3] that was bequeathed to him by Vedius Pollio. This partisan of Octavian became an embarrassment to the Princeps by his ostentatious luxury and cruelty. During a formal banquet Pollio gave in honor of Augustus, a cupbearer broke a priceless myrrhine goblet, whereupon the host ordered him thrown to the lampreys in the villa's piscina. Augustus intervened and demanded that the entire collection of myrrhina be smashed, one by one (Dio Cass. 64, 23, 1–6). When Pollio bequeathed his property to his patron, including a villa in Rome called "Pausilypon," Augustus had the mansion razed and constructed the Porticus Liviae on the site (Ovid, *Fasti* 6, 643–4). But the Neapolitan villa was spared.

After Vergil's death at Brundisium his ashes were taken to Naples and according to Donatus-Suetonius, "laid to rest on the Via Puteolana less than two miles from the city, in a tomb for which he himself had composed the distich:

> Mantua gave me the light, Calabria slew me; now holds me
> Parthenope. I have sung shepherds, the country, and wars."

The tomb has been identified with an Augustan dovecot, or columbarium, mausoleum standing alongside the entry to the Crypta Neapolitana, which passes beneath Pausilypon towards Puteoli and "Vergilian" Campania. (Fig. 44) The mausoleum, in the shape of a circular drum on a square podium, has ten niches for cinerary urns. Its location, overlooking the bay and on the slopes of Vergil's Epicurean *templa serena,* at a point where every visitor to Naples would observe the tomb and pay appropriate respect, is ideally situated for the last resting place of Naples' most distinguished adopted son. But the Suetonian evidence would locate the site near the present Park of Remembrance and Aquarium, where one must suppose that the tomb slipped into the sea during some earthquake centuries ago.

Silius Italicus and Statius accorded Vergil's tomb the reverence usually assigned to those of ancient heroes or demi-gods. According to Pliny (*Epist.* 3, 7, 1), Silius Italicus had a large collection of books, statues, and portrait busts which he tended religiously, and Vergil's bust was one of those he venerated most. (Fig. 45) He used to celebrate Vergil's birthday (October 15th) even more dutifully than his own, particularly at Naples, where he approached the poet's tomb as though it were a shrine. St. Paul allegedly visited Vergil's tomb on his way from Puteoli to Rome and wept because the poet had died before Christ's coming.[4]

Vergil was by nature *amantissimus vetustatis,* an enthusiast for antiquity (Quintilian 1, 7, 18). Aeneas' adventures at Cumae offered the poet a marvelous opportunity to research the origins of much of Rome's inheritance from the antique settlers of the peninsula.

Vergil was fully aware of the legendary and historical tradition of Cumae, for Aeneas was not the first "Mycenaean" visitor to those shores. The poet ascribes the first temples at Cumae to Daedalus, the Minoan Leonardo da Vinci who had devised the labyrinth at Cretan Cnossus where Theseus slew the Minotaur. The temple doors, which Aeneas inspects while he awaits the Sibyl, depict the exploits of Theseus and the Greeks' overthrow of Minoan tyranny; Vergil seems to construct this subject matter as much along the lines of megalographic wall painting as of gold and ivory reliefs. The parallel with the splendid doors of the Temple of Apollo Palatinus (cf. p. 135 f.) is suggestive, for both reflect themes of death and salvation, of Apollo's intervention in history and myth as redeemer and punishing deity: at Rome, the Rescue of Delphi from Celtic attack and the Fate of the Niobids; at Cumae, the Deliverance of the Athenians from their bondage to Crete and the Escape of Theseus and Daedalus. But Vergil's panels are equally pictorial and tragic, for Theseus' love for Ariadne was as ill-fated as Pasiphae's for the bull, and Daedalus' flight was ultimately as heartbreaking as Theseus': for Theseus returned to mourn his father's death, and Daedalus mourned the death of his son Icarus even while he flew towards his refuge at Cumae.

Daedalus, Theseus, Pirithous, and Hercules were numbered among the heroic invaders of the realms of death at Cumae. The exploits of these Bronze Age heroes are partly confirmed by finds at Cumae and on the neighboring island of Ischia of Mycenaean potsherds, which testify to sporadic trading with the indigenous Oscans (Opici). But until the historical period Cumae, with its adjacent Campi Phlegraei ("The Fiery Plains"), was known to most men as the fabulous home of supernatural creatures and of the dead. Homer's story of Odysseus' visit to the realm of the dead, where he encounters the prophet Teiresias and the denizens of Hell, provided the authorized picture of Hades—although it was subjected to repeated variation—until Vergil adapted the account to an entirely novel scheme, charging it with Platonic, Stoic, and Orphic significance for a Roman audience.

Vergil's description of Aeneas' arrival at the beaches of Cumae is detailed and contemporary:

> And at long last they slid to the shore of Euboean Cumae.
> The bows are swung round to face the sea, the vessels made fast with
> The biting hook of their anchors, and the sheer sterns are lining
> The beach. Now, full of excitement, the heroes tumble out
> On the Hesperian shore: some look for seeds of fire
> Hidden in veins of flint, some scour the woods, the tangled
> Haunts of wild beasts, for fuel, and point to the springs they have found.
> But the god-fearing Aeneas made for the shrine where Apollo
> Sits throned on high, and that vasty cave—the deeply-recessed
> Crypt of the awe-inspiring Sibyl, to whom the god gives
> The power to see deep and prophesy what's to come.
> Now they passed into Diana's grove and the gold-roofed temple.
>
> (A. 6, 2–13. Day Lewis)

The shoreline, the Trojan's first significant landfall on the Tyrrhenian coastline, wins an enthusiastic response from the crew. Their zest must have been matched by the Greeks who founded their settlement at Cumae in 750 after a preliminary, no doubt exploratory, venture at Pithecusae on Ischia, the island whose acropolis confronts the Cumaean hill. The mainland site was favored for its fertility, its abundant fisheries, and, even more critical at this particular historical juncture, its mineral resources. The metalliferous hills of Campania had already supplied a modest bronze industry at pre-Hellenic Cumae, and the proximity to Etruscan iron and copper outlets was certainly a prime inducement for the establishment of a firm, defensible colony on the mainland. Vergil's references to Euboean and Chalcidic associations (A. 6, 2; 6, 17; 5, 3, 182) reflect the original founding parties both at Pithecusae (770) and at Cumae, for they came from Chalcis and Eretria, and probably from Euboean Cyme off the east coast of Greece.

The cultural importance of Cumae in the development of Italian architecture, sculpture, religion, philosophy, and literature must have been known to Vergil. The tradition that Tarquinius Priscus purchased the Sibylline books of prophecy for Rome was imbedded in Roman religious tradition. Although the Etruscans no doubt affected the development of alphabetic writing in their spheres of influence, Cumae played its role as well, and in fact the earliest evidences of alphabetic writing in Italy have emerged from the excavations at Pithecusae and Cumae. The religious legacy of the Cumaeans has also been debated, but there is some consensus that Apollo worship entered Rome during the fifth century, perhaps in a time of pestilence.

After a period of tyrannical rule under Aristodemus (505–485?), Cumae returned to its oligarchical form of government and found itself beset by Etruscan hostility, both commercial and military. Finally, after gaining the assistance of Hieron, tyrant of Syracuse, the fleets of Cumae and Syracuse met the allied attack of the Etruscans and Carthaginians and emerged victorious. Their victory of 474 was won off the shores of Cumae, where Aeneas anchored his ships. Pindar lauded the victory in his first Pythian Ode; Hieron dedicated a portion of the Etruscan spoils to Zeus at Olympia and to Apollo at Delphi. One priceless relic survives from the Olympian dedication, a bronze Etruscan helmet inscribed with a legend that honors Hieron and the Syracusans as victors at Cumae (Fig. 46).

The references to the Apollo temples (Day Lewis favors a Vergilian "poetic" plural in his version) again draw on Vergil's own experience, although they are charged with imaginative additions and more awesome associations than those which persisted in his time. There are two temple foundations, of Greek origins, on separate terraces of the Cumaean acropolis. The temples Vergil described as adorned with gilded roof tiles and, in one instance, with doors decorated with bas-reliefs by Daedalus, are sorry ruins today, but enough remains to reconstruct both with some assurance of accuracy. The lower temple, which has been identified positively by inscriptional evidence as Apolline, was reached by a Sacred Way and was located about halfway up the acropolis slope. The temple, which underwent rebuilding in Augustan and Christian times, was no doubt a Doric structure, hexastyle with 12 columns along the flanks, approximately 58½ feet wide and 99 feet long in the original Greek design. (Figs. 47, 48) The upper temple was contemporary with the lower, roughly about the mid-fifth century, though perhaps both surmount earlier sanctuaries of the sixth century. It was also a Doric peripteral building, hexastyle with 14 columns along the flanks, 81 feet wide and 130 feet long. Once again, Augustan and Christian rebuildings have done much to erase the Greek structures which Vergil would have his readers recapture beneath their Samnite and Roman successors. The upper temple underwent interior alterations and changes in the long narrow cella (with side-wall niches for images and dedications), and the addition of an extensive precinct wall greatly altered its original Doric severity. The lower temple, closer to the Sibyl's grotto though never in any way connected with it, underwent alterations of a major order: the orientation was changed, a colonnaded porch was added to the side which had overlooked the Forum, and this minor axis was adapted to accommodate a triple-cella arrangement, modelled perhaps after the Augustan temple of Apollo on the Palatine. These repairs and renovations at Cumae may be considered part of Augustus' program to restore and revive the ancient cults of Italy. Diana-Hecate, central to the cults of Cumae and Avernus, had long-standing associations with the peoples of Italy but was nowhere more revered than at Cumae and Aricia. Apollo's cult, though less popular at Rome because of its foreign origins, was of central importance to the policy of Augustus, who strove to center public piety on the deity to whom, as we have seen, he attributed his success against Sextus Pompey and more recently, against Antony and Cleopatra at Actium.

When Helenus gave Aeneas instructions on the safest sea route to Italy, he also gave firm rules for Aeneas' consultation with the Sibyl at Cumae, rules which Vergil has Aeneas recall when he appears at the grotto of Apollo's prophetess:

> Now when you are safely there, close to the city of Cumae
> And the haunted lake Avernus deep in a soughing wood,
> You will find an ecstatic, a seeress, who in her antre communicates
> Destiny, committing to leaves the mystic messages.
> Whatever runes that virgin has written upon the leaves
> She files away in her cave, arranged in the right order.
> There they remain untouched, just as she put them away:
> But suppose that the hinge turns and a light draught blows through the
> 　door,

Stirs the frail leaves and shuffles them, never thereafter cares she
To catch them as they flutter about the cave, to restore
Their positions or reassemble their runes: so men who have come to
Consult the Sibyl depart no wiser, hating the place.
Here you must not grudge time spent, although it delays you—
However impatient your friends may grow, however fine
The weather for sailing, however strongly the sea calls you—
Time spent in approaching the Sibyl, asking an oracle of her,
Praying that she will graciously open her mouth and prophesy.

(A. 3, 441–57. Day Lewis)

Vergil is precise in his description of the oracular delivery:

There's a huge cave hollowed out from the flank of Cumae's hill;
A hundred wide approaches it has, a hundred mouths
From which there issue a hundred voices, the Sibyl's answers.
They had reached its threshold when "Time it is to ask your destiny"
The Sibyl cried, "For lo! the god is with me." And speaking,
There by the threshold, her features, her colour were all at once
Different, her hair flew wildly about; her breast was heaving,
Her fey heart swelled in ecstasy; larger than life she seemed,
More than mortal her utterance: the god was close and breathing
His inspiration through her.

(A. 6, 42–51. Day Lewis)

Because Aeneas is slow to perform the requisite vows and prayers, the somewhat irascible Deiphobe makes urgent demands so that the doors may open for her prophecy. Thereafter, as the nightmarish sequence continues, the hundred massive mouths of her dwelling open of their own accord, and the answers of the prophetess burst forth (A. 6, 51–101). Her voice resounds through the cavern as she wraps truth in obscurity, following the long-established procedure at Delphi and elsewhere in the Greek world.

The Sibyl's grotto was excavated and identified in 1932 (Fig. 49). The long "dromos" is reminiscent of the long entrance halls to Etruscan tombs and of the false-vaulted galleries in the monumental fortification walls of Tiryns (post-1250 B.C.). The trapezoidal passage is cut through the volcanic acropolis rock on its western side. The dimensions are awe-inspiring and testify to the engineering genius of the builders: 431 feet 4 inches long, 7 feet 9 inches wide, and an average of 16 feet 4 inches in height. Six lateral fenestrations provide light and air for the underground gallery, and it has been suggested that they were originally fitted with wooden doors or shutters. Halfway down the inner side of the grotto and directly opposite one of the lateral openings the passage opens into three large rock-cut tanks which probably served as the ritual baths of the prophetess. At the end of the gallery a triple complex opens up, a central recess where the Sibyl chanted her prophecies, a side recess at the last of the six lateral openings, and an inner room which has a vestibule with podia on either side and an entranceway which is lower than the central vaulting (Fig. 50). The marked similarity between the Cumaean grotto and the Etruscan tomb passages inclines one to believe that the design and the engineering may be Etruscan—perhaps the product of captive or enlisted Etruscan builders after the naval victory at Cumae in 474 B.C. After the religious rebuilding program was well advanced or nearly completed, the earlier grotto was probably enlarged and formalized. New fortifications also appeared on the acropolis and probably also in the lower city. The citadel wall was fashioned from squared blocks cut from the local tufa and laid without mortar. The walls had rusticated facings with drafted edges which are characteristic of late fifth-century building techniques and are probably best assigned to the Samnite occupation (post-421 B.C.).

The Greek city of Cumae, after three centuries of history, was overrun by the Samnites shortly after the fall of Capua (423 B.C.); resident Samnite sympathizers who had infiltrated during the fifth century no doubt contributed to its defeat. Some of the Cumaean refugees fled to Neapolis and found asylum in Palaeopolis—the original core of that city; others were executed or enslaved, and the rest were absorbed into the Oscan system (Diod. Sic. 12, 76, 4; Vell. Pat. 1, 14).

The new governmental system favored Samnite "democratic" forms instead of the long-established "oligarchic" ways of Hellenic Cumae. The immigration of Samnites into Cumae after the conquest required expansion beyond the old city limits, and no doubt along Hippodamian gridiron town-planning design. Greek religious practices certainly persisted, and the cults of Apollo and of the Sibylline oracle were operated on a profitable basis as before. The lower town probably housed at least one new Samnite deity, Jupiter Flagius (Flazzus or Flazius?), perhaps identical with Jupiter Fulgor (the god of lightning). The Samnite temple on the western edge of the agora, or civic center, beneath the acropolis was provided with an immense platform, based on molded tufa foundation blocks (some with Greek quarrying marks, suggesting that the Greeks provided the labor) and covering an area 186 feet long by 94 feet wide. The temple seems to date from the fourth century B.C.[6] Alterations were made to the Sibyl's grotto at the inner end, and the last building of the Samnite period may have been the early amphitheater in the neighborhood of the modern Villa Vergiliana, overseas center of the Vergilian Society of America since 1937. (Fig. 51)

Vergil's description of the grotto, once identified with the pseudo-Sibyl's grotto on the shores of Lake Avernus, later with the underground gallery in the lowermost depths of the Cumaean acropolis, is an expansion and an exaggeration of the actual cavern but still close enough to the reality to substantiate its proper identification. The reference to the effect of the sudden gusts of wind on the untidy oracular leaves (perhaps of metal or some lighter material in the shape of palm leaves), the multiple mouths—not one hundred but seven (including the main aperture to the antrum)—and the details of threshold and double doors are all careful testimony to the original form of the grotto or of its state when Vergil visited. Elsewhere Vergil assigns the altar to the forecourt of the oracular zone, and he implies that the Sibyl prophesied deep within the cavern:

> But the Sibyl, not yet submissive to Phoebus, there in her cavern
> Prodigiously struggled, still trying to shake from her brain the powerful
> God who rode her: but all the more he exhausted her foaming
> Mouth and mastered her wild heart, breaking her in with a firm hand.
> And now the hundred immense doors of the place flew open
> Of their own accord, letting out the Sibyl's inspired responses.
>
> (A. 6, 77–82. Day Lewis)

There is clear indication that Aeneas stopped at the entrance to the grotto (A. 6, 45) and that his entreaties to the priestess-prophetess were addressed from altars without specific notice of the powers to whom the altars were dedicated—a procedure which seems to accord

well with the pagan approach to worship, which was not congregational
and only rarely called for or permitted the entry of the profane into the
sanctuary proper.

A notice survives from ca. 250 A.D. with the details of a visit to the
grotto by two Christian tourists: "We inspected a place at Cumae where
we found a large 'basilica' excavated from a single rock, a magnificent
and awesome work. There the Sibyl gave her prophecies, according to
those who claimed to have inherited the account from their ancestors. In
the centre of the basilica we were shown three tanks excavated from the
same rock. They maintained that these were regularly filled with water
and that the Sibyl bathed in them. Then, after she had put on her long
robe again, she would retire into the innermost room of the basilica
which was also hewn from the same rock. Then, they stated, she would
take her seat on a raised platform in the centre of this chamber and
would pronounce her oracles."[5]

In Vergil's time, according to his own announcement, "the last age of
Cumaean prophecy had come round." (*Eclogue* 4, 1) The oracle was
moribund during the first century B.C., and enjoyed only a brief recuper-
ation under Augustus. The difficulties of the period of the Second
Triumvirate brought about numerous alterations and depredations at
Cumae. Besides the oracle's providing funds for the Triumvirate's military designs, an almost inevitable recourse in time of emergency, there
were startling structural alterations in the city. Lucius Cocceius Auctus,
the freedman architect and engineer of Agrippa and the triumvirate,
who built the tunnel through Mons Pausilypus at Naples, cut a tunnel
some two hundred yards in length from the Cumaean forum area to
the heart of the acropolis. (Fig. 52) This tunnel was linked with another
even more spectacular which ran through Mons Grillus and linked
Cumae with the shores of Lake Avernus. Both tunnels were cut to
facilitate rapid communications between the garrison and port at
Cumae and the shipbuilding base at Lake Avernus. The acropolis
tunnel, at one time mistakenly identified with the grotto of the Sibyl,
opened off a monumental vestibule, a vast reception area with steps
leading to the entrance levels of the acropolis interior. The vestibule was
lined with reticulate brick facing and had four large statue-niches which
may have been designed to accommodate, initially at least, the portrait

statues of the triumvirs and Agrippa. The tunnel was provided with openings for ventilation and daylight along its entire length, and an enormous reservoir or granary was excavated from the tufa rock towards its eastern end. Reliefs representing the axes and wedges which were used in the construction of the tunnel appear on the roof at the lower acropolis entry. The grotto of the Sibyl also went through alterations as part of the remilitarization of the area: the triple bath was lined with waterproof cement and served as a reservoir for the troops stationed on the hill. The water was brought to the basins by means of a wall aqueduct.

Vergil's creative imagination almost certainly associated these and other new tunnel constructions in the Cumae-Avernus area, labyrinthine and mysterious, with the Daedalic and historical phases of Cumae's history. His respectful, perhaps wistful, description of the antique site, with its hallowed buildings and cult associations, may very well have prompted Augustus to undertake massive rehabilitation at the site after Actium. Certainly Vergil's extensive acquaintance with the ancient citadel made his account of Aeneas' encounter both circumstantial and exact.

Later literary references suggest that the attempt to resuscitate the cult center and the community was fruitless. Cumae rapidly entered a period of stagnation, such that Juvenal could refer to Cumae as a ghost town in his lifetime, and Petronius and Ovid both suggest that the oracle was close to oblivion.

> I [Trimalchio] saw the Sibyl at Cumae with my own eyes; she was hanging in a bottle and when the boys asked her in Greek 'Sibyl, what do you want?', she gave her response in Greek, 'I want to die.'
>
> (Petronius, *Satyricon*, 48–9)

Although Vergil witnessed the brave attempt at reconstruction, he must have sensed, with regret, the gradual disintegration of the ancient center, already eight centuries old. The amphitheater, as large as that at Pompeii, the inevitable theater and the baths, the decaying sanctuaries around the freshly refurbished Apollo temples, must have catered increasingly to a tourist and summer resident population, to the superstitious farmers of the area, and to poets, like Vergil, and later Statius and Silius Italicus, who venerated the classical background of Italy.

The topography of the Campi Phlegraei was obviously known directly by Vergil throughout its entire area, which includes Cumae, the bay of Puteoli, and the Neapolitan shoreline. The most popular association with the Campi Phlegraei was the smithy of Vulcan, which the ancients located in the volcanic region of Solfatara overlooking Puteoli. The area remains active today and still emits steam, bubbling mud, lava, and sulphurous fumes which carry as far as Puteoli and support the etymology of the place-name (from the Latin *puteus,* "well," or "spring"). Such fiery and mysterious manifestations led the ancients to place the battle of the Gods and Giants here, and above all to locate the forges of Vulcan's heavy industry in this rumbling, hissing, smoking crater (cf. Petronius, *Satyricon* 67–73; Strabo 5, 4, 6). (Fig. 53)

According to the tradition, Hercules, en route to Greece with the cattle of Geryon, constructed a causeway or dike, about a mile long, across the bay of Puteoli, connecting the site of the later commercial harbor with the shore of Baiae. Strabo (5, 4, 6) described the embankment, which separated Lake Lucrinus from the bay, as broad as a wagon road. On an equally heroic scale were the modifications which Agrippa made to the Via Herculanea during the struggles with Sextus Pompey. The legendary highway was pierced with an opening towards the Baian end to admit ships into the shallow water of Lake Lucrinus and an even more impressive canal was dug to link Lake Lucrinus with Lake Avernus.[6] The new naval base could take advantage of the thickly forested slopes of Avernus and also enjoy the shipping facilities, supplies, and protection of nearby Puteoli and Cumae. Vergil extols the engineering skill demonstrated in the Portus Julius, as the new harbor complex was named, in honor of Octavian, although he does not mention the architect, who was the omnipresent Lucius Cocceius Auctus:

> Shall I tell of Italy's harbors, the breakwaters imposed on Lucrinus and the sea which thunders loudly in resentment, where the Julian water echoes far and wide as the seawater pours back and the Tyrrhenian sea races through the channels into Avernus?
>
> (G. 2, 161–4)

The canal, constructed in 37 B.C., is still visible, but the harbor complex was soon rendered useless by rapid silting in the outer basin of shallow Lake Lucrinus and had to be abandoned in favor of a similar but more practicable crater complex at nearby Cape Misenum. In prospect of his encounter with the shade of Anchises, Aeneas is advised of harbors at Cumae and at Avernus, and the latter may have particular reference to the Portus Julius, which combined Lake Lucrinus and Lake Avernus into a single complex.

Before the militarization of the area Lake Lucrinus had been a vacation site for C. Sergius Orata, M. Marius Gratidianus, M. Terentius Varro, and M. Tullius Cicero. Its salt-water fish was always a prized item in the epicure's regimen, and the oysters of Lucrinus were famous. Although the waters were fished and developed earlier, C. Sergius Orata seems to have been a particularly successful speculator in the development of the shores. Lucrinus was his source of lucre as he improved and enlarged the oyster beds, and built and sold luxuriously appointed villas along the shores. His combination of real estate development and oyster trade won him notoriety and a fortune (Pliny, *N. H.* 9, 79, 168; Val. Max., 9, 1, 1 ff.). Cicero's Cumanum, an elegant mansion which the statesman had purchased in 56 B.C. after his return from exile, was almost certainly located somewhere between the lake and the sea. The villa had a portico and landscaped garden, and Cicero called it the Academy after the prototype associated with Plato in Athens (Pliny, *N. H.* 31, 7). There, feasting on the library of his neighbor, Faustus Cornelius Sulla, son of the dictator, and on the delicious oysters of Lake Lucrinus, Cicero lived in productive retreat and composed his *Academica*. He enjoyed the quiet and semi-isolation of his pleasure villa, but he also throve on the proximity to Puteoli, with its bustling commercial harbor, and to Naples. (Fig. 80) His Cumanum welcomed many celebrated visitors—Pompey the Great, who lived in the vicinity during a period of convalescence; Lucullus, the multi-millionaire, in grandiose retreat at Naples; and most trying of all, Julius Caesar, who on one occasion transferred with his official retinue from the nearby villa of Philippus to dine with Cicero (Cicero, *ad. Att.* 4, 10; 13, 52). Gourmets, statesmen in seclusion, intelligentsia and pleasure-seekers saw their lovely mansions reflected in the glassy waters of Lucrinus—forecast of the licentious scene which Seneca later deplored with Stoic censure: "a pleasure resort . . . with adulterous women sailing by, multitudinous craft painted with various colors, roses drifting over the lake, midnight wrangles of serenaders" (Seneca, *Epist.* 51, 1). In 79 B.C. the dictator Sulla settled there to hunt and fish, and to finish his *Memoirs.* (Appian, *B.C.* 1, 12, 104; Plutarch, *Sulla* 37, 3; Cicero, *ad. Att.* 4, 10). This surprise retirement must have caused a tremor of excitement in the area. One may perhaps reasonably suppose that he bequeathed his property and library to his son, Faustus Cornelius Sulla, bibliophile and connoisseur of the arts.[7]

Nearby Lake Avernus (Fig. 54) lacked the pleasurable associations of Lucrinus. From time immemorial it was feared and reverenced as the entry to Hades, and the links of this ancient volcanic lake with the past were of almost incalculable importance for Vergil. Strabo was also deeply impressed, and his testimony on Avernus is most valuable, although it poses problems beyond our compass, the chronology and identification of the Cimmerians:

> Men before my time regularly identified the setting of the Homeric Nekyia [*Odyssey* XI] with Avernus and assigned the adventures of Odysseus to the site . . . Avernus is enclosed by steep overhanging ridges on all sides except the ship entrance. Today these hills have been heavily worked over, whereas formerly they were thickly shaded with a wild impenetrable forest of large trees. Local residents added the further fiction that birds flying over it fell into the water, asphyxiated by the mists which rose from it as is the case with all Plutonia [i.e., entries to Hades]. People also used to imagine that this was a Plutonia and that the Cimmerians had dwelt there. Only those who had completed the preliminary sacrifices and propitiated the powers of the underworld ever sailed into Avernus, and priests who instructed in such matters accepted remuneration for their advisory services. A spring of fresh water is located there by the sea but everyone abstained from drinking it since they regarded it as the water of the river Styx. The oracle was located somewhere nearby. Men also deduced from the neighboring hot springs and the Acherusian swamp that the river Pyriphlegethon was there. When Ephorus [fourth century B.C.] states that the area was Cimmerian property he claims that they lived in underground dwellings which they called *argillae* [i.e., clay-beds], that they communicated with one another by means of tunnels, and that they admitted visitors to the oracle which was established deep underground. They earned their living from mining and from consultations

and from the ruler who gave them allowances. There was an ancestral custom among those who lived in the environs of the oracle that no one should see the sun but should only leave the caverns at night time. For this reason the poet Homer has remarked about them that "the sun never shines down on them with his rays" [Odyssey 11, 15]. At a later date, according to Ephorus, they were destroyed by a ruler when an oracular response disappointed him. The oracle still survives although it has moved to another location [at Cumae].

These are the tales my ancestors told, but nowadays, since the forest has been cut down around Avernus by Agrippa and the countryside has been built up and the underground tunnel has been cut from Avernus to Cumae, all these tales have been revealed as mythical. However, the Cocceius who engineered the aforementioned tunnel and also the one from Dicearchia [Puteoli] near Baiae to Naples, probably subscribed to the Cimmerian tradition already related, and may have regarded it as an ancestral custom that roads in this area should proceed through tunnels.

(Strabo, 5, 4, 5)

Strabo's remarks recall the Mycenaean and probably the pre-Italic tradition regarding the lake. The heroic descent into the netherworld is a pattern which Vergil adopts with a full awareness of the epic counterparts to his Trojan hero. Charon cites earlier invaders of the world of the dead—Hercules, Theseus, and Pirithous; and there were others—Odysseus, Castor and Pollux, and Orpheus. Differently motivated and protected, these heroes found inspiration and an initiation into a new life through the underworld experience, and Aeneas was similarly protected and directed.

Throughout his account of the preparations and actual descent Vergil provides a detailed recital of movements, procedures, and confrontations which provide reality of setting and engagement. From the outset there is evident concern for setting—awesome, terrific, and nightmarish.

Avernus, in every Vergilian citation, seems to imply the lake as well as the infernal regions. Helenus' instructions to Aeneas at Buthrotum are lucid: he is to consult the Sibyl at Cumae (A. 3, 441–51) in the neighborhood of sanctified lakes and Avernus' rustling woods, no longer extant in Vergil's time. Anchises' shade is even more specific.

In Latium you must fight off a people both hard and rough
In their way of life. But first you must go to the home
Of Dis, down below, and then meet me in deepest Avernus.
For godless Tartarus, abode of the sorrowing shades,
Does not hold me; I dwell in Elysium and share the mild councils
Of those who are just. The chaste Sibyl will lead you there
When you in your sacrifice shed much blood of black cattle.

(A. 5, 754–60. Lind)

When Aeneas appears with Achates before the Sibyl Deiphobe, who stands like some tragic Iphigenia in the temple precinct, he requests directions, for there are several approaches to the underworld—Cumae perhaps, the Acherusian Swamp nearby (mod. Lago del Fusaro), or Avernus itself. The Acherusian Swamp suggests itself as the proper entry at the outset:

I have one request: since here is reputed to be the gateway
Of the Underworld and the dusky marsh from Acheron's overflow,
May it befall me to go into my dear father's
Presence—open the gates and show me the way!

(A. 6, 106–9. Day Lewis)

The ancients located the overflow of the River of Woe beneath the Cumaean citadel towards modern Torregaveta on the Tyrrhenian shore. The lake was once part of the defense system of Greek Cumae but in Vergil's time was a villa resort and vacation site.

Aeneas expresses concern that his entry into the Underworld by the stream of Acheron may be barred or be impenetrable for his mortal person. Deiphobe replies with precise detail:

Trojan, son of Anchises, child of divine blood, the descent by Avernus is easy; night and day the door of dark Dis stands open; but to retrace your steps, to escape to the upper air, herein lies the task, here the struggle. Only a few, through Jupiter's impartial love, or men exalted to heaven through their own glowing courage, the sons of gods, have achieved it. In between there lies a forest, the Cocytus winds darkly around the region. However, if great love inspires your purpose and your desire is strong enough to cross the Stygian waters twice, though you are eager to yield to such a senseless quest, learn what you must go through beforehand. Hidden in the enveloping shade of a tree there is a golden bough, with golden leaves and a strong stem, sacred to Proserpina. An entire forest conceals this bough and shadowy dark gorges enclose it. But no man may enter the land beneath the earth until he has plucked that gold-leaf bough from its tree.

(A. 6, 125–141)

Following the proper burial of his lost companion Misenus (see pp. 218–9). Aeneas carries out the instructions of the Sibyl to the letter. After the appropriate sacrifices he and his prophetess-'cicerone' invade the Underworld:

> A deep, deep cave there was, its mouth enormously gaping,
> Shingly, protected by the dark lake and the forest gloom:
> Above it no winged creatures could ever wing their way
> With impunity, so lethal was the miasma which
> Went fuming up from its black throat to the vault of heaven:
> Wherefore the Greeks called it Avernus, the Birdless Place.
>
> But listen!—at the very first crack of dawn, the ground
> Underfoot began to mutter, the woody ridges to quake,
> And a baying of hounds was heard through the half-light:
>   the goddess was coming,
> Hecate. The Sibyl cried:—Away! Now stand away,
> You uninitiated ones, and clear the whole grove!

(A. 6, 237–42; 255–60. Day Lewis)

The most critical experience in Aeneas' entire career befalls him in the confines of Lake Avernus and the underground passages of the defunct volcano. The crater measures today about two miles in circumference and is over two hundred feet deep. It is fed by mineral springs and is brackish to the taste. The remains of a large Roman bath on the east side of the lake, dating from Augustan times, were badly damaged during the birth of Monte Nuovo by volcanic action in September 1538. The octagonal building has a circular interior, 120 feet in diameter, with large arched windows, and its arrangements are comparable to the examples at Baiae. The building probably served as a swimming pool, the pool fed by the hot springs which gushed from the crater slopes. A communications tunnel, the so-called Sibyl's grotto, runs for 220 yards between Avernus and Lucrinus and was equipped with an apartment for the marine detachment stationed there. A more impressive tunnel, counterpart to the tunnel which ran from the heart of the Cumae acropolis into the civic center (see p. 208), runs through Mons Grillus to Lake Avernus. Like the acropolis tunnel, the one through Mons Grillus was obviously part of the overall militarization of the area ca. 37 B.C., designed to expedite and safeguard the movement of troops and supplies between the citadel at Cumae and the Portus Julius. The tunnel, which opened on the western slopes of Lake Avernus, was 1100 yards long and permitted vehicles to pass when travelling in opposite directions. Light and air entered through vents in its vaulted roof. An aqueduct ran down the north side of the Avernus grotto to augment the water supply of the marine base at Portus Julius.[8]

> Dimly through the shadows and dark solitudes they wended,
> Through the void domiciles of Dis, the bodiless regions:
> Just as, through fitful moonbeams, under the moon's thin light,
> A path lies in a forest, when Jove has palled the sky
> With gloom, and the night's blackness has bled the world of colour.
>
> (A. 6, 268–72. Day Lewis)

The account of the hero's descent in all probability owes much of its character to Vergil's experience with the tunnels, old and new, in the environs of Portus Julius. Conway once suggested that the *largior aether* and *sol suus* of Elysium may be an illustration of the comparable experience of ancient and modern travellers between Naples and Fuorigrotta (the district "outside the grotto," the tunnel beneath Posillipo) and between Cumae and the Portus Avernus. Vergil's description of Elysian Fields is rhapsodic:

> What largesse of bright air, clothing the vales in dazzling
> Light, is here! This land has a sun and stars of its own.
>
> (A. 6, 640–1. Day Lewis)

The traveller emerging from the tunnels of the Campi Phlegraei into the comparatively remote and silent "fields of light" experiences a strange sensation which cannot be unique to the twentieth century. When one emerges from the twilight of the tunnels ordinary daylight assumes a new color, and the whole landscape seems to present a sharper, clearer aspect.

The palace of Dis and the interior regions of Hades, Tartarus and Elysium, and the rivers of Hell are visualized with extraordinary attention to organization and detail. The House of Hades is a carefully designed counterpart to the Greco-Roman-style house of the upper world, as tactfully and graphically designed as a Vitruvian "domus."[9] It resembles the more elaborate houses unearthed at Pompeii, a spacious structure with atrium court, stables, salons, and cubicula, and a fearsome janitor in the shape of the three-headed Cerberus. Since Campanian Avernus is riverless, Vergil was compelled to confine Styx, Acheron, Cocytus, and Phlegython—all with peculiar volcanic associations of pitch and fire—to the underworld. Even in the depths of Hades, Vergil's ordered picture remains intact. The nightmarish bogies which Aeneas confronts in the House of Hades—Death, Agony, and Sleep, the Furies and mad Civil Strife, Centaurs, Scyllas, Briareus and the Lernaean Hydra, Gorgons, Harpies, and triple-bodied Geryon—may reflect the allegorical art of the age and the demonic subject matter of Etruscan tombs at second-century Tarquinia and elsewhere. The massive sculptures of Scylla attacking the ship of Odysseus found in the recently excavated cave at Sperlonga (anc. Spelunca) may be an enlarged version of a sculptural or pictorial work used earlier in an Augustan milieu. (Fig. 55)

Tartarus is as carefully organized as a police-department line-up or groups of criminals awaiting trial in the Roman basilicas. Ten types of criminals emerge in Tartarus: (1) religious: stock types of impiety (580–607); (2) domestic: those who despised their brothers (608); (3) parent-killers (609); (4) social: dishonest patrons (609); (5) misers (610 f., "most numerous of all are these"); (6) adulterers (612); (7) political: those who broke faith in civil war (612 f.); (8) one who sold his country and brought in a tyrant (621 f.); (9) the venal politician (622); (10) the incestuous (623). The categories of Elysium's residents are five in number: (1) those who gave their lives for their country (660); (2) pure priests (661); (3) noble poets (662); (4) inventors (663); (5) men of memorable character (664). So Vergil details the eternally damned and the everlastingly blest spirits in Hades, and the sins against Roman law are especially reprehensible.[10]

Cape Misenum, once part of the suzerainty of Cumae, was a safer anchorage for ships than the exposed shoreline under the Cumaean citadel, and it became Rome's prime naval base in Vergil's lifetime.

(Fig. 56) After the harbor facilities at Lake Avernus proved unserviceable because of silting, Agrippa transferred the naval base to the natural basin on the inner side of Mount Misenum, and once again, by means of a specially constructed canal cut through the tufaceous neck of land, united the outer basin with an almost landlocked inner basin. The freedom from silting and the easy access to the open sea, with the impressive barrier of Mount Misenum to protect and mark the harbor, made the site a distinctly attractive and eminently successful choice. The inner harbor, called Mare Morto today, served as winter quarters for the imperial fleet, as a refitting center and construction site, while the outer harbor served as reception area for incoming vessels and as a training area for the oarsmen and marines. The harbor was completed in time to permit Agrippa to make his naval preparations against Antony and Cleopatra here, and the ultimate victory, in September of 31 B.C., ushered in the Augustan Peace. Vergil's presence in the Neapolitan environs during the troubled period between 37 and 31 permitted him to see the impressive and somewhat portentous developments in the area. Just as his tribute to the Portus Julius was inspired by a growing respect for the Julian arrangements in the area, his inclusion of Misenum in the *Aeneid* no doubt owes much to Augustan connections with the site.

Misenum (Greek, "odious," "hateful") was a natural landfall for Aeneas as he ploughed the seas towards Cumae and Ostia. But Vergil delays Aeneas' visit to the commanding promontory until after his pilgrimage to the Sibyl's grotto and the Apollo temples at Cumae. Aeneas learned that the Sibyl would not escort him to the Underworld until he had completed the requisite funeral rites for the drowned Misenus, whose absence from his company had evidently not yet been detected by Aeneas. The discovery of the drowned mariner provides a moment of considerable pathos. Like the death of Palinurus, which is demanded—*unum pro multis*—by Neptune to guarantee the safe landing of the Trojans, Misenus' death seems to be a prerequisite of Aeneas' descent into and return from Hades. Vergil provides a detailed account of the cremation-burial rites of Misenus. The piety of the leader to a comrade dead in action seems to serve as symbolic preparation for Aeneas' own entry into the world of the dead and for his final confrontation with his past and his future in the presence of Anchises.

Vergil's account, here much abbreviated, emphasizes two local aspects or phenomena:

> But to-day, as he sent his horn's notes ringing over the sea,
> Most rashly challenging the gods to a musical contest,
> Jealous Triton caught him off guard—if we may credit
> The story—and plunged him down in the surf among those rocks.

> Aeneas the true now raised over his friend a massive
> Tomb, laying on it the man's own arms, his oar and his trumpet,
> Beneath that high headland which takes its name from him,
> Misenus, and preserves his fame unto all ages.
> (A. 6, 171–4; 232–5. Day Lewis)

The legend, part of a larger tradition which assigned the drowning of Baios, Odysseus' shipmate, to Baiae, finds its Vergilian inspiration in the topography of the site. The impressive configuration of the cape, some three hundred feet high, does bear a striking similarity to a monumental tumulus or mound burial, as impressive as the Etruscan mounds at Cerveteri and the Phrygian mounds at Gordium. The association with the trumpeter is also perhaps suggested by the sound of the breezes which today still rip into the caves and grasses of the cape and produce a sound which might be equated with those produced by a Triton's conch shell or a trumpet.

But there may be another, even more material inspiration for the lengthy recital of the burial rites of Misenus. Seamen of the Praetorian Fleet at Misenum were regularly buried at the site, judging by the plentiful remains of sepulchral texts relating to such men. The majority of the Imperial sailors were born in foreign parts, most of them in Alexandria or in Thrace. The fleet offered husky men an energetic outlet and some relief, too, from the oppressive poverty of backward rural zones of Italy and of the Empire. But a more important connection from a literary standpoint, and secure too in its locale, was the much-lamented death of Marcellus at nearby Baiae. (Fig. 57) When Vergil introduces Roman burial rites into the heroic funeral of Misenus, one must reflect on the passing of Marcellus. Propertius, Vergil's contemporary, brings Marcellus' death into direct association with the Misenus episode, an association which was probably inspired by Vergil's account (Prop. 3, 18, 1–16). The death of Misenus, with its poignant associations with Hector and with the Trojan past, is by Vergil's indirect reference to Marcellus brought into the context of the suffering felt when the newly consecrated Augustan order was touched with a disaster both universal and personal.

Nearby Bauli (mod. Bacoli) never claimed the opulent clientele which flocked to Baiae, but it did house some prominent persons and its shoreline must have resembled the *litus aureum,* the gold-coast of Baiae. The place name—"cattle-stalls"—was linked with Hercules' adventure with the cattle of Geryon.

The most startling archaeological discovery at Bauli was the Piscina Mirabilis, the "marvelous pool," or cistern, excavated out of a volcanic hill to house fresh water for the Augustan naval base at nearby Misenum. (Fig. 58) The dimensions of the reservoir are staggering: 230 feet long, 84 feet wide, and 49 feet high. Forty-eight pillars, arranged four abreast in twelve rows, rise from floor level to the roof far above. This vast underground cistern, excavated as recently as 1927, also has windows in the long side walls, and two entrances at the opposite extremities of the cistern with stairs leading down to the floor level. Apertures set at regular intervals in the vaulted roof permitted the removal of water and detritus by waterwheels or pulley and bucket and the entry of water by means of aqueduct or rainfall. The capacity of the vast tank was 2,775,000 gallons (12,600 cubic meters), striking evidence of the engineering capacity of Agrippa's architect and craftsmen, as well as of the menace to Italian security felt in the face of Pompey and later of Antony and Cleopatra.

Baiae, on the Bay of Pozzuoli (anc. Sinus Puteolanus), provides Vergil with his unique architectural simile; Trojan Bitias, one of Turnus' more horrendous foes, is slain by a heavy projectile and his gigantic fall is likened to villa and causeway construction at Baiae:

> That fall was like when a stone pier, constructed from huge, shaped
>   blocks
> Of masonry and built out into the sea in the bay of
> Baiae, near Cumae, collapses: the wall of it falls away, dragging
> A mass of rubble behind, slaps the water and sinks to the bottom;
> The sea is all in a welter, black sludge oozes up to the surface.
>
>   (A. 9, 711–4. Day Lewis)

The detailed picture reflects eyewitness experience. The volcanic sand on the floor of the bay still clouds and darkens the water when there is unusual activity there.

Greek myth assigned the place-name to Baios, the drowned crewman of Odysseus, although Vergil, as we have seen, preferred to accent Misenum with the more dramatic and poignant parallel incident. Baiae in Vergil's time was a Fort Lauderdale, a Torquay, a Monaco, for the wealthy and the sensation-seekers. The marvelous view, the abundant sulphur springs, and the attractive lido made Baiae the ideal resort of the vacationing Romans. The shores were lined with pretentious villas, with peristyle courts, landscape gardens, seaside porticoes and extensive piers, artificial fishpools and epicurean oyster-beds. Pompeian and Stabian wall paintings repeatedly mirror the lovely "Renaissance" villas, with their porticoes, replete with statuary and light-catching oscilla, extending out into the bay. (Fig. 59)

The charms and license of Baian society attract considerable notice in the writings of the Golden Age, and among the visitors, if not the habitués, were Vergil—for reasons of health—Catullus and his "Lesbia," Propertius and his "Cynthia," Cicero, Horace, and a host of wealthy or gain-seeking freedmen, patricians, equestrians, and panderers to the wealthy. Pavilions and palaces crowded in on the therapeutic facilities of the site, which began to attract Roman visitors from the second century B.C., no doubt to enjoy a facility already developed by the original Greek settlers from Cumae and Neapolis. Strabo's assertion that "at Baiae another city has come into being with one mansion built on top of another, a community not inferior to Puteoli in size," (5, 4, 5) has been strikingly supported by recent excavations at the site. Besides the great domical bath buildings, the earliest of which, the Bath of "Mercury," dates from Augustan times, there are residential units set into the terraced hillside, some of them with single rooms, others consisting of several expertly designed chambers, with an eastern exposure which permitted the residents to enjoy the morning sunshine and the magnificent sweep of the bay at all hours. There are long flights of steps and ramps which connect the lower pool and bay-side levels with the topmost suites. Cisterns, floor aqueducts, and the proud line of the Aqua Serino bringing fresh water from Naples supplied the residents with the proper amenity. Horace testifies to the efficacious appointments of Baiae which archaeologists have only recently unearthed. He refers to Antonius Musa, the court physician of the Julian family, whose hot- and cold-water therapy had won him fortune's favors. The cold-water prescription once required Horace to absent himself from the steaming springs and baths of Baiae, and the local entrepreneurs were resentful:

> The community complains at having its myrtle groves abandoned, its sulphur baths neglected, when they are renowned for eradicating chronic rheumatic attacks. The town resent invalids who have the temerity to plunge head and stomach under cold-water springs at Clusium [Chiusi] or make for Gabii [Castiglione] and the wintry zones.
>
> (*Epist.* 15, 3–9)

Underwater searches have revealed traces of the port town, streets, houses, and harbor-works of Baiae beneath the bay off Punta dell' Epitaffio; the search must eventually yield tangible evidence of the porticus-villas along the shore.[11]

Baiae was everyone's goal, at least once in a lifetime, but it was especially favored by the jaded members of Rome's political echelons, and by the political leaders. Cornelia, mother of the Gracchi, daughter of Scipio Africanus, lived like a Venetian duchess along the shore; Gaius Marius, L. Cornelius Sulla, Gnaeus Pompey, and Julius Caesar found the charms of Baiae congenial enough to maintain permanent residences there.

Caesar's villa, whose site is popularly identified with that of the fortress-castle of Don Pedro of Aragon, sixteenth-century Spanish viceroy, was no doubt a legacy of his aunt, wife of Marius, and it came finally into the possession of Octavian. The latter, who came frequently to Baiae for his health and to find a measure of isolation, must have found much to relish in the Neapolitan environs. His easy familiarity with Greek made him a welcome if awesome visitor in the bilingual society of the area around the Bay of Naples. However, the villa at Baiae was ultimately to witness Augustus' greatest personal tragedy, the death of Marcellus. Vergil's tribute to the heir of Augustus, an *In Memoriam* composed in 23, made a deep impression on Octavia, the youth's mother, at a private reading. The death of Marcellus awakened universal mourning:

Alas, poor youth! If only you could escape your harsh fate.
Marcellus you shall be. Give me armfuls of lilies
That I may scatter their shining blooms and shower these gifts
At least upon the dear soul, all to no purpose though
Such kindness be.

> (*Aen.* 6, 883–6. Day Lewis.
> cf. Propertius 3, 18, 1–16;
> and Dio Cass., 53, 30.)

Procida and Ischia play no major role in Aeneas' adventures and the poet gives only brief notice to them. Procida (anc. Prochyta, "off-pouring") with its barren neighbor, Vivara, lies four miles off Cape Misenum and well within sight of Ischia. Anxious to consolidate the Trojan tradition in Campania, some local mythographers sought desperately to assign Prochyta as nurse to Aeneas' family, although Vergil adopted Caieta (Dion. Hal., 1, 55; Servius, *ad. Aen.* 9, 716). Pliny and Strabo are undoubtedly more accurate and scientific in ascribing the name to the volcanic "off-pouring" of Mount Epomeo on Ischia (Pliny, *N.H.,* 3, 6, 82; 2, 89, 203). Vergil's allusion to the island is in the context of an architectural simile which describes the convulsive reaction of the bay to the sudden submersion of a prefabricated block at Baiae:

> That impact shakes to the core Prochyta and the bedrock of
> Inarime beneath which, at Jove's bidding, Typhoeus was buried.
> (A. 9, 716–6. Day Lewis)

One must suppose that nature's shudders were about the only startling sign of life on the island, which remains today a quiet fishing village of almost Arabic appearance, wresting a livelihood from the sea and from the productive vineyards and olive orchards. Certainly Juvenal's later remark testifies to quietude as well as to the menace of earthquakes:

> Personally I would even prefer Prochyta to the Subura [the teeming ghetto and slum quarter of Rome]; for what site could be so dismal or so lonely that one would not regard it as worse alternative to live in dread of fires and collapsing houses, and the thousand perils of this violent city, and of poetry-readings during the month of August?
> (Juvenal, *Sat.* 3, 5–9)

Ischia (anc. Aenaria, or Inarime in Homer, *Iliad* 2, 781–3) offers tangible evidence, at Baia San Montano, of the earliest Greek foundation in the West. The principal settlement, Pithecusae, so called after the pottery production (*pithos,* "clay vase") rather than after an unlikely community of apes (*pithekos,* "ape") was founded ca. 770 by Euboean Greek pioneers. Subsequently, as a result of *stasis* ("civic upheaval") and political division, perhaps a repercussion of the Lelantine War in their homeland, these colonists established a second settlement at Cumae on the mainland opposite (Livy 8, 22). Pithecusae, always involved in the fortunes of her successor and subsequently occupied by Oscan and Roman settlers, came to a catastrophic end in 82 B.C. Because the community had sheltered Marius and his followers in 88, Sulla ordered its destruction (Plut. *Marius* 40). The site was abandoned, although Monte Vico ("hill town") kept the memory of a settlement alive. The island thereafter was called Aenaria and so commemorated the Trojan landing in heroic times. The island was evidently regarded as Imperial property during the late Republic. Suetonius (*Aug.* 92) relates that Augustus and the Neapolitans arranged an exchange of ownership when the Emperor expressed a desire for Capri, and so, from ca. 29, Ischia became desirable Neapolitan property, offering the hot-spring therapy and tourist attractions which still provide the island's major livelihood.

The necropolis of Pithecusae has been discovered along the beach at Baia San Montano in the shadow of Monte Vico. Tumulus burials and inhumation trench-graves were common during the eighth and seventh centuries and testify to the mixed company of early settlers. Pottery imports and abundant imitation ware from the local ceramic factories testify to the quickening economy of the settlement. Most exciting among the finds are a large geometric crater of local fabric, decorated with a scene of shipwreck, and a geometric scyphus of Rhodian make, dated provisionally ca. 750–725, with an incised inscription of three lines running from right to left on its side. The Chalcidic alphabet was used in composing an iambic trimeter and two dactylic hexameters:

> Nestor's cup was a fine drinking-vessel; but whosoever drinks from this man's cup will at once be gripped with longing for lovely-crowned Aphrodite.   (*S. E. G.* 14, 604)

This Pithecusan cup and the Proto-Corinthian lekythos of Tataie found at Cumae bear the earliest examples of alphabetic writing in Italy.

Capreae (mod. Capri) was acknowledged in Vergil's catalogue of the Italian forces as ruler of extensive domains beyond the rocky isle.

> Then Oebalus must not go unhonoured and unsung—
> Oebalus whom, it is said, Telon begat on the nymph
> Sebethis, when he was king of Teleboan Capreae,
> Advanced now in years. But his son, not content with his father's
>   frontiers,
> Even at this time held sway, further afield, over
> Sarrastian tribes and the plains which the river Sarnus irrigates,
> Over the dwellers in Rufrae, Batulum, rural Celemna,
> And the dwellers below the town of apple-growing Abella . . .

> (A. 7, 733–40. Day Lewis)

Greek legend ascribes the earliest foundation on Capri to Teleboans from Acarnania and the Ionian Islands off the west coast of Greece. The assumption is that they arrived in Mycenaean times or shortly thereafter and extended their interests and settlements into Campania in the ensuing years, as did the later settlers of Chalcidic Cumae. Certainly after the rise of Cumae on the mainland Capreae would have come under mainland suzerainty and have helped to ensure the sea lanes against Etruscan intrusion and piratical attacks. It may be suggested that the twin heights of Capri and Anacapri (Upper Capreae) remained independent communities until Augustan times.

Vergil's account suggests a link between Capreae and the mainland, and the inclusion of a large sector of the Campanian hinterland behind Pompeii in the suzerainty of the island. Nola, Nuceria, Acerrae, and Pompeii were all served by the Sarnus river (Strabo 5, 4, 8) and all were estimable communities in Vergil's lifetime.

Capreae gained prominence in Roman history in 29 B.C. when Augustus acquired the island. He proceeded to build a series of villas, possibly twelve in the original design, each named after a member of the Olympic pantheon.

Remains of several villas have been discovered on the shores and peaks of the rocky island. There is some indication that they may have been part of an overall design entrusted to Augustus' architect, perhaps the African freedman Masgaba. Most notable and best favored of the villas so far unearthed is the Villa Jovis, which perches atop the eastern promontory, remote, defensible, and superbly located some 1085 feet above the azure sea. The Augustan villa was no doubt enlarged by Tiberius, who chose this site for his permanent residence between 27 and 37 A.D. Peculiar to the design is the impressive arrangement of the four large vaulted cisterns in the center of the villa. The Imperial court, or *aula,* was situated on the east side, whereas on the most elevated side, the north, looking towards Sorrento, the builders located the Imperial apartments and quarters for the Praetorian Guard. An extensive open-air promenade, or *ambulatio,* one hundred Roman feet in length, served as a solarium and belvedere. The walk was provided with rectangular alcoves for seating and a triclinium. The west side of the villa, on the lower levels, accommodated the kitchens, bakeries, storerooms, pantries, and servants' quarters. To the west of the villa an observatory, or *specularium,* catered to the astrological inclinations of both Augustus and Tiberius. A lighthouse, or *pharos,* towering seventy-five feet on the south side of the palace, helped to safeguard the passage of ships through the straits and probably also served as a signal tower for tele-communications between Capri and Cape Athenaeum on the Sorrentine peninsula, and between Capri and Cape Misenum.

Remains of two other villas have been unearthed below the summit, at Damecuta (Arabic for *Domus Augusti?*) beneath Monte Solaro on the shore, and at Palazzo a Mare (anc. Palatium), west of the modern Marina Grande and near the Bagni di Tiberio. Both villas had superb belvederes or loggias sited to catch the western breezes. The Damecuta villa's *ambulatio* runs east-west along the seashore and had a residential area and dining room at its western extremity. (Fig. 60) The site of the Imperial apartments is probably beneath a mediaeval tower. The site at Palazzo a Mare has yielded only meager remains of rock-cut cisterns and nondescript walls, but they testify nonetheless to a large-scale villa at the site (cf. Suetonius, *Aug.* 72), a porticus-villa oriented to catch the cool breezes and early shade, and with the amenity of woods and gardens.

The Blue Grotto was certainly known to the Roman occupants of Capreae, and its interior recently explored by skin-divers has yielded evidence of repeated use and traces of spectacular sculptures affixed to the walls. The Roman harbor was located on the northern side of the island, near the modern Marina Grande, at Punta Vivara.

The mainland sites which Vergil assigns to the suzerainty of Capreae are of varying importance and pedigree. Rufrae (or Rufrium, Livy 8, 25, 4) dominated a small plain alongside the Volturnus river. The site today is recalled by S. Felice a Rufo, near the town of Presenzano. The Samnite stronghold of Rufrae fell to the Romans in 326 B.C. at the outset of the Second Samnite War. Batulum and Celemna are Samnite communities which elude identification today. Abella (mod. Avella), another Samnite stronghold, which Vergil distinguishes for its apple orchards and citadel site (cf. p. 225), lies five miles northeast of Nola on the left bank of the Clanius river. In 399 Abella became an ally of Rome and remained faithful, sometimes under considerable duress, until the Civil War era. An amphitheater of Imperial date is the most impressive ruin today, and the Cippus Abellanus, ca. 165 B.C., is one of the most celebrated documents in Oscan to survive. Abella's relations with nearby Nola varied from amity to outright hostility. The Samnites tended to safeguard their mountain strongholds (cf. A. 7, 740; Abella) with "Cyclopean" masonry, and sometimes entire hill-tops were encircled with ring-walls. Remains survive at Aufidena, Saepinum, and Allifae. Salmon comments on the vulnerable nature of the fortifications and their inability to withstand a siege: "Normally built near the crest of a hill without towers or bastions or, presumably, battlements, they seem to have served principally as rallying points where the defenders could regroup. Like the Spartans, the Samnites put more trust in the arms of their men than in blocks of limestone."[12] The Sarrastes, mentioned by Vergil (cf. p. 225) but otherwise unknown, are perhaps to be associated with the Sarnus river environs, presumably in the territory facing Capreae.

Historical and archaeological allusions favor Greek origins for Surrentum (mod. Sorrento) although it was certainly a Samnite community from the fifth to the third century B.C. During late Republican and Imperial times Surrentum was greatly favored by tourists and year-round residents who were then, as today, attracted by the marvelous panorama, the fruits and vines, and the temperate climate. Vergil may have lived there at some time during his twenty-five years of residence in Campania. The *dolce far niente* tenor of Neapolitan life must have been upset by the militarization of the area during and after the war with Sextus Pompey, perhaps sufficiently to induce Vergil to transfer his residence, temporarily at least, to Siren Land (cf. Appendix Vergiliana, *Catalepton* 14). Augustus certainly maintained a villa there. The lovely *municipium* became increasingly popular after peace was regained, and the slopes of the promontory were lined with porticus-villas, parks, and shrines. Strabo's account (5, 4, 8) of the Bay of Naples, the so-called Crater, includes Surrentum as one extreme shore of the bay which owed its adornment to the cities and "partly to the residences and gardens which continue in such an unbroken succession that they give the appearance of a single city."

Campania was not immune to one of the most oppressive problems facing Octavian-Augustus in the post-war reconstruction. The enormous loss of life during the Social War and the Civil Wars of the first century B.C. aggravated the economic situation as well as the problem of under-population. Even the Pax Augusta could not reverse the tide of depression in Italy.

Vergil alludes several times to the adverse economic conditions, usually with some critical epithet attaching to a declining community. On one occasion he refers to a situation which was evidently very much a part of his experience, for the terrain was most familiar to him:

> Such is the soil that wealthy Capua ploughs, and the shores near
> Vesuvius' ridge, and the river Clanius cruel to empty Acerrae.
>
> (G. 2, 224–5)

Poetic fiction assigned the foundation of Capua to Capys, cousin of Aeneas:

> There was Capys;
> From him rose the name of Capua, Campania's city.
> (A. 10, 150–1. L. R. Lind)

(Cf. also Ovid, *Fasti* 4, 45.) Certainly the city was founded before the close of the sixth century, and archaeological evidence has shown that there was an Etruscan settlement there ca. 520. But the Trojan origin cannot be discarded, although Capys is an Etruscan name. The Etruscan, and later Samnite (post-423 B.C.), city was an industrial center, particularly a manufacturer of bronze articles which rivaled the work at Chalcidic Cumae and elsewhere in Campania. After the naval defeat off Cumae in 474 the Etruscan control weakened markedly. The Samnite shepherds and farmers in the environs of Capua gradually infiltrated into the capital city and ultimately demanded and received political rights in 438 B.C. as guarantee of their peaceful coexistence. After the overthrow of the city in 423, they proceeded to occupy Cumae in 421 and so changed the Greek to Oscan modes of life. Capua's role during the Samnite Wars was highly questionable at times, but her factories and agricultural production enabled her to reach unprecedented wealth and luxury and to experience a population explosion which brought Capua to the level of Carthage and Rome (Florus, 1, 16, 6). Her assistance to Hannibal provided him with sorely needed military assistance, weapons and supplies, and a military base near Mount Tifata (mod. Monte di Maddaloni). After a severe reprisal exacted by Q. Fabius Maximus in 216 B.C. (Livy 23, 46, 8–11), and the establishment of a Roman colony in Capua in 194 (Livy 32, 29, 3–4), the city found new vigor. Although several times the victim of land partition during the late Republic, Capua remained productive and prosperous, with agricultural produce in wheat, grapes, and Falernian wine, and industrial output of bronze articles, weapons, rope, carpets, tapestries, cosmetics, and perfumes. Suetonius, on the authority of Cornelius Balbus, an intimate friend of Caesar, reports presentiments in Capua of Caesar's assassination: "A few months before, the settlers assigned to the colony at Capua were razing some very ancient tombs preparatory to building farm houses and were doing so with even greater enthusiasm because as they poked about they found a number of vases of great antiquity. There was also discovered in a monument which was reported to be the tomb of Capys, founder of Capua, a bronze tablet inscribed with Greek words to this effect: "Whenever the bones of Capys shall be uncovered, it will come to pass that a descendant of his shall be slain at the hands of his kinsmen, and presently avenged at a cost of great slaughter to Italy." (*Deified Julius* 81, 1.)

Vergil's inclusion of Capys in his epic enables him to pay his respects to the traditional founder of what Livy (7, 31, 1) called *urbs maxima opulentissimaque Italiae*. But the city's role in the epic was inconsequential in the light of her historical career. In Vergil's lifetime Capua had been a storm center of political struggle. Cicero chose Capua as his headquarters in January 49 when he commanded the district. Antony's attempt to plant a new colony at Capua was frustrated by Cicero, but he did succeed in planting an illegal colony at Casilinum, so close to Capua that the ploughshare of the *deductio* ceremony, designating the furrow where the walls should rise, almost grazed the gates of Capua. Casilinum today is the successor to Capua on the Volturnus river; the ancient city, S. Maria Capua Vetere, lies approximately two miles distant. The controversial events involving Capua may have induced Vergil to deny it a significant role.

Capua's fertility certainly contrasted markedly with evacuated Acerrae (mod. Acerra), located some eight miles northeast of Naples. Acerrae, at one time under Capuan control, was occupied by the Samnites during the fifth century, and after allying with Rome after the First Samnite War, enjoyed the security and legal protection of a favored city (Livy 8, 17, 2). Its location on the Sarnus river (mod. Sarno) permitted it to open up prosperous trading relations with Nola and Pompeii (Strabo 5, 4, 8). After its destruction by Hannibal in payment for its spirited resistance in 216 (Livy 23, 17, 7; 19, 4), the community was rebuilt. The Roman commander L. Julius Sextus Caesar repulsed a heavy attack by the Samnite general Gavius Pontius at Acerrae in 90 B.C. (Appian, *B.C.* 1, 40–2; 45). The river Clanius during Vergil's time encroached on the town, and malaria, common to Etruscan Graviscae and Lucanian Paestum, probably hastened its evacuation and decay. The withdrawal of farmers from the once-fertile land was a symptom of the late Republican era. The drainage facilities and general maintenance deteriorated and the river was free to inundate the area and so hasten its isolation and interment.

Vesuvius (anc. Vesbius), Goethe's "peak of Hell rising out of Paradise," is described by Strabo as richly cultivated with vines, producers of the celebrated *vinum Vesvinum,* ancestor of the modern Lacrima Cristi, which was widely exported within Italy. (Cf. Fig. 61.) The crater was evidently largely extinct by 73 B.C. when Spartacus lodged his followers there during their insurrection. A wall painting found in Pompeii shows Bacchus or Dionysus, wearing a robe of grapes, standing on the terraced slopes of Vesuvius, which rises smoothly to a sharp peak. Today Vesuvius lies approximately eight miles south of Naples, is thirty miles in circumference and rises to a height of 4275 feet. Pliny's account of the eruption on August 24–5, 79 A.D., is worthy of Rome's greatest historian, Tacitus, for whom it was composed.

Oscan-speaking Nola at an earlier time controlled the entrance into central Campania from Samnium. Nola, "New-Town," may be the successor to Hyria, which is recalled on coins. Because of her interference in Neapolitan affairs, contrary to Roman desires, Nola was reduced by Rome in 313 (Livy 9, 28, 5–6). Gaius Papius Mutilus captured the city and its Roman garrison in 90 B.C., and the aftermath was cruel. Sulla was twice responsible for brutal retaliatory measures against the citizens of Nola during the Social and Civil War periods.

Nola's territory came close to Naples. Cicero records an instance during the second century when Q. Fabius Labeo, grandson of the famous Delayer of the Second Punic War, arbitrated in a boundary dispute between the cities. He appealed to the magnanimity of both contestants and then awarded to Rome the tract of land which their compliance had left in the middle (Cicero, *Brut.,* 12; *De Off.* 1, 83; *De Div.* 1, 72). There is also a notice that Vergil owned property at Nola, as well as at Naples and possibly at Surrentum. The account which Aulus Gellius (*Noct. Att.* 6, 20) provides of Vergil's relations with Nola is typical in its entertainment value and enlightening comment:

> I have discovered an entry in a commentary that the following lines were first read and released by Vergil in this form:
>> *talem dives arat Capua et vicina Vesaevo*
>> *Nola iugo et vacuis Clanius non aequus Acerris.*
> But after Vergil requested permission from the citizens of Nola to divert some of their city water into his country-estate nearby, and they declined to grant the favor which he had requested, the frustrated poet erased the name of their city from his poem, as though he were consigning it to oblivion (a kind of *damnatio memoriae*) and altered *Nola* to *Ora* and left the phrase in this form:
>> *vicina Vesaevo*
> *Ora iugo.* [G. 2, 224–5]

Such "poetic justice" from the gentle Vergil strikes one forcibly. There is no textual conflict with Aulus Gellius, and it seems that the poet may indeed have omitted Nola from his agricultural "accounting" because of a dispute over a branch aqueduct which would provide water for his acreage there. The story is equally intriguing for its chronological evidence for the poet's residence in the territory of Nola, and for his involvement with farming in Campania during the final composition of the *Georgics*. We might also believe that the same lingering resentment may have led him to exclude Nola from his "march-past" of Turnus' Italic heroes. The suggestion that Vergil's residence at Nola may have been given to him as partial or total compensation for the confiscated property at Mantua is an interesting possibility.

Sabellian Nola was the locale for the deaths of two distinguished men. Gaius Papius Mutilus, the Samnite war hero, committed suicide at Nola in 80 B.C. And in 14 A.D. the Emperor Augustus succumbed in the bedroom where his father Octavius had died.

Vergil ascribes hardy courage and aggressiveness to the Sabellians of Campania:

> Next, Agamemnon's son, Halaesus, who hated everything
> Trojan, harnessed his chariot team and brought to Turnus
> Post-haste a thousand warlike clans—hoers of the wine-rich
> Massic country. men whom their fathers had sent from the hills
> Of Aurunca, men who had come from the nearby Sidicine plains,
> Men who hailed from Cales, men who lived by the shallow
> Volturnus river; and with them, Oscan levies and warlike
> Saticulans. Their weapons were missiles with rounded handles
> Which they were used to throw with whippy thongs attached:
> A targe protected their left side; a scimitar was carried for close work.
>
> (A. 7, 723–32. Day Lewis)

Although Vergil's Samnite contingents (Figs. 62, 63) allied with Turnus came from a fairly circumscribed area, the terrain of the Samnites in mid-fourth century B.C. stretched for some fifteen miles along the west coast, from the peninsula of Surrentum to the river Silarus at Paestum, and from the river Aternus southwards for some seventy-five miles to Mons Garganus. Salmon has delineated the land-locked plateau as bounded on the north by the river Sagrus and the lands of the Marsi and Paeligni; on the south by the river Aufidus (mod. Ofanto) and the lands of the Lucanians; on the east by the plain of Apulia and the lands of the Frentani; and on the west by the plains of Campania and the territories of the Aurunci, Sidicini, and Latini.[13] The language of Samnium and the Samnites was Oscan, and although it does not appear to have been designed for literature, the system of orthography was precise, even meticulous, and it certainly served adequately for diplomacy and commerce. Although an Indo-European language related to Latin, it bears little resemblance to the language as we know it. Its lengthy life-span and its successful resistance to the inexorable spread of Latin throughout the peninsula testify to its popularity and to the national pride which kept it alive.

After the mid-fourth century, the Samnites were compelled by overpopulation and land hunger to infiltrate the fertile plains and opulent cities of Campania. The Romans took counter-measures, and so the Samnite Wars ensued. Traditionally there were three wars with Rome: the First Samnite War, 343–1 B.C., was fought to ensure that Campania would be Samnite; the Second, 327–01, though no more successful than the first, brought to the fore a skillful strategist in the person of the Samnite generalissimo Gavius Pontius, who humiliated the Romans at the Caudine Forks in 321 and again at the ad Lautulas pass in 316. The latter success encouraged the Samnites to advance from the Liris valley into Latium, as far as Ardea, which is a scant eighteen miles from Rome (Strabo 5, 3, 5). However, the final reckoning favored the Romans, and the Samnites were compelled to withdraw from Lucania and Apulia, south of Campania. To guarantee the territory against further Samnite incursions, Rome established Latin colonies at Saticula, Suessa Aurunca, and Pontiae (the island of Ponza), and another Latin colony at Interamna in the Liris valley in 312 B.C. The Third Samnite War ended all Samnite pretensions to suzerainty in central and southern Italy.

The final act of the Samnite-Roman encounter was the so-called Social War of 91–87 B.C. The grounds for war were various, but the major factors were the traditional ones of Samnite discontent with Roman arrogance and selfishness in their dealings with their less fortunate cousins, and resentment at the oppressive apartheid policy which restricted them from enjoying the rights of full citizenship and full social, legal, and political equality. They were no longer satisfied with partial assimilation, as *civitates sine suffragio* or as treaty states (*foederatae*). They desired full assimilation into the Roman governmental system.

The saga of the wars must have captured Vergil's imagination. The rebellion was under the dual direction of Q. Poppaedius Silo in the

"Marsic" territory and of Gaius Papius Mutilus in the "Samnite" counterpart. The Latin allies in central Italy and Campania, except for those in Horace's Venusia (mod. Venosa), offered no help to the brawny highlanders; Papius Mutilus, however, found useful assistance from the cities of southern Campania, Lucania, and Apulia. As token of nationalist spirit a capital was established at Corfinium, in Paelignian territory, a coinage was struck, and an army of 100,000 men was enlisted.

Papius Mutilus was markedly successful until he encountered the legions of the consul L. Julius Caesar at Acerrae. During the campaign of 89 Sulla assumed the offensive and captured Aeclanum and Compsa in southern Samnium, and later Bovianum Vetus, the Samnite headquarters. During 88, although the Samnites found the resource to resume the offensive, their entire resistance collapsed everywhere except at Aesernia and Nola. Rome had successfully and characteristically divided and conquered her foe by canny offers of Roman citizenship and privileges to states which remained loyal or to faithful citizens. The Lex Julia and the Lex Plautia-Papiria of 90–89 sealed the fate of the Samnite rebellion. In the last phases of the Social War the death toll was enormous, and the repercussions, personal, economic, and agricultural, were extremely grave. Only a few Samnites finally remained alive to enjoy the rights which they had sacrificed everything to obtain.

During the Civil War between the Marians and Sullans, the Marian faction found, as might be expected, some support among the shattered Samnite communities, particularly among those who had suffered the cruel reprisals of Sulla during the Social War. A Samnite contingent offered spirited, courageous resistance to Sulla at Rome's Colline Gate on November 1st, 89 B.C. The defeat of the Marians and their Samnite allies in their ultimate battle led to an appalling aftermath: "The vindictive Sulla, like 'Butcher' Cumberland after Culloden, had sent his soldiers into the highlands on a mission of extirpation and expulsion, his justification for such savagery being that Romans would never know peace so long as a cohesive Samnite nation survived."[14] Rome's Villa Publica in the Campus Martius became an abattoir for the Marian and Samnite prisoners. All were massacred, according to Sulla's *Memoirs,* to a total of 6,000 (Plut. *Sulla,* 30, 6); Sulla's pogrom was followed by land confiscations and the settlement of his veterans on Samnite terrain, a procedure which caused his successors to face an economic and social upheaval. Italy had never witnessed such a calculated program to erase one whole segment of the peninsula's population, a determination which has only been matched in modern times. Oscan, with Umbrian, Messapic, and Etruscan, was replaced by Latin as the official tongue in all Italic tribes and communities, although the tongue persisted into Imperial times in restricted zones.

Vergil evidently admired the resistance of the Samnites, their valor and their libertarian ideals. Gavius Pontius and Turnus have much in common: stubborn, brave and constant, obstinate in the face of Roman repression; the Samnites, like Turnus and his allies, were unquestionably the final champions of regional liberty in Italy, and their wars were decisive in the shaping of late Republican Italy.

Vergil makes no evident effort to recall the total roster of rebels against Rome in the Social War. (Appian [*B.C.* 1, 39, 185] lists them as Marsi, Paeligni, Vestini, Marrucini, Aculani, Frentani, Hirpini, Pompeiani [or Nolani?], Venusini, Iapygii, Lucani, and Samnites.) Vergil does however cite the Massic clans. The wine-producing country near Mons Massicus (mod. Mt. Massico) was famous for its "*obliviosum Massicum*" (Hor. *Odes* 2, 7, 21) and is historically noteworthy as the site where the Roman general Fabius saw the burning and pillaging of the villages by Hannibal's Punic forces (Livy 22, 14) and heard the reproaches of Minicius Rufus—as caustic as Vergil's Drances (A. 11, 343–375)—for his strategy of exhaustion and avoidance of pitched battles, "those slow plans which the timid call cautious."

The territory of the Aurunci lay below the junction of the Liris and the Rapido rivers. The Aurunci were identified with the Ausones (Strabo 5, 4, 3). Suessa Aurunca, the home of the father of Roman satire, Gaius Lucilius, lay in the valley of the Volturnus river. It was the site of a decisive defeat of the Latins and their associates in 340 during the First Samnite War. The Romans later, in 313, established a Latin colony at Suessa on what had been formerly Auruncan territory, and as part of the same policy of containment, at Saticula, on former Samnite terrain.

Saticula (mod. S. Agata de' Goti?), a Samnite fortress, dominated the route from Campania to Samnium, along the south side of Mons Taburnus (mod. Mt. Taburno). In 343 B.C. the Roman consul Aulus

Cornelius Cossus marched into the valley of the Isclero and a Samnite ambush. The army and its commander owed their escape and ultimate victory to the military tribune P. Decius Mus, who died in the subsequent engagement at Suessa Aurunca in 340. The Sidicini and the contingents from Cales and from the Volturnus river valley strongholds—probably Gallifae (mod Calvisi ?), Allifae (mod. Castello d'Alife), and Rufrae (mod. Presenzano)—provided impressive support to Turnus' allied army. Strabo states (5, 3, 9) that "after Casinum (mod. Cassino) the next community is Teanum, called Sidicine. These people are Oscans, a Campanian tribe which has disappeared, so you might call it a city of Campania even though it is the largest city on the Via Latina. So also with the city of the Calenians which comes after Teanum, another noteworthy city, although it borders on Casilium [mod. Capua]."

The geographer's comments are revealing of the mutability of frontiers in the common estimate. Teanum Sidicinum, the northernmost city of Campania, lies on the eastern slopes of Roccamonfina, north of Cales and the Ager Falernus. The Via Latina proceeded from Venafrum through both Teanum and Cales, and at Teanum linked with the Via Appia. Teanum was fifteen miles south of Rome by the Via Appia, and five miles from Cales by the Via Latina. On his return from the Mithridatic campain in 83, Sulla undertook summit talks there with the opposing army under L. Cornelius Scipio Asiaticus. During the talks Sulla's legionaries and propaganda so successfully infiltrated Scipio's army that Scipio soon found himself deserted and Sulla's victory was won without bloodshed (Appian, *B.C.* 1, 10). Traces of ancient Teanum survive in the fourth-century B.C. necropolis, a forum, basilica, theater, bath buildings, circus, and walls. All the finds testify to a prosperous, important road center in antiquity, still prosperous and populous in Vergil's time.

Auruncan Cales was the site of the first Latin colony in Campania, in 334 (Livy 8, 16, 3–4). It remained an important Roman control center in Campania, and a *quaestor navalis* was stationed there to safeguard the area against the Samnites. Black-glazed Calenian pottery, marketed first during the fourth century, was very popular subsequently. Calenian wine and metalwork in bronze and iron were widely used in Republican and Imperial times. The ancient remains include an amphitheater, a theater, two temples, and some portions of the Via Latina.

The armament Vergil ascribed to the contingent is in keeping with the regalia and weapons of the Samnites. The *aclydes* (A. 7, 730) were probably small javelins. Salmon notes that there are no indications that the Sabellians used either the battle-axe or curved swords (scimitars) in battle (*contra* A. 7, 732).[15]

In the catalogue of the Latin forces Vergil pays particular praise to Clausus, Sabine by descent, ancestor of the gens Claudia:

> With him, a big Amiternian detachment, and men from historic
> Cures, and all from Eretum and olive-growing Mutusca;
> Citizens of Nomentum, dwellers in the Rosean district
> Around Velinum, in craggy Tetrica, Mount Severus,
> Casperia, Foruli, and by the river Himella;
> Those who drink from Tiber and Fabaris, those whom frigid
> Nursia sent, with Ortine tribes and tribes of Latium.
>
> (A. 7, 710–716. Day Lewis)

The contingent under Clausus is an impressive array but one which defies accurate location. Amiternum (mod. San Vittorino) in the Apennines, about fifty miles northeast of Rome, was an important Samnite stronghold midway between Interamna Lirenas and Atina (Livy 10, 39, 5). Characteristic polygonal wall remains at San Elia Fiume Rapido provide some clue to its original location. Gaius Sallustius Crispus (86–34 B.C.), the historian and politician Sallust, was born at Amiternum. His family must have possessed adequate means and local prestige, for his works indicate that he was given a thorough education, both in Greek and Latin, and his subsequent political career as a municipal *novus homo* would suggest that his private income was large. He probably became a resident of Rome ca. 70 B.C.[16] Cures (mod. Corese) was birthplace of Titus Tatius and of Numa, and one tradition held that the honorific title *Quirites* for Romans derived from Cures. Eretum and Mutusca are nondescript Italic towns, the latter evidently distinguished in Vergil's time for its olive orchards. Nomentum, at some considerable distance from Samnium, belongs properly to Latium. The town (mod. Mentana) is set alongside the Tiber about twelve miles north of Rome and near Cures. Tetrica and Severus are clearly "craggy, stern" heights in the Apennine range. Casperia is a chilly stronghold north of Amiternum.

The mountainy district of Nursae sent forth to war Ufens,
Who had a high reputation as a successful fighter;
His clan, the Aequi, living on a thin soil and hardened
By constant hunting over the woodlands, excelled in toughness.
Armed to the teeth they are when they till the ground, and they never
Tire of carrying off new plunder, living on loot.

(A. 7, 744–749. Day Lewis)

The poet's description of the Aequi and of their durable nature as farmers, hunters, and sturdy aggressors is in keeping with his admiration for the Italic stock. The Aequi were among Rome's most ancient enemies, mountaineers who eked out a living in the thin-soiled valleys of the upper Anio, Tolenus, and Himella in central Italy (Strabo 5, 3, 1; 5, 3, 4–5; 5, 3, 9–10). They based themselves in the mountains behind Tibur and Praeneste and finally in 431 B.C. had to be expelled by force from the Alban Hills, where they had controlled the pass into Hernican territory. In 304, when they were confined to their original home-land, Rome made determined attacks on their settlements along the Liris, in the Upper Anio region, and in the areas north and west of the Fucine Lake. Their late intervention in the Second Samnite War cost them dearly, for they lost much of their territory and saw the establish-ment of two Latin colonies to restrain them for the future and to assist their rapid Romanization: one at Alba Fucens (mod. Albe) in 303, and another at Carseoli (mod. Carsoli) in 293. The Aequi had vanished as an independent nation long before Vergil's time.

For his Marsian entry in the catalogue of Italic forces Vergil com-posed one of his most poignant passages. Umbro is a fictitious name, with suggestions of Umbria in central Italy east of Etruria, but the land-scape and the religious association are historical:

Again, from the Marruvian tribe there came a priest,
His helmet adorned with a favour of fruitful olive leaf,
Sent by his chieftain, Archippus; this hero's name was Umbro:
He had a remarkable talent for hypnotising by spell
And touch the serpent kind, all evilly-breathing snakes;
He was able to charm their anger and cure their bites with his skill.
But his art was powerless to heal the wound he got from a Trojan
Spearpoint; neither his soporific spells nor the simples
He'd gathered on Marsian hills availed him when he was wounded.

The grove of Angitia wept him; Fucinus, glassy-watered,
All limpid lakes lamented him.

                                        (A. 7, 750–760. Day Lewis)

Umbro, captain of a Marsic band, was snake-charmer priest of Angitia, the Marsic goddess of healing, security, and snake-bite therapy, who was favored by Samnites and Marsi generally but had her most celebrated shrine in Marsic territory. Ashby suggested that the present-day ceremony of the snake festival at Paelignian Cocullo with its essential pagan overtone may derive ultimately from Angitia worship.[17] For all his expertise with herbs and incantations, the valiant Umbro died by a Trojan spear, possibly that of Aeneas (A. 10, 544). Although the Marsi, centered about the capital of Marruvium by the Fucine Lake, had maintained friendly relations with Rome from early times through the Second Samnite War and Hannibal's invasion, they assumed a directional role in the Third Samnite, or "Marsic," War (91–87 B.C.). When they had gained the rights they sought, they passed into oblivion as a separate nation: they gained Roman citizenship but lost their liberty. With their co-militants, they represent for Vergil the strength of Italy's past. Proud, independent, rapacious, and occasionally barbaric, they had hallowed the countryside with their strongholds and institutions—in the manner of the American Indian. But settled ways of peace and the armed might of the civilizing legionaries and colonists brought them to eclipse and left them to poets' fond reveries and to historians' accounts.

The Fucine Lake, at the heart of Marsic territory, was central Italy's largest body of water and a lifegiving support to the Marsians and the neighboring tribes. (Fig. 64) Strabo, Vergil's contemporary, gives a revealing description of the lake that lends insight too for proper appreciation of the poet's attitude: "They say that at times its waters rise to the height of the mountains which surround it, and at others subside so much that the places which had been covered with water reappear and may be cultivated; however, the subsidings of the water occur regularly and without previous warning, and are followed by their rising again; the springs fail altogether and gush out again after a time." (5, 3, 13) Vergil's picture of a lachrymose Fucine Lake (along with "all limpid lakes") bewailing the death of a local hero, is evidently an imaginative use of the recurrent floods.[18] Caesar intended to drain the lake to prevent the flooding; Claudius eventually accomplished the ambitious engineering venture by employing thirty thousand men for eleven years (Suet. *Julius* 44; *Claudius* 20 f., 32).

The Valley of Amsanctus was named by Vergil as the home of the Fury Allecto, Daughter of Night. When the Latins first came to open conflict with the Trojans, Allecto sounded the shepherd's signal, a blast on her curved horn:

> the sound rang on,
> Shaking the woods to their roots, through the deep forest baying:
> The lake of Diana heard it afar, the Nar heard it—
> That yellow sulphurous river, the springs of Velinus heard it.
>   (A. 7, 514–517. Day Lewis)

Finally, with her mischief unleashed, the Fury made for her home in the Underworld:

> There is a place in the heart of Italy, under the mountains,
> A well-known spot whose fame is told of in many countries—
> The Vale of Amsanctus. On either side, steep, wooded slopes
> Darken this vale with dense foliage, and down its middle
> A watercourse rumbles, eddying and clucking among the rocks.
> Here can be seen an awesome cave and the vents of the dreadful
> Underworld; a great chasm formed by the upthrust of Acheron
> Yawns, emitting a plague-breath: into it now disappeared
> The hateful Fury, relieving earth and sky of her presence.
>   (A. 7, 553–61. Day Lewis)

The Valley of Amsanctus (mod. Mefite) lies in the country of the Hirpini Samnites and was seemingly a Plutonium comparable to the examples at Avernus (cf. p. 212 f.) and perhaps at Baiae and Narnia. Vergil's description is vivid but, in Salmon's view, largely imaginary.[19] Servius (*ad loc.*) imagines the name to mean "altogether sacred" (*omni parte sanctus*). Pliny (*N.H.* 2, 208) indicates that there was a temple of the goddess Mefitis at the volcanic site, a shrine which would never accommodate the timorous. Although Avernus (lit. Aornus, "birdless") no longer intimidates or asphyxiates the fowls of the air, Lake Amsanctus still emits enough noxious fumes and searing steam to kill unwary birds and animals. Located near the modern village of Rocca San Felice, the cold-water lake, with bubbling mud, noxious exhalations, and treeless shores, measures about twenty-five feet in diameter during the summer, many times larger than that in the season of torrents. The temple vanished entirely about a century ago. Salmon remarks of the spirit-haunted Amsanctus and its counterparts that "upon the temperamental powers that controlled such places often depended a man's life and prosperity and the fertility and well-being of his crops and flocks. One was personally and even urgently concerned with them."[20]

When Aeneas' helmsman Palinurus sought to cross the Styx to obtain the peace of death, Deiphobe responded sharply that such a privilege was impossible for the unburied. But she also gave him strange but comforting assurance:

> I say that the neighbouring peoples, compelled by portents from heaven
> Occurring in every township, shall expiate your death,
> Shall give you burial and offer the solemn dues to your grave,
> And the place shall keep the name of Palinurus for ever.
> (A. 6, 378–81. Day Lewis)

Gaudet cognomine terra—the land rejoices in his name—is Vergil's final expression on the aetiological myth which he has devised. The Sibylline prophecy of cenotaph and place-name excited the interest of earlier readers. Servius comments on the passage and reports that the Lucanians on one occasion were oppressed with plague and were instructed by an oracle, presumably the Apolline oracle at Cumae, that Palinurus' shade must be appeased. The Lucanians dedicated a grove and a cenotaph to him not far from Velia (Servius, *ad Aen,* 6, 378). The story as Vergil tells it owes something to Timaeus and Varro, and to Homer's account of the deaths of Elpenor and Phrontis and of Odysseus' marathon swim to Calypso's island of Ogygia. The Vergilian account is distinguished for its tenderness and its evocative sympathy for the loss of the helmsman-companion of Aeneas' wanderings.

Vergil may have been personally acquainted with the Capo Palinuro, etymologically "windswept," and dangerous. The cape forms the southern arm of the bay of Velia on the west coast of Lucania and was traditionally a tricky headland for mariners to navigate. The Roman fleet returning from Panormus (mod. Palermo) in 253 B.C. was wrecked on its perilous lava outcroppings (Polybius, 1, 39, 1–6; Diod. 23, 19).

Horace was almost shipwrecked there on one occasion (*Odes* 3, 4, 28), and in 36 B.C. Octavian's flotilla came to grief along the same shores.

Recent excavations at Palinuro have disclosed remains of an indigenous settlement during the archaic period which lasted until Roman times. A necropolis on the hill of S. Paolo, dating largely to the period 525–500 B.C., seems to have been allocated for emergency burials. Vergil's prodigies and Servius' notice of a pestilence may support this opinion. The German excavators are convinced that Greek or Oenotrian Palinurus ended its life-span with this particular necropolis, although it revived under Lucanian rule during the fifth century B.C.

After the loss of the pilot Palinurus, the ships continued to sail on without incident until Aeneas became aware that his fleet was perilously close to the Sirens' islands (Fig. 65), whereupon, like some master of the Ship of State, Aeneas himself directed the fleet through the turbulent seas.

> Safe as before, the fleet was scudding upon its course—
> Nothing to fear, for Neptune had guaranteed a safe passage.
> And now, racing on, they were near the rocky place of the Sirens,
> Dangerous once for mariners, white with the bones of many;
> From afar the rasp of the ceaseless surf on those rocks could be heard.
> Just then Aeneas became aware that his ship was yawing
> Badly, her helmsman missing; he brought her back on to course
> In the night sea, and deeply sighing, stunned by the loss of his friend,
>   said:
> O Palinurus, too easily trusting clear sky and calm sea,
> You will lie on a foreign strand, mere jetsam, none to bury you.
>
> (A. 5, 862–871. Day Lewis)

The juxtaposition of Palinurus' Odyssean swim and his cruel death on the rocky shores with the "historical" account of the Sirens' isles and the devouring sea seem less casual than consequential in the light of recent research. A silver stater dating between 540 and 520 B.C, with a pearl border, a boar on the obverse and an incuse reverse, bears two retrograde legends, PAL on the obverse, and MOL on the reverse. The coin may be deciphered to read PALinurus and MOLpa. Although Molpa (or Molpe) has not yet been located, the suggestion of "song" in the name, plus Vergil's narrative, might induce one to associate the Sirens with this entire littoral. Molpa, which may be identified, at least tentatively, with the rock and river adjacent to Capo Palinuro, may in fact have been another Sirens' nest south of the Sorrentine promontory.

The Sirens, those predatory bird-maidens whose enchanting songs and prophetic omniscience proved fatal allurement to mariners, were frequently used in sepulchral art as mournful escorts for the souls of the dead on their last voyage to Hades, an underworld association which is further accentuated by the proximity of their habitat to the Phlegraean Fields and Lake Avernus. Strabo locates and describes the islands:

> Some locate the Sirens on Cape Pelorias [Capo Faro, Sicily], while others locate them two-hundred and fifty miles distant on the Sirenus-sae, the name assigned to a three-peaked rock which separates the Cumaean and Poseidoniate bays [i.e., Naples and Velia]. But this rock does not have three peaks, and in fact does not reach a peak at all; instead it is a long and narrow promontory which extends from the territory of Surrentum to the strait of Capreae, with a sanctuary of the Sirens on one side, and on the other, facing the bay of Poseidonia [mod. Positano?], there lie three little uninhabited rocky islands called the Sirens [mod. I Galli].
>
> (Strabo 1, 2, 12; also 5, 4, 8)

Besides "Paestum's roses blooming twice a year" (G. 4, 119), the city's local pest and its river awaken response in the poet:

> Around the groves of Silarus and Alburnus, evergreen with holm-oaks, there swarms a flying insect we Romans call the "asilus" [gadfly] and Greeks render as "oistros" in their language, a fierce creature with a shrill buzzing that drives whole herds scattered though the woodlands, distracted; the sky is stunned with their bellowings as are the wood-lands and banks of dried-out Tanagrus. Juno once directed her terrify-ing wrath with malice aforethought against the heifer-daughter of Inachus and plagued her with this pest.
>
> (G. 3, 146–53)

Gadflies swarming in the evergreen oak forests of Lucania and the perfume-laden air of Paestum (Greek, Poseidonia) are a modest notice for one of the most spectacular sanctuary sites in Italy. The original site was at the mouth of the river Silarus (mod. Sele), and legend ascribed the foundation to Jason the Argonaut who consecrated the site to Hera (Juno) as thankoffering. The historical settlers came from

Sybaris ca. 700 B.C. and comprised in large part Dorian Troezenians who chose to detach themselves from the Achaean colony at Sybaris. They named the colony after Poseidon, who was both patron deity of Troezene and tutelary god of the federated Acheans, worshipped at Helice.

After an indeterminate period the seaside settlement was moved inland to a fertile plain which was ringed with fortification walls. The city became prosperous from its agricultural produce—vines, wheat, and twice-blooming roses—and from its commercial involvements in pottery, terra-cotta sculpture, perfume, etc. Poseidonia served as terminus for an overland trade route which avoided the Straits of Messana, a veritable Scylla and Charybdis of Chalcidic piracy and tolls, and the menace of Etruscan piracy in the Tyrrhenian Sea.

The Doric temples of Poseidonia, the glory of southern Italy, matched only by the extravagant buildings in Sicily, are token of her prosperity and her piety to Hera above all. Vergil's failure to mention the Hera temples is not surprising, for the settlement's almost total involvement with Hera-Juno, the persecutor of Aeneas, would eliminate it from any heroic encounter in the epic. Within the central part of the *polis,* adjacent to the city center, two sacred precincts were defined: the northern zone was reserved for Athena, the southern for Hera. The Hera temples were dedicated to the fertility goddess of marriage and childbirth, of security and productivity in the state.

The earliest surviving Hera temple, the onetime "Basilica," was built ca. 530 B.C. in an unorthodox design: 9 by 18 Doric columns, with a stylobate measurement of 80 by 178 feet, divided by a central row of columns into two great "basilical" aisles. The Hera temple alongside, the best preserved and most "progressive" of the shrines, at one time believed to be a temple of Poseidon, was built ca. 460–440 in a modern design: 6 by 14 Doric columns, a stylobate measurement of 80 by 197 feet, and a double range of interior columns in two stories. (Fig. 66) Authorities still dispute whether this temple antedates or is indebted to the Parthenon, whose refinements it shares. The Athena Temple, once called the Temple of Ceres, was built, perhaps as a thank-offering by refugees from Sybaris, ca. 510–505 in an advanced design: 6 by 13 Doric columns, a stylobate measurement of 48 x 108 feet, and with a vestibule with 8 Ionic columns and an Ionic molding along the top of the architrave. The triglyphs were set into the wall, and the pedimental decoration was almost certainly an applied terra-cotta frieze rather than the usual free-standing sculpture. Eleven additional sanctuaries dedicated to Hera were found in the southern zone.

Shortly after 400 B.C., Paestum's original Sybarite settlers, lulled into a sense of security behind their handsome fortifications, fell prey to the marauding Lucanians who had clung to the hills behind, covetously eyeing the rich domains below them. Oscan replaced Greek as the local tongue, and Lucanian Paistos moved along new lines to increased productivity and trade, particularly in pottery. The name of Asteas, a local master of the pottery art, became renowned far and wide. Rome established a Latin colony at Paistos in 273 B.C., contemporary with the settlement at Cosa, and renamed the site Paestum. The colonial gridiron street plan may have been simply adapted to the existing city plan, which had no doubt been influenced by the radical Milesian townplanner Hippodamus. Although the city enjoyed Roman favor throughout most of its life-span as a colonial settlement, its fortunes were waning as early as the first century A.D. Strabo remarks that a nearby river (Salso ?) had started to encroach on the city and that spreading marshes, which must have fostered the noisome gadfly, were rendering the city unhealthy.

The Silarus (mod. Sele) river was the boundary between Campania and Lucania and marked the site of the original foundation at Poseidonia and of the earliest Hera temples. One of the shrines near the river mouth, dating ca. 575–550 B.C., had a stylobate measurement of a mere 55½ by 29 feet; the sandy shoreline has yielded up thirty-four of its thirty-six metopes—a veritable thesaurus of ancient myth reconstructed in the Museo Nazionale at Paestum. A second, larger Hera temple, ca. 510–500 B.C., 8 by 17 Doric columns, with a stylobate measurement of 61 by 127½ feet, had ninety-two sandstone metopes of which a dozen are preserved, depicting in relief pairs of maidens engaged in a ritual dance, or possibly Nereids fleeing from a contest between Heracles and the Old Man of the Sea, or the courtship struggle of Peleus with the sea-nymph Thetis.

In his appeal for the handful of dust to appease his unburied spirit, Palinurus says:

Please sprinkle
Dust on my corpse—you can do it and quickly get back to port Velia.
(A. 6, 365–6. Day Lewis)

Velia, twenty-five miles south of Paestum, offered mariners a compact and serviceable harbor between the mouths of two rivers, the Alento (anc. Heles) and the Fiumarella. The acropolis dominated extensive plains which extended towards Cape Licosia in the north and towards Cape Tresine (anc. Troezene) in the south. Founded ca. 540 by Phocaeans, with assistance from Poseidonia and Rhegium, Elea (Latin, Velia) was renowned for two academic residents, the monist philosopher Parmenides (fl. 500 B.C.) and his pupil Zeno (b. 490 B.C.). Xenophanes, the philosophic theologian, lived there and was instrumental in the establishment of the Eleatic school of philosophy which marked the advent of Ionian intellectual enlightenment into South Italy. The polis became one of the most prosperous and splendid of the cities in Magna Graecia. Unlike neighboring Poseidonia, it was never overwhelmed by the Lucanians, and even Roman occupation in the early third century did not alter its Hellenic institutions and way of life. Latin was certainly the official language of the city after 90 B.C., but Greek and Latin inscriptions testify to the bicultural make-up of the city, and Cicero records that priestesses of the Temple of Diana on the Aventine in Rome were regularly Greeks from Velia. Cicero and Brutus met at Velia after the Ides of March, probably at the villa of C. Trebatius Testa, Cicero's young protégé, a prominent lawyer and Caesarian, subsequently the friend of Horace. The harbor facilities were exceptionally good, the best available before Naples and Puteoli on the northward route, but the port was not invulnerable to winds. Octavian, en route to an engagement with Sextus Pompey in 36, was confined in the harbor at Velia and saw his ships pounded to pieces there by a sirocco (Appian, B.C. 5, 98).

Recent excavations at Velia have revealed a city with walls almost four miles in circumference, house foundations, an open-air sanctuary dedicated to Poseidon Asphaleios, "protector of sailors," and no doubt to his associate Aphrodite Euploia, "protector of sailors on voyages," and a large fifth-century B.C. altar, eighty-three feet long, recalling the Altar of Hieron II at Syracuse—both were without doubt dedicated to

Zeus. There are also sixth-century temple remains, perhaps of an Athena sanctuary, and impressive remnants of the civic center adorned with terrace walls, an arcade, a canal, and numerous fountains, and what has been tentatively identified as an ancient medical center—the ancestor of Europe's first school of medicine, the mediaeval school at Salerno, only fifty miles north of Velia. A number of statues and herms representing doctors, both male and female, former directors of the school (*pholarchoi*), have been unearthed, along with a statue of Asclepius and a headless herm bearing the inscribed name of Parmenides, the first documentary evidence of Parmenides found so far at the site. A known student of physics and physiology, Parmenides is assigned the title of Ouliades, "son of Apollo Oulios, the Healer." The discovery of the medical school at Velia accords well with the known visits of particular invalids to the site, of Lucius Aemilius Paullus (ca. 160 B.C., Plutarch, *Aem. Paull.* 39), and of the poet Horace (*Epist.* I, 15, 14–24). Horace testifies that the cold mineral waters of Velia offered stiff competition to the hot sulphur springs and baths at Baiae.

Archaeological discoveries in Campania, coupled with underwater searches in the Bay of Naples and the Bay of Pozzuoli, hold great promise of further insights into the genius of Vergil. The harbor at Cumae along the Euboean shores where Aeneas landed is starting to appear in surface explorations, suggesting that there was a port facility there at one time more refined than the present coastline beneath the acropolis would suggest. The area of the Portus Julius has begun to yield clues that Lake Lucrinus was an immense body of water, shallow but pervasive, and evidently a closer neighbor to Puteoli than was ever imagined earlier. Lucrinus was also in use as a harbor well before the Agrippan alterations. The cult associations at Baiae, surmounted to be sure by the playgrounds and accommodations of the wealthy, are starting to yield up their secrets to the tireless and courageous searches of Commander Robert F. Paget and his colleagues.[20] There is little doubt that a sixth-century temple once dominated the hilltop, that a pre-Augustan community clambered up the sides of the cliff with the pertinacity of a mediaeval hill-town or an ancient terraced sanctuary, and that there ran, deep within the heart of the hillside, a great artificially lit tunnel of initiation. Whether or not Vergil ever descended the long passage and underwent the ritual trials held there can never be known. The antrum was closed sometime between 50 and 25 B.C., probably as a consequence of volcanic action, perhaps as a consequence of Agrippa's closing of the antique cult site. Cumae had certainly experienced the depredations and sacrilegious actions of the Second Triumvirate during the time of troubles with Sextus Pompey so there was ample precedent, nearby, for comparable action at Baiae. Villa sites of known residents still await rediscovery, and their hidden designs and appointments may contribute much to our general understanding of the place and the time when Vergil traversed the area.

Unquestionably Vergil's vision of areas of southern Italy have been an inspiration and a support to the archaeologists in their process of recovering the past. Much more remains to be done, particularly in the investigation of religious cults, of Apollo, Diana, Hera-Juno, Ceres-Demeter, Dionysus-Bacchus, and Aristaeus, to name only the foremost deities. The cult of the underworld is the chief fascination for everyone who ventures into the Cumaean environs, thus passing through something of the mysterious initiation of Aeneas and of Vergil into this timeless, elusive zone. The coastal towns have their secrets still to yield, unimaginable disclosures which may assist still further in the illumination of the mysterious recesses of Vergil's poetry and his unique mind.

VII

Magna Graecia and Sicily

SOUTHERN ITALY, often called Magna Graecia, included some of the most historic and legendary sites in the entire peninsula. Calabria, Apulia, and Bruttium (Puglie and the Abruzzi in modern terms) are scanty in monuments and works of art, but the landscape is sometimes almost Greek, classical in its severity and rock-ribbed durability, and it offers some of the best remaining unspoiled views in Italy. Here is the true Mezzogiorno, a region until recently despised and overlooked as a primitive, remote, superstitious backwater of the peninsula, an embarrassment to the government for its desperate poverty, dust-laden, sordid, yet inescapable. However, since the Second World War, the government has been driven to adopt more humanitarian measures towards these less fortunate areas of Italy, and vast programs of land reclamation, drainage, housing, and a measure of instruction have brought this dramatic landscape back into prominence and into a condition where self-respect is being reborn.

Iapygia and Messapia were the antique names for these southern areas, the former regarded as the territory of the Apulian, Daunian, and Peucetian tribesmen, the latter as that of the Calabrians and the Sallentini. But the territories are, in fact, barely distinguishable from each other, and the tribes which made up the area's inhabitants were closely related in tongue and in culture. The Daunians, from whose tribal territories Horace came, occupied the district from Mons Garganus southwards, including the towns of Luceria, Vibonium, Venusia, and Gerunium. The Peucetii lived behind Bari, and the Messapians in the hinterland of Brundisium and Tarentum.

The Calabrian peninsula forms the instep and toe of the Italian boot. Three great plateaus dominate the area—the Sila in the north, the Serre in the center, and the Aspromonte in the south. These granite massifs rise to an impressive height, with steep, terraced slopes. In the area between the sea and the foothills there are usually somewhat diminutive plains, the largest of them opposite the bluffs on either seaboard. The Ionian seaboard, on the Adriatic side, offers a plain reasonable for settlement and agriculture. The entire coastline, from Taranto to the east coast, was once studded with Greek colonies, affluent and populous enough to earn the area the name of Magna Graecia.

Paucity of water has always been a matter for concern throughout the area. Southeastern Italy has the lowest rainfall of the entire peninsula, and the soil is burdened by a dry top layer of limestone. Consequently, the terrain could not be adapted to extensive agriculture, and landowners had to use their holdings as grazing lands for sheep and horses. The grasslands of Apulia, in fact, provided the best pasture land for horses in Italy. The dry but sheltered coastal area below the river Aufidus (mod. Ofanto) offered superb terrain for olive culture.

The nature of the land and its adaptability to ranching proved a mixed blessing to the natives. Politicians and businessmen found that large estates, called *latifundia*, would provide an excellent return for a modest investment and upkeep. The absentee landlords could live grandly in Rome or at the seaside resorts of Latium and Campania while a handful of shepherds or cowboys supervised their domains. Experience showed that eighty to one hundred sheep could be watched by a single shepherd.

Such ruthless exploitation of the land, and of the herdsmen, had serious repercussions. The dissident herdsmen and slave shepherds occasionally rebelled; in 185 B.C. the local courts condemned some seven thousand miscreants. But equally important, the countryside suffered terribly from this reckless treatment. Crop farming was no longer attractive. Deforestation and soil erosion had combined to make the raising of grain highly unsatisfactory. On the other hand, the profitable returns from ranching induced the wealthy landowners to put far too many animals on the ranges. The grass was too closely cropped, bushes and young trees were not given a chance to develop, and the burning-over of pastures in the spring impaired the root systems which would have helped to arrest soil erosion and to increase fertility. The movement of large herds of sheep (Pliny mentions that some ranches were burdened with as many as 257,000 head) contributed to the deterioration of the hillsides, and thus to the erosion of the soil, and through siltage, to the development of the encroaching malarial marshes up and down the coast. After Hannibal's occupation, peasants, onetime free-holders, left in ever-increasing numbers for the cities. They swelled the proletarian mob, hungry for the dole, for Juvenal's "bread and circuses," and for the excitements of foreign campaigns with hopes of gain and glory.

Horace and Vergil both mention herds in Apulia: herds which would graze richly there in wintertime and during the summer months would migrate to the mountain pastures of Samnium or Lucania. Certainly in Vergil's time one must suppose that the freeholder was mostly a creature of the past. The great private ranches—*saltus*—were largely worked by gangs of slaves, sometimes chained like criminals in Cato's time, but less constrained during the late Republic (although Spartacus' slave revolt must have instilled terror in many a southern rancher). However, the small farmer had not entirely died out, and minor holdings were still farmed in the late Republic around lonely villages and near the larger centers. Horace provides us with a touching portrait of an Apulian peasant *colonus* whose hard labor was shared and justified by his sunburnt wife—a vignette of pastoral happiness which helps to dispel the picture of vast land tracts managed by grasping absentee landlords.

Vergil's acquaintance with the region is strikingly supported by Horace's account of their mutual travels in the south, by a personal recollection of a small landholder near Tarentum, and by other allusions.

Horace's account was connected with the frantic efforts to find a balance of power between Octavian and Mark Antony after 40 B.C. Three attempts were made to reconcile the injured and ultra-sensitive parties after the breakdown of a treaty drafted at either Misenum or Puteoli in

● BARIUM

OTENTIA

●BRUNDISIUM

● TARAS

METAPONTUM ●

● SYBARIS-THURII

IONIAN SEA

●CONSENTIA

●CROTON

● HIPPONIUM

●CAULONIA

●LOCRI

SICILY AND MAGNA GRAECIA

39, a complex arrangement which involved the triumvirs, Octavian, Lepidus, and Antony, and also Sextus Pompey. Horace's *Satire* 1, 5 provides us with a log of one of these diplomatic missions to Antony in which Vergil participated. The sketch of the movements of the diplomatic party from Rome to Brundisium is highly entertaining and revealing. Vergil, Plotius Tucca, and Varius joined the party at Sinuessa and continued with Horace, Maecenas, Cocceius, and others to Brundisium. Assuming that Vergil persevered until the end of the journey, Horace is our witness for Vergil's visits to Canusium (where the bread was gritty) on the Aufidus river, to Ruvo, fishy Bari, superstitious Gnatia, and, finally, to Brundisium.

The presence of the two poet friends (Fig. 67)—for Horace regarded Vergil as his *animae dimidium meae* ("the half of my soul")—is doubtless explained by their recent literary successes and their friendship with Maecenas, Octavian's chief emissary in these negotiations. The mission probably took place in the spring of 38, when Vergil was a permanent resident in Naples and had won high praise for his *Bucolics* and was busy with his *Georgics*. In his report of the journey, Horace took occasion to record his local pride in the Apulian sector, since he was born in Venusia (mod. Venosa), and Vergil must have stored up memories of the same countryside for his subsequent writings. Horace (*Odes* 1, 3) is also the source of our knowledge that Vergil had travelled to Greece at least once before his final trip in 19, and such a passage would almost inevitably have required him to travel the same road to Brundisium.

The Aufidus, still one of Italy's most impressive rivers, receives a passing reference in Turnus' reply to Drances (A. 11, 405). The noble river, periodically violent and proverbial for a ranging torrent, rises in the Apennines, in Hirpini country, about twenty-five miles from Salerno. It meanders through Apulia between Horace's Venusia and Asculum, crosses the ill-fated plain of Cannae, and then empties into the Adriatic between Sipontum and Bari.

Canusium, center of an ancient wool industry in Vergil's time, was the most prominent town in the interior of Apulia. But the more important sites clung to the shoreline, and of these Brundisium and

Tarentum were easily the most outstanding during late Republican times.

Brundisium (mod. Brindisi), on the Adriatic side of the heel of Italy, had a fine harbor facility, both commodious and well sheltered. A narrow channel led from a funnel-shaped bay into two spacious inner basins. Although amply provided with grazing and agricultural lands, Brundisium was virtually ignored as a desirable settlement until Roman times. The port did not receive the major trading vessels, which still made for Puteoli and Ostia in Republican and Imperial times, but it did serve as the principal point of embarkation for Corcyra (Corfu), Dyrrhachium (Albania), and western Greece. The crossings of the "boisterous Adriatic" were mercifully shortest from Brundisium.

Vergil landed in Brundisium when he returned from his last trip to Greece. Stricken with fever at the time of embarkation, he died in Brundisium on September 21st, 19 B.C., in his fifty-first year.

Tarentum lies on the inner side of the heel of Italy. Its situation, astride an isthmus between a shallow, protected bay and a tidal lagoon, made it defensively sound and also a major port of call for shipping. The inner basin, which was practically land-locked, measured eleven miles in circumference. A bridge spanned the channel to the inner lagoon beneath the citadel rock. Not only was the harbor the safest and most spacious in Italy, but it also was stocked with an abundant supply of fish and had one of the most productive purple-beds in the Mediterranean, a rival for Phoenicia, Tyre, and Sidon. The combination of sheep raising, wool production and the purple-dye works made Tarentum the textile center of Italy. Clay beds also contributed to its leading position in the pottery trade of the fourth and third centuries.

The foundation of Taras (Roman Tarentum), in both legend and history, involves Greeks. The mythical tradition held that Taras, son of Neptune, was the original builder of the settlement, and that Phalanthus, a descendant of Hercules, was founding father for the colony of Lacedaemonians whose illegitimate births had made their position in Sparta untenable. Historians generally agree that the first permanent settlement was in fact made by refugees from Sparta. The traditional date of the founding is ca. 700 B.C., but pottery finds confirm earlier contacts with the Mycenaean world.

Tarentum had a number of famous citizens and on several occasions played an important historical role. During the fourth century a Pythagorean philosopher of Tarentum named Archytas became an effective "philosopher king." Livius Andronicus, the father of Latin literature, was born in the city and was taken as captive to Rome after the Pyrrhic Wars (282–272) and the fall of Tarentum. Hannibal occupied the city in 213 in order to gain a port for the transfer of men and arms from North Africa. After his withdrawal the Romans took cruel reprisals; the city, which had renounced its Roman alliance of 272, was recaptured in 209 and ruthlessly plundered. A Latin colony was established in Brundisium in the same year, and thereafter the primacy of Tarentum as a naval power and as a major port of Italy waned rapidly as Rome urged the diversion of sea traffic into Brundisium. The entrance to the inner harbor gradually silted up. Gaius Gracchus' attempt to instill new life into the moribund community in 122 B.C. by importing a sizable colony of Italians was doomed, and Tarentum settled down to become a pleasure resort and holiday escape for tired businessmen and lawyers, senators, and writers. Although the Gracchan-imported Italians did alter the outward aspects of the city, Tarentum, like Naples and Rhegium, was a bicultural city, Latin-speaking but retaining many of its original Greek *mores*. The climate, the fertility of the soil, and the still-adequate port facilities meant that Tarentum would never suffer the gradual decay and depopulation which usually overtook cities challenged by Roman colonial establishments planted nearby. Her importance as a naval station (which the city is still today) survived into the Civil War period.

Of all the cities in the extreme south, Tarentum was the poets' choice for its marvelous climate and peaceful setting, its sea breezes and romantic environs. Horace greatly favored the site and wrote enthusiastically of its excellent vineyards and olive trees, its fine honey, and its prize sheep. Vergil recalls a retired Corycian from Cilicia living there in quiet contentment, enjoying his squatter's rights on a plot of land which he had received from Pompey after the latter abruptly put an end to his lucrative but dangerous trade as pirate in 67 B.C. He wins a most enthusiastic salute from Vergil for his remarkable success with fruit and flowers and bees:

I remember once beneath the battlements of Oebalia,
Where dark Galaesus waters the golden fields of corn,
I saw an old man, a Corycian, who owned a few poor acres
Of land, once derelict, useless for arable,
No good for grazing, unfit for the cultivation of vines.
But he laid out a kitchen garden in rows amid the brushwood,
Bordering it with white lilies, verbena, small-seeded poppy.
He was happy there as a king. He could go indoors at night
To a table heaped with dainties he never had to buy.
His was the first rose of spring, the earliest apples in autumn:
And when grim winter was still splitting the rocks with cold
And holding the watercourses with curb of ice, already
That man would be cutting his soft-haired hyacinths, complaining
Of summer's backwardness and the west winds slow to come.
His bees were the first to breed,
Enriching him with huge swarms: he squeezed the frothy honey
Before anyone else from the combs: he had limes and a wealth of pine
   trees;
And all the early blossom, that clothed his trees with promise
Of an apple crop, by autumn had come to maturity.
He had a gift too, for transplanting in rows the far-grown elm,
The hardwood pear, the blackthorn bearing its weight of sloes,
And the plane that had already offered a pleasant shade for drinking.
                              (G. 4, 125–46. Day Lewis)

The undesirable tract which was converted into a productive paradise by the old man is probably a circumstantial detail, for when Pompey settled the regenerate pirates he was able to give them only property that had not been officially surveyed.

Vergil's sympathetic vignette refers obliquely to the Spartan foundation at Tarentum, for it introduces the name of the mythical Spartan king Oebalus (the historical founder was in fact Phalanthus). The Galaesus river, one of the fairest in Calabria, flowed into the harbor of Tarentum on its north side. The emphasis on hyacinths in this passage is typically Vergilian, for the flower has a link with the Spartan origins of Tarentum: botanically the Roman hyacinth is still something of a mystery, for the word is pre-Greek, but Hyacinthus, the handsome youth who gave his name to the flower, was son of the mythical founder, Oebalus.

The Cilician *senex* is testimony to Vergil's love of old age and to the delights of gardening. He is also neatly integrated into the topic which ensues immediately, for the old man is an accomplished beekeeper and nurtures his bees with the plants they favor. He appears as an example of the joys which attach to hard work, part of the theodicy of the *Georgics*.

There may also be poignant recollection of the aged gardener in Vergil's account of the first outbreak of hostilities between Latins and Trojans:

> Men's bodies lay wide about,
> And with them the old Galaesus, one of the justest
> Of men, once the richest of all in Ausonian fields.
> Five bleating flocks were his, five herds of cattle
> Returned to his barns. He plowed with a hundred plows.
> He was killed as he stepped to the center to ask for peace.
>
> (A. 7, 564–9. L. R. Lind).

Vergil's affection for the landscape of Italy is never more affectingly shown than in his use of the names of its rivers for his Italian heroes: Alma, Galaesus, Sebethis, Ufens, and Umbro, all of them in the Italian catalogue. In the case of Galaesus, the great age of the hero, his peaceful intentions, and his experience of the abundance of Italy provide an indirect but basically very sympathetic compliment to the productive waters and lands about the Galaesus river at Tarentum.

When the Trojan fleet heaves into sight of Italy, the low-lying shape of the western shores appears to the Trojan lookout at dawn. The hills of Calabria, the terminal outcroppings of the Apennines, come into view, and Achates cries "Land Ho!" The description suggests Vergil's personal experience:

> Now Aurora grew pink since the stars had been put to flight,
> When we saw from afar the dim hills and the low-lying shape
> Of Italy.
>
> (A. 3, 553–5. L. R. Lind)

The first Trojan landfall in eastern Hesperia occurs at Castrum Minervae, the modern port of Badisco, some five miles north of Castro:

The breezes we hoped for rose quickly, the port was revealed
Even nearer, Minerva's temple showed up on the heights.
We gathered the sails and twisted the prows toward the shore.
The harbor was curved like a bow by the beat of the East Wind;
Hidden rock-shoals foamed over with the salt sea spray.
The harbor lay snug; towering cliffs sent down arms from twin walls.
The temple stood back from the shore. The first omen I saw
Were four horses who browsed in a pasture, as white as the snow.

We prayed to the holy powers
Of arms-clashing Pallas, the first to welcome my men,
And we veiled heads with Phrygian mantles before the altar.
We followed the urging of Helenus, his solemn request,
And to Juno the Argive we sacrificed as he desired.
No delay: when our prayers had been uttered, in immediate sequence
We swung out the yard-arms and sails to catch every breeze,
And we left the homes of the Greek-born, the fields we mistrusted.

(A. 3, 562–69; 574–81. L. R. Lind)

The Athena temple which claimed the Trojan's worship was, in fact, a famous landmark on the coastal voyage between Hydruntum and the Iapygian promontory. Dionysius of Halicarnassus (1, 51, 3) expands the narrative by stating that the first beachhead of the Trojans bore the suggestive name of Portus Veneris, a harbor which was, incidentally, suitable only for summer anchorage. Vergil's description of the harbor is circumstantial and probably an accurate record of his own experience. Although it resembles the earlier sketch of the harbor of Carthage, the specific details—its shape, the reefs, the rocky breakwaters or moles, the cliffsides which help to make a landlocked harbor, and the temple set back from the shore—all suggest an eyewitness report. Catharine Saunders has identified the harbor with the Grotta Romanelli, near Castro.[1]

Next we spied the bay of Tarentum, where Hercules anchored
(If one can believe it); Lacinian Juno's temple
Arises across from it; here stood Caulonia's fortress
And shipwrecking Scylaceum.

(A. 3, 582–5. L. R. Lind)

Vergil's somewhat skeptical remark on Hercules' association with the site is curious considering the fondness he shows for the hero elsewhere. The rocky headland of Juno Lacinia thrusts out into the Bay of Taranto at a point six miles from ancient Croton, at the southern limit of the Bay. The temple site had been one of the great religious centers of Magna Graecia, comparable to the sanctuary at Poseidonia (Paestum) in Lucania, but today only one of the original forty-eight peristyle columns remains *in situ*. Servius supplies the ingenious tradition which derived the headland's name from a king Lacinius, who refused hospitality to the gluttonous Hercules when he was homeward bound from his struggle with Geryon. Lacinius' impolite behavior was not punished, although comparable rebuffs elsewhere brought Hercules to a homicidal frenzy. To mark his pride and to underline his piety at the same time, Lacinius raised a temple in honor of Hera, the goddess responsible for Hercules' (and Aeneas') trials. Dionysius of Halicarnassus provides testimony supporting Aeneas' landing at the site by relating that Aeneas lodged a bronze vessel inscribed with his name, probably a cauldron or a tripod, in the sanctuary. Hera-worship at the site, as the legends and the remains testify, was very ancient indeed. Nearby Cotrone, ancient Croton, has produced remains of a prehistoric settlement with traces of the earlier great goddess of Oenotria, Italy's antique name, whose symbol was the cow, later sacred to Juno and Hera. The fifth-century B.C. Hera temple has been excavated, and terra-cotta revetments of a high artistic order have been found.

Croton, the city responsible for building and embellishing the Heraeum on the promontory, was, according to legend, a foundation of Hercules. In earlier times, Croton had been one of the wealthiest and most populous cities of Magna Graecia, particularly during the sixth century. During the Punic Wars, Hannibal chose the environs as his headquarters for three successive winters because of the luxuriant pasture lands which enabled him to supply his army easily. Cicero suggests that the enormous wealth of the Hera sanctuary nearby was also an inducement for quartering there. A society of Pythagoreans at Croton, onetime residence of the philosopher-mathematician, assumed a leading role in the political and religious life of the city, and Pythagorean ideas spread throughout Magna Graecia. The fortunes of the city declined after a disastrous defeat by the Locrians and Rhegians during the fourth century and were further reduced during the wars with Pyrrhus, when the population was reduced by half. Croton had assisted Hannibal during the occupation, and this perfidious role brought punitive measures. Livy testifies that the once-proud city had dwindled to a mere village by the second century B.C., and the maritime colony planted there in answer to the threat of war with Antiochus of Syria barely assisted its recovery. Vergil's Croton must have been a very modest community indeed compared with the Croton of the great days when she destroyed her decadent neighbor Sybaris. Only the sanctuary remained as a landmark for mariners and as testimony to the former ascendancy and wealth of the area.

During his forecast of events to come, Trojan Helenus, who had settled with Andromache at Buthrotum in Epirus, provided Aeneas with a short list of places to avoid in his search for a permanent settlement:

> But the lands that lie near and this shoreline [Adriatic] of Italy,
> The closest of regions washed by the tide of our sea,
> You must fly from: its cities are peopled by hostile Greeks.
> Here Locrians of Narycium founded their walls;
> Lyctian Idomeneus occupied Sallentine fields.
> Here is little Petelia, built by the Meliboean
> Leader Philoctetes, based firm on its circling wall.
> But when you've passed by them and anchored across the sea,
> You shall set up an altar on shore and fulfill all your vows.
> You shall cover your head with a cowl of purple cloth,
> Lest amid sacred fires in honor of gods some unfriendly
> Sight shall appear and trouble the omens of heaven.
>
> (A. 3, 431–42. L. R. Lind)

Narycium, associated by Vergil with pine woods, which are under no obligation to man or his implements (G. 2, 438), was a foundation of the Locrians who lived near Euboea. According to tradition, the men of Narycium accompanied Ajax, son of Oileus, to Troy and were shipwrecked on their return at Cape Caphareus (A. 1, 40 f.) because of Athena's enmity towards Ajax. A small remnant continued to Italy and founded the city of Locri Epizephyrii in the Abruzzi.

Locri, founded between 680 and 670 B.C., was a port of call for ships passing between Sicily and the Adriatic coast. The commanding site, high above the Calabrian shoreline, made it another seaman's landmark.

Strabo the geographer says that the first settlement was on Cape Zephyrium (mod. Capo di Bruzzano), but like Poseidonia, it was later moved inland. The law code of Zaleucus, a native of Locri, was the earliest written collection of laws anywhere in the Greek-speaking world. The provisions were excessively severe, but the legal observances meant that Locri became a city which was reputedly well governed into the fourth century B.C. At the battle of the river Sagrus (mod. Allaro?), the largest river between Locri and Caulonia and a natural boundary, the Locrians administered a crushing defeat to the Crotoniates. Pyrrhus imposed heavy exactions on Locri and plundered the temple of Persephone, Locri's most celebrated shrine, although the wary commander returned the treasures after a storm arose during his evacuation of the site. After the Roman disaster at Cannae, Locri assisted Hannibal. Scipio captured the city just as Hannibal was about to leave Italy; when the Roman garrison commander, Quintus Pleminius, treated the Locrians with extreme harshness, they appealed to the Roman Senate, and the treasures Pleminius had removed from the temple of Persephone were once again restored. The city later enjoyed the special patronage of Cicero.

Remains of ancient Locri include some fortifications, originally two miles long, and temple foundations, probably to be assigned to the Persephone sanctuary. From 550–350 there was a flourishing bronze industry at Locri and a fine school of terra-cotta sculpture. Most exquisite were the clay relief panels or ex-votos, eight- to twelve-inches square, like predellas from Italian altarpieces, designed for hanging or nailing on a wall. Some scholars have argued that the Ludovisi and Boston Throne reliefs originally decorated two sides of a shallow pit in the Locrian sanctuary.

The region of the Sallentines extended to Locrian territory. It was famous in Republican times for its olives and olive-oil export. (Hor. *Odes* 2, 6, 15–6). The association of Cretan Idomeneus with the area shows Vergil's archaeologizing tendency, his desire to find suggestive antique associations for his sites (cf. Daedalus at Cumae). Idomeneus was expelled from Crete for sacrificing his son's life in obedience to a rash vow. When pestilence ensued and his exile was demanded, he went to Calabria and founded cities there. Modern Gallipoli (Kallipolis) is located on the Sallentine promontory.

Petelia lay on the coast between the Sallentini and the Locrians, twelve miles from Croton. Helenus' allusion to the community includes mention of its Mycenaean foundation by Philoctetes. Mycenaean sherds have been found at the site, but these offer no substantial support to the civic pretensions to an antique heroic foundation, part of the same mythical colonial story which brought Diomedes to Arpe, Pylians to Metapontum, and Epeius, the carpenter who built the wooden horse, to Lagaria. Petelia, in fact, first entered the mainstream of history during the fourth century when the Lucanians captured the city and made it their metropolis. Its spirited resistance to Hannibal was renowned, and this may, in fact, account for Vergil's reference. His use of the epithet *parva* (A. 3, 410), perhaps recalling the old Latin, *petilus* ("thin," "small"), may be a deliberate word-play to fix Petelia firmly in the reader's mind; the site, even in Vergil's time, was significant; Strabo comments that Petelia was one of the few cities of Bruttium still flourishing and populous in Augustan times.

When the Trojans actually make the passage advised by Helenus, they take pains to avoid Tarentum, the promontory of Lacinian Hera, the heights of Caulonia between Croton and Locri, and Scyllaceum, with its dangerous reefs (A. 3, 551–3.) Like Croton, Caulonia in Vergil's time was a sad remnant of its former greatness. Strabo remarks that the ancient Achaean site was a ghost town, the product of deterioration which set in after the Pyrrhic wars, when a company of Campanian mercenaries took the city and left it a shambles. Finally, after Hannibal's withdrawal, Rome punished the city ruthlessly for its assistance to the Carthaginian. The incuse coinage, with a nude youth holding a branch in his right hand and supporting a small running figure on his outstretched left arm, and with a stag in front, is a confirmation of the city's former prosperity and of its desire to find recognition among the great cities of Magna Graecia, even though it was never to attain major status.

Vergil's treacherous Scyllaceum was colonized, according to the mythical tradition, by Athenians under Mnestheus. Certainly there is no evidence of this enterprise; Athens was involved overseas only once, at Thurii, a Periclean Panhellenic colony, in 444–3 B.C. In 124 B.C., as part of the Gracchan program for the revival of the south, a Roman colony was established at Scyllaceum, not on the ancient site, but on that of modern Squillace. The Aurelii came from Scyllaceum; Cassiodorus Varus, who in his retirement built a new monastery on his Aurelian family estates near the ancient Greek acropolis, has left a detailed description of the site, emphasizing its superb location and productive soil. Although Scyllaceum was notorious for its shipwrecks (rather like Palinurus on the western coast), Hannibal evidently found the beach to the north of the community quite serviceable, for he used it as a refuge during his troubles in the Abruzzi.

At the outset of their hostilities with the Trojans, the Latins dispatched an embassy to seek an alliance with Diomedes, founder of Argyrippa (mod. Arpe) in Apulia, but the ambassadors returned with the news that Diomedes had refused to ally against the Trojans:

> Citizens, we accomplished our journey, surmounting all its
> Hazards: we saw Diomed in his Argive settlement,
> And pressed the hand which wiped out the country of Ilium.
> He was building a city, Arpi, named after his father's people,
> On land he had won in war round about Apulian Garganus.
>
> (A. 11, 243–7. Day Lewis)

Diomedes' role as founder of cities in the west is almost as remarkable as his career on the windy plains of Troy. After he overcame the native peoples of Mount Garganus, he founded Beneventum, Equus Tuticus, and Argyrippa, and was linked with Horace's Venusia, Canusium, and Venafrum. Very few ancient remains survive at the modern village of Arpe, near Foggia. Vergil introduces a touch of pathos into the story of the Diomedes' exile by referring to the sea-birds which still haunt the Diomede Islands off the Apulian promontory of Mount Garganus (cf. *Iliad* 5, 318 ff.). Diomedes laments his fate in the presence of the Latin mission:

> Look how the gods have grudged me a sight of the wife I long for
> And beautiful Calydon—stopped me returning to my home altars!
> Even now I'm pursued by things of ill omen, dreadful
> To look at: my own lost comrades, changed into birds, made off
> To the sky—an uncanny retribution they suffer, haunting
> The streams, and the cliffs are loud with their melancholy cries.
>
> (A. 11, 269–74. Day Lewis)

51. Cumae: remains of the amphitheater adjacent to the Mercury temple.

The amphitheater was excavated from the tufa to form a hollow arena, roughly 444 by 361 feet, seating about 15,000 spectators in 21 rows.

52. Cumae: the underground tunnel leading to the forum area.

The subterranean crypt, built under the Second Triumvirate, provided troops and supplies landed at the harbor of Cumae with rapid access to the larger facility at Portus Julius.

53. Solfatara (mod. Pozzuoli): interior of the crater.

Craters were once characteristic of the Campi Phlegraei, which is still an awesome region. The ancients regarded this crater as the Forum of Vulcan.

54. Lake Avernus, looking towards Baiae and Cape Misenum.

The sacred "birdless" crater lake, once associated with an oracle of the dead and the entry to Hades, was converted to Portus Julius in 37 B.C.

55. Terrified mariner, from Sperlonga. Early Imperial date. Sperlonga, Museo Nazionale.

This over life-size figure clutching the helm is part of a group representing Scylla attacking the ship of Odysseus; the sculptures were recently discovered in the nymphaeum-vivarium cave at the site of Tiberius' villa at Spelunca.

56. Cape Misenum and the beach of Miliscola, air view.

The prominent headland shaped like a funeral tumulus was a landmark for ships making for the Imperial harbor at Misenum and nearby Puteoli.

57. M. Claudius Marcellus (42–23 B.C.). Marble. Paris, Musée du Louvre.

The heir-designate and son-in-law of Augustus failed to respond to the medical treatment of Antonius Musa at the Baian Praetorium and died there at the age of twenty.

58. The Piscina Mirabilis at Bauli (mod. Bacoli). Late Republican date.

This monumental underground cistern, 230 feet long, was excavated in the tufa hill; the water was transported to nearby Baiae and Misenum by ship and cart and by aqueduct.

OPPOSITE PAGE, TOP:

59. Wall painting of a porticus villa and harbor. Imperial date (pre-79 A.D.). Naples, Museo Nazionale.

OPPOSITE PAGE, BELOW:

60. Capri: Villa of Damecuta. Augustan date.

The belvedere (ambulatio) *of the Imperial villa runs along the shore facing Procida and Ischia. The mediaeval tower at the far end probably stands on the site of the Imperial quarters and dining area.*

BELOW:

61. Reconstruction of the rustic villa at Boscoreale. Imperial date (pre-79 A.D.). Model: Rome, Museo della Civiltà Romana.

This large-scale country house incorporated both living quarters and factory. The elevated courtyard accommodated storage for wine and other agricultural products.

BELOW:

62. Italic warrior, found at Capestrano
in 1936. Late sixth century B.C.
Height 6 feet 9½ inches. Chieti,
Museum.

*The purpose of the over life-size image
remains an enigma.*

ABOVE:

63. Samnite warrior. Bronze.
Fifth century B.C. Height 11½ inches.
Paris, Musée du Louvre.

*This small votive figure represents a
soldier (or Mars) in full armor, with a
short-sleeved leather tunic; he has lost his
shield and lance and the crest and twin
feathers of the helmet. The crudely
rendered figure, thickset, with low
forehead and bulging eyes, seems an
admirable reflection of Vergil's primitive
highlanders.*

64. The Avezzano town relief, found in the Fucine Lake, near Alba Fucens. Mid-first century B.C. Rome, Museo della Civiltà Romana.

The relief evokes the Vergilian countryside: a well-organized town, possibly Angitia, is protected by sturdy walls and a high gate; villas dominate the landscape outside the walls.

65. The Sirens' Isles, seen from the peninsula of Sorrento.

The rocky perches of the Sirens lie off modern Positano. Aeneas managed to sail past without incident after Odysseus' passage.

66. Paestum: the Doric Temple of Hera (formerly called
Temple of Neptune). Ca. 460–440 B.C.

*The remains of thirteen Hera temples and shrines and an
impressive Athena temple attract modern visitors to Paestum;
it was a major cult center, perhaps a therapeutic or
miracle site.*

67. Livy (?), Vergil, and Horace in procession. Detail of
relief which originally decorated the Ara Pietatis Augustae.
Claudian date (41–54 A.D.). Rome, Villa Medici.

The Augustan literary triumvirate is portrayed posthumously.
Livy's prose epic of the history of Rome, sister to Vergil's
in verse, found yet another parallel in Horace's Roman Odes.
(Cf. the likeness of Vergil in Fig. 45).

68. The Strait of Messina, air view.

Sicilian Messina faced Rhegium on the Italian mainland, and both enjoyed security and prosperity because of their location. Scylla, the denizen of the strait, was legendary, but the whirlpool of Charybdis was an actual terror, although it lay outside the shipping lanes.

69. Syracuse: the Spring of Arethusa beside the Great Harbor.

Cicero described the fresh-water spring on Ortygia as "unbelievably large, teeming with fish, and so situated that it might be swamped by the waves but for the protection of a massive stone enclosure."

70. Selinus: the eastern plateau with the temple remains, air view.
The resurrected Temple E (Hera?), ca. 480, is in the foreground.

71. Mount Eryx and the town of Erice, air view.

Ancient Eryx, two thousand feet above sea level, was associated with the worship of Astarte, Aphrodite, and Venus. Vergil links Anchises' hero cult with the Elymian (some said Trojan) cult at Eryx.

72. Segesta: view from Monte Barbaro to the Doric temple.

This unusual Doric building (421–415 B.C.) has the normal peristyle and entablature, but the interior altar was probably left open to the sky, as at Eryx.

Vergil's other allusions to South Italy are in some ways more specific than most of his references to settlements. His references to "Calabrian lawns," to the forests of Sila, and to the ridge of Aspromonte seem to derive from visits. The poet conjures up the watersnakes of Calabria in a picture of mounting horror, becoming almost nightmarish at the close, which suggests some personal experience in the area:

Or take that evil watersnake of Calabrian woods
Who bowls around with upright port; his back is scaly,
His belly long and marked all over in big blotches:
That one, while streams are still issuing from their source
And earth remains dank with the wet spring and the rainy south wind,
Living in ponds, housekeeping on river-banks, will cram his
Black maw with fish and garrulous frogs immoderately.
But when the swamp dries out and a hot sun splits the earth
He darts onto dry land, rolling his flame-shot eyes,
And raves through the meadows, mad with thirst, crazy with heat.
I only hope I shall never be tempted to sleep in the open
Or repose on a forest ridge
Among the grass, when that one has cast his slough and glides out
Gleaming in youth, leaving his young or his eggs at home,
Erect to the sun, forked tongue flickering between his lips.
                                        (G. 3, 425–39. Day Lewis)

He also knows the high plateau of the Sila, the mountain ranges where cattle roamed, the dark forests and pistachio-green lakes:

A handsome heifer is grazing upon the slopes of Sila:
Two bulls begin to encounter furiously and inflict
Many gashes, until their bodies are dark with blood;
Their horns confront, lock with a crash and take the strain,
The forests and far-reaching skies roar back at them.
                                        (G. 3, 219–23. Day Lewis)

The belligerent bulls, in the same setting, appear once again when Aeneas and Turnus join in violent combat:

As on the ranges of Sila or a plateau of Taburnus
Two bulls charge at each other, head on, determined to fight
To the death; the herdsmen have backed away from the combat in
   terror,

And the whole herd stands mute with fear, the heifers wondering
Which will be lord of the forest and sultan of all the herd.

(A. 12, 715–9. Day Lewis).

The Sila mountains which rise in a mass behind Croton isolate it
from the interior and the opposite coast. Although at some places the
mountains reach 6500 feet, the slopes and foothills are extensive and
fertile, crowded with woodland, and in Vergil's time they provided rich
pasture land. The mountain torrents then, as now, enriched the low-
lying ground, although the icy-cold waters racing along in formidable
torrents have also done much to erode the productive upper reaches of
the hill country. Taburnus, referred to in the same simile, is the forested
mountain (mod. Monte Taburno, approx. 4000 feet) near the frontier
of Samnium and Campania.

Sicily's position between Europe and North Africa made her the
stepping-stone between the two continents and a battleground for powers who sought to control the Mediterranean basin. Although Sicily has
enjoyed independence in several periods, her history is mainly one of
domination by a succession of outsiders—Greek, Carthaginian and
Roman, later Vandal and Ostrogoth, Byzantine and Saracen, Norman
and Angevin, Spaniard and Austrian. The Sicilians came as immigrant
"Sicels" from the mainland peninsula and reduced the native hill-
dwellers to serfdom. The rugged topography of the island and the almost
constant state of defense which the Sicilians were forced to sustain
meant that the population tended to congregate in large groups, and
where possible, on elevated, easily defended citadels. Life on the higher,
more salubrious ground has always been more practicable than on the
grassy, often marsh-ridden lowlands because of the malarial mosquito.
Agriculture and ranching, both sheep and horse, have always flourished
in Sicily. Even today, given some rather unpromising terrain, some
ninety per cent of the island is under cultivation. Sicily, with Sardinia
and North Africa, was Rome's major granary and also contributed a
rich outpouring of wine, olive oil, and honey. Yet in this plenteous land
life for the Sicilian peasant has been a constant, often painful, struggle
for existence. In Roman times, because of the large-estate system, the
peasant toiled out his days in virtual serfdom to an absentee landlord.

Isolation, illiteracy, and the slave gangs, compounded with grinding poverty, made the life of many of the Sicilian unfortunates as unhappy in antiquity as it has demonstrably been in more recent times. Although the cities were able to muster fervent political spirit and local patriotism, the average Sicilian was probably sullen and apathetic towards changes of rule, and on only a few occasions, in the servile revolts, did the people endeavor to ameliorate their lives by united action.

Rome entered into Sicilian politics almost inevitably. After she had annexed the Greek cities of South Italy, she was almost duty-bound to adopt the views and tactics of Pyrrhus. This Epirote Greek, descendant of Alexander, had endeavored to recreate a Hellenic world in Magna Graecia and Sicily, but his efforts were ruinously costly and ultimately failed—and his name became a symbol of the too-costly victory. The Carthaginian outposts in eastern Sicily were a menace to Rome as they had been to Pyrrhus, and Rome was bound to take comparable preventive measures against them. When the Mamertines, a company of Campanian mercenaries in Messana (mod. Messina), required help against Hieron of Syracuse, they appealed first to Carthage, then to Rome. Both powers intervened in this local issue, largely to ensure the accessibility of the Straits for their shipping, and the result was the First Punic War (264–241). Rome used her allies in South Italy, more experienced in naval warfare, to assist her to ultimate victory. But the cost, particularly to the Sicilian cities, in life, property, and livestock, seemed to outweigh the gain of "liberation." Few actions approached the savagery of Rome's treatment of the ancient city of Leontini. Because the citizenry had shown sympathy for the Carthaginian cause, the town was pillaged; two thousand troops were beheaded because they had betrayed their proper loyalty. The city of Enna was also made an example because of its anti-Roman sentiments. The Roman garrison surprised the citizens as they sat unarmed and unsuspecting in their theater and massacred them. Claudius Marcellus, the destroyer of Leontini, captured Syracuse, and with apparent reluctance turned the city over to his frustrated troops for pillage; the rich accumulations of centuries, precious works of art and votive treasures, were either ruined by the ignorant, reckless troops or were loaded onto ships for Rome. Plutarch relates that Marcellus looked down from a height upon the beautiful, spacious city below and wept copiously, aware of the impending calamity. Amidst the burning and looting, the scientific genius of the age, Archimedes, fell beneath an impatient legionary's sword. Hatred, repugnance, and dread were Rome's inevitable harvest in the succeeding years. And for the Sicilians, the great suffering and destruction brought by the Punic wars was merely a prelude to the equally terrible consequences of comparable adventures by Caesar, Sextus Pompey, and Octavian, to say nothing of the depredations of rapacious governors who swaggered through their provinces like luxurious potentates, with senseless cruelty, arrogance, and thievery.

The system of provincial government, drafted with hesitation and implemented with a makeshift system in 227 B.C., ultimately proved as ruinous to the Sicilians as the conquest itself. The taxation system, which was simply an adaptation to Roman needs of the earlier Punic and Hellenistic system, proved ultimately so onerous, so liable to graft and unjust collection, that farming became a liability many would prefer to escape. The exploitation of the Sicilians between 73 and 71 by their governor Verres was notorious, and finally Rome's fear of a breakdown of the grain supply enabled Cicero to bring him to trial. (Cicero appeared as advocate for the Sicilians, who had known him as a fair financial officer in 75.) For Sicily was the "Republic's storehouse," the nurse at whose breast the Roman people fed, for more than a century and a half. Behind the eulogies to Sicily's plenty by writers from Homer and Pindar to Vergil and Horace lay the somewhat sinister reality that Rome's dependence upon Sicilian produce required constant, often extravagantly cruel, supervision and exaction.

Wracked by two slave insurrections, in 135–2 and in 104–100 B.C., Sicily had a brief breathing space of two generations before even more serious encounters. The protracted fight between Sextus Pompey and the Second Triumvirate brought repeated misfortunes. Sextus found that he could gain his desires best by embarrassing the Triumvirate where it hurt most: in the area of the food supply. By cutting off the grain supply from Sicily and from Africa, he was able to cause a famine in Rome. Treaties which were drafted hurriedly, usually out of desperation, were never effectively honored, and eventually, after years of harassment on both sides, Octavian undertook full-scale military operations against Sextus in Sicily.

Sextus had been a benevolent master of the island and so had considerable Sicilian support against the seemingly malevolent Roman government. For a number of years Sextus and his fellow commanders kept the government armies at bay. Eventually, however, the northeastern sector of the island, from Tyndaris to Tauromenium, became the area of conflict. Octavian, using the naval genius of Marcus Agrippa effectively for the first time, proceeded to launch a series of raids on the Sicilian coast. Messana suffered most in the conflict: Lepidus pillaged the city and set it partly afire in 36. No Sicilian city in this sector emerged unscathed; the damage of war and the devastation of peace were equal in their severity. Octavian punished all defectors who had assisted Sextus Pompey, and a tribute of 1600 talents was required of the islanders, in addition to the normal tithe exacted from most cities—and these exactions followed the recent requisitions of Sextus, which had grown more demanding as the war fever mounted. This "cockpit of the Mediterranean," finally, at the height of the conflict, had to support forty-five legions, twenty-five thousand mounted troops, forty thousand light-armed soldiers, and six hundred warships; the consequence was ruin and a complete breakdown of nerve and resource. Some of the islanders were actually transplanted: the Liparaeans were moved to Naples, wrenched from their homes as reprisal for assisting the nation's enemy. One must suppose that comparable measures were adopted in other communities, most likely at Tauromenium. But man's inhumanity, appalling as it was, was seemingly not sufficient: Mount Etna became unusually active in 36 B.C., the year of the Roman naval victory at Mylae (Milazzo), and in 32 a huge flow of lava damaged cities and fields in the environs.

The consequences of war, however crippling for the Sicilians, must have affected many Romans who, like Cicero, had known the island in happier days. Sicily had been a resort for Romans for centuries. Syracuse, Agrigentum, Segesta, Enna, and Lipara were their favorite ports of call and holiday resorts. Cicero referred to Sicily as Rome's suburban province, its pleasant suburban retreat, and he wrote that Syracuse was so popular with the tourist trade that a class of professional guides, *ciceroni,* came into being. Proximity to Rome was a powerful factor in the encouragement of travel and business on the island. Etna's volcanic display was a perennial attraction. Professional guides would assist the visitor to the summit, and there were hotels on the slope for those who wished to break the ascent or to witness the incomparable sunrise from the height. Mineral-spring baths were also available, rivaling the facilities at Puteoli and Baiae in Campania. Sciacca, near Selinus, and the baths adjacent to Himera were especially popular.

Vergil's biographer suggests that the poet favored Sicily (with Campania) as a retreat away from the tumult of the capital. Although some scholars have doubted Vergil's association with Sicily, the poet's enthusiastic revival and adaptation of Theocritean pastoral, which finds part of its inspiration in the Sicilian landscape, his frequent allusions to the island and to particular cities, and his graphic description of particular sites—of Catania and Syracuse, of Trapani and Segesta, and, not least, of Mount Etna in eruption—seem to indicate personal experience of the island. Vergil's descriptions of the southern shore and of sites on the coast south of Syracuse suggest that he saw them from shipboard, but in view of his evident affection for mainland Tarentum, which provided easy access to the island, it seems very likely that he was directly acquainted with certain parts of Sicily.

Vergil's familiarity with the island must have come during his years of residence in Naples. The period before 36, when the clash between Octavian and Sextus Pompey came, and the period between 30 and the settlement of 22 B.C. (when Augustus intervened in the affairs of Sicily and abolished the tithe-system in favor of a fixed levy) were both suitable for protracted visits or a tourist cruise. The later date seems particularly suggestive in view of the Anchises-Aeneas association with the northwest Sicilian coast, an association which registered strongly in the poet's mind, and presumably, too, in the mind of Augustus, descendant of those epic figures. The melancholy which attaches to the funeral games and the forthright action of Julus-Ascanius when the women attempted to burn the ships probably have poignant connections with Marcellus, who died in 23.

Vergil's allusions to Sicilian history are free of reference to past and recent depredations and conflict, and his review, admittedly set in the timeless, almost abstract world of legend and nearly forgotten history, does not leave one with the impression which Strabo, his contemporary, imparts. Nor does Cicero support the description of desolation, of dying communities, in Strabo's account, which is more appropriate to the mid-second century B.C. than to the Imperial Age. To be sure, the old *latifundia* system of large-scale ranches persisted, and there were still sizable farms for the production of grain. But Augustus had also undertaken to settle thousands of legionaries on Sicilian soil, and a new, progressive and industrious class of small landowners had come into existence. The south coast, at Agrigentum and Gela, and the northwest littoral, at Lilybaeum, still held flourishing and enterprising cities, much diminished from their grandeur and affluence in the sixth and fifth centuries, but in no way desolate or impoverished.

Sicily enters the epic narrative first with the catastrophic storm at sea which Juno contrived through Aeolus, god of the winds, in order to thwart Aeneas' destined landing in Italy. Ancient writers located the storm center, the realm of picturesque Aeolus, in the islands some fifty miles off the northeast coast of Sicily. The Aeolian group comprises seven islands, of which Lipara is the largest, but Hiera (mod. Volcano) was thought to be the site of Vulcan's smithy. Diodorus Siculus says that although all seven islands were once actively volcanic, in his time only Hiera and Strongyle (Stromboli), lighthouse of the Mediterranean, were active. The peculiar sounds of hissing steam, rockfalls, and intermittent bursts of flame did much to support the notion that here was Vulcan's home, and the modern name continues the tradition. Strabo and Pliny locate the palace of Aeolus on Strongyle.

The Aeolian islands, though not specifically ports of call for Aeneas, were certainly open to Mycenaean shipping. Obsidian, which erupted from the craters on Lipara, was used for knife blades, scrapers, and the like before metalworking techniques were perfected. Because Melos, which contained comparably large deposits, was dominated by Minoans in the early Mycenaean period, traders were driven westwards to find other deposits for their arrowheads and sharp instruments. A prosperous trade developed during the Mycenaean period and continued thereafter. Pliny and Diodorus relate that Lipara derived its name from a son of Auson, who reigned there before Aeolus. Greek colonists from Cnidus and Rhodes, ca. 580 B.C., found only five hundred inhabitants on the island. As corsairs, preying on the shipping and coastlines nearby, the Liparaeans were a match for the Etruscans, who tried on numerous occasions to wrest the islands from Greek control. In 252, after a period of Carthaginian occupation, the islands formed part of the province of

Sicily and contributed to Roman tribute on a sizable scale. The harbors of Volcano and of Strongyle served as naval bases for Agrippa during the hostilities with Sextus Pompey on the eve of the victories at Mylae and Messana. Cicero speaks of Lipara in somewhat disparaging terms, "a small community, set on an undeveloped diminutive island," but this is almost certainly a rhetorical exaggeration, for the soil remained attractive for its yield of fruits, its alum mines, and its increasingly popular steam baths and hot springs.

Vergil's account of the awesome dwellings of Aeolus and of Vulcan is memorable:

> . . . the goddess
> Came to the storm-cloud country, the womb-land of brawling siroccos,
> Aeolia. Here in a huge cavern King Aeolus
> Keeps curbed and stalled, chained up in durance to his own will,
> The heaving winds and far-reverberating tempests.
> Behind the bars they bellow, mightily fretting: the mountain is
> One immense murmur. Aeolus, aloft on his throne of power,
> Sceptre in hand, gentles and disciplines their fierce spirits.
> Otherwise, they'd be bolting off with the earth and the ocean
> And the deep sky—yes, brushing them all away into space.
> But to guard against this the Father of heaven put the winds
> In a dark cavern and laid a heap of mountains upon them,
> And gave them an overlord who was bound by a firm contract
> To rein them in or give them their head, as he was ordered.
>
> (A. 1, 50–63. Day Lewis)

> Between the Sicilian coast and Aeolian Lipare there's an
> Island, whose cliffs, sheer-rising, jet out smoke from their crannies:
> Deep within it are vaults, a rumbling volcanic cavern
> Scooped out by the action of the Cyclops' fires; you can hear
> The clang of hard blows on the anvils, the roaring when masses of ore
> Are smelted within, and a throbbing blast of flame from the furnaces.
> Here is Vulcan's place; the island is called Vulcania.
>
> (A. 8, 416–22. Day Lewis)

The volcanic origins of Hephaestus-Vulcan and his Cyclopean workers, with their crater-like single eye, are evident. Aeolus' castle may be an imaginative recollection of the Castello of Lipara, an isolated rock which soars above sea level, an almost impregnable fortress which served as the citadel for the island's inhabitants from Neolithic through Roman and mediaeval times.

Even more horrendous for seamen was the Strait of Messina (Fig. 68). Vergil subscribes, and rightly, to the belief that Italy and Sicily were once joined. Less scientifically, he also accepts the antique tradition of Scylla and Charybdis as denizens of the strait. Scylla is usually described as a sea-monster living in a cave on the Italian side, where the promontory still preserves her name. She is given six heads, each equipped with a triple row of murderous teeth, and twelve feet. Although fish were her main diet, if an unwary ship sailed by she would seize six men at a time and devour them. Etymologically, Scylla suggests Greek *skylax*—"puppy." Vergil may have this in mind when he leashes wolves to her girdle and assigns to her cave a kennel of cerulean sea-hounds. Pocock has suggested that the puppy sobriquet stemmed from the high-pitched sounds often associated with underwater eruptions.[2] Equally suggestive are the howling, barking noises made by the wind in the rocky caves. Charybdis, Scylla's notorious partner, fortunately outside the shipping lanes which led into Messana, behaves like a whirlpool which sucks in and belches water three times daily, deadly to ships. Odysseus owed his salvation to a tree which grew above the maelstrom, enabling him to escape the suction and to drop into the efflux at the right moment to be borne away. Vergil's epithet *vasta* ("yawning") is etymologically linked to the Greek Charybdis (cf. chasm). Servius tells the intriguing story that Charybdis had once been a "man-devouring" female, child of Neptune and Earth, and because she stole the cattle of Hercules, the much-travelled herd of Geryon, she was hurled into the depths of the sea, where she continued her old behavior. The legendary figure has been associated by Pocock with underwater convulsions which were peculiar to the Aeolian Islands, where volcanic phenomena, magnified versions of the monster's behavior, may still be witnessed.

Aeneas' experience with both monsters is limited, but nonetheless dramatic: an almost proleptic view of the underworld which he will one day visit in the ancient volcanic setting of Cumae and Avernus. Helenus forecasts both monsters to his Trojan audience at Buthrotum:

Scylla guards the right shore, insatiable Charybdis
The left. Three times a day the latter, down in the depths of
A whirlpool, gulps whole tons of wave into her maw,
Then spews them up again, flailing the heavens with spray.
But Scylla lurks unseen in a cavernous lair, from which
She pushes out her lips to drag ships on to the rocks.
Her upper part is human—a girl's beautiful body
Down to the privates; below, she is a weird sea-monster
With dolphin's tail and a belly of wolverine sort. It's advisable
To fetch a long compass, although it protracts the voyage, and sail
Right round the Sicilian cape of Pachynum, a southernmost mark,
Rather than to set eyes on that freakish Scylla within
Her cavern vast or the rocks where her sea-blue hounds are baying.
(A. 3, 420–32. Day Lewis)

The Trojans successfully escape Scylla, but the encounter with Charybdis is dramatic:

Yarely they all obeyed my father's command. Palinurus
Turned away first to port, the bows of his vessel creaking;
Then the whole convoy, with oars and sails, clawed off to port.
We were tossed up high on an arching surge, then down we went
In the trough as the wave fell away, down to the very Pit.
Thrice roared aloud the reefs and the caverns of rock beneath us,
Thrice we beheld the sky through a spattering flounce of spindrift.
Time passed. The wind went down with the sun. Utterly spent,
Not knowing where we were, we crept to the shores of the Cyclops.
(A. 3, 561–9. Day Lewis)

The northeastern tip of Sicily, modern Punte del Faro, was ancient Pelorus, and Vergil's account of its appearance seems evidence of his direct acquaintance with the straits:

Now when you have left that first landfall and sail to Sicily,
At the point where Pelorus begins to reveal a narrow opening
Steer for the land on your port bow, the seas to port, and make
A detour giving a wide berth to shore and breakers a'starboard.
Once on a time, they say, these two lands were a single
Country; then there came a convulsion of nature which tore them
Hugely asunder—the ages can bring such immense geological
Change—and the sea rushed violently in between them, dividing

Italy from Sicily, severing their coasts and washing
Cities and fields on either side with a narrow strait.
(A. 3, 410–19. Day Lewis)

As ships approach, the land mass on the northeast does start to thin out (*rarescere*) into the contours of two coastlines which get gradually steeper as the foothills of Mount Etna come into view. Pelorus on repeated occasions played an important role as a naval station guarding the approaches to Messana and to Sicily generally. Sextus Pompey kept strict watch on the cape during the wars with Octavian. The temple of Neptune, protector of mariners, and the complementing Pharos (lighthouse) have vanished without a trace.

Aeneas' encounter with the Cyclops and his towering brethren and with the Greek castaway Achaemenides is one of the lengthiest and most melodramatic incidents in all of Book 3. Vergil's setting for the incident, either Taormina or Catania, is designed like an extravagant stage set or dramatic landscape painting:

There lies a haven, sheltered from all four winds; it is calm
And roomy too; but, nearby, Aetna thunderously erupts.
Ever and anon it discharges at heaven a mirky cloud,
A swirl of pitch-black smoke lurid with white-hot cinders,
And volleys huge balls of flame, singeing the very stars.

So, every time he [Enceladus] turns over to rest one aching side,
Sicily quakes and rumbles, smoke hangs above like an awning.
That night we hid in the woods, enduring these gigantic
Phenomena, and unable to see what caused the din;
For the lights of the stars were out, there was no shine on the face of
Heaven from the constellations, only a fog which bandaged
Its eyes, and clouds which muffled the moon at this dead of night.
(A. 3, 570–4; 581–7. Day Lewis)

With the morning sun the Aeneadae are confronted by a helpless individual in the ragged remnants of Greek military dress, a Philoctetes-like figure, a somewhat more tragic forecast of Robinson Crusoe, or *Treasure Island*'s Ben Gunn, a veteran of a foreign war, abandoned by Ulysses and his crew during their flight from Polyphemus. Scion of a military family, with an exotic Persian or Parthian association in his name, Achaemenides appeals to Aeneas for deliverance or death. The account of his travails, as circumstantial as Sinon's earlier tale on the plains of Troy, wins the belief and the amity of Anchises and the magnanimous Trojans, and he becomes their deliverer and guide in return. The honesty of his account is dramatically substantiated by the apparition of Polyphemus—like some authentic sign, a *monstrum* in the technical sense—and his fellow Cyclopes, personifications of the volcanic death-dealing craters of Etna.

The inspiration for Vergil's description of the volcano may lie in his experience of an actual eruption, perhaps in 44, perhaps subsequently. Certainly the volcano was source of fascination for the poets of antiquity, for Homer, Pindar, Aeschylus, and for Lucretius, Seneca, and for the author of the *Aetna* which has often been ascribed to Vergil. Travellers today are still treated to periodic bursts of fire from the cone and to occasional outpourings of lava, seen most vividly at night from the shoreline of Catania and Aci Trezza or from the more theatrical viewpoint of Taormina.

Lava flows which have worked their way down to the seashore through vineyards and estates, cities and their outlying areas, are still a characteristic feature of the landscape; and the use of the abundant lava as an economical building material, by itself or stuccoed, gives a somewhat melancholy aspect to the surroundings, a gloomy reminder of past and future encounters with the titanic mountain.

Tauromenium, successor city to ancient Naxos on the promontory below, owed its prosperity to the splendid Naxian harbor and to the benefactions of Syracusan despots. Vessels bound for South Italy or the Aegean frequently used the convenient port facilities of Tauromenium and filled its coffers. Sextus Pompey made the city his naval headquarters during his struggle with Octavian. At one stage, after a naval defeat Octavian was shipwrecked and separated from his fleet and was reduced to wandering forlornly up and down Tauromenium's shores seeking assistance in the depths of night. The city was subsequently punished severely by Octavian for its defection to Pompey. The population may even have been transplanted elsewhere as reprisal before the site was resettled by a military colony.

The original inspiration for the Cyclopean story and the details of Polyphemus' action against Odysseus are probably to be found in mariners' stories, perhaps as early as Mycenaean times. These tales were

perhaps embellished subsequently by the Chalcidic Greeks who occupied Messana and Rhegium and sought by piratical attack and by these
terrifying stories to exclude other Greeks and Etruscans from their territorial trading waters. In this connection, the basaltic rocks, the so-called
faraglioni, in the sea off Aci Trezza, have often been identified with the
rocks hurled at the escaping Odysseus by the irate, blinded Cyclops.
Odysseus escaped the volcanic fall-out, a more material terror than that
Aeneas suffered—though the Trojan nervous strain was as great, and
in its way marked the culmination of an Odyssey of disappointments
and agonizing doubts about the future.

Polyphemus himself was a creature of larger associations than
Odysseus and Aeneas, for the courtship of milk-white Galatea by the
amorous giant was a favorite theme with Greek pastoral writers, with
both Theocritus and Bion, and with Vergil and Ovid. Galatea and Acis,
with the curiosity of youth and the audacity of lovers, listened in hiding
to Polyphemus' love song to the absent Galatea. They were discovered
by the giant, however, and his rage brought their love to a tragic end:
Galatea leapt into the sea, her natural habitat, but Acis was crushed
by a rock hurled by the jealous Polyphemus. Galatea thereupon turned
her beloved Acis into a river which is recalled in several of the local
place-names in the environs of Etna and Catania.

Vergil's closing words on the Polyphemus-Achaemenides episode are
among his most disturbing and memorable. Aeneas and his men view the
Cyclopean company from shipboard:

> There they stood, the fraternity of Aetna, impotent,
> With baleful eyes and their sky-scraping heads—we saw them—
> A terrifying assembly; so on some mountain top
> Head-in-air oaks are massed, or cone-bearing cypresses—
> Jupiter's own tall wood, or a grove sacred to Diana.
>
> (A. 3, 677–81. Day Lewis)

The nightmarish landscape and underworld associations of Mount Etna
are part of a larger canvas of volcanic scenes and the landscape underground at Cumae, and, equally horrendous for their sinister quiet and
grim associations, of the infernal lakes of Avernus, Amsanctus, and
Nemi.

The description of Aeneas' coastal voyage mentions several smaller sites before Syracuse. The account of the Pantagias river between Catana (mod. Catania) and Syracuse, a faithful sketch evidently based on eyewitness, emphasizes the rocky defile through which the river flows today, torrential in spring, less obstreperous at other seasons. The "Megarian bay" is a small, scenic bay which provides a safe landing for smaller ships. Megara Hyblaea, on a low grassy plateau, was reduced to village-status in Vergil's time, but was still famous for its Hyblaean honey. Founded by Megarians from the isthmus of Corinth, and subsequently itself metropolis of Selinus on the south-western shore, the city was taken by storm by Gelon of Syracuse in 481 B.C. Thereafter, Megara never regained its freedom or its onetime affluence. Although another city was built on the original territory during the mid-fourth century, its destiny was equally tragic, for Claudius Marcellus captured the city in 214 B.C., and because it had assisted Syracuse against Roman attack, it was plundered and destroyed; it never revived thereafter.

Aeneas' pilot and guide between Etna and Syracuse is Achae-menides, the very embodiment of the smooth-talking, often garrulous practitioners of the same art today. Low-lying Thapsus, the modern peninsula of Magnesi two miles north of Syracuse, may provide another instance of Vergil's association of an etymological epithet with the Greek place-name (Greek *thaptein,* "to bury, lay low"; and *iacere,* "to lie low, lie buried"). By nature Thapsus was designed to be less a colonial site than a pirate's haven. There is a modest harbor on the south side, used by the Athenians prior to their capture of the Great Harbor of Syracuse. Its recorded history, however, is brief and un-eventful. Before establishing themselves firmly at Megara Hyblaea, the Megarians had tested the resources of both Trotilon and Thapsus. According to tradition, the founding father, Lamis, died at Thapsus, and after something less than a year the colonial party transferred to the mainland opposite. Several hundred rock tombs, tholos (beehive) and rock-cut forms, mostly from the Bronze Age settlement, crop up along the shoreline and in the interior, a feature which may, in fact, have urged the place-name on the colonists. After the eighth century the site was never inhabited again.

One of the victims of Mezentius on Latin soil is strangely associated with the Sicilian river Symaethus (mod. Giarretta), a sizable river

which enters the sea about eight miles south of Catania. Vergil describes
this youth's Sicilian upbringing in remarkable detail:

> The son of Arcens stood in his excellent armor,
> His embroidered cloak red with its Spanish dye,
> Noble of face. Arcens, his father, had sent him,
> Raised in a grove of Mars by the river Symaethus,
> Where Palicus' altar, fat with slain beasts, grants favor.
>
> (A. 9, 606–10. L. R. Lind)

Vergil's account of Syracuse is both topographical and legendary:

> There's an island lies
> In front of Sicania's bay, Plemyrium the wavy:
> The ancients had named it Ortygia. They tell how Alpheus,
> A river of Elis, had forced his way under the ocean,
> And now with your spring, Arethusa, has mingled his waters.
> Obeying Anchises' command we worshipped the powers
> That rule there . . .
>
> (A. 3, 718–24. L. R. Lind)

The poet seems to recall his own view of the celebrated harbor of
Syracuse: Plemyrium is the headland on the south side of the bay,
a critical area during the Athenian siege of Syracuse (415–3 B.C.), and
Ortygia is the low, rocky island on the north side of the bay. Once again
Vergil uses an identifying epithet with the place-name: Plemyrium
("tidal") is characterized by *undosum* ("wavy"). His insertion of the
antique name, Ortygia ("quail island"), probably arises from his association of the local name with Delos, also called Ortygia, birthplace
of Apollo and Diana in the Aegean Cyclades. Diana's links are not
only with Delos, but through Arethusa with Syracuse as well. Vergil
recalls here the legend of Arethusa, perhaps as old as the eighth century:
Alpheus, the river god of Olympia, enamored of the nymph Arethusa.
During his pursuit of his beloved, Diana answered her votary's prayer
and changed the nymph into a spring which plunged into the sea and
emerged as a fresh water spring off the Syracusan shore (Fig. 69). But
Alpheus, the undaunted lover, followed her under the sea and united
his waters with hers in the bay of Syracuse. Thus Diana is associated
with Syracuse, and, of course, with the Apollo temple on Syracusan
Ortygia. The source of those instructions the Trojans follow in their

religious services at Syracuse is unexplained (unless perhaps Achaemenides is implied, or some further, unrecorded, advice of Helenus);
this was evidently Vergil's indirect way of acknowledging the formerly
splendid sanctuaries in and around the city.

The sack of Syracuse in 214, with the dispersal of its treasury, its
wealth of coin and art works, was unforgettable. But the fortunes of
the city had sufficiently revived one hundred and fifty years later to
permit Cicero to compose an account of the wonders of the ancient city
which would excite his great-hearted audience to condemn Verres'
depredations:

> You will often have been told that Syracuse is the largest of Greek
> cities and the loveliest of all cities. Gentlemen, what you have been
> told is true. Its position is not only a strong one, but beautiful to be-
> hold in whatever direction it is approached, by land or sea. Its harbours
> are almost enfolded in the embrace of the city buildings, their
> entrances far apart, but their heads approaching till they meet each
> other . . . The island [Insula] . . . is girdled by two harbours and
> extends to their two mouths of entrances. In this quarter is the house,
> once King Hiero's, which our governors regularly occupy. Here also
> are a number of temples, two much finer than the rest; namely, that
> of Diana, and the other one, that of Minerva, a place rich in treasures
> in the days before Verres arrived there. . . . Then there is a second
> town of the city called Achradina: this contains a broad market-place,
> some fine colonnades, a richly adorned town hall, a spacious senate
> house, and the noble temple of Olympian Jupiter, besides the rest
> of the town which is filled with private houses, and divided by one
> broad continuous street crossed by a number of others. There is a
> third town, called Tycha from the ancient temple of Fortune that
> once stood there: this contains a spacious athletic ground and
> several temples, and is also a crowded and thickly inhabited part of
> the city. And there is a fourth town, which being the most recently
> built, is called Neapolis: on the highest point of this stands the great
> theater; besides which there are two splendid temples, one of Ceres,
> and the other of Libera, and a large and beautiful statue of Apollo
> Temenites—which if Verres had been able to transport he would not
> have hesitated to carry off.

(Cicero, 2 *Verr.*, 4, 53. 70 B.C.)

Although Syracuse had dwindled in population by Vergil's time, it remained much favored by tourists and long-term residents. The winters were mild and the sun shone daily. After Actium, Octavian lodged a military colony of his veterans at Syracuse, according to Strabo in the area adjacent to Ortygia. Not all of Rome's associations with the city were as respectful and pietistic as Aeneas' preliminaries.

After duly worshipping the patron spirits of Syracuse, the Trojans, guided by Achaemenides, sailed around the southeastern promontory and along the southern shore of Sicily:

> The marshy mouth of Helorus with its most fertile soil.
> Next, we skirt Pachynus—a place of high rocks and jutting
> Reefs; and now, far off, is Camarina, which fate said
> Must never be reclaimed, and the Geloan plains,
> And Gela, which is named after its own wild river.
>
> (A. 3, 698–702. Day Lewis)

With his usual etymological and topographical exactitude, Vergil designates the river Helorus ("marshy") as stagnant. Today the modern Abissos river, some three miles southeast of baroque Noto, still shows the features which characterized it in ancient times. Rising in the hills above Acrae (mod. Palazzolo Acreide), it thunders down through rugged terrain into a pleasant valley, which Ovid calls Heloria Tempe, recalling the verdant vale of the Muses in Thessaly, and which Vergil describes as rich lowlands; thence it flows to a stagnant river mouth where fish once abounded, tame enough to feed from human hands. The town of Helorus, which was almost certainly a colony of Syracuse, has virtually disappeared.

Aeneas' ships skirt the projecting rocks and the deep reefs of Pachynus, the southeastern promontory of Sicily (mod. Capo di Passaro). Vergil's emphasis on the rocks and reefs enhances the tricky nature of the shoreline, which, like a turning point in a chariot race, the ships barely graze as they round the bend towards Camarina, "which the Fates said should never be moved," and the plains of Gela, with its "cruel" river. Camarina, an ancient Syracusan colony about fifty miles west of the Cape and southwest of modern Vittoria, marked the western limit of Syracusan expansion, which by the time of Camarina's foundation (ca. 598) covered an area of approximately fifteen hundred square miles. The gently sloping hills, with forests and well-watered terrain, combined to make the foundation an affluent one from the outset. Dunbabin's description of the site is precise and revealing: "Kamarina, like Gela, but on a smaller scale, is the outlet of a rich land whose other access to the sea is blocked by sand-hills. The channel between the lake and the sea formed a port, and remains of quays have been found flanking it. The marsh into which the river [Hipparis] spread defended the city effectively on one side, though it was very unhealthy. Low sandy hills are presented to the sea, and to the east the flat-topped hill is succeeded by rolling country. It was a site easy to fortify."[3]

Servius enlarges on the fatal move of Camarina. The neighboring marsh, which was also called Camarina, gave rise to pestilence, probably malaria, and the citizens consulted the Delphic oracle to inquire whether the marsh should be drained. They were instructed, somewhat less than satisfactorily, to leave the trouble-spot alone—in an expression which became as proverbial as "let sleeping dogs lie": "Do not disturb Camarina; it is better undisturbed." But the citizens chose to disregard the oracular advice in favor of public health, and they drained the marsh, whereupon the town was attacked and plundered by an enemy who approached over the dry land which once had been marsh. The city was destroyed. It was refounded twice, in 491 and in 461. The destruction at the hands of the Carthaginians during the first Punic war (258) was final, and in Augustan times the site was a ghost town.

Vergil's "log" takes note next of the low acropolis hill of Gela, a Dorian colony founded in 688 by Rhodians and Cretans, and named after the Siculan river Gelas. A century later Gela had become metropolis to Acragas (Agrigentum), the latter a colony which ultimately eclipsed its founder. Hippocrates became tyrant of Gela in 498, and with an almost Napoleonic vigor and aggressiveness he built an empire by absorbing the Chalcidic cities of northeastern Sicily, including Naxos, Zancle, and Leontini. Only Syracuse successfully resisted his attacks. When Corinth and Corcyra (mod. Corfu) arbitrated, Hippocrates accepted Camarina as compensation for his frustration before the defenses of Syracuse. After his death in 491 his cavalry officer Gelon assumed power, and assisted by malcontents in Syracuse, the Geloan forces finally took the great city. Gelon moved his residence to Syracuse and left his brother Hieron at Gela. Because it had assisted Syracuse, Camarina was destroyed, and its population, together with half of the citizenry of Gela, was moved to Syracuse. This mass deportation reduced both cities to second-rate powers until the Deinomenid tyranny was overthrown at Syracuse, and Gela regained her independence. The transplanted citizens returned, and Gela entered a period of great commercial prosperity and artistic activity. Aeschylus, who left Athens after the production of his *Oresteia* in 458 to enjoy the enlightened patronage of the Sicilian courts, died at Gela and was buried in her soil. His epitaph, supposedly by his own hand, made no mention of his career as playwright:

> This tomb the dust of Aeschylus doth hide,
> Euphorion's son and fruitful Gela's pride.
> How tried his valour Marathon may tell
> And long-haired Medes who knew it all too well.

The Athenian catastrophe at Syracuse in 413 presaged a time of troubles for Gela, culminating in 280 when Phintias, the tyrant of Acragas, removed Gela's population to his newly founded Phintias (mod. Licata) and his Mamertine mercenaries destroyed the city. In Vergil's time the site was only a sparsely inhabited ruin with few visible remains. Certainly the most impressive features would have been the fertile wheat fields and possibly some sectors of the circuit walls of the fourth century along the beach. Their discovery in the sand dunes of Capo Soprano came during the allied bombardment of Gela during World War II. The splendid walls, some five miles in length, were seemingly ineffective against the Acragantines and their Campanian troops and were left to the shifting sands for burial, no doubt almost complete by Vergil's time. Other finds made recently at Gela include architectural and votive terra cottas of unique style and mastery and some valuable examples of imitative ware fashioned by native Sicilian potters inland. The ancient city rose on a low ridge overlooking the wide plains, and there were no really adequate harbor facilities at any time.

Vergil's epithet *immanis* ("cruel, mean"; A. 3, 702) has caused commentators dismay. Servius and others have chosen to assign it to the place-name of Gela and have interpreted it as a reference to the cruel behavior of local despots. But Acragas is actually more likely than Gela to be linked with savage dynasts, and Vergil probably applies the epithet to the river Gelas, possibly referring to the torrential, destructive force of the river rampaging through the grainfields and lowlands in springtime. Coin types offer a reminder of the river's potential by representing it as a swimming, man-headed bull. But behind the "cruel" one may perhaps detect a Vergilian witticism: Gela, which has the same root as the Greek verb "to laugh" in the adjectival form, coupled with *campi*, yields an alternative meaning of "Plains of Laughter"—a nice partner for the *Campi Lugentes*, "The Fields of Mourning," of Aeneas' Underworld experience (A. 6, 441).

Acragas, Roman Agrigentum, receives due notice in the account of Aeneas' voyage:

> Acragas, lofty with walls widespread,
> Showed up afar off, once breeder of high-hearted horses.
> (A. 3, 728–9. L. R. Lind)

Acragas ("lofty," "citadel height") was founded by a combined Geloan and Rhodian colonial party in 580 B.C. The craggy acropolis, a major rise on the southern horizon, lies between the rivers Acragas (mod. San Biagio) and Hypsas (mod. Drago). The earliest personality was the diabolical Phalaris, a less-than-benevolent despot who extended the territories of Acragas to the east and west, and, in a bolder thrust, to Himera on the northern coast, the last probably as part of a design to contain Punic expansion in western Sicily. His home policy coupled oppression with intelligent town-planning and a program of splendid public works. Pindar refers to the exotic cruelty of Phalaris, who roasted men alive in a bronze bull. (The infamous oven, captured by the Carthaginians in 406, was later recovered and returned to Agrigentum by the Romans to contrast their generosity with the cruelty of the local government in the past.) Theron reigned in Acragas from 488 to 472; his beneficent rule led to a victory of the allied forces of Acragas and Syracuse against Carthage at Himera (480). This celebrated victory ushered in a golden age at Acragas, a period of great agricultural and economic prosperity. Local wines, olive oil, and grain were exported to North Africa, and Vergil echoes the praise of earlier eulogists when he remarks on the fine horses which were then still bred at Acragas. Its racehorses were frequent victors at the Panhellenic Games and were famous throughout the world. Theron also patronized the poets Simonides and Pindar at his court, and several odes of Pindar celebrate victories won by Acragantine competitors at Olympia and Isthmus between 490 and 472. Pindar refers to Acragas as "seat of Persephone," a tribute both to the cult service and to the rich grain fields, and again as "most beautiful of mortal cities that lives upon the hill of fine dwellings above the bank where the sheep graze beside the river."

The war indemnity paid by the defeated Carthaginians, the enormous spoils and droves of prisoners taken at Himera, enabled Acragas to launch an impressive building program of construction of temples, houses, and aqueducts. The ridge lying between the city and the sea supported the religious sanctuaries, an imposing line of Doric temples: the enormous and unusual Temple of Olympian Zeus (510–409), the temples of Heracles (ca. 500), of Hera Lacinia (ca. 460), and of Concord (ca. 430?). All are noteworthy today, and all were visible to Vergil's contemporaries.

Although repeatedly taken by Carthage between 406 and the third century, Acragas, renamed Agrigentum, finally came under Roman protection during the Second Punic War (210 B.C.) and became a tithe-paying community in the final settlement. During Verres' rapacious governorship of Sicily, the city served as center for the administration of the island's grain tax. Finally, in 43 B.C., Roman citizenship was conferred on the city by a grateful Roman Senate, and the city enjoyed almost two centuries of prosperity before its final decline. The fortifications—which Vergil characterizes with the epithet "lofty," though they had become somewhat dilapidated since the Punic Wars—were probably the work of Phalaris and date ca. 575–550 B.C. Cicero, in his attack on Verres' administration, frequently remarks on the wealth, the large population, the fertility of the land, the sulphur and textiles, and the fine port facilities (Porto Empedocle) of the agricultural center. Famed for its fine statuary and beautiful buildings, both public and private, and renowned as a gallant defender of Sicilian liberty against the Punic menace, the city is quite reasonably included in Aeneas' *periplus,* his coastal exploration.

After Agrigentum, Vergil brings his hero into an area of Carthaginian influence, just on the eve of Aeneas' adventures in North Africa.

And I left you, palmy Selinus, when wind-thrust was given,
And skirted Lilybaean shoals, with their harsh hidden rocks.
Then the harbor of Drepanum, shores of my sorrow, received me.
Here, driven by so many storms over ocean, I lost
Anchises my father, the solace of every misfortune
And care.

(A. 3, 730–5. L. R. Lind)

Picturesque Selinus was built on low-lying hills; today ruined temples on three ridges and shattered walls look down on the beaches. Founded by Megara Hyblaea in 628 to ease the strain on its limited territory, Selinus' site proved a mixed blessing. Though the land yielded rich crops of grapes and olives, and provided fine grazing and productive grain fields, the situation had no natural protection. Dunbabin comments judiciously on the site: "Though defensible, the low hill is not a commanding position, and needed strong fortifications. There was no port and very poor shelter. The marshes into which the two rivers run made it unhealthy."[4] But in architecture and art Selinus was unique; for bold, energetic construction and original ideas in the plastic arts, Selinus was a leading power in sixth- and fifth-century Sicily.

Selinus' remote and therefore precarious position in western Sicily made it imperative to find an understanding with both Greeks and Phoenicians. The prime enemy was Segesta on the north coast; the two cities had designs on each other's shores. Selinus obviously coveted a port on the northern shore which would be available to Carthaginian shipping from North Africa and which would service its own trading ships dealing with the Phoenician cities in northwest Sicily, as well as with Spain and Etruria. After the failure of the Athenian expedition against Syracuse in 413, Segesta turned to Carthage for protection: Selinus was captured and sacked by the Carthaginians, and it became tributary to Carthage. Eventually, in 250 B.C., during the First Punic War, Carthage evacuated Selinus and razed the ancient city. The population was removed to Lilybaeum (Marsala) and thereafter the site was largely a ghost town, prey to malaria.

The temples at Selinus were originally a match for those at Acragas: three Doric temples rose on the east plateau (Marinella), a colossal Temple of Apollo (ca. 520–450), Temple F (Athena?), and Temple E (Hera?), closest to the shore (Fig. 70). Temple E has been recently reconstructed using the ancient blocks which lay in massive disorder about the site. Among several sanctuaries on the acropolis the most noteworthy is Temple C (Heracles? 550–530).

Vergil's epithet for Selinus, "palmy," should probably be connected literally with local palm trees, although, rather ingeniously, some have thought that Vergil reflects the canting type of *apium,* a kind of parsley which appears on the obverse of the local incuse coinage. Others have argued with Servius that the adjective is meant to recall Selinuntine victories, particularly at the Isthmian Games where the prize was a garland of parsley, the "victor's palm."

Vergil pays special heed to the formidable headland of Lilybaeum (mod. Marsala), with its hidden rocks, perhaps seeing it as a fore-shadowing of the harsh tragedy which lay ahead in the death of Anchises. As remarked earlier, the western zone of Sicily, excluding Selinus and Segesta at an earlier stage, was almost entirely Punic terrain; the hundred miles of coastline between Lilybaeum and Solus (mod. Solunto) was so exclusively. The Carthaginians seem to have migrated to the area sometime after 700 B.C., and in this limited sector continued to maintain themselves, with varying fortunes, until the Roman conquest and organization of Sicily. Lilybaeum provided the Carthaginians with a superb naval base, and the city developed into a commercial and military outpost of the first rank. It resisted the attacks of Pyrrhus of Epirus (276) for two months, and even Rome was forced to mount an eight-year siege (250–242). The fate of the Carthaginian empire in Sicily was finally sealed in a naval engagement at Lilybaeum in March of 241 B.C. Lilybaeum's importance as a port servicing ships trading with Africa and Sicily increased markedly after the Roman settlement, and Cicero refers to it as "an absolutely splendid city" during his residence there as financial officer in 75.

Drepanum (mod. Trapani) was located about twenty miles north of Lilybaeum, not far from Mount Eryx. The city lay on a sickle-shaped peninsula (*drepanon,* "sickle") extending westwards, prolonged further in a southwesterly direction by a series of rocks and small islands. The excellent harbor faced south and was protected from adverse winds and currents by the island of Colombaia. The peninsula has recently been identified as the location of Homeric Scheria and the Phaeacians, on the basis of Nausicaa's description of her locality. In Vergil's time, Segesta

(Greek, Egesta), Drepanum, and Eryx were ascribed to mysterious founders called Elymi. Thucydides informs us that they were at least partly Greek-speaking, for their mixed origins included Trojan and Greek (Phocian) stock. Whatever their origins, they were, in historical times at least, subject to the Carthaginians, later to Rome. One famous anecdote attaching to the area involves the consul Publius Claudius Pulcher at the battle of Drepanum (249–8 B.C.), during the First Punic War. When the augurs reported that the sacred chickens had refused to eat on the eve of the battle, which must, therefore, be ill-omened, the consul angrily hurled the chickens into the sea with the order that they should drink, since they would not eat. But in the ensuing battle, as so often in the early years of Rome's expansion, the Roman commander met his match in Adherbal and lost one hundred ships. To add to Roman mortification, in the same year the Punic admiral intercepted another fleet of one hundred and twenty warships and eight hundred transports while it was moving cautiously along the southern coast of Sicily. The Romans were surprised and failed to realize that they were being maneuvered into dangerous waters. At the appropriate moment the Carthaginians took to the high seas, leaving the Roman armada to be battered to pieces in a storm which the enemy had sensed was coming. Eventually, the Roman commander made Lilybaeum with two ships. Rome's naval adventures in this northwestern quarter were regularly unhappy, as grief-laden as the rites which Aeneas must undertake there, as fraught with peril as the burning of the ships.

Vergil locates two events of significance in the harbor of Drepanum. The details of the first, the rowing contest in honor of Anchises, almost certainly involve specific features of the local seascape:

> Well out at sea, right opposite this spray-tossing shore,
> There is a rock, submerged and thumped by a heavy swell
> At times when the wintry nor'-westers blot out the stars from the sky:
> In a calm, it's a quiet place, lifting above still water
> A flat top, where the gulls love to perch and bask in the sunshine.
> Here Aeneas erected an ilex, leaves and all,
> As seamark for the mariners, to show them where they must turn,
> And rounding it, row back the length of the course again.
>
> (A. 5, 124–31. Day Lewis)

The turning point might well be the island of Colombaia at the entry to the harbor, or one of the more remote rocky projections beyond the sickle-shaped peninsula.

The second incident is the attempted burning of the ships. Pocock has argued recently that the tradition of the ship-burning at Drepanum may derive from an actual event in Elymian history. But the thesis that Nausicaa, "burner of ships," may somehow be related to the Vergilian ship-burning—and so support the identification of Drepanum as the locale of the *Odyssey's* Phaeacian episode and even as the home of the poet who wrote the *Odyssey*—is hardly tenable.

Aeneas' conduct at Eryx (mod. Erice and Monte San Giuliano) is almost reverentially detailed in separate notices:

>   The friendly shore
> Of your half-brother Eryx, Sicilian ports,
> Lie not far distant, I believe, if only
> I still recall the way to steer by stars
> I [Palinurus] watched before.

> Then was founded a shrine to Idalian [Cyprian] Venus on Mount Eryx,
> Close up to the stars; a priest for Anchises was added
> To tend his tomb and a sacred grove spreading widely.

> Then he [Aeneas] ordered three calves and a lamb to be slaughtered to Eryx
> And to the Tempests, to cast off the hawsers in order.
>   (A. 5, 25–9; 785–7; 798–9. L. R. Lind)

The hero's visit to the famed mountain is an act of piety, not merely to the memory of his father or to his divine half-brother, Eryx, but even more important, to his mother, Venus.

The background to the place-name is provided at some length. Eryx, guardian of the site and son of Butes and Venus, had been a celebrated boxer, onetime opponent of Hercules. His boxing gauntlets, a magnified version of the normal Roman caestus, were displayed at the anniversary games for Anchises. Acestes' invitation to Entellus, a former pupil of Eryx, to champion the Sicilians against the Trojan boxer Dares enabled Vergil to narrate in some detail the traditional stories of Eryx. But more important than the boxing master was the celebrated shrine of Venus on Mount Eryx (Fig. 71). The spot had been ground hallowed to the service of a succession of celestial love goddesses, Phoenician Astarte, Greek Aphrodite, and Roman Venus. Revered as a marine-born goddess who watched over the seas and as one who might guarantee fair sailing (Aphrodite Euploia), Venus was, above all, a goddess of love. A cult of temple prostitution rose in her service, consonant with the eastern origins of the cult.

Thucydides is the authority for the information that the town of Eryx was an Elymian foundation, and that it became a dependency of Segesta, twenty-five miles away, during the fifth century. The ancient site was probably located on the lower mountain slopes, northwest of the present community of San Giuliano. It was evacuated in 258 B.C. when the population was transferred to Drepanum. Romans and Carthaginians struggled repeatedly for possession of the hill during the First Punic War. Hasdrubal eventually captured the town site and held it until 241.

In 215 B.C., during the desperate days of the Second Punic War, the cult of Venus Erycina was transferred to Rome and lodged first on the Capitoline and then outside the Colline Gate. Roman morals were stricter than those of their Sicilian cousins, and the cult was purged of its more colorful aspects; it ultimately became one of the most venerable cults of Rome and was linked, appropriately, with the Julian family. Horace includes the cult of Venus in his appeal for saving assistance from the gods in time of trouble (*Odes* 1, 2). Archaeologically, the original cult site is today something of a disappointment, although the vista over the peninsula of Trapani to the offshore islands and to the rich lowlands two thousand feet below is extremely picturesque. The ancient cult site, still a sailor's landmark, is dominated by a Norman castle, and only a few visible remains—blocks re-used in medieval buildings—testify to the tradition of a proud and affluent sanctuary. Excavators have located, at least tentatively, a modest-sized podium oriented northeast-southwest, adjacent to a later Christian Church dedicated to Our Lady of the Snows. Portions of the sacred enclosure wall have been found, but the only architectural elements which can be attached to the Venus temple are of Claudian date. A coin of Considius Nonianus (60 B.C.) provides the best clue to the nature of the temple in Roman times. Large flocks of pigeons (the doves of

Aphrodite) were kept in the sanctuary, consecrated and untouchable, and they still gather at the site. There is some archaeological evidence to suggest that silversmiths maintained shops adjoining the temple, ready to supply votive figures for a price.

The anniversary games in honor of Anchises are seemingly assigned to the territory of Segesta, perhaps in the valley beneath the citadel hill of Monte Barbaro, where the poet might visualize a natural grassy circus for the athletic events (Fig. 72).

The chief remains at Segesta today are a temple on the lower level and a Hellenistic theater on the citadel of Monte Barbaro, with an unhampered view towards the Gulf of Castellammare. Both were intact in Vergil's time, and the stage buildings were, in fact, remodelled to cope with Roman demands ca. 100 B.C. Recently, Italian excavators working on the northeastern slopes of Monte Barbaro have come upon the remains of an archaic Greek sanctuary with a circuit wall almost intact, dating ca. 500–485 B.C. The sanctuary lies on a plateau consisting of almost three acres beneath the ancient citadel site, about a mile and a half north of the village of Calatafimi. Within the precinct wall traces of at least two Doric temples have been unearthed, along with deposits of Greek pottery and Elymian ware. Even more intriguing are pottery finds on another terrace beneath the citadel which include many fragments inscribed with Greek characters in a non-Greek language. These mysterious graffiti may be the first tangible evidence for the existence of the shadowy Elymians and the first clue to the nature of their language.

Vergil subscribes completely to the tradition of a Trojan or possibly an Elymian foundation at Segesta. When the Trojans move towards the tomb of Anchises to offer libations and other appropriate cere- monies, Aeneas is accompanied by Helymus (who entered the foot race) and Acestes (who entered the archery lists), along with Ascanius. Helymus was obviously the eponymous hero of the Elymi and Acestes of Segesta. Vergil finds them both already established among the native Sicani of the area. Acestes appears to have been settled there for some unspecified time (A. 1, 195, 570; 5, 24, 30); Helymus (5, 73) is called a Sicilian and an intimate associate of Acestes, but neither has a named settlement assigned to him, for Aeneas is to be the effective agent in establishing a community which will combine the Trojans already present, native Sicani, possibly Greeks (for Salius and Patron, from Arcadia and Acarnania respectively, are contestants in the games), and the aged and travel-weary members of Aeneas' party. Nautes advises Aeneas on the foundation:

> There is Dardanian Acestes, sprung from the gods.
> Take him as ally in your planning; he will not refuse you.
> Turn over to him the survivors of ships that are lost
> And those who are sick of your great adventure, of sharing
> Your fortunes, the old men, the mothers weary of water,
> Weak, fearful of danger, and let them have walls in this land.
> They shall call their city Acesta, when Acestes allows it."
>
> (A. 5, 736–42. L. R. Lind)

The apparition of Anchises to Aeneas strengthens his determination to found the city:

> In the meanwhile, Aeneas
> Had marked out the city by plowing and cast lots for their houses.
> He ordered this place to be called Ilium and these environs
> Troy. Trojan Acestes rejoiced in his realm and proclaimed
> A court and gave laws to the fathers when they were assembled.
>
> (A. 5, 780–4. L. R. Lind)

Whether Elymian or Trojan in origin, by the fifth century Segesta was thoroughly Hellenized. This was the epoch when the Doric temple, never completed and still unassigned, was erected, and when the Segestaeans negotiated, somewhat deceitfully, with the Athenians. The city fathers borrowed funds and treasures, probably from the temple of Aphrodite on Eryx, to impress the Athenian legation on the eve of the alliance which they hoped would assist them against inimical Selinus. Twice allied with Athens, in 426 and 416, Segesta felt compelled to seek help from Carthage after the Athenian disaster at Syracuse in 413. Always on guard against Selinus, Segesta imagined the worst after her own quisling role during the recent hostilities. The Segestaeans invited the Carthaginians to occupy their city in 410, and the latter launched a destructive attack on Selinus and also erased Himera on the north coast.

Strabo indicates that the sanctuary and the town site of Eryx were both declining in his time, in need of priests and stripped of the crowds of temple prostitutes. Vergil's suggestion that Aeneas had founded a Venus and Anchises sanctuary on the height may ultimately have impressed the Imperial house with the need to give attention to the sanctuary. Diodorus' comments are revealing:

> The Romans surpassed all people who had preceded them in the honours they paid to the goddess. . . . The consuls and praetors for instance, who visit the island, and all Romans who sojourn there clothed with any authority, whenever they came to Eryx, embellish the sanctuary with magnificent sacrifices and honours, and laying aside the austerity of their authority, they enjoy themselves and keep company with women in a spirit of great gaiety, believing that only in this way will they make their presence there pleasing to the goddess. Indeed the Roman senate has so zealously concerned itself with the honours of the goddess that it has decreed that the seventeen cities of Sicily which are most faithful to Rome shall pay a tax in gold to Aphrodite and that two hundred soldiers shall serve as a guard of her sanctuary.
>
> (Diodorus 4, 83, 4–7)

Although Augustus, curiously enough, did not involve himself with the site, Tiberius, according to Tacitus, gladly undertook repairs to the Venus temple. Claudius completed the renovations, and the cult site regained some of its old prosperity and veneration.

When Acestes, eponymous hero of Segesta, sights the Trojan fleet from a distant hilltop, he is described as wearing a Libyan bearskin, a somewhat bizarre dress even for a shipwrecked Trojan; his origins as son of Crimisus, the local river god, and a Trojan mother are equally startling.

> Afar from a high hilltop, Acestes marvelled to see
> His friends' ships bearing towards his coast: he went to meet them,
> A rough-looking man with his javelins and the pelt of the Libyan
> she-bear
> He wore—Acestes, son of a Trojan dame and the river
> Crimisus.
>
> (A. 5, 35–9. Day Lewis)

According to Servius, the hero's mother, Egesta, banished from Troy by Laomedon, was visited by his father in the guise of a dog. The coins of Segesta kept this legendary tradition alive by picturing a dog (a Phoenician link?) alongside the youthful hunter, Aegestus. The river Crimisus follows a course some five miles to the east of Segesta and empties into the Gulf of Castellammare. The river had actually played a saving role in the history of the city, for during an engagement between the forces of Timoleon and the Carthaginians in 339, the timely flood-waters of the Crimisus surprised the Carthaginians and confused their offensive, thereby enabling the Sicilians to win a victory which, for the time being, saved Sicily from further warfare with Carthage.

Liberated by Timoleon in 339, Segesta was later captured and destroyed by Agathocles in 307 and occupied by Pyrrhus in 276. The city's difficulties ended with the First Punic War. Once again relying upon an outside power to buttress her fortunes, Segesta allied with Rome, citing, among other compelling reasons, their common Trojan ancestry. The city went into a decline during the first century B.C., when, according to Strabo, it was overshadowed by Emporium, its port town, and by the sulphur springs near modern Calamelti.

Galinsky's searching analysis of the Sicilian episode in the *Aeneid* yields many fresh insights and brilliant conjectures—not least that "it was in Sicily that the Romans became fully aware of their claim to Trojan descent; it is in Sicily that Aeneas begins to understand the implications of his mission. . . . Vergil deliberately stressed that aspect of the Trojan legend which was most realistic for the Romans: its mobilization against the Carthaginians during the Punic Wars. This accounts for the importance of Sicily in the epic, which many scholars have considered excessive or, at least, unprecedented."[5]

VIII

Conclusion

VERGIL'S abiding faith in the renascence of Italy, the government, the people, and the land, is constantly evident. Alive to the realities of injustice and cruelty during the civil war era, bearing himself the imprint of the confiscations, Vergil yet realized that the agony of exile was part of a maturing process, that the violent upheavals, however traumatic, were part of the traditional process of growth and heightened sensibility.

Octavian himself exemplified such growth. As triumvir, he had shown the brutality, the opportunism, and the arrogance of his partners and predecessors. But after Actium, by calculation and inspired counsel, Octavian developed a charisma which inspired men to follow him and to keep the peace. Julius Caesar had failed to assess the response to his monarchic designs and he had died by the hands of patriotic, reactionary senators; Augustus, in undertaking his imperial reorganization, faced the same problem of a city-state mentality, in which traditions, prejudices, and deeply felt Italic republican sentiments were antagonistic to a monarchical solution. With the persistence of Vergil's Saturnian Juno, Augustus contrived a compromise: a restoration of the Republic, with the paraphernalia of Senate, magistrates, and assemblies, along with the discrimination between Roman citizens and subjects that answered a deep-seated prejudice. He also accepted Cicero's concept of the leading citizen, the *princeps,* but widened its scope to include his own extraordinary position as a statesman deriving special powers from the Senate and Roman People as their political agent. His powers rested in his proconsular *imperium* which assigned him command of the armies and control over the provinces—practically speaking, for life; in his tribunician powers, regularly conferred, which gave him legislative powers of control; and in his influence and prestige, the *auctoritas* which the title "Augustus" underlined, through which he maintained control in all affairs of state. The Augustan solution was the culmination of some five centuries of engagement with the problems of national and ecumenical government. The achievements, the failures, and the dreams of statesmen like Pompey, and Cicero, and Caesar were the *exempla* for this final, practical organization—a conservative Augustan classicism which was a durable amalgam of the political thought and experience of Periclean Greece, of the Hellenistic kingdoms, and of Rome itself.

Vergil's devotion to the new Romulus, the restorer of peace and prosperity and the guarantor of law and order throughout the world, is repeatedly evidenced in his later works, the *Georgics* and the *Aeneid*. Yet in these works there are occasional suggestions of hesitation regarding Augustus' means of attaining his goals; and there is certainly regret for time past, for people and institutions lost, and some indignation at the terrific expenditure of life, the travails of civil war, and the amoral, irreligious direction that Italy had taken at certain stages. Vergil is no servile poet laureate, any more than was Horace. But both poets witnessed a remarkable conversion in their leader, and they respected the evident improvements in the state after the fall of the Republic. The good government of Augustus therefore enlisted Vergil's sometimes reluctant but eventually consistent support. His death-bed wish that the *Aeneid* be burned was inspired not by a desire to recant or to demonstrate disillusionment with Augustus and the Imperial society, but by an artist's awareness of the imperfect composition, and reluctance to commit to his Princeps a testament which would be incomplete and flawed.

This book has dealt with Vergil's Italy, the fundamental object of the Mantuan's piety and patriotism. An exile from his native fields, Vergil found inspiration and comfort in the multiple aspects of Saturnian Italy as a whole, and his works are secular gospels on the blessings, the strengths, and the eternal pattern of nature, and on the tragic but durable and responsible pattern of man's life.

With almost evangelical fervor Vergil hymns the glories of his fatherland as though he were himself celebrating its millennium:

> But not the groves of Media, wealthy land,
> Nor lovely Ganges, nor the golden streams
> Of Lydia match Italy in praise;
> Not India, Afghanistan, nor isles
> Of Araby with incense-bearing sands.
> No fiery bulls ploughed Italy's black soil
> To sow a crop of giant dragon's teeth,
> No human warriors sprang full-armed from her fields:
> But teeming fruit and wine of the Campagna
> Filled our Italian fields; fat herds and olives
> Found their place in Italy's rich land.
> Hence, the charger prancing in the plain;
> Hence, white sheep and sacrificial bull,
> So often plunged in Umbria's sacred streams,
> Precede our Roman triumphs to the temples.
> Here Spring persists, and Summer makes her way
> Through foreign months: the flocks bear twice a year,
> And twice the useful tree yields up her apples;
> No raving tigers, savage lion cubs:
> No poison wolfsbane fools the poor herb-gatherers.
> No scaly reptile hustles huge coils across
> The ground—or stops and winds his train in spirals.
> See our noble cities, labor's crown,
> Built breathlessly upon steep mountainsides,
> Deep rivers flowing under ancient walls!
> Shall I name the seas on either side?
> Our inland lakes you, Larian Como, the greatest,
> And you, oh Garda, whose sea-waves plunge and roar?
> Recall the Julian Port at Lake Lucrine
> Where the channeled Tyrrhene flows into Avernus,
> And the jetties thrust against the indignant sea
> With a hissing surge, where Julian water sings
> Its distant tones of tidal solitude?
> Our land is veined with silver, copper, gold.

> Italian soil has bred a race of heroes,
> Marsians, Sabines, toughened generations
> From the Western Coast, and tribes of Volscians
> Handy with the spear. Great family names,
> Camillus, Decius, Marius, Scipio,
> And chief of all, Octavianus Caesar,
> Who triumphs now on Asia's farthest shore,
> And defends the hills of Rome from the timid foe.
> All Hail, Saturnian Land, our honored Mother!
> For thee I broach these themes of ancient art
> And dare disclose the sacred springs of verse,
> Singing Hesiod's song through Roman towns.
>
> (G. 2, 136–76. Palmer Bovie)

Keats, Frost, Bromfield, Eliot, Day Lewis, and Auden share Vergil's proud devotion to the land—its beauty, its history, its life-giving, philanthropic nature, its diversity, and its ageless character. Italy's natural features and its man-made works are part of an inexhaustible repertoire. The fertility of earth and the productivity of beast, and the timeless progression of the seasons are always at the heart of Rome's greatest poetry. A private and a public aspect are involved: the admission of a personal affection for the land, and a concern with the welfare and status of the Italian farmer. In R. D. Williams' phrase, "to project his own enthusiasm of rural life in a stabilized society to a wide audience was a political and social service which the poet was most ready to perform."[1]

The most impressive testimony to Vergil's concern for the soil of Italy and the need for peace appears at the end of the first *Georgic,* where the Italian deities, protectors of Tiber and Rome, are invoked to enable Augustus to save his generation from recurrence of the past, and so permit the cycle to advance to a Golden Age, to a regenerated Saturnian Italy freed from civil war, a land invested with the productivity and peace of an Arcadia:

> O my country's gods, my homeland's heroes,
> And Romulus, and Vesta, who protect
> The Tuscan Tiber, Roman Palatine:
> May our young Octavian Caesar right this world
> That our disastrous age has overturned!

We have atoned in full for perjured Troy,
And long enough has heaven's court complained
That Caesar celebrates his triumphs here
On earth, where right and wrong have been reversed.
So many wars, so many shapes of crime!
The plough dishonored, fields left lying waste
Now that their men are drafted; curving scythes
Are pounded into shape for ruthless swords.
War in Germany, and in the East:
Neighbouring towns dissolve their legal bonds,
Unholy Mars bends all to his mad will:
The world is like a chariot run wild
That rounds the course unchecked and, gaining speed,
Sweeps the helpless driver on to his doom.
                              (G. 1, 498–514. Palmer Bovie)

Not Rome alone, but Italy, carried Augustus and the City to ultimate triumph. In the *Aeneid,* Vergil arrays the tribes and towns on the side of Trojan Aeneas or Rutulian Turnus, and there is intense local and national patriotism among the hosts opposing the invader Aeneas. The gathering of the clans underlines the poet's concern to involve as many as possible in the birth of the Trojan Italian nation. For though he himself occasionally reveals his regional pride, his fullest patriotism is to Italy—the nation, rather than the land. In interpreting for a national audience the antique strengths of Italy, his antiquarian zeal and scholarly virtuosity are tempered by fondness for his unusually catholic subject matter; the experiences, the thoughts and feelings of Everyman—as shepherd and lover, as farmer, as political animal—are in Vergil's compass. In choosing the elements for his mosaic of Italy, the poet seems to have been motivated by various factors. Generally the choice of places which Aeneas touches emphasizes a peculiar relationship—family, political, or diplomatic—with the Roman Commonwealth and its *maiores,* the ancestral heroes, from the earliest times. Eduard Fraenkel has grasped the implications and the technique of Vergil's emphasis on peoples and places in his epic, an emphasis which is nowhere more obvious or exciting than in passages concerning his beloved Campania Felix and southern Italy, the *Mezzogiorno* generally, land of his adoption and his ultimate resting place: "Vergil planned and executed the *Aeneid* on such a scale as to name it the national epic, not of Rome only but of Italy. If this end was to be achieved, it was highly important that the inhabitants of the whole peninsula, including its half-forgotten rural districts and many *municipia* of little fame, should in the great poem find at least some passage which immediately appealed to the pride they derived from their local traditions and customs. All of them should be made to feel that this was not merely the story of a conflict between a Trojan hero and a young prince of Ardea and his Etruscan ally but something in which they had a share themselves."[2]

ABBREVIATIONS

—

AJA   *American Journal of Archaeology*
AJP   *American Journal of Philology*
AUMLA   *Journal of the Australasian Universities Modern Language Association*
CJ   *Classical Journal*
CP   *Classical Philology*
CQ   *Classical Quarterly*
G&R   *Greece and Rome*
HSCP   *Harvard Studies in Classical Philology*
JRS   *Journal of Roman Studies*
PBSR   *Papers of the British School of Archaeology at Rome*
PCA   *Proceedings of the Classical Association*
PVS   *Proceedings of the Virgil Society*
TAPA   *Transactions of the American Philological Association*
VS   *Virgil Society (London)*
YCS   *Yale Classical Studies*

NOTES

I
THE ACHIEVEMENT OF VERGIL

1. T. S. Eliot, *On Poetry and Poets* (London, 1957), 70. See also Sir John Lockwood, "Vergil and his Critics," *PVS* 2 (1962–3), 53–71.

2. *Ibid.*, 131. See also C. N. Cochrane, *Christianity and Classical Culture* (New York, 1940), 61–73, on Vergil's philosophy of history and his vision of cosmic justice.

3. See T. S. Eliot, "What is a Classic?," in *On Poetry and Poets*, 53–71. Consult also W. F. Jackson Knight, "T. S. Eliot as a Classical Scholar," in *T. S. Eliot: A Symposium for his Seventieth Birthday*, Neville Braybrooke, ed. (New York, 1958), 119 ff.; and David J. De Laura, "The Place of the Classics in T. S. Eliot's Christian Humanism," in *Hereditas: Seven Essays on the Modern Experience of the Classical*, Frederic Will, ed. (Austin, 1964), 155 ff.

4. Brooks Otis, Introduction, *The Aeneid*, verse trans. by Frank O. Copley (Indianapolis, 1965), xx.

5. Otis, *Virgil: A Study in Civilized Poetry* (Oxford, 1963).

6. Otis, *Virgil*, 393.

7. Robert Graves, "The Virgil Cult," *Virginia Quarterly Review* 38:1 (1962), 13–35; and "The Anti-poet," in *Oxford Addresses on Poetry* (London, 1962), 27–53.

8. E. M. Forster, Introduction, *Virgil's Aeneid*, trans. and annotated by Michael Oakley (London, 1957), ix.

9. E. A. Havelock, "History and Counter-History in the Aeneid," *Ventures: Magazine of the Yale Graduate School* (Spring, 1967), 46.

10. Consult, *inter alios*, E. L. Brown, *Numeri Vergiliani: Studies in "Eclogues" and "Georgics"* (Brussels, 1963); R. W. Cruttwell, *Virgil's Mind at Work* (Oxford, 1946); G.

E. Duckworth, *Structural Patterns and Proportions in Vergil's Aeneid* (Ann Arbor, 1962); W. F. Jackson Knight, *Roman Vergil* (London, 1944); V. Pöschl, *The Art of Virgil: Image and Symbol in the Aeneid* (Ann Arbor, 1962); M. C. J. Putnam, *The Poetry of the Aeneid* (Cambridge, Mass., 1965); *Virgil: A Collection of Critical Essays*, Steele Commager, ed. (Englewood Cliffs, N.J., 1966); Kenneth Quinn, *Virgil's Aeneid, a critical description* (Ann Arbor, 1968); G. E. Duckworth, "The 'Old' and the 'New' in Vergil's *Aeneid*," in *The Poetic Tradition: Essays on Greek, Latin, and English Poetry*, Don Cameron Allen and Henry T. Rowell, eds. (Baltimore, 1968), 63–80; and Otto Skutsch, "Symmetry and Sense in the Eclogues," *HSCP* 73 (1969), 153–70.

11. Gavin Maxwell, *The Ten Pains of Death* (London, 1959), 47, 49, 50.

12. Most scholars deny the Vergilian authorship of the *Appendix Vergiliana* and regard them, except for certain poems of the *Catalepton*, as post-Vergilian imitations. For divergent views consult: E. K. Rand, "Young Virgil's Poetry," *HSCP* 30 (1919), 103–85; T. Frank, *Vergil, A Biography* (New York, 1922); N. W. DeWitt, *Virgil's Biographia Litteraria* (Toronto, 1923); A. Rostagni, *Virgilio Minore. Saggio sullo svolgimento della poesia Virgiliana* (Torino, 1933); H. W. Prescott, "The Present Status of the Virgilian Appendix," *CJ* 26 (1930–31), 49–62; Duckworth, *Structural Patterns,* 93–102; Eduard Fraenkel, "The

Culex," *JRS* 42 (1952), 1–9; and Duckworth, "Studies in Latin Hexametric Poetry," *TAPA* 97 (1966), 67–113, especially 86–101.

13. *Eclogues* 1, esp. 6–10, and 4, 21 ff., the peace and plenty of the Julian dispensation. See also H. J. Rose, *The Eclogues of Vergil* (Berkeley, 1942); E. A. Hahn, "The Characters in the *Eclogues*," TAPA 75 (1944), 196–241; and L. R. Taylor, *The Divinity of the Roman Emperor* (Middletown, 1931), 149 f.

14. Consult A. S. F. Gow, *Theocritus*, Vols. I and II (Cambridge, 1950); and Wendell Clausen, "Callimachus and Roman Poetry," *Greek, Roman and Byzantine Studies* 5 (1964), 181–96. Clausen highlights Parthenius, who provided Cornelius Gallus, Vergil's poet friend, with Greek erotic poems for translation into Latin.

15. Consult T. B. L. Webster, *Hellenistic Poetry and Art* (London, 1964), 156–77.

16. See especially *Eclogues* 1, 6, and 9. For comment consult C. P. Segal, "*Tamen cantabitis Arcades*—Exile and Arcadia in Eclogues One and Nine," *Arion* 4:2 (1965), 237–66; L. P. Wilkinson, "Vergil and the Evictions," *Hermes* 94 (1966), 320–4; and Otis, *Virgil*, 98–143.

17. *Eclogue* 9, 27–8.

18. The Golden Age theme is cognate to the Christian doctrine of the Fall (Genesis III) and implies a loss of innocence and a progressive degeneration, with a hardening of the conditions of life. The "classical" versions appear in Hesiod, *Works*

and Days, 109–21, Aratus, *Phae-
nomena,* 96–136; and in the Roman
poets Horace, *Epode* 16, Vergil,
Georgic I, 121 ff., Tibullus I, 3, 35
ff., and Ovid, *Metamorphoses* 1, 89–
150. For discussion of the Golden
Age in classical poetry see M. E.
Taylor, "Primitivism in Virgil," *AJP*
76 (1955), 261–78; I. S. Ryberg,
"Virgil's Golden Age," *TAPA* 89
(1958), 112–31; K. J. Reckford,
"Some Appearances of the Golden
Age," *CJ* 54 (1958–9), 79–87; G.
Boas and A. O. Lovejoy, *Primitivism
and Related Ideas in Antiquity*
(Baltimore, 1935); W. K. C.
Guthrie, *In the Beginning* (Ithaca,
1957), Ch. 4; T. P. Harrison, ed.,
The Pastoral Elegy (Austin, 1939).

19. Bruno Snell, "Arcadia: The Discovery of a Spiritual Landscape," in
*Virgil: A Collection of Critical
Essays,* Steele Commager, ed., 14–
27 (esp. 23).

20. On matters of structure consult:
L. Richardson, *Poetical Theory in
Republican Rome* (New Haven,
1944), 101–32; Paul Maury, "Le
Secret de Virgile et l'architecture des
Bucoliques," *Lettres d'Humanité* 3
(1944), 71–147; Duckworth, *Struc-
tural Patterns,* 3–4 (with notes); and
Otis, *Virgil,* 128–31, and 216.

21. *Ibid.,* 130–1.

22. The literature on the Messianic
Eclogue is extensive and exhausting.
The best discussions are provided
by: H. J. Rose, *op. cit.,* 162–217,
253–65; K. Büchner, *P. Vergilius
Maro, der Dichter der Römer* (Stutt-
gart, 1956), 175–93; Duckworth,
"Animae Dimidium Meae: Two
Poets of Rome," *TAPA* 87 (1956),

287–90; J. J. Savage, "Apollo-Her-
cules: Two Themes in the Fourth
Eclogue," *Vergilian Digest* 2 (1956),
5–10; Colin G. Hardie, *The Fourth
Eclogue (VS Lecture Summaries,*
No. 42, 1957); E. T. Salmon, "The
Fourth Eclogue Once More," *CP*
34 (1939), 66–8. For a broader
view of the topic consult A. J.
Toynbee, *A Study of History,*
abridged by D. C. Somervell (Oxford, 1946), 219 ff.

23. E. Paratore, "Il bimillenario
della guerra di Perugia e della pace
di Brindisi," *Studi Romani* 8 (1960),
523–34, suggests that Vergil gleaned
Messianic ideas from Herod the
Great, Pollio's friend, and from the
Jewish legation at Rome. See also
N. W. DeWitt, *Vergil's Biographia,*
172–89.

24. E. V. Rieu, *Virgil: The Pastoral
Poems* (Penguin ed., 1949), 103.

25. On Hesiod, see Richmond
Lattimore, *Hesiod: The Works and
Days, Theogony, The Shield of
Herakles* (Ann Arbor, 1959), Intro-
duction (1–10) and verse transla-
tion; A. R. Burn, *The World of
Hesiod* (London, 1936); F. Solmsen,
Hesiod and Aeschylus (Ithaca,
1949).

26. *Works and Days,* 274 ff.

27. For details on Alexandrian didactic poets and the popularization
of scientific subject matter, consult
M. Hadas, *A History of Greek Literature* (New York, 1950), 196–214;
and A. S. F. Gow and A. F. Schol-
field, *Nicander: The Poems and Poetical Fragments* (Cambridge, 1953).

28. For text, translation, and commentary, consult C. Bailey, ed. and

trans., *De Rerum Natura Libri Sex,* 3 vols. (Oxford, 1947); N. W. DeWitt, *Epicurus and his Philosophy* (Minneapolis, 1954).

29. Cf. L. P. Wilkinson, *Horace and his Lyric Poetry* (Cambridge, 2nd ed., 1951), 21 ff., 26 ff.

30. B. Farrington, "Polemical Allusions to the De Rerum Natura of Lucretius in the Works of Vergil," in *Geras: Studies Presented to George Thomson* (Prague, 1963), 87–94, esp. 88.

31. *De Rerum Natura,* 5, 206–12 (R. E. Latham).

32. M. Porcius Cato "Censorius" (234–149 B.C.), and Marcus Terentius Varro (116–27 B.C.): consult W. D. Hooper and H. B. Ash, *Cato and Varro, De Re Rustica* (Boston, 2nd impr., 1934).

33. *Georgic* 1, 121–4 (Day Lewis). See also L. P. Wilkinson, "Virgil's Theodicy," *CQ* 13 (1963), 75–84; and Antonio La Penna, "Esiodo nella cultura e nella poesia di Virgilio," in *Hésiode et son influence* (*Entretiens sur l'antiquité classique,* Tome VII), (Genève, 1960), 213–70.

34. Servius, the fourth-century commentator on Vergil, suggested that the original draft of *Georgic* 4 ended with a tribute, of undisclosed length, to Cornelius Gallus, Vergil's poet friend, celebrated for his love elegies to Lycoris, and first Prefect of Egypt after Actium. After his recall from Egypt for hubristic behavior and his suicide in 22 B.C., Vergil allegedly revised the final *Georgic,* replacing the tribute with the Alexandrian tale. The problem is debated frequently.

Representative arguments for and against the Servian account include the following: T. J. Haarhoff, "Vergil and Cornelius Gallus," *CP* 55 (1960), 101–8; R. Coleman, "Gallus, the Bucolics, and the Ending of the Fourth Georgic," *AJP* 83 (1962), 55–71; Duckworth, "Vergil's *Georgics* and the *Laudes Galli,*" *AJP* 80 (1959), 225–37; and Otis, *Virgil,* 408–13.

35. Otis, *Virgil,* 146.

36. On the structure of the *Georgics,* consult: Otis, *Virgil,* 144–214; Duckworth, *Structural Patterns,* 41–2; Sir James Mountford, "The Architecture of the Georgics," *PVS* 6 (1966–7), 25–34, L. P. Wilkinson, *The Georgics of Virgil* (Cambridge, 1969), 71–120.

37. R. G. Austin, *PCA* 46 (1949), 124.

38. On the Neoterics (*Novi Poetae*) and the epyllion ("miniature epic") consult, *inter alios:* C. W. Mendell, *Latin Poetry: The New Poets and Augustans* (New Haven, 1965); Kenneth Quinn, *The Catullan Revolution* (Melbourne, 1959), 44–69; F. O. Copley, trans., *Catullus, the Complete Poetry* (Ann Arbor, 1957), Introduction, v–xv; R. A. Swanson, trans., *Odi et Amo: The Complete Poetry of Catullus* (New York, 1959), Foreword, vii–xvi; L. Richardson, *Poetical Theory in Republican Rome,* 1–16. On the "Orpheus" episode consult, especially, M. Owen Lee, "Virgil as Orpheus," *Orpheus* 11 (1964), 9–18; Otis, *Virgil,* 196–210; Duckworth, *Structural Patterns,* 42 ("The pattern is tripartite, with the death

of Eurydice [453–66], Orpheus in the Underworld [467–98], and the lament and death of Orpheus [499–527]"); Wilkinson, *op. cit.* 108–20, 213–22.

39. *Aeneid* 6, 645–7 (Day Lewis). There are additional references to Orpheus in *Eclogues* 3, 46; 4, 55 ff.; 6, 30; 8, 55 f. On possible Neo-Pythagorean influence on Vergil's philosophy and method of poetic composition, see Duckworth, *Structural Patterns,* 73–7 ("his use of mathematical ratios [Golden Mean] can serve as a supporting argument").

40. Consult I. M. Linforth, *The Arts of Orpheus* (Berkeley, 1941); W. K. C. Guthrie, *Orpheus and Greek Religion* (London, 1952), 40: "The influence of Orpheus was always on the side of civilization and the arts of peace. . . . He taught men . . . the arts of agriculture and in this way inclined their natures towards peace and gentleness."

41. Cf. S. Palmer Bovie, "The Imagery of Ascent-Descent in Vergil's *Georgics*," *AJP* 77 (1956), 337–58. For derivative versions of the Orpheus myth see M. Owen Lee, "Orpheus and Eurydice: Some Modern Versions," *CJ* 56 (1961), 307–13 (Cocteau, Anouilh, Williams, Camus); Michael Grant, *Myths of the Greeks and Romans* (New York, 1962), 266–84.

42. For military terms see *Georgics* 1, 99, 104–5; 2, 369–70, etc.

43. *Georgic* 4, 67–87. Cf. *Georgic* 3, 219–41 (the duel between the bulls).

44. R. G. Austin, *PCA* 46 (1949), 124.

45. *Georgic* 3, 13 ff.

46. Cf. Duckworth, "The Architecture of the Aeneid," *AJP* 75 (1954), 1–15.

47. See V. Pöschl, "The Poetic Achievement of Virgil," *CJ* 56 (1960–1), 290–9.

48. On the Hellenistic epic consult Otis, *Virgil,* Ch. II, *passim;* T. B. L. Webster, *Hellenistic Poetry and Art,* Ch. II; and J. Carspecken, "Apollonius Rhodius and the Homeric Epic," *Yale Classical Studies* 13 (1952), 33–143.

49. On early Roman epic consult Otis (*supra*); W. F. Jackson Knight, *Roman Vergil,* Ch. IV.

50. See note 38.

51. Propertius 2, 34, 65 f.

52. C. M. Bowra, *From Virgil to Milton* (London, 1945), Ch. I.

53. Cf. M. Hadas, "Aeneas as a National Hero," *AJP* 69 (1948), 408–14; Otis, *Virgil, s.v.* Aeneas; E. M. Blaiklock, *The Hero of the Aeneid* (Auckland, 1961); R. D. Williams, "The Purpose of the Aeneid," *Antichthon* 1 (1967), 29–41.

54. V. Pöschl, *The Art of Vergil* (Ann Arbor, 1962), 3.

55. *Ibid.,* 19–21, 24 ff. (on *Aeneid* 1, 8–296, the storm at sea).

56. For suggestions of the Civil War and Vergil's conceivable insecurity or frustration, consult: F. W. Dupee, "Virgil and War," *Partisan Review* (Winter, 1944), 122–4; A. M. Parry, "The Two Voices of Vergil's

Aeneid," *Arion* (Winter, 1963), 66–80; Wendell Clausen, "An Interpretation of the *Aeneid*," *HSCP* 68 (1964), 139–47; and L. A. MacKay, "Hero and Theme in *Aeneid*," *TAPA* 94 (1963), 157–66. The articles by Parry and Clausen appear also in *Virgil: A Collection of Critical Essays,* Steele Commager, ed. (Englewood Cliffs, N.J., 1966).

57. On matters of structure consult: W. A. Camps, "A Note on the Structure of the *Aeneid*," *CQ* 4 (1954), 214–5; *id.,* "A Second Note on the Structure of the *Aeneid*," *CQ* 9 (1959), 53; Duckworth, "The Aeneid as a Trilogy," *TAPA* 88 (1957), 1–10; *id.,* "Tripartite Structure in the Aeneid," *Vergilius* 7 (1961), 2–11; and *id., Structural Patterns, passim;* Otis, *Virgil, passim.*

58. W. F. Jackson Knight, "Poetic Sources and Integration," *Vergilius* 5 (1940), 7–16; "Integration of Plot in the Aeneid," *ibid.,* 6 (1940), 17–25; "Vergil's Secret Art," *PVS* 1 (1961–2), 1–14; "Poetic Sources and Integration—Continued," *Vergilius* 8 (1962), 2–7; and M. C. J. Putnam, *The Poetry of the Aeneid* (Cambridge, Mass., 1965).

59. See Pierre Grimal, *Pius Aeneas* (London, 1959), *VS* Lecture.

60. Cf. *Aeneid* 8, 678 ff.

61. See G. Karl Galinsky, "The Hercules-Cacus Episode in *Aeneid* VIII," *AJP* 87 (1966), 18–51.

62. On the character of Aeneas, in addition to observations by Blaiklock, Pöschl, Duckworth, Grimal, Maguinness, MacKay, Otis, etc., see also D. R. Dudley, "A Plea for Aeneas," *G&R* 8 (1961), 52–60.

For an adverse estimate see Mark Van Doren, *The Noble Voice* (New York, 1946), 86–121.

63. For discussion of Vergil's "new" dramatic style, both emphatic and editorial, consult Otis, *Virgil, passim.*

64. *G&R* 3 (1933), 20.

65. On the four Augustan virtues, consult M. P. Charlesworth, "The Virtues of a Roman Emperor: Propaganda and the Creation of Belief," *Proceedings of the British Academy* 23 (1937), 105–33, esp. 111–4; and I. S. Ryberg, "Clupeus Virtutis," in *The Classical Tradition, Studies in Honor of Harry Caplan,* L. Wallach, ed. (Ithaca, 1966), 232–8.

66. W. S. Maguinness, *Some Reflections on the Aeneid* (London, 1951), 13, *VS* Lecture.

67. Lucan, *Pharsalia,* 1, 218: *Victrix causa deis placuit, sed victa Catoni* [my substitution, *Maroni*].

68. Otis, *Virgil,* 265.

69. K. Quinn, *Latin Explorations: Critical Studies in Roman Literature* (New York, 1963), 35.

70. *Aeneid* 4, 68–73.

71. On the character and tragedy of Turnus, see: W. W. Fowler, *The Death of Turnus* (Oxford, 1919); Duckworth, "Turnus as a Tragic Character," *Vergilius* 4 (1940), 5–17; E. L. Highbarger, "The Tragedy of Turnus: A Study of Vergil *Aeneid* XII," *Classical Weekly* 41 (1947–8), 114–24; J. B. Garstang, "The Tragedy of Turnus," *Phoenix* 4 (1950), 47–58.

72. On Mezentius, see F. A. Sullivan, S.J., "Virgil's Mezentius," *Classical Essays . . . J. A. Kleist* (St.

Louis, 1946), 118–20; K. Quinn, *Latin Explorations*, 212–4. On the comparable tragedy of Evander, see G. R. Manton, "Virgil and the Greek Epic: The Tragedy of Evander," *AUMLA* 17 (1962), 5–17.

73. Consult Duckworth, "The Significance of Nisus and Euryalus for *Aeneid* IX–XII," *AJP* 88 (1967), 129–50.

74. See Duckworth, "The Aeneid as a Trilogy," *TAPA* 88 (1957), 1–10; and *Structural Patterns*, 11–3.

75. See B. C. Fenik, *The Influence of Euripides on Vergil's Aeneid* (Princeton, 1960) (microfilmed dissertation); W. F. Jackson Knight, *Roman Vergil*, 135–7.

76. On Camilla, see Otis, *Virgil*, 362 ff.; T. G. Rosenmeyer, "Virgil and Heroism: *Aeneid* XI," *CJ* 55 (1959–60), 159–64 ("the motif of heroism in a non-heroic world"); H. H. Huxley, *Virgo Bellatrix* (London, 1960) (*VS* Lecture Summaries, No. 52).

77. N. W. DeWitt, "Vergil and the Tragic Drama," *CJ* 26 (1930–1), 26–7.

78. On the characterization of Dido, see Quinn, *Latin Explorations*, 29–58; Gordon Williams, "Poetry in the Moral Climate of Augustan Rome," *JRS* 52 (1962), 28–46, esp. 43–5; A. S. Pease, *Vergil: Aeneid* IV (Cambridge, Mass., 1935), Introduction, and *passim;* R. G. Austin, *Virgil: Aeneid* IV (Oxford, 1955), Introduction, and *passim*.

79. Cf. Duckworth, "*Animae Dimidium Meae:* Two Poets of Rome," *TAPA* 87 (1956), 287–90.

80. See A. J. Gossage, "Vergil in Exile," *PVS* 1 (1961–2), 35–45.

81. *Ibid.*, 45.

82. Consult C. Bailey, *Religion in Virgil* (Oxford, 1935); E. Tavenner, "Roman Religion with Especial Relation to Virgil," *CJ* 40 (1944–5), 198–220; M. L. Clarke, *The Roman Mind* (Cambridge, Mass., 1956), 66–88; Duckworth, "Fate and Free Will in Vergil's Aeneid," *CJ* 51 (1955–6), 361–3.

83. For Apollo's role in the epic see R. B. Lloyd, "*Aeneid* III; A New Approach," *AJP* 78 (1957), 133–51; W. F. Jackson Knight, *Some Divine Monitions and Revelations in Vergil* (London, 1958) (*VS* Lecture Summaries, No. 45).

84. On the Palatine Temple see *Aeneid* 6, 675–728; and S. B. Platner and T. Ashby, *A Topographical Dictionary of Ancient Rome* (Oxford, 1929), 16–29.

85. Apolline prophecy is foremost in the first half of the epic. For an extensive treatment of Apollo in the Augustan Age, see J. Gagé, *Apollon Romain. Essai sur le culte d'Apollon et le développement du "ritus Graecus" à Rome des origines à Auguste* (Paris, 1955), 421–637.

86. *Aeneid* 6, 743.

87. *Aeneid* 1, 33.

88. See A. G. McKay, "Aeneas' Landfalls in Hesperia," *G&R* 14 (1967), 3–11.

89. Maguinness, *Some Reflections on the Aeneid*, 8.

90. Cf. *Georgics* 4, 153 ff.

91. For a review of the century's bloodshed, see R. S. Conway, *New*

Studies of a Great Inheritance (London, 1921), 49 ff.

92. Horace, *Epistles* 2, 156–7.

93. Cicero, *Ad Att.* 13, 27, 1.

94. For detailed information on the British and Parthian questions, consult Hans D. Mayer, *Die Aussenpolitik des Augustus und die Augusteische Dichtung,* "(*Kölner Historische Abhandlungen,* Bd. 5 Cologne, 1961).

95. *Res Gestae Divi Augusti* (3): "I undertook civil and foreign wars by land and sea throughout the whole world, and as victor I showed mercy to all surviving citizens. Foreign peoples, who could be pardoned with safety, I preferred to preserve rather than destroy. (26): I have extended the boundaries of all the provinces of the Roman people which were bordered by nations not yet subjected to our sway."

96. E. Fraenkel, "The Culex," *JRS* 42 (1952), 1–9.

97. See G. B. Townsend, "Changing Views of Vergil's Greatness," *CJ* 56 (1960–1), 67–77.

98. For Vergil in mediaeval times consult: D. Comparetti, *Vergil in the Middle Ages* (London, 1908); J. W. Spargo, *Virgil the Necromancer* (Cambridge, Mass., 1934); J. H. Whitfield, *Dante and Virgil* (Oxford, 1949).

99. For the influence of Vergil on subsequent European literature consult: C. M. Bowra, *From Virgil to Milton* (Oxford, 1945); G. Highet, *The Classical Tradition* (New York, 1949); J. A. K. Thomson, *The Classical Background of English Literature* (1948); *Classical Influence on English Poetry* (1951); R. R. Bolgar, *The Classical Heritage and its Beneficiaries* (Cambridge, 1954); D. P. Harding, *The Club of Hercules. Studies in the Classical Background of Paradise Lost* (Urbana, 1962); L. P. Wilkinson, "The Georgics in After Times," *PVS* 6 (1966–7), 22–5.

100. *The Eclogues, Georgics, and Aeneid of Virgil,* trans. by C. Day Lewis (London, 1966), Foreword, vii.

101. Gilbert Bagnani, "The Classical Technique: Virgil, Dante, and Pope," *Phoenix* 2 (1947–8), 2–14; A. G. McKay, "Virgilian Landscape into Art: Poussin, Claude and Turner," in *Virgil,* D. R. Dudley, ed., Studies in Latin Literature and Its Influence (London, 1969), 139–60.

II

CISALPINE GAUL
AND LOMBARDY

1. Mary L. Gordon, "The Family of Vergil," *JRS* 24 (1934), 1–12.

2. *Op. cit.,* 12.

III

ETRURIA

1. Louise A. Holland, "Place Names and Heroes in the Aeneid," *AJP* 56 (1935), 204–5, suggests that Aulestes, who shares the leadership of the Mantuan troops (A. 10, 207–12), recalls by his death (A. 12, 289–97) the slaughter at Perusia. For details consult Suetonius, Augustus 15; Dio Cass., 48, 14; Appian, *B.C.* 5, 48; and Velleius Paterculus 2, 74.

2. Colin G. Hardie, JRS 54 (1964), 250. See also Hugh Hencken, *Tarquinia and Etruscan Origins* (New York, 1968), 26 f. and *passim;* H. H. Scullard, *The Etruscan Cities and Rome* (London, 1967), 84–92.

3. Caere's alias, Agylla, may derive from Phoenician trading contacts with Tuscany (cf. Punicum, mod. Santa Marinella, farther north). Agylla may derive from the same Canaanite word-root as Gilgal (= circle, or ring wall, of a fortified city).

4. Pyrgi, "gateway" in Greek, may have been the Phoenician port of entry to the Tiber basin before Rome displaced Caere's trading monopoly in her environs.

5. See Emeline Richardson, *The Etruscans* (Chicago, 1964), 127–30; Scullard, *op. cit.*, 102–4. Vergil's Trojan nursemaid, Pyrgo (A. 5, 645), may have been imaginatively linked with Etruscan Pyrgi and the cult of Eileithyia, goddess of childbirth.

6. G. Dennis, *Cities and Cemeteries of Etruria* (London, 1883) I, 133.

7. G. D. B. Jones, "Capena and the Ager Capenas," *PBSR* (N.S.17) (1962), 116–210.

8. G. Karl Galinsky, *Aeneas, Sicily, and Rome* (Princeton, 1969), 133 ff., argues that the mid-fifth- or early fifth-century ex-votos provide no indication that the cult at Veii centered around Aeneas (136).

9. G. M. A. Hanfmann, "The Etruscans and their Art," *Bulletin of the Museum of Art,* Providence, Rhode Island 28 (1940), 31.

IV
ROME

1. Vergil confounds the fortunes of Priam (A. 2, 554–8) and Pompey (Plutarch, *Pompey* 80) in his account of Priam's end.

2. R. G. Austin, *P. Vergili Maronis Aeneidos. Liber Secundus* (Oxford, 1964), ix.

3. W. A. Camps, "A Second Note on the Structure of the *Aeneid,*" *CQ* 9 (1959), 53–6; *id., An Introduction to Virgil's Aeneid* (Oxford, 1969), 153, n. 14.

4. Henry T. Rowell, *Rome in the Augustan Age* (Norman, Oklahoma, 1962), 192.

5. J. W. Mackail, "Virgil and Roman Studies," *JRS* 3 (1913), 13.

6. Cf. W. A. Camps, *An Introduction to Virgil's Aeneid* (Oxford, 1969), 98–100.

7. *Ibid.,* 100–2. "This recollection of honours paid by Octavian to his father Caesar explains the references to Anchises as *divinus* and awaiting the dedication of a temple, and establishes the analogy between the filial piety of Aeneas and the filial piety of Octavian" (102).

8. Emeline Richardson, *The Etruscans* (Chicago, 1964), 221 f., suggests that the stories of Vergil's fire-breathing demon and Livy's powerful robber (I, 7) may record hostility between a prince of Campania (Cacus) and the Etruscans of Tarquinia; the Latins were involved because Rome controlled the Tiber crossing.

9. Mackail, *op. cit.*, 19.

10. On the vexatious question of identification of the "Italian" panel, consult G. Karl Galinsky, *Aeneas, Sicily, and Rome* (Princeton, 1969), 191–241.

11. The original painting by Apelles was in the Temple of Mars the Avenger in the Forum of Augustus (Servius, *ad Aen.* 1, 294; Pliny, *N.H.* 35, 93).

V

LATIUM

1. E. T. Salmon, "Rome and the Latins II," *Phoenix* 7 (1953), 123–35, esp. 134 f.

2. B. Tilly, "Albunea," *JRS* 24 (1934), 25–30 (3 plates), esp. 28 f.

3. F. Castagnoli, "Lavinium and the Aeneas Legend," *Vergilius* 13 (1967), 4.

4. See G. Karl Galinsky, *Aeneas, Sicily, and Rome* (Princeton, 1969), 141–90.

5. Links between Saturnus and Turnus are suggestive. Both ruled in Latium: Saturnus was the consort of Urania; perhaps Turnus was once consort of Turan, the Etruscan Aphrodite, whose altars were common in Latium. Turnus may simply be a Latinized form of an Etruscan name for Turan's consort. It is noteworthy that Turnus was allied with the Etruscans against the Latins and Trojans (cf. Livy 1, 2).

6. B. Tilly, "Vergil's *Periplus* of Latium," *G&R* 6 (1959), 194–203.

7. *Ibid.*, 200.

8. Vergil's *damnatio memoriae* upon Veii is explained by one indisputable allusion in the *Aeneid:* Lars Tolumnius, the fifth-century king of Veii, executed four Roman *legati* at Fidenae (Livy 4, 17); Cicero (*Philippics* 9, 2) mentions seeing statues of the victims on the Rostra at Rome. In *Aeneid* 12 (258–68), it is the augur Tolumnius who treacherously launches the final conflict, thus recalling his historical counterpart. Halaesus, son of Agamemnon (A. 7, 723 ff.), the legendary founder of the Faliscans (Servius, *ad Aen.* 7, 695), comes, like Tolumnius, with Juno on his side, for the Faliscans, like the people of Veii, worshipped Juno in particular.

V I

CAMPANIA, LUCANIA, AND CENTRAL ITALY

1. Vita Donati, 36: Mantua me genuit, Calabri rapuere, tenet nunc Parthenope; cecini pascua rura duces.

2. Cf. T. Frank, *Vergil: A Biography* (New York, 1922), 47–63; A. Rostagni, *Virgilio Minore* (2nd printing, Rome, 1961), 169–83; R. G. M. Nisbet, ed., *M. Tulli Ciceronis in L. Calpurnium Pisonem Oratio* (Oxford, 1961), 183–8.

3. For Vedius Pollio, consult R. Syme, *The Roman Revolution* (Oxford, 1939); *id.*, "Who was Vedius Pollio?" *JRS* 51 (1961), 23–30; R. T. Günther, *Pausilypon: The Imperial Villa Near Naples* (Oxford, 1913), *passim*.

4. Stanzas used in the Mass for the Festival of St. Paul at Mantua suggest that the Apostle, perhaps dur-

ing his sojourn at nearby Puteoli (Acts 28, 11–14; A.D. 61), visited the poet's tomb at Naples. The highly debatable lines are:

Ad Maronis mausoleum,
Ductus, fudit super eum
   Piae rorem lacrimae;
Quem te, inquit, reddidissem
Si te vivum invenissem,
   Poetarum maxime.

Brought to Maro's mausoleum [Paul] wept pious tears for him and said; "What I might have made of you had I found you alive, mightiest of poets." For discussion see Bruno Nardi, *Mantuanitas Vergiliana* (Rome, 1963), chapter entitled "Ad Maronis Mausoleum"; see also review by Colin G. Hardie, *JRS* 54 (1964), 250, who argues that the verses originated in twelfth-century Paris; and Bernard M. Peebles, "The Ad Maronis Mausoleum: Petrarch's Virgil and two fifteenth-century manuscripts," in *Classical, Mediaeval, and Renaissance Studies in Honor of B. L. Ullman,* Charles Henderson, Jr., ed., Vol. I (Rome, 1964), 169–85.

5. Cf. *Patrologiae Graecae*, Vol. 6, Ch. 37 (4th cen. A.D.).

6. Consult R. F. Paget, "The Ancient Ports of Cumae," *JRS* 58 (1968), 152–69; "Portus Julius," *Vergilius* 15 (1969), 25–32.

7. The villa site is disputed between (a) Puteoli: Val. Max., 9, 3, 8; Plutarch, *Sulla,* 37, 3; *De Viris Illustribus* (4th cen. A.D.), 75, 12; (b) Cumae: Appian, *B.C.,* 1, 12, 104; and (c) Posillipo: G. Della Valle, "La Villa Sillana ed Augustea Pausilypon," *Campania Romana* (Naples,

1938), 207–67 (but this last location seems highly improbable).

8. Consult R. F. Paget, "The Ancient Harbours at Cumae," *Vergilius* 14 (1968), 4–15.

9. See Erik Wistrand, "Virgil's Palaces in the Aeneid," *Klio* 38 (1960), 146–54.

10. See Clyde Murley, "The Classification of Souls in the Sixth Aeneid," *Vergilius* 5 (1941), 17–27.

11. Joan du Plat Taylor, ed., *Marine Archaeology* (London, 1965), 178–85. Punta dell'Epitaffio seems to have supported a smaller complex comparable to the "Palatium" at Baiae. Underwater finds of potsherds suggest that the Baian shoreline was submerged by the third century A.D., probably by the time Alexander Severus made monumental changes at the site.

12. E. T. Salmon, *Samnium and the Samnites* (Cambridge, England, 1968), 135.

13. *Ibid.,* 26–7.

14. *Ibid.,* 387.

15. *Ibid.,* 110, n. 6.

16. Cf. G. M. Paul, "Sallust," in *Latin Historians: Studies in Latin Literature and its Influence,* ed. by T. A. Dorey (London, 1966), 85–113.

17. T. Ashby, *Some Italian Scenes and Festivals* (London, 1929), 109–22 (Cocullo). Cf. Pl. 92.

18. Cf. Adam Parry, "The Two Voices of Virgil's Aeneid," *Arion* 2:4 (1963), 66–9.

19. Salmon, *op. cit.,* 150 and Pl. 4.

20. Cf. note 6 (*supra*); consult R.

F. Paget, *In the Footsteps of Orpheus* (London, 1967), *passim; id.,* "The Great Antrum at Baiae," *Vergilius* 13 (1967), 42–50.

VII
MAGNA GRAECIA
AND SICILY

1. Catharine Saunders, *Vergil's Primitive Italy* (New York, 1930), 7.
2. L. G. Pocock, *The Sicilian Origin of the Odyssey* (Wellington, New Zealand, 1957), 59–61.

3. T. J. Dunbabin, *The Western Greeks* (Oxford, 1948), 104.
4. *Ibid.,* 301–2.
5. G. Karl Galinsky, *Aeneas, Sicily, and Rome* (Princeton, 1969), 190.

VIII
CONCLUSION

1. R. D. Williams, *Virgil,* Greece and Rome, New Surveys in the Classics No. I (Oxford, 1967), 17.
2. *JRS* 35 (1945), 8.

BIBLIOGRAPHY

VERGILIAN STUDIES

J. P. Brisson, *Virgile: son temps et le nôtre*. Paris, 1966.

Karl Büchner. *P. Vergilius Maro: der Dichter der Römer*. Stuttgart, 1956.

W. A. Camps. *An Introduction to Virgil's Aeneid*. Cambridge, England, 1969.

Steele Commager (ed.), *Virgil: A Collection of Critical Essays*. Englewood Cliffs, New Jersey, 1966.

R. W. Cruttwell. *Virgil's Mind at Work*. Oxford, 1946.

N. W. DeWitt. *Virgil's Biographia Litteraria*. Toronto, 1923.

G. E. Duckworth. "Recent Work on Vergil (1940–1956)," *CW* 51 (1957–58), 89–92, 116–7, 123–8, 151–9, 185–93, 228–35, reprinted in 1958 by the Vergilian Society of America under the title *Recent Work on Vergil. A Bibliographical Survey*, 1940–56.

"Recent Work on Vergil (1957–1963)," *CW* 57 (1963–64), 193–228, reprinted in 1964 by the Vergilian Society of America under the title *Recent Work on Vergil. A Bibliographical Survey*, 1957–63.

Structural Patterns and Proportions in Vergil's Aeneid. Ann Arbor, Michigan, 1962.

Vergil and Classical Hexameter Poetry: A Study in Metrical Variety. Ann Arbor, Michigan, 1969.

D. R. Dudley, ed. *Virgil*. Studies in Latin Literature and its Influence. London, 1969.

D. L. Drew. *The Allegory of the Aeneid*. Oxford, 1927.

Tenney Frank. *Virgil: A Biography*. New York, 1922. Reprint, New York, 1967.

Gilbert Highet. *Poets in a Landscape*. London, 1957.

W. F. Jackson Knight. *Roman Vergil*. London, 1944.

F. Klingner. *Römische Geisteswelt.* 3rd ed. Munich, 1956.

Virgil. Bucolica Georgica Aeneis. Zurich/Stuttgart, 1967.

G. N. Knauer. *Die Aeneis und Homer: Studien zur poetischen Technik Vergils mit Listen der Homerzitate bei Vergil.* Göttingen, 1964.

Egil Kraggerud. *Aeneisstudien.* Symbolae Osloenses Fasc. Supplet. XXI. Oslo, 1968.

A. G. McKay, "Vergilian Bibliography." *Vergilius* 9 (1963), 33–6; 10 (1964), 40–44; 11 (1965), 40–47; 12 (1966), 39–45; 13 (1967), 35–41; 14 (1968), 16–27; 15 (1969), 42–52.

Brooks Otis. *Virgil: A Study in Civilized Poetry.* Oxford, 1963.

J. Perret. *Virgile.* 2nd ed. Paris, 1965.

V. Pöschl. *The Art of Vergil: Image and Symbol in the Aeneid* (trans. by Gerda Seligson). Ann Arbor, Michigan, 1962.

M. C. J. Putnam. *The Poetry of the Aeneid: Four Studies in Imaginative Unity.* Cambridge, Mass., 1965.

Kenneth Quinn. *Virgil's Aeneid: a critical description.* Ann Arbor, Michigan, 1968.

L. P. Wilkinson. *The Georgics of Virgil: A Critical Survey.* Cambridge, 1969.

R. D. Williams. *Virgil:* Greece and Rome. New Surveys in The Classics, No. 1. Oxford, 1967.

F. J. Worstbrock. *Elemente einer Poetik der Aeneis: Untersuchungen zum Gattungsstil Vergilianischer Epik.* Münster, 1963.

GENERAL STUDIES
Geography, Topography, and Ethnography

Anna G. Blonk. *Vergilius en het landschap.* Leiden, 1947.

R. S. Conway. *The Italic Dialects.* 2 vols. Cambridge, 1897.

Elizabeth C. Evans. *The Cults of the Sabine Territory.* Rome, 1939.

A. Geikie. *Landscape in History.* London and New York, 1905 (esp. 308–52).

A. von Hofmann. *Das Land Italien und seine Geschichte.* Berlin and Stuttgart, 1921.

P. Jal. *La Guerre civile à Rome: Étude littéraire et morale.* Paris, 1963.

J. Jung. *Grundriss der Geographie von Italien.* 2nd printing. Munich, 1897.

F. Milone. *L'Italia nell'Economia delle Sue Regioni.* Turin, 1955.

H. Nissen. *Italische Landeskunde.* Berlin, 1902.

S. Puglisi. *La Civiltà Appenninica.* Florence, 1959.

E. Pulgram. *The Tongues of Italy.* Cambridge, Mass., 1958.

Bernhard Rehm. *Das Geographische Bild des alten Italien in Vergils Aeneis.* (*Philologus,* Supplementband XXIV, Heft II.) Leipzig, 1932.

F. E. Sabin. *Classical Associations of Places in Italy.* Menasha, Wisconsin, 1921.

P. Schmitz. *Die Agrarlandschaft der italischen Halbinsel.* Berlin, 1938.

R. Syme. *The Roman Revolution.* Oxford, 1939.

A. J. Toynbee. *Hannibal's Legacy.* 2 vols. Oxford, 1965.

R. Thomsen. *The Italic Regions.* Copenhagen, 1947.

D. S. Walker. *A Geography of Italy.* London, 1958.

J. Whatmough. *The Foundations of Roman Italy.* London, 1937.

CISALPINE GAUL AND LOMBARDY

E. Abbe. *The Plants of Virgil's Georgics.* Ithaca, N.Y., 1965.

R. L. Beaumont, "Greek Influences in the Adriatic Sea before the fourth century B.C." *JHS* 56 (1936), 159–204.

H. Bennett, "Vergil and Pollio." *AJP* 51 (1930), 325–42 (especially 328–30).

H. Bennett, "The Restoration of the Virgilian Farm." *Phoenix* 5 (1951), 87–95.

G. E. F. Chilver. *Cisalpine Gaul.* Oxford, 1941.

R. S. Conway. *Harvard Lectures on the Vergilian Age.* Reprint, New York, 1967.

A. L. Frothingham. *Roman Cities in Italy and Dalmatia.* New York, 1910.

Mary L. Gordon, "The Family of Vergil." *JRS* 24 (1934), 1–12.

A. J. Gossage, "Virgil in Exile." *PVS* 1 (1961–62), 35–45 (VS Lecture No. 57).

G. A. Mansuelli and R. Scarani. *L'Emilia prima dei Romani.* 1961.

Bruno Nardi. *The Youth of Virgil,* trans. by Belle Palmer Rand. Cambridge, Mass., 1930.

Bruno Nardi. *Mantuanitas Vergiliana.* Rome, 1963.

H. Nettleship. *Ancient Lives of Vergil.* Oxford, 1879.

T. G. E. Powell. *The Celts.* London, 1958.

C. P. Segal, "Tamen cantabitis Arcadis—Exile and Arcadia in *Eclogues* One and Nine." *Arion* 4:2 (1965), 237–66.

A. N. Sherwin-White. *The Roman Citizenship.* Oxford, 1939.

K. Wellesley, "Virgil's Home Revisited." *Vergil Society Lectures,* 67 (1964).

R. E. H. Westendorp Boerma, ed. *P. Vergili Maronis Catalepton* (Pars altera). Assen, 1963.

ETRURIA

A. Alföldi. *Early Rome and the Latins.* Ann Arbor, 1965.

Luisa Banti. *Il mondo degli Etruschi.* Rome, 1960.

R. Bloch. *The Etruscans.* London, 1958.

J. Bradford. *Ancient Landscapes: Studies in Field Archaeology.* London, 1957.

R. F. Cruttwell. *Virgil's Mind at Work.* Oxford, 1946.

G. Dennis. *The Cities and Cemeteries of Etruria.* London, 1878 etc.

P. T. Eden, "The Etruscans in the Aeneid." *PVS* 4 (1964–65), 31–40.

Etruscan Culture, Land and People. Columbia University Press, and Allhelm, Malmö, 1963.

H. Hencken, "A View of Etruscan Origins." *Antiquity* 40 (1966), 205–11.

J. Heurgon. *La Vie quotidienne chez les Etrusques.* Paris, 1961.

Guido A. Mansuelli. *Etruria and Early Rome.* London, 1966.

M. Pallottino and M. Hurlimann. *Art of the Etruscans.* London, 1955.

M. Pallottino. *The Etruscans.* Middlesex, 1955.

M. Pallottino. *Etruscan Painting.* Geneva, 1952.

L. R. Palmer. *The Latin Language.* London, 1954.

F. Poulsen. *Etruscan Tomb Paintings: Their Subjects and Significance.* Oxford, 1922.

Emeline Richardson. *The Etruscans.* Chicago, 1964.

G. M. A. Richter. *Ancient Italy.* Ann Arbor, Mich., 1955.

H. H. Scullard. *The Etruscan Cities and Rome.* London, 1967.

J. B. Ward-Perkins. *Landscape and History in Central Italy.* The Second J. L. Myres Memorial Lecture. Oxford, 1964.

G. E. W. Wolstenholme and C. M. O'Connor, eds. *Ciba Foundation Symposium on Medical Biology and Etruscan Origins.* London, 1959.

ROME

A. Alföldi. *Early Rome and the Latins.* Ann Arbor, 1964.

Franz Altheim. *A History of Roman Religion,* trans. by Harold Mattingly. London, 1938.

J. R. Bacon, "Aeneas in Wonderland: A Study of *Aeneid* VIII." *CR* 53 (1939), 97–104.

R. Bloch. *The Origins of Rome.* New York, 1960.

H. Boas. *Aeneas' Arrival in Latium.* Amsterdam, 1938.

Axel Boethius. *The Golden House of Nero: Some Aspects of Roman Architecture.* Ann Arbor, 1960. Especially Chapter IV.

Jerome Carcopino. *Daily Life in Ancient Rome,* edited, with bibliography and notes by Henry T. Rowell, and trans. from the French by E. O. Lorimer. New Haven, 1940.

D. R. Dudley, *Urbs Roma:* A Source Book of Classical Texts on the City and Its Monuments Selected and Translated with a Commentary. Phaidon, 1967.

Tenney Frank, "Roman Buildings of the Republic: an Attempt to Date Them from Their Materials." *Papers and Monographs of the Amer. Academy in Rome* 3 (1924).

G. Karl Galinsky. *Aeneas, Sicily, and Rome.* Princeton, 1969.

E. Gjerstad. *Legends and Facts of Early Roman History.* Lund, 1962.

P. Grimal. *In Search of Ancient Italy,* trans. by P. D. Cummins. London, 1964.

C. Huelsen. *The Forum and the Palatine,* trans. by Helen H. Tanzer. New York, 1928.

G. Lugli. *Roma Antica: il Centro Monumentale*. Rome, 1946.

G. Lugli. *I monumenti antichi di Roma e suburbio*. 3. Rome, 1938.

G. Lugli. *Monumenti minori del Foro Romano*. Rome, 1947.

P. MacKendrick. *The Mute Stones Speak*. New York, 1960.

Ernest Nash. *Pictorial Dictionary of Ancient Rome*. London, 1961–2.

R. Ogilvie. *A Commentary on Livy, Books 1–5*. Oxford, 1965.

E. Pais. *Ancient Legends of Roman History*. London, 1906; repr. 1950.

J. Perret. *Les Origines de la légende troyenne de Rome*. Paris, 1942.

S. B. Platner and T. Ashby. *A Topographical Dictionary of Ancient Rome*. Oxford, 1929.

M. C. J. Putnam. *The Poetry of the Aeneid*. Cambridge, Mass., 1965. (Chapter 3, "Aeneid Book VIII: History's Dream.")

M. Reinhold. *Marcus Agrippa*. Geneva, N.Y., 1933.

Dorothy M. Robathan. *The Monuments of Ancient Rome*. Rome, 1950.

M. I. Rostovtzeff. *The Social and Economic History of the Roman Empire*. 2nd ed. Oxford, 1957. 2 vols. Especially Chapter II.

Inez Scott Ryberg, "Rites of the State Religion in Roman Art." *MAAR* 22 (1955). (Augustan religious art, especially the Ara Pacis.)

Inez Scott Ryberg. *An Archaeological Record of Rome from the Seventh to the Second Centuries B.C.* London, 1940.

Inez Scott Ryberg, "The Procession of the Ara Pacis." *MAAR* 19 (1949), 79–101.

M. R. Scherer. *Marvels of Ancient Rome*. New York and London, 1955.

F. G. Scott, "Early Roman Traditions in the Light of Archaeology." *MAAR* 7 (1929), 7–116.

J. M. C. Toynbee, "The Ara Pacis Reconsidered and Historical Art in Roman Italy." *Proceedings of the British Academy* 39 (1953), 67–95.

C. C. Van Essen, "L'Architecture dans l'Enéide de Virgile." *Mnemosyne* 7 (1939), 225–36.

W. Warde Fowler. *Aeneas at the Site of Rome*. Oxford, 1917.

LATIUM

A. Alföldi. *Early Rome and the Latins*. Ann Arbor, 1965.

A. Alföldi, "Diana Nemorensis." *AJA* 64 (1960), 137–44.

T. Ashby. *The Roman Campagna in Classical Times*. London, 1927.

S. Aurigemma and A. De Sanctis. *Gaeta, Formia, e Minturno* (Itinerari dei Musei e Monumenti d'Italia). Rome, 1955.

Gilbert Bagnani. *The Roman Campagna and its Treasures*. New York, 1930.

C. Bailey. *Religion in Virgil*. Oxford, 1935.

Henriette Boas. *Aeneas' Arrival in Latium*. Amsterdam, 1938.

A. Boethius. *The Golden House of Nero*. Ann Arbor, 1960.

B. Brotherton, "Virgil's Catalogue of Latin Forces." *TAPA* 62 (1931), 192–202.

J. Carcopino. *Virgile et les origines d'Ostie*. Bibliothèques des Écoles françaises 116 (1919).

F. Castagnoli, "I luoghi connessi con l'arrivo di Enea nel Lazio." *Archaeologia Classica* 19 (1967), 235–47.

R. S. Conway. *The Italic Dialects*. Cambridge, 1897. 2 vols.

E. Fraenkel, "Some Aspects of the Structure of Aeneid VII." *JRS* 35 (1945), 1–14.

R. Gardner, "The Siege of Praeneste." *Journal of Philology* 35 (1919), 1 f.

J. Göhler. *Rom und Italien*. Breslau, 1939.

E. A. Hahn, "Vergil's Catalogue of the Latin Forces." *TAPA* 63 (1932), lxii–lxiii.

Louise A. Holland, "Place Names and Heroes in the Aeneid." *AJP* 56 (1935), 202–15.

Jotham Johnson. *Excavations at Minturnae*. Philadelphia, 1935. 2 vols.

G. D. B. Jones, "Capena and the Ager Capenas." *PBSR* 30 (1962), 124 ff., 191–202.

Hans Kühner. *Latium-Land im Schatten Roms*. Cologne, 1967.

G. Lugli. *Forma Italiae: Regio I: Circeii*. Rome, 1926.

G. Lugli. *Forma Italiae: Anxur-Tarracina*. Rome, 1926.

A. H. McDonald. *Republican Rome*. New York, 1966.

A. G. McKay, "Aeneas' Landfalls in Hesperia." *G&R* 14 (1967), 3–11.

R. Meiggs. *Roman Ostia*. Oxford, 1960.

R. M. Ogilvie. *A Commentary on Livy, Books 1–5*. Oxford, 1965.

G. Säflund, "Ancient Latin Cities of the Hills and Plains." *Opuscula Archaeologica*, 1 (1934), 64–86.

E. T. Salmon, "The Coloniae Maritimae." *Atheneum* 41 (1963), 3–38.

E. T. Salmon, "The Beginnings of the Latin World." *Report of the Canadian Historical Association* (1960), 33–43.

E. T. Salmon, "Roman Expansion and Roman Colonization in Italy." *Phoenix* 9 (1955), 63–75.

Catharine Saunders. *Vergil's Primitive Italy*. New York, 1930.

Hans Jorg Schweizer. *Vergil und Italien. Interpretationen zu den italischen Gestalten der Aeneis*. Aarau, 1967.

A. N. Sherwin-White. *Roman Citizenship*. Oxford, 1939.

B. Tilly, "Virgilian Cities of the Roman Campagna." *Antiquity* 19 (1945), 125–34.

B. Tilly. *Vergil's Latium*. Oxford, 1947.

B. Tilly, "Vergil's *Periplus* of Latium." *G&R* 6 (1959), 194–203. (Vergil, A. 7, 797–802.)

B. Tilly, "The Topography of Aeneid 9, with reference to the way taken by Nisus and Euryalus." *Ar-*

cheologia Classica 8 (1956), 164–72. (Ostia.)

B. Tilly, "More Excursions into Virgil's Country of the Clans." *VS Lecture Summaries,* No. 36 (1955).

A. W. Van Buren. *A Bibliographical Guide to Latium and Southern Etruria.* 5th printing. Rome, 1953.

W. Warde Fowler. *Virgil's Gathering of the Clans.* Oxford, 1918.

W. Warde Fowler. *The Death of Turnus: Observations on the Twelfth Book of the Aeneid.* Oxford, 1919.

J. B. Ward-Perkins. *Landscape and History in Central Italy.* The Second J. L. Myres Memorial Lecture. Oxford, 1964.

J. B. Ward-Perkins, "Veii: Historical Topography of the Ancient City." *PBSR* 29 (NS 16) (1961), 25 ff.

CAMPANIA, LUCANIA,
AND CENTRAL ITALY

P. E. Arias, et al., *La Ricerca Archeologica nell'Italia Meridionale.* Naples, 1960.

K. J. Beloch, *Campanien: Geschichte und Topographie des antiken Neapel und seiner Umgebung.* 2nd printing. Breslau, 1890.

K. J. Beloch, "Le fonti di Strabone nella descrizione della Campania." *Atti dei Lincei: Memorie,* ser. 3, x (1882), 429–48.

John Boardman. *The Greeks Overseas.* Harmondsworth, 1964.

G. Buchner and A. Rittman. *Origine e Passato dell'Isola d'Ischia.* Naples, 1948.

Giorgio Buchner, "Pithekoussai: Oldest Greek Colony in the West." *Expedition* 8:4 (1966), 4–12.

G. P. Caratelli, M. Napoli, *et al.,* "Napoli Antica." *La Parola del Passato* 25–27 (1953), 243–453.

F. Castagnoli. *Ippodamo di Mileto e l'urbanistica a pianta ortogonale.* Rome, 1956.

G. Consoli-Fiego. *Cumae and the Phlegraean Fields* (trans. by Alma Reed). Naples, 1927.

Alfonso de Franciscis, "Underwater Discoveries Around the Bay of Naples." *Archaeology* 20 (1967), 209–16.

T. J. Dunbabin. *The Western Greeks.* Oxford, 1948.

S. Eitrem, "La Sibylle de Cumes et Virgile." *Symbolae Osloenses* 24 (1945), 88–120.

C. Dubois. *Pouzzoles antiques—Histoire et Topographie.* Paris, 1907.

M. W. Fredricksen, "Republican Capua: A Social and Economic Study." *PBSR* 27 (NS 14) (1959), 80–130.

G. Gàbrici, "Cuma." *Monumenti Antichi* 22 (1913–4). 2 vols.

P. Grimal. *In Search of Ancient Italy,* (trans. by P. D. Cummins). London, 1964.

R. T. Günther. *Pausilypon: The Imperial Villa Near Naples.* Oxford, 1913.

E. H. Haight, "Cumae in Legend and History." *CJ* 13 (1917–8), 565–78.

J. Heurgon. *Recherches sur l'histoire, la réligion, et la civilisation* de Capoue préromaine des origines à la deuxième guerre punique. Paris, 1942.

G. Lugli. *Forma Italiae: Campania.* Rome, 1926–8.

E. Magaldi. *Lucania Romana,* Vol. I. Rome, 1947.

A. G. McKay. *Naples and Campania: Texts and Illustrations.* Hamilton (Canada), 1962.

Amedeo Maiuri. *Passeggiate Campane.* 3rd printing. Florence, 1957.

Amedeo Maiuri. *Saggi di varia antichità.* Venice, 1954.

Amedeo Maiuri. *The Phlegraean Fields,* (trans. by V. Priestley). 3rd printing. Rome, 1958.

Amedeo Maiuri. *Capri: its History and Monuments,* (trans. by V. Priestley). Rome, 1956.

G. O. Onorato. *La Ricerca Archeologica in Irpinia.* Avellino, 1960.

R. F. Paget. *In the Footsteps of Orpheus.* London, 1967.

R. M. Peterson. *The Cults of Campania.* Rome, 1919.

E. D. Phillips, "Odysseus in Italy." *JHS* 73 (1953), 53–67.

C. Picard, "Pouzzoles et le paysage portuaire." *Latomus* 18 (1959), 23–51.

D. Randall-MacIver. *Greek Cities of Italy and Sicily.* Oxford, 1931.

E. de Saint Denis. *Le Rôle de la Mer dans la poésie latine.* Paris, 1935. Ch. 7: *Virgilius Nauticus,* 183–278.

E. T. Salmon. *Samnium and the Samnites.* Cambridge, 1967.

P. C. Sestieri. *Paestum. La Città, La Necropoli Preistorica in Contrada Gaudo, Lo Heraion alla foce del Sele.* 9th printing. Rome, 1966.

P. C. Sestieri. *Museo di Paestum: Breve Guida.* Terni, 1958.

Lord William Taylour. *Mycenaean Pottery in Italy and Adjacent Areas.* Cambridge, England, 1958.

A. G. Woodhead. *The Greeks in the West.* London, 1962.

P. Wuilleumier. *Tarente, des origines à la conquête romaine.* Paris, 1939.

MAGNA GRAECIA
AND SICILY

Jean Bérard. *Bibliographie topographique des principales cités grecques de l'Italie méridionale et de la Sicile dans l'antiquité.* 1941.

Jean Bérard. *La colonisation grecque de l'Italie méridionale et de la Sicile dans l'antiquité.* Paris, 1957.

Jean Bérard. *L'Expansion et la colonisation grecque jusqu'aux guerres médiques.* Paris, 1960.

John Boardman. *The Greeks Overseas.* Penguin Books, 1964.

L. Bernabo Brea. *Sicily before the Greeks.* 2nd printing. London, 1966.

A. de Franciscis, "Ancient Locri." *Archaeology* 11 (1958), 206–12.

T. J. Dunbabin. *The Western Greeks.* Oxford, 1948.

M. I. Finley. *Ancient Sicily to the Arab Conquest.* New York, 1968.

E. A. Freeman. *Sicily, Phoenician, Greek and Roman.* Oxford, 1892–1894.

G. Karl Galinsky. *Aeneas, Sicily, and Rome.* Princeton, 1969.

Peter Green, "The First Sicilian Slave War." *Past and Present* 20 (1961), 10–29.

P. Griffo and L. von Matt. *Gela: The Ancient Greeks in Sicily.* Greenwich, Conn., 1968.

Margaret Guido. *Sicily: An Archaeological Guide.* London, 1967.

A. G. McKay, "Aeneas' Landfalls in Hesperia." *G&R* 14 (1967), 3–11.

B. Pace. *Arte e civiltà della Sicilia antica.* 1935–49. 4 vols.

H. W. Parke, "The Sources of Vergil, *Aeneid* III, 692–705." *AJP* 62 (1941), 490–2.

E. D. Phillips, "Odysseus in Italy." *JHS* 73 (1953), 53–67.

L. G. Pocock. *The Sicilian Origin of the Odyssey.* Wellington, N.Z., 1957.

L. G. Pocock. *Odyssean Essays.* Oxford, 1965.

D. Randall-MacIver. *Greek Cities in Italy and Sicily.* Oxford, 1931.

G. A. Ruggieri, "Motya and Lilybaeum." *Archaeology* 10 (1957), 131–6.

V. M. Scramuzza. *Roman Sicily,* in T. Frank, *An Economic Survey of Ancient Rome,* III (Baltimore 1937; repr. Paterson, N.J. 1959).

E. Sjöqvist, "Heracles in Sicily." *Opuscula Romana* 4 (1962), 117–23.

Gertrude Slaughter. *Calabria: The First Italy.* Madison, Wisconsin, 1930.

Vincenzo Tusa, "An archaic sanctuary found at Segesta, Western Sicily, etc." *Illustrated London News* 243 (19 October, 1963), 632–5.

R. van Compernolle, "Ségeste et l'Hellénisme." *Phoibos* 5 (1950–51), 183–228.

R. D. Williams. *P. Vergilii Maronis "Aeneidos" Liber Quintus.* Oxford, 1960.

R. D. Williams. *P. Vergilii Maronis "Aeneidos" Liber Tertius.* Oxford, 1962.

R. D. Williams, "Vergil and the Odyssey." *Phoenix* 17 (1963), 266–74.

A. G. Woodhead. *The Greeks in the West.* London, 1962.

GENERAL INDEX

Numbers in bold face type refer to the illustrations

INDEX OF CITATIONS

Numbers in italics refer to pages on which a poem or passage is quoted or discussed